I0031781

The Seeds of Change

Because psychotherapy is confidential, its inner workings often remain a mystery to those considering it. *The Seeds of Change: How Therapists Cultivate Personal Growth* lifts the veil on the therapeutic process, demystifying approaches, highlighting the importance of tailoring therapy to the individual, and revealing how it can enhance well-being.

Drawing on the author's extensive experience as a psychotherapist, and enriched with case studies and practical exercises, the chapters explore key themes through the lens of the therapeutic journey:

- Alchemy as a metaphor for psychotherapy, illustrating how ancient processes reflect personal growth within therapy.
- The four elements as a dynamic model of change for those engaging in inner work.
- The importance of boundaries and balance—helping readers honour their own needs while fostering healthy relationships.
- Interpreting emotional and physical symptoms as meaningful messages.
- Uncovering the hidden attitudes that influence how we live, work, and relate.
- Exploring dreams as a powerful tool to understand the unconscious.

Whether you're a mental health professional, a student of psychotherapy or counselling, a life coach, wellness practitioner, or someone committed to personal growth, this book offers the insight, tools, and inspiration to support your path.

To find out more about Lynn's psychotherapy practice and workshops, access her website at: https://www.lynnsomerfield.com.

Lynn Somerfield is a psychotherapist with over 25 years of experience. She runs a thriving private practice, guiding clients through life's complexities with warmth and insight. She also supervises other psychotherapists and leads workshops for both professionals and the general public. In her practice and writing, she brings a deep belief in our innate capacity to heal and grow.

The Seeds of Change

How Therapists Cultivate Personal Growth

Lynn Somerfield

Routledge
Taylor & Francis Group

LONDON AND NEW YORK

Designed cover image: © Getty Images

First published 2026
by Routledge
4 Park Square, Milton Park, Abingdon, Oxon OX14 4RN

and by Routledge
605 Third Avenue, New York, NY 10158

Routledge is an imprint of the Taylor & Francis Group, an informa business

© 2026 Lynn Somerfield

For Product Safety Concerns and Information please contact our EU representative GPSR@taylorandfrancis.com. Taylor & Francis Verlag GmbH, Kaufingerstraße 24, 80331 München, Germany.

British Library Cataloguing-in-Publication Data
A catalogue record for this book is available from the British Library

ISBN: 978-1-041-14586-8 (hbk)
ISBN: 978-1-041-14585-1 (pbk)
ISBN: 978-1-003-67509-9 (ebk)

DOI: 10.4324/9781003675099

Typeset in Galliard
by SPi Technologies India Pvt Ltd (Straive)

Contents

Acknowledgements

Writing this book has been an intensely enriching journey—one I could never have undertaken alone. I am deeply grateful to those who have walked beside me, offering their support, wisdom, and encouragement along the way. First and foremost, to my husband and life's great love, Kevin Reynolds—thank you. Your unwavering belief in me has carried me through the hardest chapters. For your loving kindness, your endless patience, and your quiet, steady encouragement—knowing exactly when to bring me a cup of tea and when to let me be, I am profoundly thankful. To the Centre for Counselling and Psychotherapy Education (CCPE) in Little Venice, London—where my psychotherapeutic journey began and took root—thank you. Those formative years of training, supervision, facilitation, and refinement of my craft shaped not only my work but also my very being.

I owe a particular debt of gratitude to Nigel Hamilton, founder of CCPE, for creating a visionary transpersonal curriculum and an experience that continues to inspire me. My thanks also go to Annie Lloyd, my psychotherapist before and during training—a wise and remarkable woman whose presence was both grounding and transformative. I'm deeply grateful to all the facilitators and supervisors who supported me in those formative years. Your questions, your steadiness, and your guidance helped shape the therapist I would become. A special acknowledgement goes to Maggie Kafton, my supervisor for over 20 years. Her insight, clarity, and unwavering presence have influenced my work more than she may ever know. To Richard Stewart—friend and colleague for over 25 years—thank you for your brilliant mind, your humour, and your steadfast presence. I'm deeply grateful our paths crossed; your companionship has lifted me more times than I can count. To Samantha Llewellyn, psychotherapist and cherished colleague, thank you for your thoughtful encouragement and for gently checking in on my writing along the way. And to the friends who have believed in me with such fierce loyalty—you know who you are; my heart overflows with appreciation. I also remember two extraordinary teachers whose souls are so luminous they've never truly departed: Allan Pimentel and Atum O'Kane. Their presence continues to influence my work. Allan's use of music during my foundation year broke through layers of defence, gently opening a space for something long kept hidden. His Taoist grace and quiet wisdom left a lasting mark on me. The memory of a silent retreat in Cape Cornwall with Atum stays with me like a perfect spell of weather—calm, expansive, and quietly transformative. My heartfelt thanks go to Amy Mindell and her late husband, the extraordinary Arnold Mindell. It was through your workshops that I first glimpsed the depth of the dreaming body, and your teachings continue to echo through my thinking, my practice, and the very fabric of this work.

To my editor, Lauren Redhead, my peer reviewers, and the team at Routledge: thank you for recognising the potential of this book and for helping to bring it to fruition. Though my name appears on the cover, the spirit of this book bears the fingerprints of all who helped shape it. For your presence, influence, and generosity, I am deeply grateful.

Making the Most of this Book

Welcome to a journey of self-discovery and transformation. Whether you're here as a curious reader, a student just beginning to explore the human psyche, a seasoned graduate deepening your understanding, learning anew, or an academic seeking fresh insight, this book invites you to read in your way, for your reasons.

This is a space where psychology meets life, and theory comes alive in the personal. You don't need to read the book from start to finish; feel free to jump straight to the topics that interest you. Each chapter offers practical insights and tools you can apply immediately, along with recommended reading for the insatiable seeker.

I aim to clarify the psychotherapy process by providing insights into various types of therapy, the challenges clients often encounter, and how therapists assist clients in overcoming these challenges. I have also included case examples and methods for personal growth, utilising techniques I regularly employ in my practice.

This book is built for flexibility. If you're a general reader, you'll find Recommended Reading sections throughout the book where I've shared some of my favourite books with summaries to help you decide whether to purchase them.

For professionals, enthusiastic researchers, and academic readers, I have included references and citations that cater to their needs, neatly gathered at the end of the chapters so that the book's flow is not interrupted by endless footnotes.

To enhance the clarity and accessibility of this book, I have utilised Grammarly Beta to refine and polish certain sections of the narrative. I have also relied on ChatGPT 4o to curate relevant book recommendations and distil key takeaways at the end of each chapter, ensuring that core insights are both engaging and easy to remember.

Confidentiality

With my clients' permission, I've provided anonymised examples to aid the reader in grasping the concepts discussed. To safeguard my clients' privacy,

I have modified their ages and genders, replacing them with comparable professions or roles where appropriate. The dialogues have been recreated to represent conversations as accurately as possible.

Like many fields, psychotherapy has its insider language—helpful for professionals, but often confusing for those outside the field. I've included a dedicated "Jargon Buster" chapter to unpack these terms for curious readers. Additionally, I've tried to avoid technical language throughout the book, keeping things clear, down-to-earth, and engaging, so anyone interested in therapy can follow along easily.

I hope you enjoy reading it as much as I enjoyed writing it.

Introduction

It had been raining for weeks. The city felt waterlogged and weary.

Returning from lunch along the Grand Union Canal in Little Venice, I passed a moored canal boat, and something unusual caught my eye. Perched on the rudder was a curious patchwork nest—an intricate weave of twigs and leaves interlaced with cable ties and scraps of discarded snack wrappers in flashes of blue, green, yellow, and red. A shelter constructed from nature and the remnants of the city. A waterbird's rough-hewn masterpiece; a recycling triumph. Mr and Mrs Coot took turns sitting atop their nest, sheltering five speckled eggs beneath their feathers. They shared the task with quiet devotion, expectant parents watching for something sacred.

Their quiet constancy transformed them into local celebrities. Local workers and walkers paused to marvel at the nest's unlikely beauty and the coots' vigilance. In a busy city where eye contact is rare and casual conversations rarer still, these coots stirred something in us. Strangers gathered along the towpath, drawn into an unexpected community by the promise of new life.

One by one, five tiny chicks cracked their way into the world, brightening the grey drizzle of a damp spring. Born of scrap and storm, these little lives reminded us that beauty often arises from what has been discarded. They revealed the poetry hidden in the prosaic.

Can we, too, uncover the poetry woven into our being? Does the Self exist, or is it only an illusion? And what of the Soul—does it have form, or is it just a whispered longing? Are Self and Soul the same, or do they dance as distinct forces within us? These questions have echoed through time, stirring the minds of philosophers, psychologists, and mystics.

As a psychotherapist, I often return to the potent metaphor of the seed—an image of the Soul's slow, unfurling, healing journey and the sacred process of becoming whole.

Across psychological traditions, the seed reappears, but nowhere more vividly than in James Hillman's archetypal psychology. In *The Soul's Code* (1996), Hillman suggests that we are born with a unique seed of purpose, just as an acorn holds the blueprint of the oak tree. He says our task is not to invent this destiny but to remember it, nurturing it through life's joys and hardships,

DOI: 10.4324/9781003675099-1

allowing it to grow upwards through the body and into the world. The seed is not a goal to chase but a mystery to unfold.

Freud (1923), the father of psychoanalysis, offered a different vision: the Self as a composite of desire (id), reason (ego), and morality (superego).

In contrast, Carl Jung, the renowned Swiss psychotherapist, viewed the Self not as a fixed entity but as a dynamic unfolding—life's inner drive towards wholeness, which he referred to as *individuation*. In *The Development of Personality* (1954), Jung even likened this unfolding to a seed or "germ" of personality that must be nurtured into being.

Gestalt therapy emphasises process and growth. Its founders rejected the notion of the Self as a hidden treasure. Instead, they perceived it as something created moment by moment—a fluid, ongoing process they called *selfing*. Wholeness wasn't something to be discovered, but something to be enacted repeatedly in response to the ever-changing dance of life.

Philosophy has offered answers: Plato believed that our true Self was our reason, separate from the body. Aristotle viewed the Soul and body as inseparable. Descartes (1637) reduced the Self to thought—"*I think, therefore I am.*" David Hume (1739), the Scottish philosopher, saw no enduring Self at all, only a flickering bundle of sensations. Journeying eastward, Buddhist thought dissolves the Self entirely—a mirage, a dance of impermanence. Hinduism offers the Atman, a spark of divine essence, eternal and indivisible from Brahman, the infinite whole.

In spiritual traditions, the Self is often viewed as something to transcend or as a sacred and luminous entity. Mystics speak of surrendering the ego to merge with the divine, the universe, or a deeper truth that lives beneath the skin of things.

In this book, I embrace these many threads, inviting you to explore who you are, who you might become, and what may be standing in the way of your unfolding.

We often enter therapy when something inside us feels fractured. We sense a disquiet, a storm beneath the surface, a longing for a centre we cannot name. We ask, *Who am I?* But even as we seek our Self, we may wonder if it truly exists.

We are not just minds or bodies. Not our successes or failures. Others glimpse only fragments of us, while some parts remain hidden—even from ourselves. When we silence or deny parts of ourselves, we fracture. A disconnect grows. We wear a mask and fear being seen, yet don't fully know what lies behind it.

The truth is: we are not one, but many. Within us live different selves, each with its own voice and longing. When one dominates and others are ignored, tension builds. But these parts are not threats—they are vital, necessary. They are the raw materials of wholeness.

No one sees the world exactly as you do. The "I" you know—your ego—is merely a single mountaintop on a vast inner mountain range. Suppressed parts do not vanish; they lie in wait. And when we're ready—or not—they rise, often in ways that catch us by surprise.

Therapy invites us to reclaim what we have lost or exiled. It offers more than solutions—it provides a path home.

Yes, many seek therapy for help with anxiety, grief, relationships, or illness. However, what often begins as a quest for relief evolves into something more profound: a journey towards meaning, transformation, and inner coherence.

Starting therapy can feel daunting, like showing up to a first date with your soul. You may wonder: What will it be like? Will it work? Is it selfish, especially in a world so broken?

But healing oneself isn't selfish. As Gandhi (1964: 156) said,

> We but mirror the world. All the tendencies present in the outer world are to be found in the world of our body. If we could change ourselves, the tendencies in the world would also change. As a man changes his own nature, so does the attitude of the world change towards him. This is the divine mystery supreme. A wonderful thing it is and the source of our happiness. We need not wait to see what others do.

This quote encapsulates Gandhi's conviction that inner transformation is the seed of outer change, an idea that resonates profoundly with therapeutic work and spiritual growth.

The ripple effects of personal change are real. Over two and a half decades of practice, I've witnessed it happen again and again.

We must look inward to grow, but we cannot do it alone. The unconscious requires a relationship to become known. Therapy is a brave collaboration in the art of becoming.

Becoming a therapist is a long journey. Years of training, experience, and continuous learning have shaped me. In these pages, I hope to share what I have learned: how therapy works, what it can achieve, and why personal growth is important.

This book is both practical and spiritual, serving as a bridge between the inner and outer worlds—a harmonious blend of heart and mind. I offer it as a companion for those who yearn for more: more wholeness, more truth, and more moments of beauty, even in the rain.

My Training

My psychotherapy training was just as much about personal transformation as it was about professional development.

I studied various theories, honed techniques, and practised the art of listening. Psychoanalytic models taught me to look beneath the surface; humanistic approaches reminded me of the power of empathy; cognitive methods offered valuable tools for untangling thoughts. Each modality had its wisdom—a lens through which to understand suffering and growth. I learned to sit with stories of trauma, anxiety, grief, and tangled relationships.

But sometimes, often, there was a missing piece. Clients spoke of dreams that felt like messages, moments of stillness that cracked them open, grief so vast it felt cosmic, or joy so sudden it felt like a gift of grace. These experiences didn't quite align with clinical language. They were numinous, mysterious— what some might call spiritual.

That's where transpersonal psychotherapy comes in.

Transpersonal describes experiences and perspectives that transcend the ordinary. *Trans* means "beyond", thus *transpersonal* means "beyond the personal". Transpersonal psychotherapists seek to understand, in the words of Pir Vilayat Inayat Khan,[1] "That which transpires behind that which appears" (1991).

Transpersonal therapy doesn't discard what came before—it builds on it. It honours the insights of Freud, Jung, Rogers, Perls, and others. And it dares to ask the big questions, such as: *What if healing is not just about fixing what's broken but about discovering who we are?*

Transpersonal psychotherapy views the psyche as part of something larger and invites the Soul into the room. It holds space for altered states, synchronicities, dreams, and that quiet inner knowing that often goes unnamed.

When I sit with a client, I drop into my heart and listen from there—from the quiet intelligence of feeling. In that attunement, something gentle often arrives.

This kind of therapy isn't about shining a harsh torchlight on the psyche; it's more akin to lighting a candle—a gentler flame, one that reaches into the unseen corners of the Self. The aim isn't just insight; it's illumination. And yes, it may sound poetic. That's because it is. Poetry is one of the Soul's native tongues.

In the transpersonal frame, the Self is a seed of potential. The journey is not from dysfunction to function but from fragmentation to wholeness.

Transpersonal psychology extends its exploration beyond the confines of the ordinary mind, delving into realms where altered states of consciousness can reveal secret gardens waiting to be discovered. It seeks to illuminate the profound moments when, through the stillness of meditation, the fluid rhythm of yoga, the nurturing presence of nature, or myriad other practices, the boundaries of the Ego dissolve. In these instances, a sense of unity emerges—a fleeting yet profound harmony that connects us to all living beings and resonates with the infinite. This discipline invites us to explore the sacred vastness within and beyond, urging us to embrace the deeper currents of our existence.

In many non-Western cultures, the transpersonal has long been intricately woven into the fabric of psychological healing, embracing the interconnectedness of Self, community, nature, and Spirit.

Shamanic practices among Indigenous tribes, Sri Lankan Buddhist healing ceremonies, and the ancient wisdom of traditional Chinese medicine all attest to this holistic approach. In Indigenous traditions, healing is seldom a solitary journey. Mental health is intricately linked to the community's well-being, representing a collective responsibility that extends beyond the individual. The African Ubuntu philosophy, for example, views healing as a communal effort. Individual emotional challenges are considered to be rips in the social fabric that require repair through unity and shared care. In this context, the mind, heart, and Spirit are not isolated; they are interconnected with the broader environment and the sacred, reminding us that true well-being is a harmony of the whole.

In the West, transpersonal psychology emerged as a significant field during the 1960s and 1970s, driven by the human potential movement and the rise of humanistic psychology. Over time, it has evolved to combine psychological theories with insights from disciplines such as high-energy physics, presenting the mind as an integral part of a vast network of cosmic energy. This innovative perspective goes beyond the boundaries of traditional psychology, delving into the profound spiritual dimensions of human existence.

Transpersonal psychotherapists recognise that all humans are on a spiritual path, whether or not they are aware of it. We are not merely our minds and bodies; we also possess Souls. As Pierre Teilhard de Chardin (1881–1955), the French Jesuit, scientist, and philosopher, is commonly believed to have said: *"We are not human beings having a spiritual experience. We are spiritual beings having a human experience"*.

Although fewer people attend church these days, many still feel a strong sense of spirituality, but without the rules, rituals, or labels that usually accompany organised religion. Nonetheless, for many of us, outdated notions about being "sinful" or "not good enough" can linger in the background, shaping how we perceive ourselves. Therapy examines how these lingering beliefs manifest in our inner world and how we can begin to address them, primarily through a process known as *shadow work*—a method of confronting the parts of ourselves we typically keep hidden.

Regardless of its form, spirituality can be a powerful inner tool. Many people overlook it or deny it, but it can help us heal and grow, especially when we tap into what some call the "inner guide", that wise, quiet voice inside us. However, we must first acknowledge its existence. Through case examples, this book illustrates what that inner guide might look like and how we can connect with it to discover strength, insight, and genuine change.

Spirituality is not a means of avoiding real life, with all its challenges and limitations; rather, it is an intrinsic part of life. Living a spiritual life entails cultivating genuine, authentic relationships that connect you with others on a deeper level. It involves viewing your problems from a broader perspective, staying true to your values and morals when making decisions, and not unquestioningly conforming to what everyone else believes, especially if it contradicts your principles.

The spiritual path is vibrant, dynamic, and anything but dull. It involves seeking meaning in life, attuning to the quiet wisdom of your Soul, and allowing your intuition and imagination to guide you. This journey may encompass exploring the messages in your dreams or understanding what your physical and emotional symptoms are attempting to communicate. It also entails staying connected to your instincts, embracing joy and laughter, and feeling linked to something greater—nature, the planet, the cosmos, or a higher power. The spiritual journey is an ever-evolving process of remaining open, curious, and deeply connected.

Not all clients seeking psychotherapy with a transpersonal therapist are attracted to its spiritual dimension, and that's perfectly fine. Everyone is approached with respect for their personal journey, values, and goals. The therapeutic process adapts to meet clients precisely where they are, prioritising their needs and preferences above all else. This ensures that spiritual elements, while available as resources, are never introduced forcibly or in a manner that misaligns with the client's comfort level.

So, how do integrative and transpersonal psychotherapy coexist? Therapy often begins with well-worn tools—talking, uncovering, and reframing. Psychodynamic therapy explores your past, cognitive behavioural therapy (CBT) reshapes your thoughts, humanistic therapy nurtures your sense of self, and so forth.

Transpersonal therapy uses all of these, but then poses a deeper question: *What is your Soul trying to communicate through this emotional disturbance or physical symptom?*

It perceives symptoms not merely as issues to resolve, but as messages—calls from something greater within or beyond. In this context, therapy becomes more than just healing; it can be a journey towards meaning, purpose, and the mystery of who you truly are.

The approach employed in integrative therapy relies on various factors, such as the client's mental and emotional state, their stage of life, and the contributions they bring to the sessions. It emphasises viewing the individual as a whole rather than merely their symptoms. This holistic process may integrate art, literature, science, philosophy, mythology, indigenous wisdom, and bodywork to facilitate healing and personal growth. Sessions are customised to resonate most with the client and may include talking therapy, guided imagery, visualisations, sand-tray work, Gestalt's Empty Chair technique, meditation, mindfulness, or chakra balancing. The aim is to create a personalised, meaningful experience that supports the client's unique journey towards healing, self-discovery, and personal transformation.

This may all seem a bit far-fetched for anyone rolling their eyes at spiritual matters—the chakras, breathwork, visualisations, or those significant "aha" moments. However, I agree with Ken Wilber[2] on this; he suggests that dismissing spiritual concepts as unreal is akin to the tail (material science) pretending the dog (spiritual realities) doesn't exist (Wilber, 2000).

Everything is interconnected, whether we recognise it or not. Theoretical physicist David Bohm observed that believing all parts exist in isolation is a clearly false idea, one that inevitably leads to conflict and confusion (Bohm, 1980).

This idea encapsulates Bohm's vision—that what we perceive as separation is, in fact, an illusion. Beneath the surface of things lies a deeper, undivided wholeness. His work establishes a powerful bridge between physics and philosophy, with far-reaching implications for our understanding of the mind, spirituality, and the interconnected systems that shape our world.

The psychotherapist's role resembles that of a Sherpa, the native guide who escorts travellers to the summit of Mount Everest. Countless paths traverse the psyche, and each therapeutic journey is unique. For some, the direction of consciousness moves upwards; for others, it descends. There are peaks and valleys, and one can see things from various perspectives.

Psychotherapists, most of whom undergo years of therapy as part of their training, have traversed this terrain many times and guided numerous others. Like climbing and descending Mount Everest, psychotherapy is a grand adventure, a significant challenge that stretches and exhilarates you; it is transformative. To engage in it, you must genuinely find the human condition captivating. It centres on being curious enough to explore the profound questions people often overlook, such as how we develop a personality, what we desire, what inspires us, and what drains our energy. Can we uncover meaning in life? What plunges us into despair, and what uplifts us with joy? How do we instigate change, and what can we do to facilitate it?

These are the profound, thought-provoking questions that therapists wrestle with daily. Therapy involves living an examined life; delving into this with others is a joy and a privilege.

Notes

1 Vilayat Inayat Khan (19 June 1916–17 June 2004) was a teacher of meditation and of the traditions of the East Indian Chishti Sufi order. His teaching derived from the tradition of his father, Inayat Khan, founder of The Sufi Order in the West (now named the Ināyati Order), in a form tailored to the needs of Western seekers.
2 Kenneth Earl Wilber II (born January 31, 1949) is an American theorist and writer on transpersonal psychology and his own integral theory.

References

Bohm, D. (1980). *Wholeness and the implicate order*. Routledge.

Descartes, R. (1637). *Discourse on the method*. Edinburgh: Sutherland and Knox.

Freud, S. (1923). *The ego and the id*. In J. Strachey (Ed.), *The standard edition of the complete psychological works of Sigmund Freud* (Vol. 19). Hogarth Press.

Gandhi, M. (1964). *Collected works of Mahatma Gandhi*, vol. 12. The Publications Division, Ministry of Information and Broadcasting, Government of India.

Hillman, J. (1996). *The soul's code*. Random House.

Hume, D. ([1739]2004) *A treatise of human nature*, Book I, part IV, sec.6. Penguin.

Jung, C. G. (1954). *The development of personality*. Pantheon Books.

Khan, V. I. I. K. (1991). *That which transpires behind that which appears: The experience of Sufism*. Omega Publications.

Wilber, K. (2000). *A theory of everything: An integral vision for business, politics, science and spirituality*. Shambhala Publications.

Chapter 1

How Therapy Begins

Establishing a trusting relationship with clients is central to effective psychotherapy.

All therapists have their methods for establishing a therapeutic relationship, yet initial sessions typically follow a similar trajectory. The early sessions emphasise the importance of building a robust therapeutic alliance and understanding the client's personal narrative. Together, the therapist and client explore the reasons for seeking therapy, the challenges faced, and how these difficulties impact the client's emotional and psychological well-being. The client's history includes significant life events, family dynamics, cultural influences, and pivotal childhood experiences. Through this examination, the therapist and client collaboratively articulate goals and the client's vision for positive change, thereby laying the groundwork for meaningful, personalised therapy.

Much of what a client communicates extends beyond mere words. Therapists attentively observe body language, facial expressions, and other subtle cues that may uncover hidden emotions. Trusting their intuition, therapists recognise when words and actions do not fully align. For example, if a client, when asked about their relationship, says, "It's fine!" but turns away slightly and clenches their fists, the therapist will notice the discrepancy between the client's words and body language. Depending on the moment, they may gently address it then or explore it later, as timing is crucial in therapy.

This initial phase does not focus on diagnosis; it emphasises building a relationship, understanding the client's world, and collaboratively setting a course. Goals are revisited and refined as therapy progresses to align with the client's growth and evolving needs.

Examining a client's past illuminates how early experiences have shaped their beliefs about themselves, others, and the world. These ingrained patterns influence thoughts, feelings, and behaviours in the present moment, often without conscious awareness.

Once this foundation-building phase concludes, the therapist possesses a rich map to guide the journey ahead, allowing them to navigate more confidently, recognising promising paths and potential dead ends. Additionally, as

DOI: 10.4324/9781003675099-2

healing is a dynamic process, new insights will naturally emerge as the work continues to evolve.

After the initial sessions, clients sometimes wonder how to optimise their therapy hours. My advice is to come as you are, bringing whatever is on your mind that week. Sometimes, therapy involves firefighting—addressing the immediate flare-ups of daily life. At other times, there may not be an urgent issue at all. These quieter moments can be the most fruitful. There's a quiet kind of magic in silence. Without the noise and drama that usually occupy the mind, deeper, unconscious material is free to surface, finally given the space to speak where the busy mind once kept the Self quiet. It can be tempting to fill the space with words, but sometimes the most significant work occurs in the pauses. Your therapist may ask you to slow down or sit with a feeling, rather than talk around it. This approach allows both of you to attune more deeply to what's happening.

Keeping a daily journal and recording your dreams can be incredibly valuable if you wish to deepen your therapeutic journey. You'll find more on this in Chapter 10, "You May Say I'm a Dreamer: Working with Your Dreams".

It's also helpful to acknowledge any unhelpful thoughts that arise—about yourself, others, or the world in general. If you find yourself particularly averse (or strongly drawn) to specific individuals, note that as well. These small observations can become significant gateways for exploration. Chapter 12, "Carry My Gold: Retrieving Projections", explores this in more detail.

As time passes, you'll begin to feel more at ease in the therapeutic space—learning to trust, to soften, and to yield to the process itself.

Chapter 2

A Brief History of Psychotherapy

Numerous types of psychotherapy exist, and an understanding of how the field has evolved may be helpful if you're considering training or seeking a therapist; familiarity with how the different modalities function is beneficial.

Psychologists and psychotherapists debating theories resemble less a quiet academic discussion and more an intellectual cage fight, with footnotes and passive-aggressive citations instead of punches and roundhouse kicks. One proposes a sweeping theory of the mind, while the others line up with metaphorical scalpels, eager to dissect, dispute, or flat-out demolish it in the following journal issue. It's a world where Freud gets accused of being obsessed with sex, Jung is called too mystical, and behaviourists are mocked for pretending feelings don't exist at all. At the same time, everyone insists *they're* the ones being entirely objective.

But that's part of the beauty of progress—ideas are meant to be challenged, reshaped, and tested. While the chronology below is not exhaustive, it captures some of the key turning points where ground-breaking theories collided, diverged, or evolved, all contributing to the development of psychotherapy into the rich and complex field we know today.

Psychoanalytical Psychotherapy (Freudian)

The ancient Greeks were among the first to recognise the importance of talk therapy. However, modern talking therapies gained traction due to Sigmund Freud (1856–1939), an Austrian neurologist who began his practice in Vienna in the 1880s. Freud believed that dialogue could effectively address mental health issues. He developed psychoanalysis and introduced revolutionary techniques, such as free association (saying whatever comes to mind without censorship) and transference (when a client projects feelings for another person onto their therapist).

Freud also proposed that dreams unveil unconscious, repressed desires, using this notion to develop his theories on symptom formation and repression.

DOI: 10.4324/9781003675099-3

This culminated in his renowned model of the psyche, which divides the mind into the id (your instincts), ego (your reality-checker), and superego (your moral compass). For further details, refer to Chapter 3, "Jargon Buster: Telling It Like It Is".

In 1900, Freud published *The Interpretation of Dreams*, a seminal book that introduced his ideas to a broader audience.

A few years later, in 1919, his associate Ernest Jones established the British Psychoanalytical Society, promoting the spread of Freud's work throughout the English-speaking world.

Recommended Reading

Burgo, Joseph (2012). *Why Do I Do That?* New Rise Press. (A clear, beginner-friendly guide to defence mechanisms from a psychodynamic perspective.)

Freud, Sigmund (1916–1917). Introductory Lectures on Psycho-Analysis. In J. Strachey (Ed.), *The Standard Edition of the Complete Psychological Works of Sigmund Freud* (Vols. 15 & 16). Hogarth Press. (Freud's introduction to his theories; an excellent book for the basics of psychoanalysis.)

Freud, Sigmund (1923). The Ego and the Id. In J. Strachey (Ed.), *The Standard Edition of the Complete Psychological Works of Sigmund Freud* (Vol. 19). Hogarth Press. (An essential overview of Freud's structural model: Id, Ego, and Superego.)

Kottler, Jeffrey A. (1986/2022). *On Being a Therapist* 6th ed. Oxford University Press. (A rich, reflective look at the therapist's inner world—ideal for thoughtful practitioners.)

Lanyado, Monica (2004). *The Presence of the Therapist: Treating Childhood Trauma*. Routledge. (Explores countertransference in relational psychoanalysis—essential for intersubjective practitioners.)

Laplanche, Jean & Pontalis, Jean-Bertrand (1988/2018). *The Language of Psychoanalysis*. Routledge. (A comprehensive reference for psychoanalytic terms and concepts; ideal for students and practitioners.)

Wallin, David J. (2007). *Attachment in Psychotherapy*. Guilford Press. (A practical integration of attachment theory with relational and intersubjective therapy—widely used in contemporary practice.)

Winnicott, Donald W. (1971/2005). *Playing and Reality*, 2nd ed. Routledge. (Introduces concepts like the "transitional object" and the "true/false self; a thought-provoking and accessible book.)

Individual Psychology (Adlerian)

Alfred Adler (1870–1937) was an Austrian medical doctor and psychotherapist who began his career working alongside Freud. However, over time, he carved out his path, developing a distinct approach known as Individual Psychology. While Freud focused on the "will to pleasure"—our drive to seek enjoyment and avoid pain—Adler believed we're primarily motivated by a "will to power", a deep desire to overcome challenges and strive for mastery or superiority.

Adler focused on the role of family dynamics in human development. He observed that children often feel "less than" early in life—perhaps due to being the youngest, facing physical challenges, experiencing failures, or lacking sufficient emotional support. He coined the term "inferiority complex". Adler recognised that these feelings of inadequacy could also act as a motivating factor, driving individuals to overcome their weaknesses (Adler, 1925).

Adler transformed the therapeutic experience by replacing the traditional psychoanalytic couch with two chairs, fostering a setting of equality and collaboration between therapist and client. This shift towards a more open and less hierarchical relationship established the foundation for the modern therapeutic approaches we recognise today.

Recommended Reading

Adler, Afred (1927/2013). *Understanding Human Nature*. Routledge. (One of Adler's most accessible original works, introducing his concepts through practical examples and plain language.)

Adler, Alfred (1931/2015) *What Life Could Mean to You*. CreateSpace. (A more philosophical and inspirational take on how Adler's psychology applies to everyday life.)

Mosak, Harold H. & Maniacci, Michael (2015). *A Primer of Adlerian Psychology*. Routledge. (A clear and concise overview of Adler's key ideas, including social interest, inferiority, and lifestyle.)

Sweeney, Thomas J. (2009). *Adlerian Counseling and Psychotherapy: A Practitioner's Approach*. Taylor & Francis. (A practical guide for therapists, blending theory with application in modern settings.)

Analytical Psychotherapy (Jungian)

In 1913, Carl Jung (1875–1961), a Swiss psychiatrist and psychologist, took a bold step that would shape the future of psychology: he broke away from his mentor, Sigmund Freud. This split was not merely personal; it was philosophical in nature. Jung disagreed with Freud's assertion that sexuality was the primary force behind our thoughts and behaviours. He believed that the human mind was far more mysterious and expansive.

Jung agreed that we all have a personal unconscious, where forgotten memories, emotions, and life experiences quietly shape our thoughts and actions. But he felt Freud stopped there, missing something more profound. Jung introduced the concept of the collective unconscious—a shared psychological inheritance that all humans are born with. This hidden layer of the psyche holds what he called archetypes: ancient images and patterns that show up in dreams, myths, and stories across all cultures, from every era.

To Jung, the mind was not merely about repressed desires; it was a dynamic, evolving landscape filled with meaning, mystery, and the potential for personal transformation. He viewed the conscious mind as the tip of the iceberg, while the unconscious, particularly the collective unconscious, represented a vast and powerful force beneath the surface. The section on "The Psyche" in Chapter 3, "Jargon Buster: Telling It Like It Is" further explores these ideas, examining how Jung's concepts continue to influence our thinking today.

Jung developed Analytical Psychology, and his concepts of the collective unconscious, archetypes, and individuation established him as one of the most prominent psychologists in the history of psychology (Jung, 1964).

Recommended Reading

Butler, Jason A. (2014). *Archetypal Psychotherapy: The Clinical Legacy of James Hillman*. Routledge. (Brings Hillman's poetic, soul-centred approach into therapeutic contexts, rich with metaphor and imagination.)

Fordham, Michael (1978/2018). *Jungian Psychotherapy: A Study in Analytical Psychology*. Routledge. (A bridging text between classical Jung and modern clinical practice, written by a key figure in the post-Jungian tradition.)

Johnson, Robert A. (1986/2009). *Inner Work: Using Dreams and Active Imagination for Personal Growth*. Harper Collins. (A practical guide for engaging with dreams and inner imagery; for clients and therapists alike.)

Jung, Carl Gustav (1921/2016). *Psychological Types*. Routledge. (A key introduction to Jung's personality types—foundational for analytical therapy.)

Jung, Carl Gustav (1933/2001). *Modern Man in Search of a Soul*. Routledge. (A classic, accessible introduction to Jung's ideas, including dream analysis, the unconscious, and psychotherapy.)

Jung, Carl Gustav (1954/1993). *The Practice of Psychotherapy*. In *The Collected Works of C. G. Jung*, 2nd ed. Routledge. (Part of Jung's *Collected Works*; focuses on Jung's clinical method, including case material.)

Jung, Carl Gustav (1959/1991). *The Archetypes and the Collective Unconscious*. In *The Collected Works of C. G. Jung*. Routledge. (A foundational text for understanding analytical psychology, exploring mythic patterns and symbolic structures in the psyche.)

Stein, Murray (2010). *Jungian Psychoanalysis: Working in the Spirit of C. G. Jung*. Carus. (A collection of essays by contemporary analysts exploring the therapeutic process from a Jungian lens.)

Feminine Psychology

In 1922, a German psychoanalyst named Karen Horney (1885–1952) practised in the United States during her later career. She introduced a fresh, more holistic, and humanistic perspective, emphasising how cultural and social differences shape us globally. Karen Horney boldly challenged Freud's theories, particularly his views on women. She criticised the male bias inherent in psychoanalysis and dismissed the notion of intrinsic psychological differences between genders. Instead, Horney contended that these differences arose from cultural and societal influences rather than biological factors. Her work contributed to a more inclusive understanding of the human psyche and experience. Freud's concept of penis envy was also challenged by Horney, who introduced the idea of "womb envy": the notion that men may envy women's ability to bear children.

By presenting these innovative ideas, Horney paved the way for the development of feminist psychology. She authored several papers on the subject, which were later compiled into her book, *Feminine Psychology*, in 1967—an essential read for anyone interested in the evolution of psychological thought concerning gender (Horney, 1967).

Recommended Reading

Baker, Miller Jean (1976/1992). *Toward a New Psychology of Women*. Beacon Press. (A feminist classic, exploring how connection and relationality shape female psychological development.)

Horney, Karen (1993). *Feminine Psychology* (H. Kelman, Ed.). W. W. Norton & Company. (A pioneering psychoanalytic critique of Freud's theories, offering a new lens on women's inner lives and development.)

Johnson, Robert A. (1976/2009). *She: Understanding Feminine Psychology*. Harper Collins. (A short, elegant introduction to the feminine archetype through the myth of Amor and Psyche.)

Jung, Carl Gustav (1982/2003). *Aspects of the Feminine*. Routledge. (A collection of Jung's writings on the feminine archetype, the anima, and the animus.)

Monaghan, Patricia (1981). *The Book of Goddesses and Heroines*. Dutton. (This is a beautiful reference book on the feminine in world cultures, useful in symbolic and mythic work.)

Pinkola, Estés Clarissa (1989). *Women Who Run With the Wolves*. Rider. (A bestselling exploration of wild feminine archetypes through myths and fairytales, grounded in Jungian depth psychology.)

Woodman, Marion (1982). *Addiction to Perfection*. Inner City Books. (Examines how women may internalise cultural ideals that suppress the feminine body and soul.)

Woodman, Marion (1985). *The Pregnant Virgin: A Process of Psychological Transformation*. Inner City Books. (A deeply symbolic and poetic exploration of the feminine journey towards individuation.)

Client-Centred Therapy

Carl Rogers (1902–1987) was the founder of humanistic psychology and developed an approach known as Client-Centred Therapy (1951; also referred to as Person-Centred Therapy), which was influenced by Adler's method and featured a direct and relational working style.

Rogers illustrated his therapy model with a childhood story about his farm experience. One day, he ventured into the dark cellar and noticed some potatoes in storage. The potatoes had sprouted, reaching towards a small crack of light from a window. This served as a metaphor for his therapy model: people are naturally driven to grow towards their full potential, even in unfavourable conditions.

Rogers viewed the therapist's role as accepting and valuing the client without judgement, comprehending the client's feelings and experiences while accurately reflecting them, and being genuine in their communication. The central concepts of Client-Centred Therapy are:

- **Actualising tendency**: Individuals possess an innate motivation to grow, heal, and fulfil their full potential.
- **Self-concept** refers to how we perceive ourselves (our "self-image"). Issues often arise when our self-concept does not align with our actual experiences.
- **Conditions of worth**: When people believe they must meet specific conditions to be loved or accepted (like "I'm only good if I succeed"), it hinders their growth.

- **Unconditional positive regard**: The therapist offers complete acceptance and warmth without judgement, regardless of the client's experiences.
- **Empathy**: The therapist fully understands the client's feelings and experiences from their perspective and accurately reflects them.
- **Congruence (Genuineness)**: The therapist is authentic and transparent, not behaving like a "blank screen" or "expert". Their external behaviour aligns with their inner feelings.
- **The therapeutic relationship**: Healing occurs through the quality of the relationship, which is rooted in trust, empathy, and acceptance, rather than in techniques or advice.

Client-centred therapy suggests that individuals heal most effectively when they feel safe, understood, and accepted, allowing their natural self-healing abilities to flourish.

Recommended Reading

Di Malta, Gina, Cooper, Mick, O'Hara, Maureen, Gololob, Yana, & Stephen, Susan (eds) (2024). *The Handbook of Person-Centred Psychotherapy and Counselling*, 3rd ed. Bloomsbury. (An academic and comprehensive guide, featuring chapters from various experts in the field. Useful for professionals, students, and researchers.)

Mearns, Dave & Thorne, Brian (1988). *Person-Centred Counselling in Action*. Sage. (A clear, practical guide, often recommended for students and trainees. Introduces theory with real-life case examples.)

Mearns, Dave & Thorne, Brian (1994). *Developing Person-Centred Counselling*. Sage. (A deeper dive into the process of becoming a person-centred counsellor and dealing with challenges in practice.)

Rogers, Carl R. (1951). *Client-Centred Therapy: Its Current Practice, Implications and Theory*. Houghton Mifflin. (The classic foundational book outlining the theory and techniques of client-centred therapy. Essential reading for anyone studying or practising this approach.)

Rogers, Carl R. (1954). *On Becoming a Person: A Therapist's View of Psychotherapy*. Houghton Mifflin. (A profoundly humanistic and accessible collection of essays reflecting Rogers' philosophy and insights into therapy, growth, and authenticity.)

Gestalt Therapy

Friedrich Salomon Perls (1893–1970), better known as Fritz Perls, was a German-born psychiatrist, psychoanalyst, and psychotherapist. Laura Perls (née Lore Posner; 1905–90) was a German-Jewish psychologist and psychotherapist. The couple are most notable for developing the Gestalt therapy approach in collaboration with the intellectual Paul Goodman (Perls et al., 1951). Frustrated with Freudian psychotherapy, they founded a humanistic and person-centred approach known as Gestalt Therapy and established The Gestalt Institute in New York.

The term Gestalt is German and has no direct translation, although it is similar to "whole" or "form". Gestalt practitioners contend that the reductive approach of psychoanalysis overlooks the broader perspective. They argue that a proper understanding arises from grasping the whole person—mind, body, emotions, and Spirit—and their unique experience of reality.

At its heart, Gestalt is about seeing things holistically and understanding that patterns, relationships, and perceptions are key to human experience. A significant aspect of Gestalt thinking is the belief that "the whole is greater than the sum of its parts". In other words, when you look at a picture, you don't just see lines and colours separately—you see an image, a feeling, a scene. Your brain fills in the gaps, connects the dots, and naturally makes sense of the information.

Gestalt psychology is based on the idea that we experience life as whole, as meaningful patterns rather than mere random bits and pieces. When we observe the world, our minds automatically organise what we see into shapes, patterns, and stories without conscious effort. It's not something we control deliberately—it's inherent to our brains. For instance, imagine driving and seeing a few road signs partially obscured by trees. Even though sections of the signs may be hidden, you still instantly recognise them—perhaps a stop sign or a speed limit—without needing to see the entire shape or every letter.

That's Gestalt in action: your mind automatically fills in the missing pieces (employing the Principle of Closure) and helps you grasp the entire message without requiring all the details.

Gestalt psychologists also discovered some fundamental rules regarding how we group items. For instance, we tend to perceive objects that are situated close together as belonging to the same group, a concept known as *proximity*. As an illustration, consider a collection of 12 circles arranged like this:

OOO   OOO   OOO   OOO

Even though all the circles are identical, your brain automatically groups them into sets of three because the circles that are closer together are perceived as belonging together. **Gestalt's principle of proximity** states that elements that are near each other are perceived as a group.

Gestalt's principle of similarity refers to items that appear to belong together. Imagine you are watching a football match. One team is wearing blue shirts, while the other is in red. Even though the players are scattered all over the pitch, you instantly group the blue-shirted players as one team and the red-shirted players as the other, because they look similar. That's Gestalt's principle of similarity: when things resemble each other (in colour, shape, size, etc.), we perceive them as part of the same group.

Here's an example of how this manifests in the consulting room. Imagine a client discussing various life situations—trouble at work, conflict with a friend, tension with a parent. Initially, these appear to be separate problems. However, similar emotional patterns emerge throughout the conversation; perhaps the client feels unheard or disrespected in each instance.

As these emotional experiences are similar, the therapist and the client naturally begin to group them, recognising a broader pattern of the client feeling overlooked in relationships, instead of addressing each event in isolation. Similarity aids in organising emotional experiences.

If a shape is nearly complete, our minds will "finish" it for us (closure). We instinctively follow lines and patterns in a smooth, flowing manner (continuity). Typically, we separate objects from their backgrounds without even realising it (this is Gestalt's **figure–ground principle**). A classic real-life example of Gestalt's figure–ground principle is when you're reading text on a page. The letters are the figure (what you focus on), and the white page is the ground (the background you ignore). Your brain naturally separates the words from the background, allowing you to read with ease.

Another example is **road signs**: the symbols or words (figure) stand out against the flat background colour (ground), assisting drivers in quickly understanding the message.

As an illustration of how this operates in therapy, consider someone attending therapy and expressing that they're stressed about work deadlines. Initially, work-related stress is the most apparent issue they recognise. The ground (the background) encompasses everything else: feelings about family, physical sensations, memories, and so on.

As the therapist gently explores with them, the client may notice a tight sensation in their chest. Perhaps a sense of sadness arises when they discuss their fear of disappointing their boss; at that moment, they might recall a memory of their father criticising them as a child. Suddenly, an old fear of failure emerges from the background like a new figure.

Now, therapy can shift its focus, addressing not only deadlines but also healing that deeper wound from childhood. The deeper truths often surface naturally when the person is ready.

Another essential idea is that nothing we experience occurs in isolation; everything is influenced by the larger situation or "field" in which we live. The context, the environment, the moment—all these factors are significant. Figure 2.1 is an example involving Gestalt and the field.

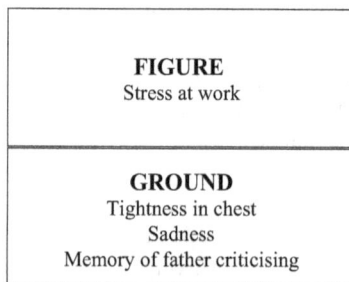

```
┌─────────────────────────────────────┐
│                                     │
│              FIGURE                 │
│           Stress at work            │
│                                     │
├─────────────────────────────────────┤
│                                     │
│              GROUND                 │
│          Tightness in chest         │
│               Sadness               │
│      Memory of father criticising   │
│                                     │
└─────────────────────────────────────┘
```

Figure 2.1 Gestalt principle of figure–ground.

A client feels anxious during a session. Rather than treating the anxiety as merely "inside" the client, the Gestalt therapist examines the entire field:

Perhaps it is raining outside (heavy, gloomy field).
Maybe the therapy room feels cold and distant.
Perhaps the therapist's posture seems closed off today, and the client unconsciously senses it.
Maybe the client's partner sent a harsh text earlier.

The anxiety isn't just "their issue"—it arises from the entire field of experiences surrounding them. Therefore, the therapist doesn't go through a tick list, suggesting possible contributory factors. Instead, they might say: "I wonder if you're picking up something in the room or something between us that's adding to this anxious feeling?" Rather than focusing solely inward, they explore the *field conditions* together.

When it comes to learning and problem-solving, Gestalt psychology suggests that we do not always figure things out by working slowly and step by step. Sometimes, understanding strikes us in a flash—a sudden "aha!" moment when everything falls into place.

Being in the present. Gestalt therapy places a strong emphasis on the present moment. Rather than dwelling endlessly on the past, clients are encouraged to speak in the present tense to explore how things feel now, rather than how they were in the past. For example, instead of "I felt angry when she ignored me," the client is invited to say, "I feel angry now, remembering how she ignored me."

First-person language. Clients are encouraged to take ownership of their experiences and avoid using passive or detached language. For example, "You feel ignored when that happens" becomes "I feel ignored when that happens."

Awareness statements. Gestalt therapy encourages the use of "I notice ..." or "I am aware of ..." to enhance self-awareness, such as "I'm aware that I'm clenching my fists right now."

Descriptive rather than interpretive. Clients are asked to describe sensations, actions, and emotions directly, rather than interpret or analyse them. For example: "My chest feels tight" instead of "I think I'm anxious." If a client has a headache, they might be invited to speak in the first person as the headache: "I am pounding, I am piercing, I am persistent," and so on. This technique enables the client to understand the symptom's message directly.

Dialogue with parts. Gestalt therapy employs tools such as the Empty Chair Technique to facilitate internal dialogues between conflicting aspects of the self or with others. An example of this might involve a client role-playing by conversing with their critical inner voice, which they place in an empty chair. Here's an example of the Empty Chair Technique:

Client:	I keep thinking about how my boss embarrassed me in that meeting.
Gestalt therapist:	Can you say more about what you're feeling right now as you remember that?
Client:	I feel my stomach tighten. I'm clenching my jaw. I guess I'm angry.
Therapist:	Say it in the first person—"I am angry." And notice what's happening in your body as you say that.
Client:	I am angry. My hands are clenching. I want to shout at him.
Therapist:	Let's put your boss in that empty chair. Tell him how you feel right now ...

This exchange brings the experience into the present, deepens awareness, and helps the client process emotions more directly and authentically.

At its core, Gestalt provides insight into the intrinsic human tendency to seek patterns, wholeness, and meaning, often without even realising that we are doing so.

Gestalt psychology suggests that we do not merely see individual pieces of the world; instead, we instinctively perceive whole patterns and shapes. Our minds are structured to connect the dots, fill in gaps, and make sense of things effortlessly. It's akin to a built-in shortcut for understanding life. In short, Gestalt is about seeing life as a whole, not in pieces, and trusting that our minds are built to find meaning.

Key Takeaways: Gestalt Therapy

Founders and Origins

- **Fritz Perls, Laura Perls, and Paul Goodman** were the founders of Gestalt therapy.
- Gestalt Therapy is a **humanistic** and **person-centred approach**, focusing on the whole individual.
- The **Gestalt Institute** was established in New York.

Core concept: **The whole is greater than the sum of its parts**

- We instinctively perceive **wholes** rather than isolated elements.
- Our brains **fill in the missing information** to make sense of incomplete images or experiences.

Gestalt Principles in Perception

1 **Closure**: We complete incomplete shapes.
2 **Proximity**: Things that are close together are perceived as a group.

3 **Similarity**: Similar items, such as colours and shapes, are grouped.
4 **Continuity**: We follow smooth lines and patterns.
5 **Figure–ground**: We identify a primary object (figure) against the background (ground).

Application in therapy:

- **A holistic perspective** reveals that **problems are not isolated**; rather, they reflect broader emotional patterns.
- **Field theory**: Emotions are shaped by the **entire environment**, not just the individual's inner world.
- **Here and now**: Focus is on the **present moment** rather than past experiences.
- **Insightful moments**: Understanding often comes in sudden, intuitive flashes ("aha!" moments).

Therapeutic Techniques

- First-person statements.
- Descriptive rather than interpretive.
- Awareness statement.
- Dialogue with parts.
- Empty Chair Technique.

Relevance

- Gestalt therapy encourages us to trust our inherent ability to create meaning.
- It integrates **thoughts, feelings, and the environment** to understand behaviour.
- It emphasises the client's active role in comprehension and healing.

Recommended Reading

Clarkson, Petruska (1989). *Gestalt Counselling in Action*. Sage. (A concise, practical introduction for students and practitioners, illustrating Gestalt in contemporary counselling contexts.)
Kepner, James I. (1987). *Body Process: A Gestalt Approach to Working with the Body in Psychotherapy*. Gestalt Institute of Cleveland Press. (Explores somatic awareness and body process as pathways to integration.)
Perls, Fritz (1969). *Gestalt Therapy Verbatim*. Real People Press. (Transcripts from Perls' workshops, illustrating Gestalt techniques in vivid, spontaneous dialogue.)
Perls, Fritz S., Hefferline, Ralph F., & Goodman, Paul (1951). *Gestalt Therapy: Excitement and Growth in the Human Personality*. Julian Press. (The original text that launched Gestalt therapy—blending existential philosophy, field theory, and phenomenological practice.)

Polster, Erving, & Polster, Miriam (1973). *Gestalt Therapy Integrated: Contours of Theory and Practice*. Brunner/Mazel. (A clear and accessible overview of Gestalt therapy's principles and methods—ideal for trainees.)

Yontef, Gary M. (1993). *Awareness, Dialogue, and Process: Essays on Gestalt Therapy*. Gestalt Journal Press. (Explores awareness, contact, and the I–Thou relationship in depth. Integrates Buber's philosophy with relational Gestalt—essential reading on presence, empathy, and the therapeutic field.)

Zinker, Joseph (1977). *Creative Process in Gestalt Therapy*. Brunner/Mazel. (A classic on imagination, experimentation, and creativity in the therapeutic process.)

Rational Emotive Behaviour Therapy (REBT)

Albert Ellis (1913–2007) was an American psychologist and Psychotherapist. In 1955, he introduced Rational Emotive Behaviour Therapy (REBT; Ellis, 1994).

At the centre of the model is Ellis's ABC model, the foundation of Rational Emotive Behaviour Therapy (REBT). From this centre, three key branches extend: A, B, and C, which represent the flow of emotional and behavioural experience.

A **stands for Activating Event**. The situation or trigger that occurs first could be something as simple as being criticised at work or being stuck in traffic. It's important to remember that the *event itself doesn't directly cause our emotional reaction*.

B **stands for Beliefs**. These are our interpretations, assumptions, and beliefs regarding the activating event. For instance, after being criticised, we

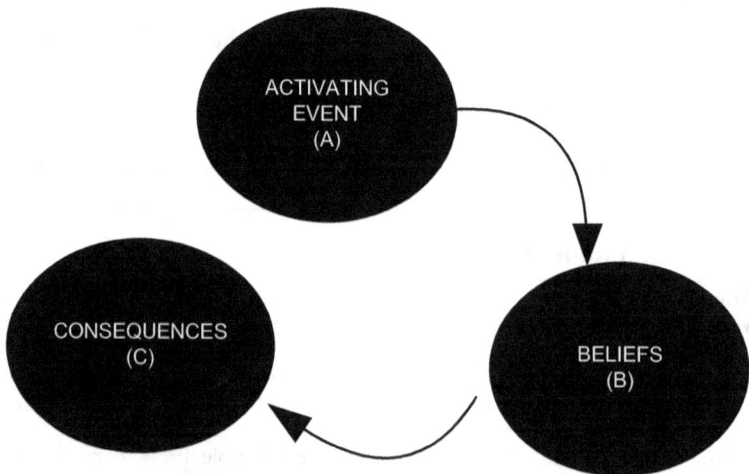

Figure 2.2 Ellis's ABC model.

might believe, *"I must be perfect and never make mistakes."* It is our beliefs, not the event, that truly shape how we feel and act.

C   **stands for Consequences**, which are the emotional, physical, and behavioural outcomes resulting from our beliefs. If we hold rigid, harsh beliefs about ourselves after receiving criticism, we may feel shame, anger, or depression and might withdraw from future challenges. In this model, Ellis powerfully highlights that altering the belief (B) can transform the emotional and behavioural consequences (C)—even when the activating event (A) remains unchanged.

Key Takeaways: REBT

Founder and Framework

- **Albert Ellis** founded **REBT** (Rational Emotive Behavior Therapy), which was introduced in **1955**.
- REBT focuses on altering irrational beliefs to improve emotional well-being.

Ellis's ABC model:

- **A stands for Activating Event,** which refers to a triggering situation (e.g., criticism, traffic). It is important to note that **the event itself does not directly cause emotional responses.**
- **B stands for Beliefs**: the interpretations or thoughts regarding the event. For instance: "I must never make mistakes." This is known as a **dogmatic belief,** one of many types of distorted thoughts. It is not the event itself that determines how we feel and react, but rather the thought.
- **C stands for Consequences.** Consequences can be summarised as the **emotional, physical, and behavioural outcomes.** If beliefs are irrational or rigid, the consequences may include feelings of shame, depression, or avoidant behaviour.

Core concept of REBT:

- **Altering beliefs can lead to changes in emotional and behavioural outcomes, even if the triggering event remains unchanged.**
- This model empowers individuals by demonstrating that they can **reframe their thinking** to alter how they feel and behave.

Recommended Reading

Dryden, Windy (2008/2014). *Rational Emotive Behaviour Therapy: Distinctive Features*, 2nd ed. Routledge. (A concise overview highlighting 15 key principles distinguishing REBT from other approaches.)

Ellis, Albert (1962/1994). *Reason and Emotion in Psychotherapy.* Kensington Publishing. (The original 1962 text where Ellis lays out the theory and method of REBT. Essential reading for students and professionals.)

Ellis, Albert (1988). *How to Stubbornly Refuse to Make Yourself Miserable About Anything—Yes, Anything!* Citadel. (Witty and direct. Offers practical tools to challenge irrational beliefs and build emotional resilience.)

Ellis, Albert (2001). *Overcoming Destructive Beliefs, Feelings, and Behaviours: New Directions for Rational Emotive Behaviour Therapy.* Prometheus Books. (Tailored to general readers looking to apply REBT in real life, with updated insights and examples.)

Ellis, Albert & Harper, Robert A. (1973). *A Guide to Rational Living.* Wilshire Book Company. (Accessible and popular, it introduces REBT principles for everyday life and emotional well-being. Great for clients and newcomers.)

Garcy, Pamela D. (2009). *The REBT Super-Activity Guide* (A workbook-style format with exercises for applying REBT concepts; for use in therapy or independently.)

Cognitive Behavioural Therapy (CBT)

REBT became one of the main pillars of Cognitive Behavioural Therapy (CBT), developed by Aaron T. Beck (1921–2021), an American psychiatrist and professor in the Department of Psychiatry at the University of Pennsylvania. Beck is recognised as the father of CBT, which focuses on understanding the connections between thoughts, feelings, and actions. Beck noted that individuals with depression often harbour numerous negative thoughts about themselves, others, the world, and the future.

Beck built on these insights by introducing the concepts of distorted thinking, negative automatic thoughts, and negative core beliefs. He elucidated how these unexamined thought patterns could profoundly disrupt an individual's life. Furthermore, Beck developed practical exercises to challenge unhelpful beliefs and replace them with more constructive alternatives. His work established the foundation for many therapeutic techniques we utilise today (Beck, 1976).

Key Takeaways: CBT

1 **The influence of REBT on CBT**: Rational-Emotive Behaviour Therapy (REBT) emerged as a fundamental aspect of Cognitive Behavioural Therapy (CBT).

2 **Aaron T. Beck**, an American psychiatrist and professor at the University of Pennsylvania, is recognised as the father of CBT.

3 CBT emphasises understanding the interplay between thoughts, feelings, and behaviours.

4 **Negative thought patterns in depression**: Beck observed that individuals with depression often harbour persistent negative thoughts about themselves, others, the world, and the future.

5 **Key concepts introduced by Beck**:

- **Distorted thinking**
- **Negative automatic thoughts**
- **Negative core beliefs**

6 **Therapeutic techniques**: Beck devised practical tools for identifying and challenging unhelpful beliefs, promoting the adoption of more constructive thinking patterns.

7 **Legacy**: Beck's theories and methods underpin many contemporary therapeutic practices.

Recommended Reading

Beck, Aaron T. (1976). *Cognitive Therapy and the Emotional Disorders*. International Universities Press. (The original 1976 text that laid the groundwork for cognitive-behavioural therapy (CBT). Still an essential for students and professionals.)

Beck, Judith S. (2011/2021). *Cognitive Therapy: Basics and Beyond*, 3rd ed. Guilford Press. (A gold-standard training manual used worldwide. Clear, structured, and full of clinical examples.)

Beck, Judith S. (2020). *Cognitive Behavioural Therapy: Theory and Practice*, 3rd ed. Guilford Press. (Technical and thorough, suitable for advanced students and clinicians.)

Greenberger, Dennis & Padesky, Christine A. (1995/2016). *Mind Over Mood: Change How You Feel by Changing the Way You Think*, 2nd ed. Guilford Press. (A widely used client workbook—ideal for introducing CBT concepts and tools in an accessible, practical format.)

Riggenbach, Jeff (2012). *The CBT Toolbox: A Workbook for Clients and Clinicians*. PESI Publishing and Media. (Packed with exercises, worksheets, and strategies—applicable in therapy or self-help contexts.)

Logotherapy

In 1959, Viktor Frankl (1905–1997), an Austrian neurologist, psychologist, and philosopher, published his landmark book, *Man's Search for Meaning*. In it, Frankl shares how his unwavering commitment to finding meaning amid the unimaginable suffering of Nazi concentration camps helped him survive. He learned that everything can be taken from a person except their right to choose their set of circumstances. Through this deeply personal narrative, he introduces Logotherapy, an existential and humanistic approach to psychology grounded in a powerful idea: the search for meaning is the primary driving force in human life.

Unlike Freud, who emphasised the will to pleasure, and Adler, who emphasised the will to power, Frankl proposed the concept of the "will to meaning". He believed that even in the face of suffering, pain, and adversity, we are capable of discovering purpose—and that doing so gives us the strength not just to survive, but to live with greater resilience, dignity, and inner peace.

Logotherapy helps individuals uncover personal meaning through their experiences, values, relationships, and hardships, demonstrating that we can endure almost anything when we find meaning in life (Frankl, 1959).

Key Takeaways: Logotherapy

1 **Viktor Frankl and his legacy**:

- Viktor Frankl was an Austrian neurologist, psychologist, and philosopher.
- He authored *Man's Search for Meaning* (1959), which recounts his experiences in Nazi concentration camps.

2 **Core concept of Logotherapy—"will to meaning"**: Frankl introduced Logotherapy, based on the idea that the primary drive in human life is the search for meaning, not pleasure (Freud) or power (Adler).

3 **Key insight from Frankl's experience**:

- Even in the face of extreme suffering, we retain the freedom to choose our attitude.

4 **Purpose through suffering**:

- Frankl believed meaning can be found in pain, adversity, and hardship, and this search for purpose enables resilience and dignity.

5 **Practical guidance of Logotherapy**:

- Helps individuals find meaning through their experiences, values, relationships, and even suffering.
- Suggests that when we discover purpose, we can endure nearly anything.

Recommended Reading

Frankl, Viktor E. (1959/2021). *Man's Search for Meaning*. Penguin. (Frankl's classic blends Holocaust memoir with logotherapy, centred on the will to meaning.)

Frankl, Viktor E. (1969/2014). *The Will to Meaning: Foundations and Applications of Logotherapy*. Penguin. (A theoretical companion to *Man's Search for Meaning*, outlining the clinical and philosophical roots of logotherapy.)

Behavioural Psychology

In the mid-twentieth century, Behavioural Psychology and Psychoanalysis were the dominant schools of thought in American psychology, often referred to as the First and Second Forces. One of the key figures in behaviour therapy was B. F. Skinner (1904–1990), an American psychologist, behaviourist, inventor, and social philosopher. Behaviourists suggest that our environment shapes behaviour and that it is learned through experience. They focus on observable and measurable aspects, dismissing the intangible, conceptual, and intellectual. Their premise is straightforward: behaviours can be modified using rewards or punishments. It is based on the idea that behaviour is learned through interaction with the environment, mainly through conditioning.

Behavioural psychologists argue that behaviour can be shaped, modified, or eliminated by adjusting the environment using reinforcement techniques, without exploring a person's inner mental world (Skinner, 1953).

Recommended Reading

Clear, James (2018). *Atomic Habits.* Penguin. (Another engaging behavioural read with practical applications, focusing on habit loops, reinforcement, and behavioural shaping.)

Duhigg, Charles (2012). *The Power of Habit.* Random House. (Though not a technical psychology text, it draws heavily on behavioural principles to explore how *everyday* habits are formed and changed.)

Hull, Clark L. (1943). *Principles of Behavior.* Appleton-Century. (A historical classic introducing stimulus–response theory and motivation within behaviourism.)

Miltenberger, Raymond G. (2016). *Behavior Modification: Principles and Procedures.* Cengage Learning. (A widely used university-level textbook. Clear explanations of behaviourist principles with lots of real-life applications.)

Skinner, B. F. (1953). *Science and Human Behavior.* Macmillan. (A cornerstone of behaviourism by one of its founders. Explores how environmental factors shape human behaviour. Still widely cited.)

Humanistic Psychology

Abraham Maslow (1908–70) critiqued behaviourism for neglecting fundamental aspects of being human, such as love, faith, and morality, alongside the darker elements of greed, cruelty, and the lust for power. He also raised concerns about psychoanalysis due to its excessive focus on individuals facing mental health challenges and personality disorders.

Like Rogers, Maslow believed in humans' intrinsic drive to realise their full potential and self-actualise. He centred his work on the positive, transformative aspects of humanity, which led to the development of Humanistic Psychology, often referred to as the Third Force. This field offered an optimistic perspective on comprehending the human experience, emphasising the higher functions of the psyche, such as creativity and purpose. This approach quickly became popular among mental health professionals and the general public in the UK.

Humanistic Psychology revolutionised psychotherapy, encouraging clients to look beyond the past and focus more on the present, examining what they felt and experienced in the moment. These therapies gained traction because they often resulted in immediate emotional breakthroughs and profound insights (Maslow, 1954).

Recommended Reading

Assagioli, Roberto (1965). *Psychosynthesis: A Manual of Principles and Techniques.* Hobbs, Dorman & Company. (Bridges Humanistic and Transpersonal psychology—placing the will, love, and Self at the centre of personal growth.)

Hoffman, Eve, & Maslow, Abraham H. (1996). *Future Visions: The Unpublished Papers of Abraham Maslow.* Sage. (Reveals Maslow's later writings on transcendence, creativity, and the emerging "fourth force" of psychology.)

Maslow, Abraham H. (1968). *Toward a Psychology of Being* (2nd ed.). Van Nostrand. (Introduces self-actualisation and peak experience—the positive, growth-oriented vision that inspired the human potential movement.)

Rogers, Carl R. (1961). *On Becoming a Person: A Therapist's View of Psychotherapy.* Houghton Mifflin. (A cornerstone of Humanistic Psychology, Rogers's warmth, humility, and faith in the client's capacity for growth remain relevant today.)

Rowan, John (2001). *Ordinary Ecstasy: The Dialectics of Humanistic Psychology* (3rd ed.). Brunner-Routledge. (A lively, comprehensive exploration of humanistic, transpersonal, and integrative currents.)

Transpersonal Psychology

In the 1960s, a group that included Abraham Maslow, Stanislav Grof, and Tony Sutich explored how psychology could incorporate spiritual elements. Maslow introduced his Hierarchy of Needs, describing human motivation as a progression through five levels, moving from the most basic to the most advanced. At the foundation are physiological needs—the essentials for survival, such as food, water, and shelter. Once these are met, individuals seek safety, striving for security, stability, and protection. The next level centres on love and belonging, emphasising the importance of relationships, friendships, and human connection. As people establish strong social bonds, they turn their attention to esteem needs, seeking respect, recognition, and a sense of self-worth. Ultimately, at the highest level, individuals strive for self-actualisation, seeking to reach their full potential and foster personal growth. According to Maslow, people typically must satisfy the needs at each lower level before advancing to higher stages of need development. The spectrum of human needs, according to Maslow, ranges from survival to the ultimate goal of self-actualisation—becoming the fullest version of oneself.

Stanislav "Stan" Grof (b. 1931), a Czech-born American psychiatrist, further explored the human mind. As a pioneer of transpersonal psychology, Grof opened doors to understanding non-ordinary states of consciousness, demonstrating how altered states can be powerful tools for healing, deep self-discovery, and spiritual growth.

Alongside him stood Tony Sutich (1907–76), often referred to as the Stephen Hawking of psychology. Despite living with a significant physical disability, Sutich made extraordinary contributions that helped shape and fuel the humanistic and transpersonal movements, leaving a legacy of courage, vision, and profound insight into the human spirit. He proposed a new direction for psychology—one that would go beyond traditional frameworks to include spirituality, transcendence, and elevated states of consciousness. This "Fourth Force" would focus on studying and thoughtfully integrating peak experiences and spiritual dimensions that earlier psychological models had largely overlooked or dismissed.

The group aimed to develop a holistic, spiritually inclusive approach to comprehending the human psyche. They believed that non-ordinary states of consciousness could provide profound insights, helping individuals gain a deeper understanding of themselves.

Stanislav Grof introduced the term "transpersonal psychology", which is often referred to as the Fourth Force in psychology. Maslow, already a key figure in psychology, played a significant role in this movement.

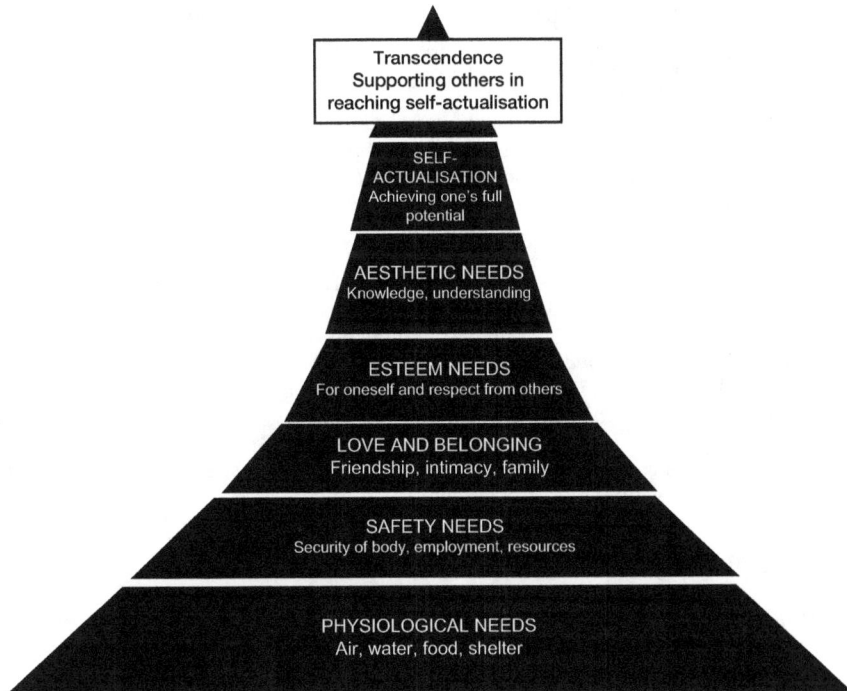

Figure 2.3 Maslow's expanded Hierarchy of Needs.

In 1943, Maslow's renowned Hierarchy of Needs was introduced in his paper "A Theory of Human Motivation". The original five-tier model outlined how basic needs—such as food, water, and safety—must be met before individuals can focus on higher needs, including love, self-esteem, and, ultimately, self-actualisation. Maslow later expanded the hierarchy to include transcendent or spiritual experiences, reflecting the movement's emphasis on non-ordinary states of consciousness. He advocated for an expanded vision of psychology— one that transcended conventional approaches by embracing spiritual insight, transcendent experiences, and higher states of awareness.

This emerging "Fourth Force" aimed to explore and meaningfully incorporate these profound human experiences, which earlier psychological schools had often neglected or excluded.

By integrating Maslow's insights with the transpersonal focus on spiritual and transcendent experiences, this group established the foundation for a new approach to comprehending the human mind and spirit.

Recommended Reading

Ferrer, Jorge N. (2001). *Revisioning Transpersonal Theory: A Participatory Vision of Human Spirituality*. SUNY Press. (A rigorous yet accessible overview of the field. Ferrer critiques traditional hierarchies and offers a participatory vision of spirituality in psychology.)

Grof, Stanislav & Grof, Christina (1989). *Spiritual Emergency: When Personal Transformation Becomes a Crisis*. Penguin. (Explores spiritual emergencies—like kundalini awakenings—and how to support those in crisis.)

Grof, Stanislav & Grof, Christina (1990). *The Stormy Search for the Self: A Guide to Personal Growth Through Transformational Crisis*. Penguin. (Companion book to *Spiritual Emergency*, blending case studies and practical guidance.)

Rowan, John (1993/2006). *The Transpersonal: Spirituality in Psychotherapy and Counselling*, 2nd ed. Routledge. (A clear, practical introduction to transpersonal therapy. Bridges psychodynamic, humanistic, and spiritual approaches. Widely used in training.)

Singer, Michael A. (2007). *The Untethered Soul: The Journey Beyond Yourself*. New Harbinger Publications. (Popular and deeply spiritual. While not academic, it aligns with transpersonal themes of awareness and liberation.)

Washburn, M. (2003). *Embodied Spirituality in a Sacred World*. State University of New York Press. (A rich, integrative theory of human development from a depth-psychological and transpersonal perspective.)

Wilber, Ken (2000). *Integral Psychology: Consciousness, Spirit, Psychology, Therapy*. Shambhala Publications. (Maps human development across cognitive, emotional, and spiritual lines. Integrates Eastern and Western models.)

Integrative Psychotherapy

During the 1940s and 1950s, therapists began to explore the integration of various therapeutic methods. At that time, the prominent schools of thought— such as psychoanalysis, behaviourism, and humanistic psychology—operated in isolation. However, therapists such as George Kelly and Carl Rogers began experimenting with combining techniques to meet their clients' needs better.

By the 1960s, humanistic therapy, emphasising personal growth and self-actualisation, was gaining popularity. This movement fostered a vibrant exchange of ideas, integrating elements from Gestalt and Person-Centred Therapy approaches. The result was a richer, more adaptable framework for helping clients navigate their challenges. It marked the beginning of a more integrative approach to psychotherapy.

Integrative psychotherapy combines various therapeutic styles to create a treatment plan tailored to each individual. This approach flourished in the 1970s and 1980s as therapists realised that a singular method could not adequately encapsulate the complex nuances of human emotions and behaviours.

Arnold Lazarus (1932–2013) was a South African-born clinical psychologist and researcher who specialised in cognitive therapy and is best known for developing Multimodal Therapy (MMT).

In 1973, MMT was developed to encourage therapists to customise their techniques by drawing upon a range of therapeutic practices that align with each client's needs. This method adopts a holistic perspective, considering every aspect of a person's experience—thoughts, emotions, behaviours, physical sensations, and more—creating a comprehensive and personalised framework for therapeutic healing (Lazarus, 1981).

Around the same time, American professor and clinical psychologist John Norcross (b. 1957) and others promoted an eclectic approach that incorporates techniques from various therapeutic models according to clients' needs. The eclectic approach weaves together methods from different schools, rather than adhering to a single, rigid framework. This flexibility enables therapists to create a personalised, client-centred plan tailored to each individual's unique challenges and aspirations. This concept evolved into what we now refer to as integrative psychotherapy. By the 1990s and 2000s, integrative therapy had become a respected approach within modern psychotherapy. Its strength lies in its adaptability; it has continuously evolved to include techniques such as mindfulness, cognitive-behavioural therapy, and trauma-focused methods.

Recommended Reading

Erskine, Richard (2011). *Integrative Psychotherapy in Action*. Routledge. (Blends psychodynamic, cognitive, body-oriented, and existential approaches. Focuses on contact, awareness, and the therapeutic relationship.)

Feltham, Colin & Horton, Ian (2000). *The Handbook of Counselling and Psychotherapy*. Sage. (Comprehensive reference text covering various approaches, integration methods, ethics, and contemporary issues.)

Gilbert, Maria & Evans, Ken (2005). *An Introduction to Integrative Psychotherapy*. Bloomsbury. (Provides a solid theoretical foundation for working integratively, including relational, developmental, and humanistic elements.)

Gilbert, Maria & Evans, Ken (2010). *Integrative Psychotherapy: 100 Key Points and Techniques.* Routledge. (A concise and practical guide offering core concepts and tools across various modalities. Excellent for trainees and practitioners alike.)

Knox, Rosanne, Wiggins, Susan, Murphy, David, & Cooper, Mick (eds) (2012). *Relational Depth: New Perspectives and Developments.* Palgrave. (While rooted in person-centred work, this book explores relational integration that applies across modalities.)

Ogden, Pat, Minton, Kekuni, Pain, Claire (2006). *Trauma and the Body: A Sensorimotor Approach to Psychotherapy.* W. W. Norton & Company. (While grounded in somatic work, this book offers integrative methods that incorporate neuroscience, attachment theory, and relational theory.)

Van der Kolk, Bessel (2014). *The Body Keeps the Score.* Penguin. (A widely read text that integrates psychology, neuroscience, bodywork, and trauma theory into a coherent, holistic view of healing.)

References

Adler, A. (1925). *The practice and theory of individual psychology.* Routledge.

Beck, A. T. (1976). *Cognitive therapy and the emotional disorders.* International Universities Press.

Ellis, A. (1994). *Reason and emotion in psychotherapy.* Carol Publishing Group.

Frankl, V. E. ([1959]2006). *Man's search for meaning* (I. Lasch, trans.). Beacon Press. (Original work published 1946.)

Freud, S. ([1900]1953). *The interpretation of dreams.* Hogarth Press.

Horney, K. (1967). *Feminine psychology.* W. W. Norton & Company.

Jung, C. G. (1964). *Man and his symbols.* Aldus Books.

Lazarus, A. A. (1981). *The practice of multimodal therapy: Systematic, comprehensive, and effective psychotherapy.* McGraw-Hill.

Maslow, A. H. (1943). A theory of human motivation. *Psychological Review*, 50(4): 370–396.

Maslow, A. H. (1954). *Motivation and personality.* Harper & Row.

Perls, F. S., Hefferline, R. F., & Goodman, P. (1951). *Gestalt therapy: Excitement and growth in the human personality.* Julian Press.

Rogers, C. (1951). *Client-centred therapy: Its current practice, implications and theory.* Houghton Mifflin.

Skinner, B. F. (1953). *Science and human behaviour.* Macmillan.

Chapter 3

Jargon Buster

Telling It Like It Is

Like any profession, psychotherapy has jargon—shorthand that professionals use for quick and precise communication. To make this book more accessible to those unfamiliar with the terms, I have included a glossary of the psychological concepts featured throughout, providing easy-to-understand definitions.

Let us begin with the psyche, the central focus of psychotherapists' work. I will explain this concept in straightforward steps.

The Psyche

People often confuse the terms "psyche" and "personality", but they are distinct concepts. The psyche encompasses your entire mental, emotional, and spiritual world, including your conscious knowledge and the aspects that lie beneath the surface in the unconscious. In contrast, personality reflects how this inner content manifests *externally*—how you behave, interact with, and respond to the world around you. Your psyche represents your inner Self, while your personality is what others perceive based on your internal experiences.

The term "psyche" comes from the Greek word *psyche*. In psychotherapy, it denotes an individual's mental or psychological framework; transpersonal psychotherapists (and some others) also include the concept of the Soul. The origins of the psyche and its intricate contents raise profound metaphysical questions that may never be fully resolved. Carl Jung, the eminent Swiss psychiatrist and psychoanalyst, characterised the psyche as a dynamic system in constant pursuit of equilibrium between opposing forces, evolving through a transformative journey he referred to as individuation (1923).

Pliable and ever-changing, the psyche learns from experiences, adapts to new challenges, and seeks equilibrium amidst conflict. The rules and roles within our families, societal norms, and interactions with others shape our psyche, influencing our identity and our relationship with the world. Our experiences leave footprints on our psyche; we form biases and perceptions that affect how we interpret and respond to our surroundings. Traumas and

DOI: 10.4324/9781003675099-4

unresolved conflicts can leave a lasting mark, impacting mental health and well-being. The most enduring footprints are often made during the first seven years of life. The world comprises many opposites, and our psyches also encompass opposing forces—inner and outer, conscious and unconscious. Conflict, although often uncomfortable, is an integral part of our existence and plays a crucial role in our development. The psyche's inherent drive is to balance these opposing forces, encouraging our evolution. When we confront the clash between these contrasting elements, we create space for something new to emerge—something that respects and harmonises both sides—a third way. This transformative process, known as self-realisation, actualisation, or individuation (take your pick), leads us towards discovering life's deeper meaning and our sense of wholeness. It is referred to as individuation or selfing—the goal towards which human beings aspire. Psychotherapy involves understanding and exploring the complexities of the unconscious mind. Therapists unravel its mysteries in various ways, assisting clients in illuminating unconscious material and navigating their thoughts, emotions, and behaviours to foster healing and growth. Exploring this intricate landscape can lead to self-discovery, personal development, and a deeper appreciation of our shared human experience.

Figure 3.1 presents a simplified map of the psyche, as depicted by Jung (1960a), illustrating the Self as both a process and a psychic entity. Don't

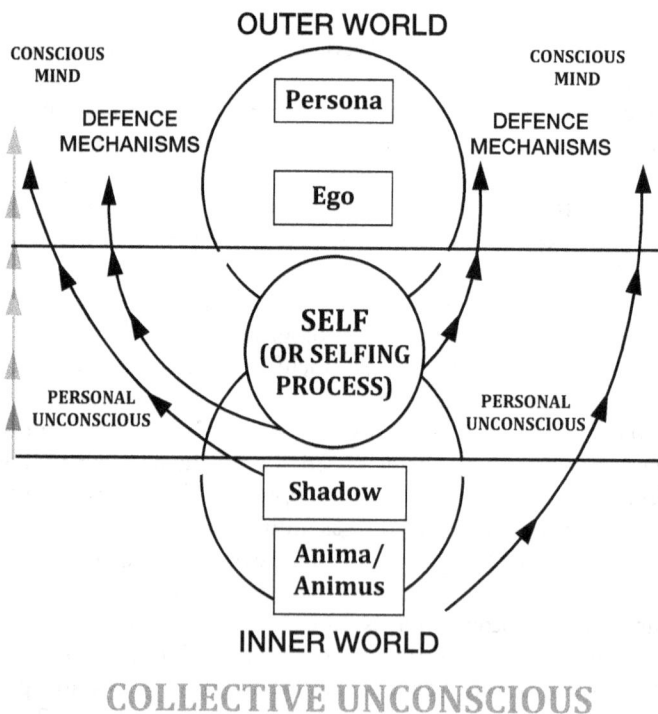

Figure 3.1 Simplified Jungian map of the psyche.

worry—it's not as complex as it may seem. I will explain the basics and elaborate on them throughout this chapter and the book.

You cannot see or touch the psyche, and no X-ray can reveal it. The psyche is a theoretical framework that encompasses our thoughts, emotions, behaviours, and experiences.

It comprises several interconnected zones and polarities, such as consciousness and unconsciousness, the outer world and inner world, and the Ego and Shadow. Envisage it as a living, ever-shifting terrain with peaks of clarity and valleys of obscurity, constantly reshaping our self-perception and worldview. Each component operates as a secondary self, contributing uniquely to our mental landscape.

Consciousness

The psyche encompasses both consciousness and the unconscious. Consciousness is a vast and intricate subject. Throughout history, some have maintained the belief that everything in the universe contains elements of consciousness—a perspective that has persisted across various cultures and philosophies.

Ibn Arabi (1165–1240), a twelfth-century Andalusian Arab scholar, Sufi mystic, and philosopher, was highly influential in Islamic thought. He stated, "God sleeps in the rock, dreams in the plant, stirs in the animal, and awakens in man."

In the mid-1600s, Baruch Spinoza (1632–77), a Dutch philosopher of Sephardic Jewish origin, had a bold and radical vision: he viewed God not as a distant, human-like figure watching over the world, but as the world itself. To him, God and nature were the same—everything that exists expresses this singular, infinite reality. There is no separation between the divine and the universe; everything from stars to thoughts forms part of the same substance.

This sweeping idea is *pantheism*—the belief that God is the universe. In Spinoza's view, if you want to understand God, you don't look up; you look around. Though Spinoza was branded a heretic in his own time—cast out by his community and dismissed by many—his ideas refused to die. Instead, they quietly took root and flourished, influencing some of the most powerful minds in history. Hegel admired his logic, Nietzsche respected his strength of thought, Einstein called him a kindred spirit, and Deleuze saw him as a philosopher of joy and freedom. Today, Spinoza remains a cornerstone of modern philosophy. His rationalism, characterised by clear-eyed insight and a profound belief in the natural order, has significantly influenced our understanding of ethics, the universe, and our place within it.

Similarly, Giordano Bruno (1548–1600), an Italian philosopher, poet, and alchemist, examined the universe from a mystical perspective. He proposed that the universe was composed of a single substance infused with Spirit or consciousness (Bruno, 1998). The Inquisition accused Bruno of heresy and ultimately executed him by burning him at the stake and scattering his ashes in the Tiber.

During that era, the prevailing view, particularly among those in power, was that all matter was lifeless and that humans occupied a superior status. Challenging this notion often had serious consequences. These historical conflicts underscore the ongoing debate about the nature of consciousness and humanity's place in the universe.

These ideas have existed for centuries, emerging in ancient Greek philosophy, Hinduism, Buddhism, Taoism, and Christian mysticism. For instance, St Francis of Assisi, an Italian mystic and Catholic friar who founded the Franciscan religious order, famously spoke to flowers and birds, embodying a profound connection with all living beings.

This philosophical perspective is known as panpsychism, which combines the Greek words "*pan*" (meaning "all") and "*psyche*" (meaning "soul"). It posits that, at a fundamental level, everything in the universe possesses some form of consciousness. As the Canadian philosopher William Seager (2020: 9) stated, at a very basic level, the world is awake.

Enter quantum physics: the science that says, "Reality? Good luck pinning that down." When physicists zoom in on the universe's tiniest building blocks, they don't find neat little bricks. They find shimmering energy fields where particles pop into existence like surprise guests at a party—borrowing energy, busting a few moves, hanging around for a nanosecond, and then vanishing like Cinderella at midnight.

In this view, consciousness and energy aren't separate; they're part of the same strange and possibly sentient universe.

Some scientists and philosophers have speculated that the strange, unpredictable behaviour of quantum particles might be linked to our minds. In the quantum realm, particles can simultaneously exist in multiple states until they are observed; at that point, they "collapse" into a definitive state. It's as if nature plays coy until someone asks, "What's happening?" and then quantum potential becomes reality because we looked.

Let's put it this way: Imagine you are playing hide-and-seek with a quantum cat. Until you peek, it's not just behind the curtain or under the bed—it's hiding in *all* the spots simultaneously. Closet? Yes. Inside the box? Also, yes. But the moment you lift the lid and look—BOOM!—The cat picks a spot. Suddenly, it's *just in the box*. That magical moment of choosing is what physicists refer to as *wave function collapse*.

And yes, it remains a contentious issue. Physicists, philosophers, and theorists are engaging in fierce debate. They argue with more passion about this than some couples I've observed in therapy. And that's saying something.

This raises the provocative question: Could our consciousness influence this process? It is almost as if the universe is a vast "choose-your-own-ending" story, where our observations determine which reality comes to pass.

The notion that consciousness might shape reality has sent imaginations spiralling, not just among sci-fi writers and conspiracy theorists. Some speculate that your thoughts could influence the fabric of the universe. If true, this means that your bad mood could be more potent than you realise. However, mainstream physicists aren't convinced. They argue that quantum effects are so tiny that they barely tickle an atom, let alone bend the power of your brainwaves.

Still, the mystery of consciousness continues to tug at the edges of science. It isn't entirely proven science, not quite philosophy, but wonderfully in between, a place where curiosity thrives, and conclusions remain just out of reach.

So, we return to the big question again: Could consciousness be more than we think it is?

Let me summarise the above and explain why this is significant from a therapeutic perspective. In quantum physics, wave function collapse occurs when a particle that exists in many possible states suddenly "chooses" one of them the moment it is observed. Before that moment, it's all potential, *a cloud of possibilities*. However, when we observe it, reality crystallises into a single outcome.

Some interpretations suggest that consciousness plays a role in this collapse—that our *attention* or *observation* is not merely a passive act of witnessing reality, but actively contributes to shaping it.

If the universe holds multiple possibilities at once, and our observation brings one into being, then perhaps, just perhaps, we're not just participants in reality, but co-creators of it.

In this regard, your choices, focus, and awareness not only reflect your world but also play a role in its creation.

Moving on from quantum physics now (as I've exhausted my knowledge of it), at the individual level, consciousness is the experience of awareness. It is the part of you that recognises that you are thinking, feeling, and perceiving the world around you. When you are awake and alert, you remain conscious. Consciousness diminishes when you are in a deep sleep, listening to a dry lecture, reading this book (I'm just checking to see if you're still with me), under anaesthesia, or otherwise unaware.

Consciousness defines you, offering a sense of self and allowing you to reflect on your thoughts and experiences. Consciousness has two primary aspects:

1 **Awareness of the world**: This represents your built-in reality radar. It's how you register the warmth of sunlight on your skin, catch the scent of a blooming rose, or hear your favourite song and tap your foot. In those moments, you aren't merely existing—you're aware of the experience, and actively tuned in to the world around you.
2 **Self-awareness**: This is your ability to step back and say, "Hey, that's me feeling this." It's recognising yourself as a distinct being—separate from your surroundings—with the capacity to reflect on your own thoughts, emotions, and existence. It's your inner witness, quietly asking (usually at

3 a.m.), "Why do I feel this way?" or "What does it all mean?" These two aspects work together to create your conscious experience. Carl Jung compared consciousness to the eye: it can focus on only a limited number of objects at any moment. Likewise, consciousness's activity is selective. Jung argued that selection necessitates intentional direction, which inevitably excludes other aspects considered irrelevant to the immediate focus.

Sigmund Freud employed the iceberg analogy, suggesting that the mind resembles an iceberg.

The brain plays a vital role in consciousness. Various regions of the brain process information, such as sights, sounds, and memories, which shape your conscious experience. Scientists suggest that consciousness may operate like a spotlight in the brain—only certain information is illuminated, which you are aware of at any given moment.

There are vast oceans of unknowns surrounding the concept of consciousness. For instance, we can understand how the brain perceives red or blue, but we don't know why seeing red or blue *feels* as it does. Scientists and philosophers have proposed various ideas about how it operates:

- **Global Workspace theory** envisions consciousness as a stage in a theatre, where numerous thoughts and perceptions compete for centre stage, and those that prevail are what you consciously recognise.
- **Consciousness as a form of energy**: This hypothesis posits that consciousness, like other forms of matter, constitutes a type of energy, as matter and energy can manifest in various forms.
- **Integrated Information theory** posits that consciousness emerges from the brain's ability to connect and integrate information. The more interconnected and unified the brain's information processing is, the richer and more complex consciousness becomes.
- **Panpsychism** posits that consciousness may be an inherent aspect of everything in the universe, not solely limited to our experiencing brains. From this perspective, even simple entities like atoms might possess a small degree of consciousness, though not in the same manner as we do.

Consciousness manifests in various ways, two of which are emotional tension and contemplation.

Consciousness Arising through Emotional Tension

I recall complaining to my therapist about an acquaintance I shall call Jane, who often asked me for a hug. "She's so childish, the way she uses a baby voice to request a hug," I remarked scornfully. "Show me what she does," my therapist prompted. I extended my arms, imitating the woman's body language. As I raised my arms towards my therapist, I unexpectedly felt tears welling up.

I was taken aback. I had been irritated, yet now I felt a wave of sadness wash over me. What was happening?

Encouraged by my therapist, I kept my arms outstretched and remembered moments from my childhood when I sought a hug while feeling upset, only to be told to stop crying. Reflecting on my somatic responses to the experience of outstretched arms, I realised an essential truth: vulnerability had sometimes gone unrewarded in my childhood, leading me to marginalise that part of myself. Jane had unearthed a long-suppressed piece of my past. She had shown me a part of myself I had consigned to the shadows, and I had a visceral reaction to her. She inadvertently helped me recognise a facet of myself I had avoided for years. Why could she display that emotionally needy part while I couldn't? I unconsciously envied her, and my envy was causing a destructive response, albeit one I masked.

The emotional tension created by criticising her and my outstretched arms ignited a flash of association, heightening my consciousness and enabling an emotional release.

I became aware of a marginalised part of myself: the needy child. The culture I was raised in largely denied this aspect of me, and I had concealed it so effectively that I no longer recognised it as part of "me".

What happens to these marginalised aspects? We cannot surgically remove them; they must be "heard", leading us to project them onto others unconsciously.

So, if you have a strong aversion to someone or their behaviour, ask yourself, "In what ways am I like that?" This is an entirely free and effective self-help technique.

Consciousness Arising through Contemplation

During a ten-day silent retreat, I experienced consciousness arising through contemplation. My retreat guide invited me to lie in the sunlight in the meadow connected to her house as part of a meditative spiritual practice. Having lived in cities all my life, this presented a challenge, yet I complied. I lay quite still, feeling as if I were doing something wrong, realising that I had never lain down in a meadow during my 45 years on this planet. I had always been concerned that I might be guilty of trespassing.

I stayed there for two hours or more, contemplating how the Earth spins on its axis and completes a full rotation every 24 hours, creating a rhythm of day and night through spring, summer, autumn, and winter, while cradling every creature upon it. My rational mind assured me that it wasn't a mystery keeping us all here, but gravity.

I had what I can only describe as a spiritual experience as I lay there. I felt smaller and smaller until I was not lying in a meadow but in a vast pair of hands. Cradled by Mother Earth, I wept quietly. I became acutely aware of my place in the cosmos—small yet significant and, above all, supported.

The Conscious and the Unconscious

The **conscious mind** is just the tip of the iceberg—the part of you that's alert, aware, and actively thinking in this very moment. It's where your focus resides, enabling you to take in your surroundings, solve problems, and make choices with clarity and intention. Like a spotlight, it shines on what matters most right now, guiding your thoughts, shaping your beliefs, and powering your ability to reason and plan. Though it's only a small slice of your mental landscape, it plays a decisive role in helping you respond to life with logic, purpose, and control.

Picture yourself sailing across a vast, glittering ocean when, on the horizon, a shimmering white peak catches your eye—an iceberg gleaming in the sunlight like a crown of ice rising from the deep. Its grandeur strikes you. "It's massive ... breathtaking," you gasp. But as your boat glides closer and you lean over the side for a better look, a startling truth emerges: what you see above the surface is just a tiny fragment. Beneath the waves lies an immense hidden world of ice, far larger than you imagined.

The striking image in Figure 3.2 is Sigmund Freud's powerful metaphor for the human mind; we know only the tip of the iceberg. The *real force* lies beneath, in our unconscious's vast, unseen depths (Freud, 1915).

The tip of the iceberg, above the waves, signifies your *conscious mind*—everything you are aware of in this moment. What you perceive, hear, think, and feel right now exists here.

Just beneath the surface lies your *preconscious*. It's akin to a mental waiting room where memories and thoughts linger quietly in the background, inactive yet readily accessible, like your best friend's birthday or how to ride a bike. You aren't actively thinking about them, but they're within reach.

The term "subconscious" is more modern than "preconscious". While it is not a formal Freudian term, it is sometimes used interchangeably with "preconscious"; however, distinct differences exist between the two. The subconscious encompasses both preconscious material and deeper, automatic processes, such as learned responses like flinching when a ball is thrown towards you or feeling uneasy in a situation without understanding why.

The conscious mind, where our immediate awareness resides, represents only a fraction of our thoughts, beliefs, and opinions. It functions with self-awareness, actively engaging in the present moment. It sharpens our focus, directing our thoughts, intentions, and perceptions to navigate life with purpose and awareness. This mental clarity empowers us to plan, reason, and process information logically, making it essential for overcoming challenges and making well-informed decisions. It operates alongside other facets of our mental life, such as the subconscious and unconscious mind, which often influence our conscious thoughts and behaviours in ways we may not fully understand. For instance, habits, implicit biases, and emotional triggers rooted in past experiences can subtly shape our decisions, even when we believe we are acting rationally.

FREUD'S ICEBERG THEORY

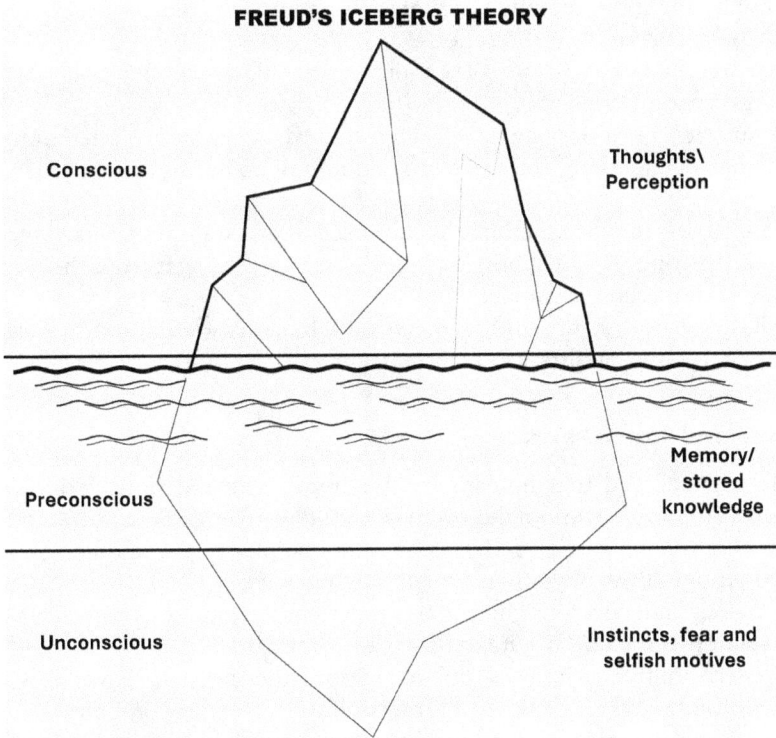

Figure 3.2 Freud's iceberg theory.

The Unconscious Mind

Deep beneath your awareness lies the *unconscious mind*—the deepest, most mysterious part of who you are. It's a vast, shadowy reservoir filled with hidden memories, desires, fears, and instincts. Although you may not sense it directly, it quietly shapes your thoughts, emotions, and behaviours, like powerful ocean currents steering a ship without the captain ever noticing.

This hidden inner world encompasses everything from buried childhood memories to intense emotions, including joy, grief, fear, love, and rage. You cannot see these forces, and you may not even realise they exist; however, they influence your daily choices in ways that often defy logic or explanation.

In therapy, we begin to explore this inner terrain through tools that open the door to the unconscious:

Free association—speaking freely, without filtering, to uncover hidden truths.
Dream analysis—decoding the rich symbolism of your dreams to reveal unconscious conflicts or desires.

Insight and interpretation—recognising patterns in your thoughts, behaviours, and emotional reactions.

Resistance work—exploring the topics you avoid, which often point directly to what is buried.

Transference—observing how feelings toward others are projected onto the therapist, offering clues to past relationships and unconscious dynamics.

We also listen to what the body communicates through physical symptoms, slips of the tongue, and subtle gestures. These are messages from the unconscious, awaiting understanding.

This journey into the unseen is not easy, but it is where deep self-understanding, healing, and transformation begin.

Outer and Inner Worlds

Carl Jung believed that humans inhabit both inner and outer worlds. He regarded the inner world—the realm of thoughts, emotions, and the unconscious—as infinite and as rich in depth and complexity as the outer physical world (Jung, 2009). When we remain unaware of our unconscious patterns, they quietly influence our choices and experiences, leading us to believe that life is simply unfolding by fate, rather than by design.

Western culture prioritises and emphasises the external, physical world, which is often regarded as the ultimate reality. This outer world encompasses our daily lives—where we work, interact with family, friends, and colleagues, and engage with the tangible aspects of existence. These aspects include the physical environment, thoughts, emotions, desires, relationships, domestic routines, professional obligations, hobbies, and interactions with animals and companions. This focus shapes our perceptions and values regarding our experiences.

Recognising the existence of our inner world enhances our understanding of ourselves. This often-unconscious inner world has far more influence over our lives than we typically realise. Neglecting this inner realm can be just as harmful as disregarding the external events that surround us. This concealed domain is deeply personal, filled with our core values, long-held aspirations, unspoken daydreams, and fantasies that shape our inner reality. It is the space where we envision projects, inventions, ambitions, and dreams—ideas that can eventually manifest in the outer world.

The inner and outer worlds are profoundly interconnected. This concept is beautifully articulated in the Emerald Tablet, an ancient text from the sixth to eighth centuries that was highly regarded by European alchemists. It states, "As within, so without; as above, so below; as the universe, so the Soul" (Trismegistus, 1999). This phrase suggests that our actions and experiences in the physical world are reflected in the spiritual realm and vice versa, emphasising the reciprocal relationship between the two.

The Hopi Indians, Indigenous peoples residing in the arid expanses of northwestern Arizona, believe in a connection between the mental patterns of the psyche and their physical world counterparts. This concept is reflected in various spiritual traditions and belief systems, including Vedanta, Neoplatonism, Sufism, Kabbalah, Zoroastrianism, Buddhism, and Taoism. Each offers its interpretation of the theme of interconnectedness.

Persona

If you've ever felt like a different person in various settings—one version of yourself at work, another at home, one personality with friends, and yet another with your in-laws—you have experienced your Persona.

The concept of the Persona is a fundamental idea in Jung's analytical psychology. The term originates from ancient Latin and translates to "mask." It signifies our social face when interacting with the world—a version of ourselves shaped by culture, society, and personal experiences. Just as an actor dons a mask to portray a role, our Persona helps us adapt to various social situations, fosters connections with others, and manages relationships.

The Persona is merely one facet of who we are, not the entirety of our being. Over-identifying with it can disconnect us from our authentic Self—our psyche's deeper, unseen layers. This attachment to the Persona may also hinder us from recognising and integrating our "Shadow"—the hidden, often uncomfortable aspects of ourselves. Embracing these aspects is essential for personal growth and self-realisation; this does not entail discarding the Persona entirely but rather achieving a balance.

Becoming aware of our Persona encourages us to question the societal masks we wear and the roles we are expected to play. With greater understanding, we can consciously choose whether to keep these masks, as they serve us in specific ways, or to explore the deeper aspects of our unconscious. By integrating these hidden parts of the Self, we unlock a pathway to greater authenticity and authentic self-expression.

You can find further information on the Persona in Chapter 11, "A Tale of Two Faces: Persona and Self".

Id, Ego, and Superego

Freud identified three components of the psyche: the Id, the Ego, and the Superego (1923). These elements constantly interact, striving to balance our desires, reality, and moral values.

The Id can be viewed as an inner toddler—impulsive, demanding, and centred entirely on immediate gratification. It represents raw instincts, desires, and the pursuit of pleasure, operating without logic, boundaries, or consideration for consequences. It's the "wild child" of the psyche.

The Ego represents the responsible, adult aspect of our psyche. Originating from the Latin word for "I", it develops during childhood and provides us with a sense of personal identity. The Ego serves as a "home base", encompassing our thoughts, feelings, sensations, intuitions, and memories. A healthy Ego functions as a mediator, balancing our desires with society's constraints and expectations.

For instance, consider the feeling of envy towards a colleague who has received a promotion. To protect your self-esteem and manage this envy, your Ego might unconsciously employ a defence mechanism such as rationalisation. You may convince yourself that your colleague succeeded due to connections or luck rather than acknowledging their abilities. Imagine learning to suppress your anger, possibly because expressing it often leads to conflict. Consequently, your Ego may turn to sublimation, redirecting that suppressed aggression into something more socially acceptable, like competitive sports. Thus, the intense energy of anger is channelled into a healthy, productive outlet.

The Ego plays a vital role in managing the Id's unrealistic demands. It functions like a middle manager, seeking balance instead of outright denial. For example, rather than saying, *No, you can't watch another hour of television*, the Ego might compromise by suggesting, *Yes, but only after you finish the work due tomorrow morning.*

The Ego can help us navigate life's challenges and smooth our path. However, significant life choices can push certain aspects of our personality into the unconscious, where they may act as opposing forces to our conscious mindset. The unconscious seeks balance, often expressing itself through dreams, symbols, "accidents", or physical and emotional reactions and symptoms.

When the Ego becomes excessively rigid or controlling, it disconnects us from the deeper layers of our psyche. This rigidity can impede our ability to integrate these unconscious elements, ultimately obstructing the path to self-realisation, inner peace, and harmony. Coming into contact with the deeper self is a kind of surrender for the Ego—it challenges its control and reveals its limits.

The Superego is akin to a very strict parent who constantly informs you of what is right and wrong. It represents the internalised voice of society and your culture. It is often associated with terms like *should, have to, ought to*, and *must*. When you feel guilty over trivial matters, that is the voice of the Superego.

In summary, the Id seeks immediate gratification, the Superego demands flawless behaviour, and the Ego finds itself caught in the middle, striving to mediate the outcome.

Personal Unconscious

Carl Jung (1969) clearly distinguished between the personal and collective unconscious, emphasising their distinct roles in shaping the human psyche.

The personal unconscious is like a hidden chamber within our minds, brimming with forgotten or repressed experiences, emotions, and memories, particularly from early childhood. This facet of our unconscious encompasses an intensely personal narrative recounting our journey through life. However, this narrative is not isolated—the collective unconscious, a shared realm abundant with universal symbols and archetypes, shapes it. Moreover, our cultural context influences how we interpret the world. Together, these elements create a wonderfully intricate dance within our psyche.

For instance, an individual might experience a deep, seemingly irrational fear of small spaces. This fear may stem from a forgotten childhood incident lodged in the personal unconscious, which continues to influence their emotional and behavioural responses to similar situations. Viewed through this lens, the personal unconscious reflects the past and actively shapes the present.

The personal unconscious also includes emotionally charged associations known as complexes. These complexes, arising from unresolved emotional conflicts, traumas, or unmet desires, significantly influence our thoughts and actions. They often manifest as deeply entrenched beliefs or intense emotional reactions that shape behaviour, decisions, and relationships. Moreover, significant Jungian concepts such as archetypes, the Anima, and the Animus also interact with the personal unconscious (these are discussed in greater detail below).

The personal unconscious is partly shaped by the limitations of conscious awareness. Life constantly presents us with choices, each requiring us to leave other possibilities behind. Every decision entails a specific form of loss. For instance, an individual might dream of excelling as a renowned musician and a successful athlete. However, the practical limitations of time and resources suggest that they must prioritise one path—perhaps athletics—while relegating their musical aspirations to the unconscious. These excluded possibilities do not vanish but instead counterbalance the conscious choice, generating tension in the psyche.

This tension isn't merely sitting quietly in the background—the unconscious is constantly working to reintegrate those neglected parts. It sends us small nudges, such as insights, warnings, or "aha" moments. These can manifest subtly, such as daydreams, nightmares, random images surfacing in your mind, or even physical symptoms. It's as if the unconscious is waving its hand, attempting to capture our attention so we can acknowledge these hidden pieces, grow, and become more balanced.

Dreams, in particular, are deemed essential windows into the personal unconscious. Freud called dreams "the royal road to a knowledge of the unconscious activities of the mind" (Freud, 1900).

Consider your dreams as the late-night talk show of your unconscious—starring unresolved conflicts, surprise guest appearances by repressed emotions, and reruns of desires you thought you'd cancelled. It's your psyche's way of saying, "Hey, we need to talk."

Exploring the personal unconscious—through therapy, dreamwork, creative expression, and quiet contemplation—can be profoundly transformative. When we attune ourselves to the whispers of symptoms and the peculiar poetry of life's minor disturbances, we begin to uncover the deeper narrative attempting to surface.

The Collective Unconscious

Among the deepest mysteries of the human mind is Carl Jung's concept of the collective unconscious—a vast, inherited layer of the psyche that lies beneath our memories and experiences (see Figure 3.1).

While your unique life story shapes the personal unconscious, the collective unconscious represents the psychological inheritance we all share, much like a psychic family album passed down through the millennia. It constitutes a vast inner archive of symbols, archetypes, and emotional blueprints that emerge across cultures, myths, dreams, and fairy tales.

This idea offers us a powerful way to understand what unites us as humans. It suggests that beneath our quirks lies a deeper script—an ancient story still playing out in our imaginations, behaviours, and the narratives we tell ourselves.

At the heart of this collective unconscious are **archetypes**—timeless figures and motifs that recur in myths, dreams, fairy tales, and art. These include the Hero, the Shadow, the Wise Old Man and Woman, the Anima and Animus, the Child, the Trickster, the Maiden, the Persona, and many others. They form an internal cast of characters that help shape our perception of ourselves, others, and the world.

These archetypes embody fundamental human experiences and emotions, resonating with shared aspects of the human condition. They shape the lens through which we interpret the world, guiding our responses and actions. By examining these symbols and uncovering their deeper meanings, we can gain invaluable insights into our internal struggles, unmet desires, and unresolved issues, offering clues for growth and healing.

The Influence of the Collective Unconscious

The collective unconscious does not simply emerge through our dreams, it resounds through our myths, religions, and the very foundation of society. Throughout cultures and centuries, we observe remarkably similar themes: heroic quests, divine punishments, cosmic floods.

Take, for instance, Plato's *Timaeus*. Around 360 BCE, he recounts the tale of the Bronze Race—humans so consumed by violence that they provoke Zeus to cleanse the world with a catastrophic flood (2008). Only Deucalion, warned by clever Prometheus, survives by constructing an ark. After nine days adrift, his vessel comes to rest on a mountain peak—a story that echoes through time, surfacing repeatedly in the flood myths of other cultures. It's as if humanity shares a deep-sea memory that we continue to retell in various tongues.

This tale resonates powerfully with the much older *Epic of Gilgamesh* (c. 1600–1155 BCE), in which the gods, weary of humanity's chaos and corruption, decide to reset everything with a great flood. However, one of them—Ea—struggles to keep quiet about the plan. He secretly warns Utnapishtim, who constructs a massive boat, loads it with his family and every kind of animal, and weathers the watery apocalypse. When the storm subsides, life is preserved, and a new beginning emerges. Sound familiar? It's yet another chapter in the world's recurring dream of floods, warnings, and second chances.

The biblical story of Noah's Ark—written sometime between the fifth and third centuries BCE in the Book of Genesis—tells a well-known tale of divine disappointment and watery do-overs. Fed up with humanity's wickedness, God decides to cleanse the earth with a flood. However, one man, Noah, stands out as a beacon of virtue. He is given a celestial heads-up and the ultimate DIY project: build an ark, load it with family and animals two by two, and ride out the storm. When the waters finally retreat, life returns to dry land—cleansed, renewed, and ready to begin again.

These myths may differ in detail and deity, but the deeper pattern remains consistent: divine judgement, chosen survival, and the hope for a new beginning. They reflect not only theological traditions but also a profound psychological truth—our enduring belief in second chances, the purifying power of crisis, and the soul's longing to be saved and reborn. They illustrate how the collective unconscious shapes humanity's storytelling and moral frameworks.

Many such examples reflect the universality and significance of symbols in our collective psyche. Exploration of the collective unconscious can offer deep insights into human behaviour, creativity, and spirituality. Understanding why specific themes and symbols resonate universally and hold deep meaning across cultures can remind us of the underlying similarities that bind us as a species, irrespective of geographical, cultural, religious, and physical differences.

Archetypes

Archetypes are elusive entities—difficult to define, yet instantly recognisable, like déjà vu dressed in mythic attire. Whether they manifest in our dreams, favourite Netflix dramas, or awkward family gatherings, they resonate deeply within us, as if our subconscious is whispering, "Ah yes, I know this one."

Archetypes serve as our inner guides, acting as timeless navigation systems within the psyche. They have accompanied us through the ages, manifesting in myths, art, literature, fairy tales, and films across diverse cultures and eras. They provide profound insights and shape our understanding of the human experience.

Archetypes are universal symbols and patterns rooted in the collective unconscious. According to Carl Jung, they are not learned but are inborn, woven into the fabric of our psyche from birth. These deep psychological templates shape how we perceive the world, interact with others, and understand ourselves. They carry the inherited wisdom and emotional experiences of countless generations, silently guiding our thoughts, behaviours, and personalities.

At a certain point in our lives, we may become "possessed" by a particular archetype. For instance, you might suddenly feel drawn to a cause. Perhaps you feel compelled to attend a march in support of this cause, even at the risk of arrest. The archetype of the **Knight** is calling you. A prominent example of the Knight archetype is **Batman**. Knights are elite warriors; they have a mission to fulfil: to rescue or conquer evil. They are courageous, loyal, gallant, and single-minded. In films, a character embodying both the **Rebel and Knight** archetypes might be **Atticus Finch** in *To Kill a Mockingbird*. He defies his community to defend a black man unjustly accused of rape. He fits the Knight archetype as he has a mission to rescue his client.

The archetype of the **Shadow** embodies the repressed aspects of one's personality—those difficult-to-acknowledge, hidden parts. In films, characters such as **Darth Vader, Dr. Jekyll, Mr. Hyde**, and **Dexter** illustrate the struggle encountered when confronting the Shadow.

The **Trickster** archetype embodies chaos, playfulness, and disruption. It often catalyses change and transformation while challenging societal norms and conventions. Characters such as **Loki, Bart Simpson**, and the **Cheshire Cat** personify this archetype, offering alternative perspectives and defying expectations in surprising and thought-provoking ways. Tim Burton's films frequently explore trickster themes, weaving narratives that emphasise the archetype's mischievous and transformative essence.

Archetypal energy can assert itself in our lives, whether we are prepared for it or not. For me, this began in my mid-thirties. I found myself in a high-paying advertising job that, on the surface, appeared to offer everything I could desire—money, travel, daily challenges, and a creative environment. However, something was lacking. There was a persistent feeling that my work lacked meaning. Then, quite unexpectedly, the notion of becoming a masseuse began to surface. It felt like my hands were on fire—so real and pressing. Massage therapy paid very little, and I had no safety net. Changing careers felt like a significant risk, and most of my friends thought I was mad for even contemplating it. They feared I would not be able to support myself, and to be honest, I shared those concerns as well. But the urge to initiate a change would not disappear.

It was not a straightforward decision; in truth, it was likely reckless, but I made the change nonetheless. The archetype of the **Healer** was calling to me. I worked as a masseuse for several years, developing what became a holistic healthcare practice that incorporated reflexology, aromatherapy, Indian head massage, and Reiki. I loved it. After a few years in this field, and now engaging in psychotherapy, I again felt the stirrings of dissatisfaction. I wished to study psychotherapy. I was beckoned by **Athena**, the Greek goddess of wisdom, an archetypal pattern for those guided by their intellect. The desire to learn consumed me.

There are hundreds of archetypes, and to assist you in recognising them, I've provided a few examples.

The Innocent archetype represents the part of us that places trust in others, in life, and ourselves. It embodies hope, loyalty, and a desire for safety, yet it also harbours a fear of abandonment. At times, the Innocent may resist harsh truths, clinging to denial and wishing to be rescued from difficulties. **Dorothy in The Wizard of Oz** embodies the spirit of innocence perfectly. She embarks on her journey wide-eyed and full of wonder, guided by a pure heart and a steadfast belief that goodness will ultimately prevail. Her dream of a place "somewhere over the rainbow" reflects the Innocent's timeless longing for peace, safety, and a better world. Even as she faces challenges and encounters characters with unclear intentions, Dorothy maintains her trust in others and never loses sight of her hope to return home. Her innocence isn't a weakness— it's her quiet strength. Yet, she needs to develop other qualities as she moves towards the **Hero** archetype, integrating traits such as courage, awareness, and maturity—key steps on the path of individuation.

The **Orphan** archetype symbolises the plight of a child who has been abandoned, neglected, or cast aside, thrust into a world where they must fend for themselves from an early age. Often feeling like perpetual outsiders, orphans harbour an intense longing for connection, belonging, and unconditional acceptance. A classic example of the Orphan archetype is **Harry Potter** from J. K. Rowling's books. At the start of his journey, Harry is a true orphan— abandoned, unloved, and mistreated by his adoptive parents. However, the orphan archetype extends beyond the absence of parents. It represents a universal experience of loss, betrayal, or disillusionment, and the ensuing need to navigate the world without the safety of early innocence. Harry's journey from Orphan to Hero is about overcoming his wounds, developing inner strength and resilience, and building genuine relationships.

The **Rebel archetype** defies convention, questions authority, and resists the pressure to conform. Driven by a deep dissatisfaction with the status quo, Rebels often spark meaningful change, whether as activists, disruptors, or outspoken visionaries. They don't just break rules for the sake of it—they challenge systems to propel society forward. A powerful real-world example is **Rosa Parks**. Though often portrayed as a weary seamstress who, in 1955, refused to give up her seat, her decision was anything but passive. It represented a conscious act of resistance against the injustice of segregation laws. Her quiet courage on that Montgomery bus ignited the Montgomery Bus Boycott, a pivotal moment in the Civil Rights Movement. Parks's defiance wasn't loud, but it changed history.

The **Creator** archetype thrives on innovation and artistic expression. Whether as artists, inventors, or visionaries, Creators channel their boundless creativity to shape ideas and bring their unique visions to life. **Steve Jobs** was a Creator, a visionary who saw technology as a function *and* art. He imagined what didn't yet exist—the iPhone, the sleek and stylish Mac—and brought it to life with bold creativity. Refusing to settle for the mundane, he blended design with innovation, reshaping how we live and connect; he created a new way of thinking.

The **Hero** archetype embodies bravery, strength, a keen sense of justice, and unwavering determination to overcome challenges. Heroes are drawn to noble causes, often stepping into leadership roles and advocating for societal change. **Nelson Mandela** spent 27 years in prison for standing up against apartheid. When he was finally released, he didn't seek revenge; instead, he led South Africa towards peace and unity. His courage, patience, and vision transformed a nation. Mandela's heroism wasn't loud or flashy—it was steady, unwavering, and deeply human.

The **Martyr** archetype derives its name from the Greek word for "witness". True Martyrs are called to bear witness to their beliefs and often endure persecution. Historical examples include **Joan of Arc, St. John of the Cross,** and **Martin Luther King Jr.**, all of whom made significant sacrifices for their principles.

The **Self** is a fundamental archetype in Jungian psychology. While Freud regarded the Ego as the centre of consciousness, Jung expanded on this concept by viewing the Self as the essence of the total personality, encompassing the conscious mind, the unconscious, and the Ego. Jung also characterised the Self as a psychic structure, developmental process, and archetype representing wholeness and integration.

Just as we cannot grasp a single wave in the ocean, we cannot fully perceive the Self. It remains mysterious and elusive, never entirely knowable, as we rely on the Ego to perceive it, much like trying to see one's own eyes without a mirror! The Self is not a static entity but a dynamic, ever-evolving process.

The Self can be likened to a crucible in which the alchemical integration of opposites occurs. This inner "chemical reaction" generates transformative energy that propels growth and development. It also serves as the crossroads between the conscious and the unconscious, a meeting point where various aspects of one's personality converge and harmonise.

Ultimately, the Self represents the culmination of self-realisation, the process through which an individual becomes a fully integrated, independent, and unique being. The journey of *selfing* is the essence of personal growth and wholeness.

The **Shadow** represents the hidden aspects of ourselves—qualities we have marginalised and pushed out of awareness, much like a cartoon robber dragging a bag of stolen goods behind them. Although the term may suggest darkness, the Shadow is not inherently harmful. It is an archetype that encompasses both positive and negative traits deemed unacceptable or incompatible with the Persona (the version of ourselves we present to the world or aspire to become).

The Shadow encompasses the aspects of ourselves that we've repressed—unwanted traits, impulses, emotions, and desires. However, it is not merely a repository for our "bad bits". When we confront what we've disowned, the Shadow transforms into a source of creativity, vitality, and insight. Integrating the Shadow is essential for psychological growth and personal wholeness. For instance, someone who perceives themselves as strong and invulnerable may unveil buried vulnerability, while someone who feels weak might discover untapped strength. By acknowledging and embracing these hidden parts, we enhance our self-understanding and progress towards greater balance and authenticity.

"Until you make the unconscious conscious, it will direct your life and you will call it fate." This well-known quote, often attributed to Carl Jung, encapsulates the essence of his teachings on the Shadow and the hidden forces that shape our lives. If we don't bring our unconscious patterns into awareness, they'll continue to shape our lives without us realising it—and we'll assume that's just how things are meant to be. The Shadow often manifests through dreams, projections onto others, or sudden, intense emotional reactions that appear disproportionate to the situation. When the Shadow is suppressed or rejected, it can create inner conflict and a sense of disconnection from one's true Self. (Jung, 1953).

Exploring the Shadow involves delving into the unconscious to identify, accept, and integrate these marginalised or disowned aspects of the psyche. This process is anything but easy—it necessitates profound self-reflection and courage to confront uncomfortable truths about oneself. However, acknowledging and embracing the darker aspects of our being enables us to discover light, as genuine growth and understanding arise not through avoidance but through a willingness to integrate the parts of ourselves we might prefer to ignore.

Carl Jung extensively developed the concepts of Anima and Animus—a man's unconscious feminine side and a woman's unconscious masculine side—mainly in his work on individuation and the collective unconscious (1969). The Anima and Animus echo ancient ideas of duality within the human psyche. In Plato's *Symposium*, written c. 385 BCE, the myth of the androgynous offers a poetic origin of love and human incompleteness.

According to the myth, there were originally three types of humans: males, descended from the sun; females, descended from the earth; and androgynous beings, descended from the moon. These androgynous beings were a perfect blend of male and female, possessing two heads, four arms, four legs, and two sexes.

These powerful, perfectly round beings barrelled around the Earth in a relentless, circular motion that mirrored the orbits of their celestial parents.

Disorderly and indomitable, they defied the very gods. Enraged by their impudence, Zeus struck them down, cleaving each in two. To mend their wounds, Apollo gathered the severed skin at the midsection, creating the navel, and turned their heads so they could see their scars, ensuring they would never forget their punishment. From this division arose our deep longing for the elusive other half who can restore the wholeness we once knew.

This metaphor signifies an intense yearning for wholeness, reflecting the interplay of masculine and feminine aspects. This theme is central to Jung's exploration of the Anima and Animus archetypes. It serves as a metaphor, illustrating how the interaction between our inner masculine and feminine elements shapes our personalities and influences our romantic relationships. When these inner dynamics are unbalanced, they can create chaos; however, when understood and integrated, they pave the way for genuine happiness and fulfilment.

Gender identity is a profoundly personal aspect of oneself. Some individuals identify as male, others as female, some as non-binary, and some as questioning their gender identity. People identify in unique ways that may not conform to traditional binary notions of gender. Psychological research by Sandra Bem reveals that all humans possess an inherently androgynous nature, blending traits typically associated with masculinity and femininity (Bem, 1974).

Anthropology further emphasises this truth, as diverse cultures embrace more than two genders, challenging rigid binary definitions of identity.

The concept of androgyny has deep historical and symbolic roots. The idea of the Adamic Hermaphrodite—that the first human, Adam, was neither male nor female but a perfect blend of both—is a powerful and recurring symbol in esoteric and mystical traditions. From the hidden teachings of Kabbalah to the cryptic writings of Renaissance alchemists and Hermetic philosophers, this image of a primordial, androgynous being represents unity, wholeness, and humanity's divine origin.

In Greek mythology, Hermaphroditus, the offspring of Hermes and Aphrodite, is depicted as possessing both male and female characteristics—often illustrated as a winged youth with feminine thighs, breasts, and hair alongside male genitalia. These representations underscore humanity's enduring exploration of gender and identity as fluid and multifaceted. The Anima (the feminine aspect within the male psyche) and the Animus (the masculine aspect within the female psyche) embody qualities, behaviours, and traits traditionally associated with femininity and masculinity. These archetypes, central to Jung's theories, reflect the cultural and historical context in which he lived—a time when notions of gender roles and characteristics varied significantly from contemporary perspectives. While these concepts may be debated, particularly regarding the evolving definitions of masculinity and femininity, it is important not to interpret them literally or as value judgements. Instead, they should be understood as *symbolic polarities within the psyche,* representing the interplay and balance of opposing forces essential to personal growth and self-realisation. *The unconscious mind counterbalances the conscious mind, aiding in the growth and development of consciousness.* It is not an *either/ or* situation but an *and/and.*

Carl Jung referred to these archetypal patterns of masculinity and femininity—transcending biological gender—as the Anima, derived from the Latin word for "Soul" or "breath of life" (that which animates), and the Animus, which can signify "Spirit", "mind", "courage", or "anger". These archetypes embody inherited psychological patterns shaped by the collective experiences of different sexes. In Jung's framework, the Anima represents the feminine aspects of the male unconscious, including qualities such as receptivity, emotional depth, empathy, and sensitivity. In contrast, the Animus embodies the active, analytical, and assertive traits of the female unconscious. These archetypes often shape how we project our inner world onto potential partners, forming an idealised image of the "unknown Self". In relationships, challenges frequently emerge when these projections begin to fade, revealing each partner's authentic, complex self.

This moment offers a choice: to engage in a deeper, more conscious relationship or to walk away. However, leaving without integrating one's unresolved Anima or Animus often leads to a repetition of old relational patterns, hindering authentic growth and lasting connection. When the Anima and Animus are not integrated, they unconsciously influence our relationships, leading to unresolved conflicts and dissatisfaction. Integrating these aspects— reclaiming the qualities we project outwards—fosters healthier, more conscious, and fulfilling connections. In Jungian psychology, incorporating the Anima and Animus into the conscious Self, known as *syzygy*, is essential for achieving wholeness and balance within the psyche.

Defence Mechanisms

Sigmund Freud, his daughter Anna Freud, and numerous post-Freudians developed the concept of defence mechanisms, a form of self-deception that is typically unconscious and protects individuals from anxiety stemming from unwanted thoughts or feelings. We often utilise defence mechanisms without encountering long-term complications or issues. They can be placed on a spectrum; more mature defences can assist in managing anxiety, whereas less mature ones may cause harm. This is because less mature defences may obscure the underlying issue, exacerbating the situation when used repeatedly without addressing the root anxiety.

Defence mechanisms operate in the following manner: the subconscious evaluates its potential to inflict harm when a distressing event occurs. If the situation is deemed emotionally hazardous, it instinctively engages a coping strategy to safeguard the individual. This process occurs beneath the surface, without conscious awareness, and while various mechanisms exist, some are considerably more prominent than others. Here are a few examples:

- **Denial** is the refusal to accept reality or facts to avoid painful emotions or experiences. For instance, someone in an abusive relationship may deny the abuse by insisting that their partner is kind-hearted, attributing their harmful behaviour to external stressors, such as difficulties at work.
- **Displacement** involves redirecting negative emotions from their source to a safer or more convenient target. For example, if you have had a stressful day at work, you might come home and shout at your children instead of expressing frustration about the work situation. This redirection allows you to avoid potential negative consequences at work but shifts the emotional impact onto others.
- **Intellectualisation** is a defence mechanism whereby we emotionally detach from a stressful situation by focusing on logic and analysis, using reason to bypass feelings. For instance, after a relationship breakup, rather than confronting the emotional pain, an individual might create a list outlining everything wrong with the relationship and the advantages of being single, concentrating on rational explanations to avoid facing the sadness or sense of loss.
- **Isolation (of feeling)** occurs when an individual recalls a distressing situation but dissociates it from the associated emotions, effectively averting painful feelings.
- **Projection** is an unconscious process in which we attribute our thoughts, feelings, or beliefs to others. For example, suppose you feel unworthy or out of place. In that case, you may unconsciously project this belief onto others, assuming they dislike or reject you, even when there is no evidence to support such a conclusion.
- **Repression** is an unconscious defence mechanism that protects the mind from thoughts, memories, or emotions that are too painful or distressing to confront. A person might be terrified of a particular situation or type of animal but have no recollection of the event or experience that instigated this fear, as their mind has concealed it to shield them from the associated distress.
- **Regression** is a defence mechanism whereby a person experiencing stress or anxiety reverts to behaviours from an earlier stage of development to feel more secure. In children, this may occur following a traumatic event, leading to actions such as bedwetting or thumb-sucking. Adults can also regress, often reverting to earlier coping behaviours such as overeating, chain-smoking, or nail-biting—habits linked to Freud's "oral stage" of development.
- **Rationalisation** is a defence mechanism that justifies unacceptable behaviour by providing logical or socially acceptable explanations. It helps prevent feelings of guilt and evade criticism. For instance, someone might say, "I punched him because he asked for it, and if I hadn't done it, someone

else would have." This shifts the focus away from their wrongdoing and makes their behaviour seem reasonable.

- **Reaction formation** is when we display behaviour that contradicts our true feelings or impulses. For example, being overly friendly towards someone you dislike acts as a way to hide your real emotions.
- **Sublimation** is a defence mechanism in which negative or socially unacceptable impulses are redirected towards acceptable, productive activities. For instance, after being shouted at by their boss, a person might channel their frustration into a long run. Sublimation is considered a healthy and mature coping strategy, as it allows emotions to be expressed safely and constructively. However, while sublimation helps manage immediate emotions, it does not address the root of the issue. In the example above, directly addressing the boss's behaviour and its impact could yield a more enduring resolution.
- **Splitting** is a defence mechanism in which we view people, ourselves, or situations in extreme terms—either entirely "good" or entirely "bad". This black-and-white thinking arises when we struggle to manage conflicting emotions or complexity, making it difficult to perceive things in a balanced manner. For example, someone might initially see a new acquaintance as perfect—a "hero"—but if they feel let down, their view might shift completely, now seeing that person as worthless—a "zero." This oversimplification distorts reality and hinders our appreciation of the whole, nuanced nature of people and experiences.
- **Undoing**, similar to reaction formation, is a defence mechanism in which we attempt to "cancel out" a harmful or unwanted thought by engaging in behaviour that opposes it. For instance, if you feel annoyed with a friend and secretly wish they would stop contacting you, you might act against this impulse by reaching out to arrange a meeting. This action is driven by an unconscious desire to neutralise negative feelings and maintain balance.

These are just a few examples of defence mechanisms. When we encounter stress, these mechanisms activate automatically, helping us to remain within our comfort zone. However, relying on them can occasionally become counterproductive or self-defeating over time. Recognising and understanding your defence mechanisms is key to greater self-awareness, authenticity, and improved communication.

Complexes

In psychology, a complex refers to a collection of emotions, thoughts, and memories that can influence one's actions, even if one is unaware of their presence (Jung, 1960b).

Carl Jung introduced the concept, describing complexes as unconscious patterns linked with themes such as power, love, or abandonment. He believed they often stemmed from emotional trauma or intense experiences that leave a lasting imprint on the psyche. Complexes reside in the unconscious mind, but they can emerge when something triggers them. When this occurs, they can interfere with your thoughts, feelings, and behaviour, occasionally causing you to react in ways that seem excessive or out of character. There's a saying that perfectly encapsulates this: "What's hysterical is historical," indicating that our intense emotional reactions often stem from unresolved issues of the past.

Let us begin with two significant complexes—the mother and father complexes. Mother and father complexes are emotional imprints left by our early experiences with our parents. These issues silently shape our choices until we bring them into the light and rewrite the story. James Hollis emphasises the importance of confronting these complexes to achieve personal growth, saying that we come to understand that our mother's anger or our father's distance reflected their own limitations, not our worth (Hollis, 1996).

The Mother Complex

Everyone experiences a mother complex, as she is typically the first and most significant attachment figure in their life. We are carried in her womb and nurtured by her; she often serves as the primary caregiver. The mother archetype fundamentally shapes our self-image and relationships. At its core lies the mother complex, which Carl Jung described as encompassing both a nurturing side—symbolising care, safety, and emotional nourishment—and a negative side, representing possessiveness, overdependence, or emotional neglect and abandonment. How these aspects manifest in an individual's life depends significantly on their early relationship with their mother and how they subsequently process those experiences (Jung, 1959).

There are positive and negative aspects of the mother complex, and they may develop differently in men and women.

The Positive Mother Complex

If all goes well in early life, and you share a healthy emotional bond with your mother, you will likely develop a positive mother complex. This complex develops from feeling loved, cared for, and supported during early childhood, which fosters a strong sense of security and self-worth. Such security often allows individuals to cultivate healthier relationships as they become more comfortable with trust and intimacy. They can be nurturing and supportive towards others, passing on the same warmth and compassion they experienced.

Now, let us examine the effect of the positive mother complex on different genders.

Men with a positive mother complex often enjoy significant benefits that shape their emotional and relational lives. They typically possess a stronger sense of self and a secure masculine identity, enabling them to be emotionally present in relationships without feeling threatened by the strength or independence of a female partner. They are receptive to receiving support when needed, which can lead to deeper connections. Emotionally, these men are better equipped to express a broad range of feelings—love, joy, anger, or sorrow. This openness fosters emotional resilience and empathy, enabling them to approach life's challenges with greater sensitivity. Their emotional connection enables them to open their hearts, fostering meaningful and supportive relationships.

Moreover, men with a positive mother complex often excel in forming genuine friendships. They are capable of creating close bonds with both men and women, fostering trust and mutual respect. This ability for authentic connection contributes to a balanced and emotionally healthy life.

Women with a positive mother complex are likely to have had a good relationship with their mothers, which fosters balance and resilience. This complex equips women with nurturing strengths grounded in stability and creativity. Women with this complex can cultivate supportive environments, both personally and professionally. Their energy nurtures meaningful relationships, enhancing the world around them.

Such women often demonstrate inner stability, confidence, strong self-worth, and emotional grounding, enabling them to navigate life's challenges with dignity. They maintain meaningful connections with others while preserving their independence and managing relationships through a healthy exchange of love. However, they sometimes struggle with the urge to over-nurture or seek constant approval, which can lead to emotional exhaustion and challenges in expressing assertiveness or ambition.

The key for these women is balance, merging nurturing energy with autonomy. This enables them to flourish as sources of strength, creativity, and love for themselves and others. By embracing their whole selves, they embody the best of the mother archetype in a life-affirming and fulfilling way.

The Negative Mother Complex

A negative mother complex arises from unresolved conflicts or negative experiences with the mother, leading to feelings of insecurity, anxiety, or a distorted sense of self. When the mother is neglectful, controlling, critical, distant, or absent due to issues such as emotional wounds, depression, or substance abuse, this dynamic often affects how a person navigates relationships and interacts with others. Individuals with a negative mother complex may struggle with trust issues, fear of abandonment, or feelings of inadequacy and emptiness.

Men with a negative mother complex often face emotional and behavioural challenges, particularly in their relationships. They may struggle to express their needs, having learned to suppress them to accommodate their mother's demands. This can lead to feelings of resentment towards their mother or others who rely on them, such as a partner, while simultaneously grappling with unresolved emotions, caught between affection for their mother and feeling overwhelmed by her expectations. Some men with this complex experience an emptiness within—a sense of hollowness that they can hardly articulate. To fill this void, they may resort to self-soothing behaviours such as drinking, drug use, gambling, overeating, or engaging in meaningless relationships and casual sexual encounters.

Aggression can also manifest, leading these men to become hostile or defensive in their relationships, often without fully comprehending the reasons behind their behaviour. Trust issues are also prevalent—they may struggle to rely on others or to believe in the stability of their connections and relationships.

On the flip side, some men become excessively reliant on women, seeking constant support and validation. Others swing in the opposite direction, avoiding emotional closeness entirely to protect themselves from being hurt.

Women with a negative mother complex often develop this due to an unhealthy relationship with their mother or a maternal figure. This complex can influence how they perceive themselves, relate to others, and manage matters of nurturing and care.

Some women might feel confined by their mother's influence, overly guided by her values or expectations. This can complicate their understanding of their true identity and lead them to prioritise the needs of others over their own.

Conversely, some women resist their mother's influence, rejecting all that they embody. This can lead to tension in relationships, mistrust of other women, or even a disconnection from qualities such as vulnerability and nurturing.

Growing up with criticism or a lack of support may leave a woman with a profound sense of inadequacy. She could grapple with low self-esteem, consistently second-guess herself, or find it challenging to trust her instincts. A negative mother complex might render a woman uncomfortable with caregiving or even caring for herself. She may avoid roles that feel overly maternal or simply feel disconnected from that aspect of her identity.

For women facing this, the aim is to discover who they are beyond their mother's influence. It's about healing those old wounds, finding balance, and embracing the nurturing side without losing themselves in it.

The Father Complex

The father archetype plays a crucial role in shaping an individual's personality, particularly during childhood. It serves as a universal symbol that embodies authority, protection, structure, and guidance. This archetype is evident in mythology, religion, psychology, and everyday life. As a powerful influence, it shapes our perceptions of leadership, responsibility, and our relationship with authority.

The father archetype embodies protection and provision, fostering stability and security for growth. It represents a guiding force that instils wisdom and encourages achievement while establishing necessary boundaries for development and self-reliance. In many spiritual traditions, this archetype aligns with divine attributes, resembling a God-figure that embodies moral authority, wisdom, and enduring strength.

All archetypes possess a shadow side. The father archetype can lead to control, rigid authority, and tyranny when distorted. Conversely, an absent or neglectful father may leave an individual feeling unsupported. The shadow of the father archetype may also manifest as perfectionism, creating unattainable expectations that hinder feelings of self-worth.

On a personal level, the father archetype embodies the journey of learning responsibility, discipline, and the empowering sensation of standing on one's own two feet. It invites us to reflect on our feelings regarding authority—be it real-life father figures, bosses, or even that inner voice we all possess. When balanced, this energy provides stability, inspiring us to lead with integrity, protect those in our care, and nurture through thoughtful action. Its influence is deeply woven into mythological narratives: Zeus, the ultimate patriarch in Greek mythology, personifies authority, while Odin of Norse mythology combines wisdom, foresight, and protection to guide his people. In Christianity, there is God the Father, who exemplifies guidance and unconditional love. More recently, Will Smith in *The Pursuit of Happyness* strives to be a good role model for his son. In the 2016 film *Moonlight* by Barry Jenkins, Chiron is a bullied child of a single mother who is a drug user and abusive towards her son; his father is absent, leaving him without role models. One day, Chiron meets Juan, a drug dealer who, despite his profession, is psychologically well adjusted. Juan becomes the parental figure that Chiron desperately needs. Occasionally, we encounter non-biological parental figures who positively impact our lives.

In therapy, the father archetype often emerges when individuals confront issues related to boundaries, leadership, or their relationship with discipline and authority. It centres on balance—offering guidance without being overbearing, creating structure while allowing freedom, and blending responsibility with compassion. The father archetype plays a pivotal role in shaping who we are and how we navigate the world.

The father complex is powerful and can manifest differently in men and women.

Positive Father Complex

Men with a positive father complex often carry forward the strength and wisdom gained from a healthy relationship with their father or father figure. Even if the relationship was imperfect, they internalise a supportive, encouraging, and guiding presence that positively influences their self-perception and interactions. They typically feel grounded and confident, having likely developed a strong sense of responsibility and accountability—qualities that assist them in navigating challenges with resilience and determination. This foundation makes them natural leaders whom others trust and seek guidance from, whether at work, in friendships, or within their families.

This dynamic also manifests in men's approaches to relationships. Men with a positive father complex typically find a healthy balance between independence and connection. They can establish boundaries when necessary while remaining emotionally present and supportive. They have often learned to provide encouragement and protection without being overbearing or controlling.

At its core, a positive father complex nurtures a profound sense of security and self-worth. Men who resonate strongly with this energy often possess an unwavering moral compass and a genuine desire to make a positive impact on the world. They embody strength, stability, and wisdom while remaining open to collaboration and personal growth, illustrating the archetype's capacity for development and adaptability.

However, men with a positive father complex may sometimes struggle with perfectionism or taking on too much responsibility. Overall, this dynamic establishes a solid foundation for a life grounded in purpose, confidence, and healthy relationships.

Women with a positive father complex often embody the strengths and encouragement they have derived from nurturing relationships with their father or father figure. This does not suggest that everything was perfect, but it indicates they have internalised positive traits such as stability, confidence, and a sense of security that assist them in navigating life. Such women typically possess a strong sense of self-worth. They have grown up feeling valued and supported, which often translates into confidence in their abilities and decisions. They are comfortable standing on their own two feet while remaining open to collaboration and connection. A positive father complex often manifests as a healthy balance between independence and the awareness of when to seek support from others.

In relationships, women with this dynamic seek partnerships grounded in mutual respect and emotional support. They are more inclined to trust their instincts and establish boundaries, having experienced a strong model of guidance and protection. Their father's influence may also encourage them to pursue their goals, confront challenges with resilience, and maintain confidence in their ability to succeed.

A positive father complex provides a solid foundation for leadership, confidence, and emotional security. Such women often demonstrate a quiet strength that reflects the finest qualities of the father archetype: protection, encouragement, and a consistent sense of direction.

Of course, like anyone else, they can struggle. At times, they might rely too heavily on external validation or set excessively high standards for themselves to make their father proud. Nonetheless, this dynamic acts as a powerful asset, enabling them to navigate life with confidence, balance, and a sense of purpose.

Negative Father Complex

Men with a negative father complex often carry emotional baggage from a problematic or strained relationship with their father or father figure. This may arise from a father who was excessively critical, absent, controlling, neglectful, or simply emotionally unavailable. Such experiences can have a lasting impact, shaping how a man perceives himself, manages relationships, and interacts with authority and responsibility.

For some men, this may manifest as a persistent sense of inadequacy. Perhaps they grew up hearing more criticism than encouragement, which could lead to struggles with self-doubt or a constant need to prove their worth. Others might adopt a different strategy by rebelling against authority figures, avoiding responsibility, or dismissing anything that reminds them of their father.

Then there's the emotional aspect. Men with a negative father complex may struggle to express vulnerability or connect emotionally with others. If their father was not emotionally present, they may have learnt to suppress their feelings as a coping mechanism, which can hinder intimacy and trust.

In personal relationships, this dynamic may present as difficulty in asserting boundaries or an overwhelming urge to overcompensate, often arising from a desire to avoid repeating negative paternal behaviours. Conversely, a lack of nurturing experiences during one's upbringing can lead to challenges in being dependable or embracing supportive roles.

This complex doesn't have to define a man. Recognising the patterns is the first step. Therapy, self-awareness, and building healthier relationships can help break the cycle. With effort, men with a negative father complex can uncover their own sense of strength, security, and emotional balance, stepping out of the shadow of the past and forging their path forward.

Women with a negative father complex often carry emotional wounds stemming from complicated relationships with their fathers or father figures. These men may have been absent, critical, emotionally distant, controlling, or neglectful. Such experiences shape how women perceive themselves, relate to others, and manage trust and authority, often manifesting in their relationships. Women affected by a negative father complex might find it difficult to trust, either becoming overly protective or excessively reliant on validation from partners. They may attract emotionally unavailable or controlling individuals, reflecting their relationship with their fathers, even if it causes them pain. Furthermore, a deep-seated fear of abandonment can impede their sense of security in intimate relationships.

This dynamic can influence self-esteem. A father who is overly critical or emotionally unavailable can profoundly impact a woman's sense of self-worth, fostering patterns of self-doubt and difficulties in asserting her needs. In some instances, this situation prompts rebellion, where independence is pursued so fervently that it leads to burnout and personal sacrifice.

Gaining awareness is the first step towards healing. Engaging in therapy, practising self-reflection, and connecting with supportive, healthy relationships can help you change your narrative. Gradually, you can regain trust, establish healthy boundaries, and nurture emotionally fulfilling and secure relationships. While a negative father complex may loom large, it doesn't have to dictate your journey. With time and self-compassion, you can carve out a path based on self-confidence and personal empowerment.

Key Takeaways: Mother and Father Complexes

Mother Complex

1   *General Overview*

- Everyone forms a mother complex, shaped by early relationships with the primary caregiver.
- Rooted in the **mother archetype**, it includes both nurturing and destructive potential.
- It significantly impacts self-esteem, emotional stability, and future relationships.

2   *Positive Mother Complex*

- **Men** can be emotionally open, secure in their masculinity, and capable of deep, balanced relationships.
- **Women** may be emotionally grounded, nurturing, and resilient, but they may struggle with over-nurturing or seeking approval.
- Fosters secure attachments, compassion, and a balanced sense of independence and connection.

3   *Negative Mother Complex*

- It arises from neglect, criticism, emotional unavailability, or excessive control.
- **Men** may display emotional repression, addiction, relationship avoidance or dependency, and issues with trust.
- **Women** may either over-identify with or completely reject maternal traits, resulting in low self-worth, mistrust, or emotional disconnection.
- Healing entails reclaiming autonomy, processing early experiences, and embracing a balanced sense of care.

Father Complex

1 General Overview

- The father complex arises from the father archetype, symbolising authority, structure, guidance, and moral leadership.
- It influences identity, responsibility, boundaries, and interactions with authority.
- The archetype encompasses both positive qualities, such as wisdom and security, and shadow traits like tyranny, neglect, and perfectionism.

2 Positive Father Complex

- Men possessing a positive father complex may demonstrate leadership, resilience, emotional balance, and integrity.
- Women can be confident, secure, and capable of healthy independence and interdependence. They are responsible decision-makers and goal-setters with a strong moral compass.

3 Negative Father Complex

- Arising from absent, abusive, critical, or controlling fathers.
- **Men** may experience feelings of inadequacy, emotional detachment, rebellion against authority, or a lack of direction.
- **Women** might experience trust issues, attract unhealthy relationships, or develop low self-esteem and confusion about their identity.
- Healing centres on self-trust, redefining authority, and cultivating a strong core.

Therapeutic insights on complexes

- Both complexes have a profound influence on emotional development and adult relationships.
- Therapy aids in uncovering these patterns, fostering self-awareness, and constructing healthier relational models.
- The aim is integration—embracing nurturing and guiding forces without being dominated by past wounds.

Recommended Reading

Chodorow, Nancy (1978). *The Reproduction of Mothering*. University of California Press. (**A feminist-psychoanalytic classic that explores how early mothering influences gender identity, relational patterns, and the perpetuation of family roles.**)

Hollis, James (1994). *Under Saturn's Shadow: The Wounding and Healing of Men*. Inner City Books. (A powerful guide for men exploring how unresolved father wounds impact identity, purpose, and emotional life.)

Jung, Carl Gustav (1959/1991). *The Archetypes and the Collective Unconscious*. In *The Collected Works of C. G. Jung*. Routledge. (This book introduces the mother and father archetypes and explores how these deep psychological patterns shape our inner and outer worlds.)

Kalsched, Donald (1996). *The Inner World of Trauma: Archetypal Defenses of the Personal Spirit*. Routledge. (**Kalsched explores how early trauma gives rise to inner protectors—psychic defences shaped by wounded parental archetypes.**)

Neumann, Erich (1955). *The Great Mother: An Analysis of the Archetype*. Pantheon. (Neumann, a close follower of Jung, dives into the powerful imagery and influence of the mother archetype through mythology, dreams, and cultural symbols.)

Woodman, Marion (1985). *The Pregnant Virgin: A Process of Psychological Transformation*. Inner City Books. (A soulful exploration of feminine transformation, showing how the mother complex shapes a woman's path to wholeness and creativity.)

Inferiority Complex

This enduring sense of inadequacy often feels like a continuous struggle with self-worth. It is more than just fleeting self-doubt; it represents a profound belief that one is inferior, less valuable, or unworthy in comparison with others. More information on this is provided in Chapter 13, "When OK Is Not OK: What's Your Position?".

This complex can influence your self-perception, interactions with others, and approach to challenges. You may find yourself shying away from challenges to avoid feelings of inadequacy. Conversely, you might drive yourself excessively, striving for achievements, seeking affirmation, or exhibiting excessive competitiveness.

Inferiority complexes often begin in early life. You may have encountered criticism, comparisons, or challenges that left you feeling inadequate. Factors such as being the youngest sibling, experiencing sibling rivalry, facing academic struggles, dealing with social rejection, or having physical differences can contribute to these feelings. These experiences can gradually lead to a cycle of negative self-talk and a decline in self-esteem. Although bearing an inferiority complex can feel burdensome, it is possible to overcome it. Cognitive Behavioural Therapy (CBT) can help address negative thought patterns by encouraging you to focus on your strengths rather than dwelling on your shortcomings. Celebrating your achievements, practising self-compassion, and seeking support from a therapist, coach, or wise friend can be beneficial.

Recommended Reading

Adler, Alfred (1927). *Understanding Human Nature*. Greenberg. (Adler introduces the concept of the inferiority complex, explaining how feelings of inadequacy can motivate growth or lead to suffering when left unresolved.)

Adler, Alfred (1929). *The Practice and Theory of Individual Psychology*. Routledge & Kegan Paul. (This book is a key text on Adlerian psychology. It delves into how feelings of inferiority shape behaviour, personality, and our pursuit of significance.)

Bly, Robert (1990). *Iron John: A Book About Men*. Addison-Wesley. (Bly explores male inferiority through myth, linking it to father wounds and cultural pressures.)

Branden, Nathaniel (1994). *The Six Pillars of Self-Esteem*. Bantam Books. (Building resilience against feelings of inferiority. This practical guide explores how low self-worth develops and offers strategies for fostering authentic self-esteem.)

Brown, Brené (2012). *Daring Greatly*. Gotham Books. (Brown's research on vulnerability, shame, and worthiness addresses the root emotional terrain behind many inferiority issues.)

Harter, Susan (1999). *The Construction of the Self: A Developmental Perspective*. Guilford Press. (A developmental take on inferiority. Harter investigates how self-concept and feelings of competence evolve throughout childhood and adolescence.)

Hillman, James (1997). *The Soul's Code: In Search of Character and Calling*. Random House. (Hillman reframes inferiority as a path to hidden potential and calling, revealed through early struggles.)

Rogers, Carl (1961). *On Becoming a Person*. Houghton Mifflin. (A humanistic response to inferiority. Rogers emphasises self-acceptance and unconditional positive regard, offering tools to overcome deep-seated feelings of inadequacy.)

The Oedipus Complex and Electra Complex

Between the ages of 3 and 6, children often develop strong, unconscious feelings towards their parents. Freud (1924) referred to this as the Oedipus complex: a young boy's attachment to his mother and rivalry with his father, inspired by the Greek myth of Oedipus, who unknowingly killed his father and married his mother. Freud regarded this as a crucial stage in forming identity and morality, as the child eventually identifies with the same-sex parent and internalises social norms.

For girls, Carl Jung coined the term Electra complex, drawn from the myth of Electra, who helped avenge her father by plotting against her mother. It describes a daughter's profound attachment to her father and tension with her mother. Though Freud provided his own controversial explanation, both he and Jung viewed these dynamics as central to how children develop a sense of self, gender roles, and relational patterns.

Today, these complexes are regarded more symbolically than literally; yet, they continue to highlight how early emotional bonds shape the way we love, relate to, and understand ourselves.

The God Complex

God is sitting on His heavenly throne. Before Him stand a dog and a cat, waiting to be admitted into Heaven.

*God turns to the dog and asks, "**Have you been a good dog?**"*

*The dog wags his tail eagerly. "**Oh yes, Lord! I came when called, offered my paw in exchange for treats, and wagged my tail to make my master smile. I was loyal and loving every day.**"*

*God nods approvingly and turns to the cat. "**And you—have you been a good cat?**"*

*The cat looks at Him, blinks slowly, and says: "**You're in my seat.**"*

The God complex, while not an official diagnosis, describes an exaggerated sense of self-importance that leads individuals to behave as though they are infallible. It signifies a heightened confidence that conveys an illusion of omniscience and authority. Such individuals often resist questioning or challenges, viewing themselves as incapable of error, even in areas where they may lack knowledge. They strive to exert control over everything and everyone, frequently disregarding the needs and perspectives of others. Their lack of empathy causes them to overlook the impact of their actions on those around them. Consequently, they typically come across as arrogant, condescending, and dismissive of others' feedback. This mindset often manifests in authoritative roles, such as a manager who micromanages or a physician who dismisses differing opinions. It can also surface in personal relationships, where some individuals expect others to conform to their direction without consideration.

Multiple factors contribute to this issue. One key reason may be a narcissistic wound that makes an individual feel inherently superior or entitled. In addition, insecurity can play a role, prompting a person to overcompensate. Another significant factor is unchallenged power, arising from a position where they face neither questions nor accountability.

Engaging with someone like this can be draining. They can undermine relationships by making others feel neglected or unappreciated. In a workplace, they create tension and obstruct teamwork by disregarding others' contributions. Friends and family may feel belittled, exhausted, or emotionally distant from one another.

Change can occur when individuals are open to reflecting on and recognising their behaviour. Cultivating self-awareness is essential, and receiving honest feedback from trusted individuals can guide this process. Therapy helps to identify underlying issues and promote healthier methods of interaction. Embracing humility, particularly through active listening, can have a profoundly positive impact on relationships.

Recommended Reading

The God Complex is not a formal clinical diagnosis but is explored under themes like narcissism, grandiosity, and power pathology.

Adler, Alfred (1929). *The Practice and Theory of Individual Psychology*. Routledge & Kegan Paul. (*Adler on superiority and compensation for inferiority*. Adler's ideas are essential—what looks like a god complex may mask deep insecurity.)

Freud, Sigmund (1914/1974). On Narcissism: An Introduction. In J. Strachey (Ed.), *The Standard Edition of the Complete Psychological Works of Sigmund Freud* (Vol. 14). Hogarth Press. (*The foundation of inflated self-identity*. Freud lays the groundwork for understanding grandiosity and self-idealisation, key components of the god complex.)

Kohut, Heinz (1971). *The Analysis of the Self*. International Universities Press. (*Self-psychology and the grandiose self*. Kohut's theory of narcissistic development explains how an inflated self-image may form due to unmet early needs for validation.)

Lasch, Christoper (1979). *The Culture of Narcissism.* W. W. Norton & Company. (*A cultural critique of grandiosity in modern society.* Lasch argues that Western culture fosters narcissistic traits that echo the god complex—entitlement, detachment, and megalomania.)

Malkin, Craig (2015). *Rethinking Narcissism.* Harper Wave. (*Understanding the spectrum of narcissism—from healthy to harmful.* Malkin describes narcissism as a continuum, explaining when confidence turns into dangerous grandiosity.)

The Guilt Complex

This occurs when individuals experience a persistent, intense sense of guilt, even if it is unreasonable or unearned. It goes beyond feeling remorse for one's actions; it involves continuously carrying guilt, regardless of its justification.

If you struggle with a guilt complex, you might constantly feel that you have done something wrong, even when you haven't. You may find yourself rehashing past mistakes, no matter how insignificant they may have been. It is common to take responsibility for issues that are not your fault, such as other people's struggles, and you may find it challenging to forgive yourself for even minor missteps. An inclination to apologise excessively can also emerge to ensure you have not offended someone. This behaviour can be incredibly draining, making it difficult to concentrate on anything else or truly enjoy life.

A guilt complex often arises from early life experiences. Children raised in strict households or environments where love appears contingent on perfection may carry a deep-seated sense of unworthiness into adulthood. Trauma survivors frequently internalise guilt, believing they could have prevented the harm or that they do not deserve their recovery.

Certain cultural or religious beliefs can instil feelings of guilt when one fails to meet specific standards or expectations. If you are naturally empathetic, perfectionistic, or overly self-critical, you may be more prone to developing a complex of guilt. Mental health issues such as depression, anxiety, or obsessive-compulsive disorder (OCD) can intensify or distort feelings of guilt.

Living with a guilt complex is draining. It can strain relationships by fostering an incessant need to apologise or a crippling fear of being a burden. It may lead to chronic indecision, as self-doubt undermines confidence. Over time, this relentless self-questioning can sap self-esteem and lead to burnout, especially when individuals feel compelled to take on unnecessary responsibilities.

To address a guilt complex, identify its root causes and examine the origins of these feelings. It's vital to challenge unproductive thoughts and question whether your guilt is justified. Are you genuinely at fault, or are you being overly critical of yourself? Cognitive Behavioural Therapy (CBT) can help confront excessive responsibility and negative thought patterns. Consider discussing your feelings with someone you trust, or ideally, with a therapist who can offer a clearer perspective. Everyone makes mistakes; try not to dismiss yourself based on a single misstep and learn to let go of what's beyond your control. You aren't accountable for everything and everyone.

Recommended Reading

Brown, Brené (2010). *The Gifts of Imperfection*. Hazelden Publishing. (Reframing guilt through self-compassion, Brown offers tools to move from guilt-induced perfectionism to authentic, wholehearted living.)

Freud, Sigmund (1923). *The Ego and the Id*. In J. Strachey (Ed.), *The Standard Edition of the Complete Psychological Works of Sigmund Freud* (Vol. 19). Hogarth Press. (Freud explains how guilt arises from internal conflict between the ego and the harsh judgments of the superego.)

Jung, Carl Gustav (1954). *The Development of Personality*. Pantheon Books. (Jung's perspective on moral guilt and individuation. Jung discusses how guilt is not just neurotic but can be a meaningful signal in the journey toward psychological wholeness.)

Klein, Melanie (1948). *Envy and Gratitude and Other Works 1946–1963*. Hogarth Press. (Klein explores how guilt emerges from internalised fears of harming loved ones, even in infancy, and its role in shaping our moral development.)

Miller, Alice (1981). *The Drama of the Gifted Child*. Basic Books. (Miller illustrates how guilt often stems from unmet emotional needs in childhood, mainly when children are parentified or over-responsible.)

A Saviour Complex or Hero Complex

This illustrates a powerful urge to assist or "save" others, often becoming a core part of one's identity. While helping others is commendable, a hero complex goes beyond that; it isn't just about being kind—it entails the belief that you are the one who must tackle problems. At times, it also centres on validating your self-worth through your capacity to "rescue" others.

If you have a hero or saviour complex, you may often rush to resolve others' issues, even if they haven't requested help. You likely see yourself as the only person capable of managing certain situations effectively. Those with a "saviour" mindset tend to take on too much, even when it becomes exhausting, because declining feels like a mistake. You find it difficult to allow others to navigate challenges independently; you prefer being in control, with your sense of fulfilment stemming from the validation and admiration you receive from your assistance. It's not always about being selfless; at times, it's about feeling significant, indispensable, and even esteemed.

A saviour complex can arise from several factors. Perhaps you were praised for your helpfulness or sense of responsibility while growing up, or maybe you took on caregiving duties at a young age, making helping others an instinct.

Even with good intentions, a saviour complex can become problematic. By consistently overextending yourself, you put yourself at risk of burnout. This may lead to strained relationships, where others can feel overwhelmed or treated like children, hindering their growth and fostering dependency instead.

Wanting to help others is commendable, but balance is essential. Helping because it's the right choice is excellent; however, if your motivation stems from a desire to feel needed or in control, that can be detrimental. Genuine assistance involves empowering others rather than merely taking over tasks for them.

If you suspect you have a saviour complex, consider your motivations for helping. Are you doing it for their benefit, or is it about how it makes you feel? Learning to say no is vital; you cannot fix everything, and that's perfectly fine. Sometimes, the best way to support others is to step back and allow them to face their challenges independently. Neglecting self-care can diminish your ability to assist effectively. By consulting a therapist, you can explore the origins of these feelings and strive for a more balanced and sustainable way to offer help.

Recommended Reading

Beattie, Melody (1986). *Codependent No More.* Harper & Row. (A classic look at the hero complex as codependency—rescuing others to meet one's own unmet emotional needs.)

Campbell, Joseph (1949). *The Hero with a Thousand Faces.* Pantheon Books. (Campbell's "Hero's Journey" maps the universal hero archetype and its psychological roots.)

Johnson, Robert (1991). *He: Understanding Masculine Psychology.* HarperCollins. (A brief and insightful examination of the hero myth as a mask for men's deeper need for emotional growth and integration.)

Jung, Carl Gustav (1959/1991). *The Archetypes and the Collective Unconscious.* In *The Collected Works of C.G. Jung.* Routledge. (Jung explores the hero as an archetype of the ego's struggle with the unconscious, seen in dreams and myth.)

Lerner, Harriet (1989). *The Dance of Anger.* HarperCollins. (Lerner shows how rescuing can mask unresolved anger or the avoidance of one's emotional work.)

Moore, Robert & Gillette, Douglas (1990). *King, Warrior, Magician, Lover.* HarperCollins. (Explores the hero archetype in men, showing how it must mature to avoid self-serving or destructive patterns.)

References

Bem, S. L. (1974). The measurement of psychological androgyny. *Journal of Consulting and Clinical Psychology, 42*(2), 155–162. https://doi.org/10.1037/h0036215

Bruno, G. (1998). *Cause, principle and unity: And essays on magic.* Cambridge University Press.

Freud, S. (1900). *The interpretation of dreams* (J. Strachey, Trans.). Basic Books.

Freud, S. (1915). The unconscious. In J. Strachey (Ed. & Trans.), *The standard edition of the complete psychological works of Sigmund Freud* (Vol. 14, pp. 159–215). Hogarth Press. (Original work published 1915.)

Freud, S. (1923). *The ego and the id* (J. Riviere, Trans.). W. W. Norton & Company.

Freud, S. (1924). The dissolution of the Oedipus complex. In J. Strachey (Ed. & Trans.), *The standard edition of the complete psychological works of Sigmund Freud* (Vol. 19, pp. 173–179). London: Hogarth Press.

Hollis, J. (1996). *Swamplands of the soul: New life in dismal places.* Inner City Books.

Jung, C. G. (1923). *Psychological types: Or the psychology of individuation.* Harcourt, Brace.

Jung, C. G. (1953). *Two essays on analytical psychology* (R. F. C. Hull, Trans., 2nd ed., Vol. 7). Princeton University Press. (Original work published 1928.)

Jung, C. G. (1959). *Aion: Researches into the phenomenology of the self* (R. F. C. Hull, Trans., Vol. 9, Part 2). Princeton University Press. (Original work published 1951.)

Jung, C. G. (1960a). *The structure of the psyche* (R. F. C. Hull, Trans.). In H. Read, M. Fordham, G. Adler, & W. McGuire (Eds.), *The collected works of C. G. Jung* (Vol. 8, pp. 139–158). Princeton University Press. (Original work published 1916.)

Jung, C. G. (1960b). *The psychogenesis of mental disease* (R. F. C. Hull, Trans., Vol. 3). Princeton University Press. (Original work published 1907.)

Jung, C. G. (1969). *The archetypes and the collective unconscious* (R. F. C. Hull, Trans., 2nd ed., Vol. 9, Part 1). Princeton University Press. (Original work published 1934.)

Jung, C. G. (2009). *The red book: Liber novus* (S. Shamdasani, Ed., M. Kyburz, J. Peck, & S. Shamdasani, Trans.). W. W. Norton & Company.

Plato (2008). *Timaeus* (D. J. Zeyl, Trans.). Hackett Publishing Company. (Original work written c. 360 BCE.)

Seager, W. (2020). Introduction: A panpsychist manifesto. In W. Seager (Ed.), *The Routledge handbook of panpsychism* (pp. 1–9). Routledge.

Trismegistus, H. (1999). *The Emerald Tablet: Alchemy for personal transformation* (D. Hauck, Trans.). Penguin Group. (Original work c. sixth–eighth century.)

Chapter 4

Physician, Heal Thyself

Shirley was my very first client. It was my initial year of psychotherapy training, and I was probably the more anxious of the two of us. The steps I needed to follow to be in the therapist's role felt elusive; I recalled my supervisor saying, "Relax and be yourself. Create space for the client and ask open questions. Don't have an agenda and avoid attempting to fix anything." I clung to that last piece of advice about not fixing anything. It was a guideline I thought I could follow since I suddenly had no idea what to do.

Psychotherapists in training are required to undertake hundreds of hours of free or low-cost therapy. I volunteered at a homeless shelter in London, which allowed me to apply my counselling skills in real-life scenarios. It was during a drop-in session that I met Shirley. She arrived looking weather-beaten by life—her clothes threadbare, hair unwashed, fingernails chipped and darkened with grime, and several teeth missing. I hesitated, struck by a quiet doubt: what could I offer her?

Faced with such visible fragmentation, I felt the insignificance of my presence. What comfort could therapy provide when survival itself seemed the most urgent task? A deep wave of powerlessness washed over me.

Shirley was in her mid-fifties. Her life had been shaped by hardship—placed in foster care at an early age, she had encountered a long series of difficulties. She ran away at 14 and learned to survive on her own, working on farms around London during the summers and in kitchens during the winters.

But as she sat before me, she waved all of that away. "That's not what I came to talk about," she said.

I leaned in a little and said, "OK—what brings you here today?"

She told me she'd decided to come and see me after noticing me at the homeless centre, where she often spent her afternoons keeping warm and getting some lunch.

Curious, I asked, "What made you want to talk to me, Shirley?" I imagined she might say I seemed kind, approachable ... maybe even a little wise.

She looked at me plainly and said, "You looked depressed." Then added, "I thought it might be nice for *you* to have someone to talk to."

DOI: 10.4324/9781003675099-5

I burst out laughing—the kind of laugh that sometimes erupts when life shatters your illusions on the Rock of Truth. With that one sentence. Shirley reminded me not to take myself too seriously.

Unshackled from the niceties of polite society, she sliced through my spiritual posturing like a hot knife through butter. So much for my budding wise woman/therapist persona—Shirley saw right through it. At the time, I was knee deep in my therapy, grappling with complex issues. Physically off kilter and emotionally frayed, I hadn't realised I was broadcasting it—but clearly, I wasn't fooling anyone.

Naturally, my fledgling therapy brain wondered whether Shirley might have intended to discuss something but ultimately decided against it, opting instead to project her feelings onto me to maintain her control. Nevertheless, despite her struggles, she recognised mine.

Shirley didn't attend another session; however, I occasionally saw her around the centre, and we would wave to each other, woman to woman.

Therapy isn't merely about lying on a couch while someone with a degree nods wisely and asks, *"And how do you feel about that?"* (Though yes, we do ask that—because it works.) Real therapy, which fosters genuine change within you, occurs in a space that resembles less a science lab and more an emotional jazz duet. This space is referred **to as intersubjectivity**—but don't let the syllable count intimidate you! It simply means a shared experience.

Intersubjectivity means the therapist isn't some robot scanning your psyche for errors. They're an actual human, sitting across from you, who brings their thoughts, feelings, and—*brace yourself*—even insecurities into the room. You're not just being "analysed"—you're in a relationship. A weird, struc-tured, boundaried and at times emotionally intense relationship, sure. But a *relationship*, nonetheless.

Say you walk into your session carrying a storm cloud of sadness. The therapist might not say anything at first, but they feel it. Maybe their chest tightens, or they suddenly crave chocolate. That's intersubjectivity: your inner weather system affecting theirs. And when they name that feeling, saying, "Something feels heavy here", they didn't *read your mind*; their emotional radar picked up your signal.

At times, it may certainly feel clumsy. You might feel misunderstood. The therapist may say something that lands like a bad joke at a funeral. However, when you discuss it—voilà—you're mending the relationship. Rupture, followed by repair. The essence of healthy relationships: making mistakes, tun-ing in, and trying again.

Ultimately, intersubjectivity reminds us that change doesn't occur in isolation. It happens when two messy, meaning-making humans sit together, feel stuff, and try to make sense of it all, together. With tissues. And OK, yes, *the occasional* "How do you feel about that?"

This is *relational* therapy. We meet our clients without knowing what they might seek from the session. We sit in a room, and 50 minutes later, we conclude the session, forever changed by our encounter to a greater or lesser extent. Healing is not a one-sided process—both therapist and client are impacted by the depth of presence, honesty, and transformation that can emerge in the therapeutic space. Every true meeting is a mutual unfolding. In the space between, both are shaped, both are changed. Even in therapy, it is never a one-way deal; the journey reshapes both.

The lesson I learned from Shirley, the Truth Teller, was my baptism of fire into being myself in the role of therapist, rather than just playing the role. The reciprocal healing process in therapy isn't often discussed, but my clients have changed and healed me as much as I have them.

As the American spiritual teacher Baba Ram Dass said, we're all just walking each other home.

Recommended Reading

Almaas, A. H. (1996). *The Point of Existence: Transformations of Narcissism in Self-Realization*. Shambhala Publications. (From the Diamond Approach, this book examines the relational dynamics of narcissism, wounding, and awakening. It delves deeply into the spiritual dimensions of the self-other field, offering a penetrating insight into the soul's intersubjective journey.)

Bion, Wilfred (1962). *Learning from Experience*. Heinemann. (Introduces the concepts of "reverie" and unconscious containment between therapist and patient.)

Bion, Wilfred (1965). *Transformations: Change from Learning to Growth*. Tavistock Publications. (Essential for understanding the mysticism of unconscious communication and "thinking in the presence of another". Opaque but profound.)

Bollas, Christoper (1987). *The Shadow of the Object: Psychoanalysis of the Unthought Known*. Columbia University Press. (Examines how early relational experiences influence unconscious communication. Poetic, evocative, and clinically insightful.)

Keleman, Stanley (1985). *Emotional Anatomy*. Center Press. (Somatic psychology classic—explains how emotions develop and are expressed through posture, gesture, and internal movement. It describes the somatic link between unconscious impulse and interpersonal expression.)

Ogden, Thomas (1992). *The Matrix of the Mind: Object Relations and the Psychoanalytic Dialogue*. Joseph Aronson. (Grounded in object relations, Ogden examines unconscious communication and intersubjectivity through "the analytic third".)

Stern, Daniel (2004). *The Present Moment in Psychotherapy and Everyday Life*. W. W. Norton. (Brings developmental and neuroscience-informed insights into how unconscious communication occurs in micro-moments. Brilliant on moment-to-moment attunement.)

Chapter 5

Alchemy

A Journey of Transformation

Psychotherapy is the midwife of the soul's rebirth. In this unfolding, old selves are shed like snakeskin, and something more authentic begins to breathe. When clients consider therapy, they often ask: How long does it take? How do you know where you are on this so-called journey? Does the therapist know what they're doing or where they're leading you? And if you're feeling worse before you feel better, how can you be sure you'll ever actually feel better? These are valid questions.

There's a process to psychotherapy—a sort of alchemy, if you will. But don't worry, I'm not here to hand you a cauldron and a pointy hat or lead you down an alchemical rabbit hole. I'll keep it grounded and relatable.

Alchemy has a peculiar way of making you feel like a genius one moment and completely mystified the next. Even with my best explanations, the subject may, at times, seem as though it is carved in water. That is perfectly normal. Alchemy isn't exactly known for being straightforward. Therefore, when you feel bewildered, take a breath, allow it some time, and revisit it when you are ready. The more you read and engage with it practically, the more it will all begin to click. And don't forget—the case example is there to offer you a lifeline!

As you read this chapter, it may be helpful to consider the alchemical symbols provided in each section and observe whether they appear in your dreams or daily life. To understand the use of alchemy as a metaphor for psychotherapy, we should start with some history.

The practice of alchemy dates back thousands of years, spanning from Ancient Egypt to Greece, as well as the Middle and Far East. Alchemy spread to Europe during the Middle Ages, a time when alchemists were often regarded as mad scientists. The Holy Grail of alchemy was a mythical substance known as the Philosopher's Stone, believed to be the most perfect of all substances, capable of turning lead into gold and granting immortality. However, the pursuits of alchemists were not solely centred on acquiring wealth, although for some, that was likely part of it. Almost from the outset, a spiritual aspect also emerged. Alchemists believed that everything in nature had an ideal form, with gold symbolising the pinnacle of perfection. Their experiments aimed to

DOI: 10.4324/9781003675099-6

unveil the universe's mysteries, blending early scientific methods with philosophical and spiritual inquiry. They employed symbols, ancient texts, and practices that merged science and magic. While they never succeeded in turning base metals into gold, they provided new perspectives on materials and reactions. Their work, passion, audacity, and tenacity gave rise to modern chemistry, metallurgy, and pharmacology.

In his research into the concept of the collective unconscious—a shared layer of the mind filled with universal symbols or archetypes—Jung noticed striking similarities between these symbols and those found in ancient Gnostic and alchemical traditions. Then he stumbled upon an ancient Latin alchemical text, the *Rosarium Philosophorum*, and everything fell into place. Jung realised that alchemical symbols and processes—like *solutio* (dissolution), *coagulatio* (solidifying), and *conjunctio* (sacred union)—perfectly mirrored the psychological transformations he observed in his patients and experienced in his work. It was like finding a symbolic guidebook for inner growth and self-discovery—a spiritual roadmap for navigating the unconscious and unlocking the hidden aspects of the psyche. He believed alchemy offered clues about the deeper, spiritual aspect of the psyche (Jung, 1963).

The Self is often likened to a crucible or container where the alchemical work of integrating opposites occurs, producing a reaction that creates a dynamic force to drive growth. As we struggle to reconcile opposing factions—conscious and unconscious, inner and outer worlds, masculine and feminine, Persona and Shadow—and as we retrieve our projections onto others and accept them as our own, we perform what the alchemists called the magnum opus, the Great Work. In *Psychology and Alchemy*, Jung discusses the dual nature of alchemy, which encompasses both the chemical aspect and its corresponding mystical element (Jung, 1968).

Alchemy as a Metaphor for Transformation

While some alchemists focused on the properties of metals and chemicals, others adopted a more mystical and reflective approach, interpreting laboratory results as an outward sign of inner transformation. They believed that the real "gold" they were searching for wasn't something one could hold in one's hands but something one could find within oneself; turning lead into gold served as a metaphor for transforming the human psyche. The process of breaking down and purifying metals mirrored what alchemists believed could be done with the Soul or mind. They discussed stages like *nigredo* (the dark, chaotic part where everything feels as if it's falling to pieces) and *albedo* (when clarity and light break through). They perceived the psyche as something that could be refined, and employed the transformation of base metal into gold as a metaphor. Today, we utilise mindfulness, meditation, psychotherapy, yoga, retreats, and more in the pursuit of personal growth. The tools have evolved, but the search for transformation remains eternal.

These alchemists were trailblazers, laying the groundwork for Jung and his followers. They were pioneering, exotically dressed Soul doctors in secret laboratories who communicated their knowledge using mysterious symbols.

Carl Jung played a key role in unravelling the mysteries of alchemy, connecting its symbolic language to personal transformation. Marie-Louise von Franz expanded on his work, illuminating the significance of alchemy in modern psychology. Thinkers like James Hillman, Barbara Somers, and many others have since made this once-hidden world of symbols and inner exploration accessible to anyone curious.

At its core, alchemy is a journey of transformation, whether that involves actual metals or self-discovery. Depth psychotherapy stimulates intense and sometimes perplexing experiences, which can feel disorientating, but the alchemical stages and processes provide a roadmap. Relying on the alchemical process can bring comfort; knowing that others have undergone a similar process can help you maintain your faith.

The Four Stages and Seven Processes of Alchemy

Alchemy may appear to be an entry into a mystical and intricate realm, and indeed it is. Ancient alchemists communicated their discoveries through fantastical drawings and symbols so that the "wise" could comprehend while the "ignorant" remained unknowing. Historically—and even today—secrecy has functioned as a powerful instrument of control. Monarchies, religious institutions, and governments often restricted access to knowledge, limiting what the general public could learn and understand. By centralising this power, they fostered dependency, stifled dissent, and maintained inequality, preventing ordinary individuals from making decisions that impacted their lives. However, history shows that knowledge cannot be confined indefinitely. Movements towards enlightenment, democracy, and education have gradually dismantled this control, steering society towards greater openness and inclusivity.

Although I describe alchemy in stages and processes, don't be misled into thinking it is a linear process. Alchemy does not unfold in a straight line; it unfolds in a spiral. Each stage blends into the next, with earlier processes repeating in deeper ways.

It begins in the darkness of *nigredo*, where the old self breaks down through fire (*calcinatio*) and decay (*putrefactio*). From there, *albedo* brings emotional clarity—a cleansing through water (*solutio*) and gentle reformation (*coagulatio*).

As light returns in *citrinitas*, insight begins to rise. You see with new eyes, lifted by perspective (*sublimatio*) and refined awareness (*distillatio*).

Finally, in *rubedo*, the work becomes real. Spirit and matter unite. What was once fragmented now lives in you—whole, embodied, and awake.

And even then, the spiral turns again.

A guide to the alchemical process, presented in stages, demonstrates how it works within the therapeutic journey. Understanding that a process exists can assist you, and recognising your stage can be beneficial.

The alchemical process comprises **four main stages**, each with distinctive Latin names: *nigredo* (blackening), *albedo* (whitening), *citrinitas* (yellowing), and *rubedo* (reddening). I use Latin terms to differentiate the psychological process from the chemical one.

Within those stages are seven main *processes*—the practical components that enable the process to occur.

The seven processes of alchemy are:

1 calcination or *calcinatio* (burning away the ego)
2 dissolution or *solutio* (emotional release and letting go)
3 separation or *separatio* (sorting beliefs, boundaries, and truths)
4 conjunction or *conjunctio* (integration of the opposites)
5 fermentation or *fermentatio* (spiritual rebirth)
6 distillation or *destillare/distillatio* (refinement of insight)
7 coagulation or *coagulatio* (solidification of new identity).

Let's explore the stages and processes in greater detail.

The Four Stages

I've illustrated what each stage might feel like and included some related alchemical symbols. You may be surprised to discover that these symbols can appear in your daily life or dreams. I've also proposed a few tasks that could be beneficial while navigating each stage.

Nigredo: The Blackening

The Dark Night. Jung's Psychological Stage of Confession

> There can be no rebirth without a dark night of the Soul, a total annihilation of all that you believed in and thought you were.
>
> (Hazrat Inayat Khan)

In alchemy, *nigredo* represents decomposition or decay. It signifies the first stage of the "Magnum Opus" or "The Great Work", where a substance is deliberately putrefied until it reaches a deep black state, symbolising a period of disintegration and darkness before potential transformation. Many alchemists believed that all alchemical ingredients had to be cleansed and thoroughly cooked into a uniform black matter as the initial step on the pathway to the philosopher's stone.

- **Chemically**: *Nigredo* denotes a phase of extreme decomposition in which the original material is broken down into its essential elements through intense heating or destructive processes, resulting in a visual appearance that resembles a black mass.

Carl Jung described *nigredo* as the *psychological stage of confession*. It represents a time for self-examination, where one confronts and articulates one's inner world. This entails facing the Shadow—the concealed or repressed parts of oneself. This phase is highly challenging and is often referred to as the Dark Night of the Soul. Linked to the earth element, *nigredo*, or the blackening, relates to breakdown and decay. It is frequently the stage one finds oneself in when entering therapy, typically triggered by a life crisis. *Nigredo* symbolises the first stage of psychological or spiritual transformation, a phase during which outdated beliefs and illusions are dismantled. This process of dismantling the old is essential for creating space for renewal.

In *nigredo*, everything seems dark, and there is no guiding light to be found. The ground beneath your feet has vanished, and you no longer know what holds you up. You feel like everything is falling apart; the existing order is being destroyed—it's dark, but it's necessary. You may experience anxiety, paranoia, panic, eating disorders, substance abuse, nightmares, rage, suicidal ideation, hearing voices, and, in extreme cases, even psychosis.

A part of your psyche must die for something new to be born. But to do so, a baptism of fire is required.

Support often diminishes during this stage of our journey. We may be offered medication or solution-oriented therapies to address our challenges. While there is value in confronting difficulties, such as examining detrimental thought patterns and behaviours, there are also times when we must step back.

At this time, it is essential to pause and reflect deeply on what is happening in our lives, as it may signify that deeper issues require attention—a time for *being* rather than *doing*. There is no need to worry about knowing when to act or when to be. Action becomes almost impossible when it is genuinely a time for being. This is when we must turn inward, listen to our inner selves, and confront what we might prefer to avoid. Whatever is occurring in your life right now is part of your Soul's journey, and your Soul has come into this existence to learn.

If you get stuck in the *nigredo* stage, it can be profoundly detrimental, leading to feelings of hopelessness, confusion, and loss of purpose. While it is a necessary part of growth, prolonged lingering in *nigredo* can lead to despair, inertia, or a sense of being overwhelmed by negativity. This stagnation can prevent you from recognising the possibility of renewal and transformation, thereby creating a cycle of self-pity or rumination.

Over time, this can drain energy and lessen motivation, causing you to feel trapped in a cycle of victimhood or resignation. If this state persists for a long time, it can obscure the path to the *albedo* phase, where clarity, renewal, and healing begin to emerge. Transitioning through *nigredo* requires appropriate support, resilience, and the willingness to confront and work through discomfort rather than allowing it to dictate your state indefinitely. Don't hesitate to seek support.

During the blackening, or *nigredo*, one loses one's innocence, as in the biblical story of Adam and Eve. There is a fall and an experience of a shock to the system as they become aware of their Ego and Shadow. The Ego (which is who we believe ourselves to be) suffers a blow as it realises that other parts, long banished to the unconscious, now struggle to take the wheel.

A Case Example

Lizzie's Nigredo

A year earlier, Lizzie had experienced two devastating losses: her parents died just months apart—her father in a car accident and her mother shortly thereafter from a heart attack. Soon after these events, she discovered that her husband, the father of their two young children, had been unfaithful for several years with another woman. Overwhelmed by these challenges, Lizzie felt lost and hopeless.

Lizzie often turned to her father for significant life decisions, consulting him regularly. She regarded her father as "perfect", offering sage advice and unwavering support. He was her rock, and they shared dinner weekly—a routine her husband disapproved of. In contrast, her relationship with her mother was more complex; her mother was emotionally distant and rarely warm.

Lizzie sat in the chair facing me, slumped over, inconsolable and confused. She wanted to understand why this had happened to her and how she could move on from it. She had never expected her parents to die—certainly not at this stage. She believed her marriage was happy; that proved to be a false assumption.

Lizzie barely managed to drag herself out of bed, yet she insisted on persevering, for the sake of her children. She had tried her utmost to remain strong for them, forcing a smile, turning up at work, and pushing herself beyond her limits, yet nothing felt right anymore. It was as though a shadow loomed over her, a curse she couldn't escape. Every time she turned around, she was inundated with messages urging her to "live your best life", be positive, and "manifest your dreams". However, these expectations only intensified her feelings of inadequacy, leaving her feeling distanced and defeated.

"What do you do when you get knocked down?" she asked. "You get up again," her Instagram posts told her. Sometimes, this is the answer.

We needn't always roll over. However, there are times when the assault to the mind and body is so violent that the usual ways of responding do not suffice. Furthermore, there's little point in adding insult to injury by blaming yourself and insisting you should be coping. Taoism, the alchemy of China, compares life to a river. A river has a course, and once we are in it, we can resist, scramble for the bank or a tree branch, or let go and allow the current to carry us.

This undeniable life crisis propelled Lizzie into therapy. She attended her sessions regularly, crying and expressing rage. She felt utterly exhausted and slept soundly for long periods. I suggested she keep a dream diary, and many of her dreams were dark and disturbing, at least until we began working with them as messages from the unconscious.

She often dreamed of searching for a toilet, yet every time she looked, the facilities were blocked and overflowing with others' waste; typically, it was her husband or unfamiliar men who caused the mess. This dream symbolised her Shadow, representing her "shit", and her refusal to confront it. The masculine figures in the dream represented that part of her that strove stoically to carry on. Despite continuing to feel disgusted by the images, she found herself laughing at the symbolism.

Lizzie began to embrace the possibility of guidance from her inner world. She dreamed of bodies in various stages of putrefaction—"more death", she said. We explored which part of her psyche needed to die. (This is not as negative as it sounds, because a rebirth always follows death in the psyche.)

She identified one part as the dependent child. The reality of their deaths meant she was now truly on her own. It was time to be an adult, she said. Another she had been unaware of was the one that didn't realise her marriage was in trouble; she had been oblivious to how her husband's attention and energy had shifted elsewhere. A part she wanted to give birth to was the aspect that wasn't a wife, mother, worker, or friend, but rather the part she felt she'd never explored: herself. "Whoever that is," she said.

Lizzie described another dream:

I'm an adult, lying on my back in one of those old-fashioned baby carriages. I'm dying, and my husband, or some man, is pushing me. We're heading to the place where people go to die. Before we get there, I have to cover myself in grey ash.

I look down at my arms and hands—my skin is dry and wrinkled, and the ash makes me appear even worse. I'm grey all over, and the sadness feels overwhelming. My husband chats casually with old friends, telling them, "Lizzie's off to die now," but no one seems to care—as if I don't matter at all.

Lizzie's dream was a *mortificatio* dream. The *mortificatio* process is part of the *nigredo* stage in alchemy, symbolising a period of profound transformation. During this phase, old structures break down and dissolve, much like how fruit rots or a body decomposes into soil. Alchemists viewed this process of decay and *mortificatio* as a necessary first step in the journey towards renewal and spiritual growth—the beginning of the "Great Work". In the psyche, death is followed by rebirth.

In alchemy, ashes symbolise the culmination of fire, earth, water, and air—the union of diverse elements in a transformative process. *Mortificatio* often feels like utter defeat and failure; however, it also signifies change and renewal. We do not willingly embrace *mortificatio*; it is imposed upon us by life's challenges, whether through internal turmoil or external events.

During this time, Lizzie and her husband separated but continued couples therapy to support their co-parenting. Simultaneously, she and I pushed through the *nigredo* phase, towards *albedo*.

In alchemy, *nigredo* marks the beginning of the journey—the dark night of the soul. It's a phase of unravelling, where old structures break down and familiar aspects of the Ego begin to fall away. During this time, you may feel lost, disoriented, or devoid of meaning. The symbols that manifest often reflect this inner descent. A raven or black crow may signify a kind of death, not of the body, but of the ego or outdated identities. A skull might appear as a stark reminder that endings are necessary before something new can take root. The black sun, seemingly lifeless, suggests a hidden light—an inner fire quietly glowing beneath despair. And **ashes** denote the moment when everything has been consumed, leaving only the bare essence. Though *nigredo* can feel dark and weighty, it isn't the end—it's the essential ground-clearing before new life can begin. Look out for some of these signs in your life.

Alchemical Symbols for Nigredo

- A **raven or a black crow**. In myth, literature, and folklore, ravens and crows are often seen as harbingers of death or transition; creatures that dwell at the boundary between life and death. In alchemy, this "death" is symbolic: the death of the old self, the false self, or ego-attachment. The appearance of the crow signals that the soul is entering the dark night, where transformation begins.
- A **skull**. The skull is a stark reminder that everything eventually comes to an end. In alchemy, *nigredo* is the stage where things fall apart—when the Ego breaks down and old identities or beliefs that no longer serve us begin

to die off. The skull isn't just a symbol of physical death—it points to the **inner deaths** we all face, the ones that clear the way for something new to emerge.

- **The black sun.** Unlike the golden sun that shines with warmth and clarity, the black sun appears dark and lifeless—yet in alchemical symbolism, it holds a hidden light, a secret fire glowing deep within the darkness. *Nigredo* is the stage of confusion, despair, and breakdown, but it is also the beginning of real change. The black sun reminds us that even in the darkest moments, something is quietly taking shape.
- **A pile of ashes.** Ashes are what's left after something has been entirely consumed by fire—stripped down to its bare essence. In alchemy, *nigredo* is that same process: the burning away of Ego, identity, and everything we thought defined us. Ashes mark the point where the breakdown is complete—when there's nothing left to hold on to, and nothing left to hide behind.

Tasks for Nigredo

During this phase, you may find it helpful to embrace the mood of *nigredo* by:

- Keeping a dream journal.
- Listening to emotional music.
- Reading poetry.
- Walking in the rain.
- Visiting graveyards to reflect on mortality.
- Reflecting on your life choices (but keep that inner critic at bay; be compassionate with yourself; just be curious and notice any themes).

Albedo: *The Whitening*

The Light Breaks Through. Jung's Psychological Stage of Illumination

- **Chemically**: In its alchemical origins, *albedo* means "whitening" and is all about purification and clarity. In modern chemistry, although it is not a commonly used term, the concepts of cleaning, refining, and creating something pure align with albedo. Bleaching provides a tangible parallel to the albedo process, symbolising literal whitening. Just as bleach removes stains or colours, distillation and extraction purify substances by isolating the "good stuff" from the unwanted.
- **Psychologically**: In psychology, the *albedo* stage, associated with the water element, follows a tumultuous phase known as Shadow work or *nigredo*.

Albedo represents the purification and illumination of the Self. During this time, you unveil hidden aspects of your psyche, enhance your self-awareness, and embark on the path to wholeness. It is a transformative period marked by the release of old habits and negative patterns, paving the way for a heightened state of consciousness.

The whitening phase resembles that first sunny morning after a long storm. You're not completely healed, but there's a sense of lightness. You are sifting through the wreckage left by the blackening stage, mentally and emotionally clearing things out to give yourself a fresh start. Clarity begins to emerge, pinpointing what's happening and what's behind your struggles.

But it's important to remember that *albedo* is merely a *part* of the journey. What you uncover and learn here must be carried forward into the next stage—the yellowing (*citrinitas*). Fixating too heavily on purity or illumination can become a trap, hindering progress. The allure of a spiritual bypass may tempt you into believing you've completed your journey. It might seem like the endpoint, but true transformation lies in pressing forward, embracing new challenges, integrating every aspect of yourself, and continuing the work of self-discovery. This stage is simply a stage, not the pinnacle.

Lizzie's Albedo

Initially, I encouraged Lizzie to express her grief; she mourned the life she had always known—the one she had built with her husband—and the shattering of her envisioned future. She navigated through the grief cycle (which resembles more a pinball machine than a cycle), experiencing denial, anger, bargaining, depression, and acceptance. The sixth stage, finding meaning, remained distant. Her grief encompassed not only the loss of her parents but also the end of her marriage and all that stemmed from it.

From a position of blaming God, the world, and her husband, Lizzie gradually became more introspective and reflective. She sought to understand her role in this situation and what lessons she could learn from it. She was determined not to revert to her former self, as that had led her to the current predicament. We began exploring her polarities—inner and outer, spiritual and physical, conscious and unconscious, Shadow and Persona—and gradually, she transformed.

With the painful experience of losing her parents still fresh, she began to understand that life is limited. "How did I not see that? I never considered it. I thought they were too young to pass away and closed my eyes to the possibility—no, the likelihood—that they might die before me. I was unaware. Life is brief, and there are no certainties."

Lizzie gradually adapted to the upheaval following her parents' passing and her divorce. She learned how to navigate life without their guidance. We discussed the admirable qualities she valued in her parents—steadiness, dependability, security, and affection. However, she realised that she had relied too heavily on her father for decision-making, which affected her confidence in making choices herself. Now confronted with significant decisions, she often felt unsure.

As our discussions deepened, Lizzie spoke more realistically about her parents, recognising their strengths alongside the traits she disliked. This shift signified a step towards greater authenticity—an acceptance that life didn't need to be filtered through the lens of perfection. As she contemplated this, memories of her father came flooding back. His relentless demands for academic excellence left her feeling perpetually inadequate, as though no achievement would ever truly meet his expectations. He often questioned her choices; she felt infantilised, a topic she never addressed with him.

Lizzie conveyed that her mother preferred to hear only positive news. When Lizzie opened up about her difficulties with work and parenting, her mother became upset and redirected the focus onto herself. This realisation prompted Lizzie to explore her family background to understand her parents better. By recognising her parents' flaws and frailties and their causes, she was able to move beyond blame or idealisation. She discovered that it is possible to identify where responsibility lies while also accepting that parents are imperfect and carry their wounds. In beginning to understand them, she unlocked a deeper level of compassion and self-awareness.

Lizzie grappled with guilt as she contemplated her parents' flaws, filled with conflicting emotions.

The idea that we shouldn't speak ill of the dead can offer comfort in the early stages of grief, helping people focus on love and connection. But in therapy, it can become a barrier, especially when someone has had a complicated, difficult, or painful relationship with the person who has passed. If we feel we can't express anger, hurt, or mixed feelings, it can stop us from fully processing the loss. In many cases, healing means telling the whole truth about the relationship, not just the good parts. Therapy creates space for that honesty, allowing us to make peace with what was and move forward more freely.

With our growing understanding of intergenerational trauma, it is evident that trauma survivors often need to speak openly about the harm caused, even when those individuals are deceased. This honest reflection is crucial for fully comprehending and addressing the impact of generational trauma. Such openness can be a vital aspect of the healing process, enabling survivors to break the cycle and prevent trauma from being passed on to future generations.

Lizzie had not been traumatised by her parents; however, there was unfinished business that needed to be addressed. We employed the Gestalt Empty Chair technique to explore Lizzie's unresolved conversations—both positive and negative—with her parents. This method helped her confront unresolved issues. Engaging in this manner plays a crucial role in the *albedo* process.

As Lizzie delved deeper into this work, she began to recognise her strengths—her consistency, reliability, sharp mind, and ability to make independent decisions. She also started to reclaim positive qualities she had previously attributed solely to her father.

During her journey, Lizzie recognised that the unconditional love she believed her parents had for her often came with hidden conditions. Their affection seemed to rely on traditional measures of success: a happy marriage, a stable job, and being a good mother. Whenever she voiced her dissatisfaction with her life, they tended to dismiss her feelings and tried to uplift her mood. "They always claimed their goal was my happiness—yet what about those moments when I wasn't happy?" Lizzie pondered, "I know they would've done anything for me, but I felt the need to appear as though I had everything under control."

With this newfound awareness, Lizzie recognised the many beliefs and behaviours she had adopted uncritically from her parents. Now, she was ready to analyse them more closely and reflect on her life.

Lizzie demonstrated an impressive ability to engage with her Shadow. For instance, when she criticised others for their flaws and I prompted her to consider how she might embody those traits, she reflected thoughtfully on the question. She approached it with curiosity, eager to uncover deeper truths about herself, even when the revelations were uncomfortable. Having spent a lifetime being friendly and pleasing to others, she embraced the prospect of bringing her Shadow into the light. As I told her, there's a price for always being "nice"; you risk being inauthentic and sacrificing your growth.

In alchemy, *albedo* follows the darkness of *nigredo*, bringing a sense of cleansing, clarity, and emotional renewal. Its symbols reflect this gentle turning point. Be mindful of these in your dreams or daily life.

Alchemical Symbols for Albedo

- **A white dove**: Once everything has fallen apart, *albedo* brings a sense of cleansing, clarity, and emotional renewal. The white dove, often seen as a symbol of peace and spiritual purity, beautifully captures this shift. It's the calm after the storm, the quiet grace that follows the unravelling.
- **The moon**: *Albedo* follows the dark descent of *nigredo*, when everything familiar has fallen away. In this quieter phase, the moon's soft, silvery light helps guide us through the inner night. It doesn't flood us with answers, but gently illuminates the path, bringing clarity in a calm, subtle way, like moonlight shimmering on still water.
- **Water**: After the breakdown and chaos of *nigredo*, *albedo* marks a turning point—a stage of washing away the ashes, of purifying what remains. Water is the natural element of cleansing, both physically and symbolically. In alchemy, this is often referred to as the "ablution" or spiritual baptism that prepares the soul for further transformation.
- **The lily**: Lilies often grow from murky, muddy waters, yet they rise and bloom in perfect whiteness above the surface. In many ways, this mirrors the alchemical journey: after the soul has passed through the darkness and turmoil of *nigredo*, it begins to re-emerge, lighter and more transparent.

The lily doesn't reject the mud it came from; it rises through it, blooming clean and whole, despite the mud.

Tasks for Albedo

During this phase, you could:

- Find solace in swimming.
- Consider what you need to let go of—unwanted behaviours, relationships, and so forth. Sit by a river and imagine letting go of unwanted habits, relationships, and traits and welcome new ones.
- Clean your house.
- De-clutter.
- Practise pranayama[1] yoga.
- Be in nature.
- Visit the mountains.

Citrinitas: *The Yellowing*

The Golden Hour. Jung's Psychological Stage of Education

The yellowing stage, or *citrinitas*, associated with the air element, marks a pivotal moment when understanding transitions from a purely intellectual realm to something that is felt and lived. In alchemical philosophy, the yellowing signifies the emergence of the "solar light" within the substance, representing a spiritual awakening or a step towards enlightenment. The clarity and insights gained in the whitening stage (*albedo*) settle into a more profound and intuitive wisdom. James Hillman concisely describes the first three of the four stages of alchemy, linking *nigredo* to a time of suffering and confusion, *albedo* to the relief that comes with reflection and insight, and *citrinitas* to the deeper pain that comes from truly understanding oneself (Hillman, 2017).

During *citrinitas*, we incorporate and internalise the insights we have gathered and the burdens we have released from previous phases. This process often ignites a wave of creativity, enhancing clarity and confidence while harmonising our thoughts, emotions, and actions in a new way.

It is also a time for balancing opposites, such as your conscious and unconscious mind, masculine and feminine traits, or logical thinking and intuition. *Citrinitas* is all about grounding your transformation, stepping into authenticity, and moving closer to feeling whole. This stage is associated with enlightenment, wisdom, and the awakening of your true Self. It represents a period of personal growth during which the conscious mind begins to absorb insights and energies from the unconscious; it is characterised by clarity, creativity, and the cultivation of inner harmony.

However, it is not the end of the road. This stage lays the groundwork for the final phase, *rubedo*, where all the changes and insights become integral to your everyday life.

Hillman (2017) critiques contemporary psychotherapists for clinging to their "silvery peace" (in *albedo*), comfortably analysing and reflecting without engaging in the messy, chaotic yellowing phase. He argues that they avoid this stage because it resembles a regression to the raw, tumultuous energy of earlier phases, such as *nigredo*. Therefore, do not be enticed by the silvery peace of *albedo*; *citrinitas* is essential to complete the process!

Lizzie's Citrinitas

Early in therapy, Lizzie started keeping a journal.

Although journalling has existed for centuries, it gained popularity in the 1960s with the introduction of Dr Ira Progoff's Intensive Journal Method.[2] This structured writing approach examines the fundamental aspects of life, encompassing relationships, health, and personal development. It goes beyond note-taking by facilitating self-discovery and addressing personal challenges.

As journalling gained popularity, researchers began to take notice. Psychologist Dr James Pennebaker discovered that spending just 20 minutes daily writing about emotions can enhance immune function—a remarkable health benefit (Pennebaker & Beall, 1986). Research also indicates that labelling emotions can soothe the brain. In one study, observing angry or fearful faces activated the amygdala (the brain's alarm system), but identifying those emotions reduced its reaction (Lieberman et al., 2007). It's clear why journalling has emerged as a favoured tool for personal development and healing.

Lizzie described her journalling practice like this:

My thoughts often feel like a whirlwind—ways to improve, progress, or pause and reflect. At times, this can be quite overwhelming. However, everything calms down once I crawl into bed and begin writing. I typically begin feeling disorganised, but clarity begins to take shape as I write more. It's like a steady presence that arises from the chaos. It's grounding.

Lizzie was transforming her insights into tangible forms through writing about them. This exemplifies one method of manifesting the spiritual. Chapter 6, "The Chakras and the Subtle Body", provides further information on this topic.

In the alchemical stage of ***citrinitas***, the soul begins to awaken more fully. Following the cleansing and reflection of *albedo*, this phase signifies the return of clarity, vitality, and inner light. The symbols that manifest here convey insight taking form—not borrowed or reflected, but arising from within. Be aware of these in your dreams or waking life.

Alchemical Symbols for Citrinitas

- **The rising sun**: While *albedo* is about reflection and emotional clearing, *citrinitas* is when real insight begins to rise. It's the light of direct knowing—of intuition and inner truth taking shape. The rising sun captures this shift: it's not someone else's light you're reflecting anymore—it's your own beginning to shine.
- **A golden eagle** symbolises vision and spiritual elevation. The eagle soars high above the world, taking in the bigger picture. In *citrinitas*, we start to do the same—we begin to see with greater clarity, spotting patterns and truths that were hidden before. The eagle reflects this expanded vision, a perspective that comes only after deep inner work.
- **The colour amber**: Unlike opaque stones, amber allows light to pass through. This mirrors *citrinitas*, in which we begin to perceive ourselves and the world with clarity and depth. The psyche becomes more transparent and less shadowed, more integrated. Amber feels warm to the touch, and when rubbed, it can even carry a hint of electric charge—an echo of energy returning to life. After the quiet stillness of *albedo*, this reflects the shift of *citrinitas*: a return of vitality, gentle strength, and the first stirrings of inner will.
- **A glowing orb**—or **halo**—speaks to illumination and inner fire. Its round shape suggests wholeness, while its gentle radiance hints at something within beginning to shine. This is the essence of *citrinitas*: insight that doesn't come from outside, but from within.

Tasks for Citrinitas

During this phase:

- Keep a journal of your self-discoveries and insights.
- Based on your insights, create a vision board to visualise your goals. Use a corkboard and attach photos, images, or words representing your goal.
- Consider any traits, relationships, etc., that you wish to release, and set your intention to do so. Charles Duhigg's *The Power of Habit* is worth the investment to help with this process (Duhigg, 2012).
- Stroll in the sun, bask in it, and feel the warmth of its light.
- Reflect on this question: What brings out the sun in you?

Rubedo: **The Reddening**

Full Bloom. Jung's Psychological Stage of Transformation

The final stage, known as *rubedo* or the reddening, corresponds to the element of fire. It is the moment when all aspects come together, allowing you to realise the gifts from your journey. This phase signifies completion, wholeness, and balance, marking the convergence of all elements—the pinnacle of your inner journey. Following the tumult of *nigredo*, the enlightening clarity of *albedo*, and the balance achieved in *citrinitas*, *rubedo* represents the moment when everything aligns and things begin to fall into place.

Learning something new is a lot like learning to drive. At first, you're unconsciously incompetent—you don't know what you don't know. Then you hit the conscious incompetence stage, where you suddenly realise how much you *don't* know, which can feel overwhelming. Next comes conscious competence—you start getting the hang of it, but must focus on every step. Finally, with enough practice, you reach unconscious competence, where it all becomes second nature—you're doing it almost without thinking!

Rubedo represents the final phase of personal development. All aspects of yourself—light and shadow, conscious and unconscious—integrate in this stage, allowing you to live as a more authentic and whole individual. Being yourself becomes more instinctive and requires less effort than before.

This stage often involves seeking purpose and aligning with your authentic identity. It goes beyond fundamental self-awareness, incorporating the expression of your integrated Self in the world. This leads to a deep sense of fulfilment, indicative of a life lived with intention and significance, rather than just responding to circumstances as they arise.

Rubedo is not about being perfect—it is about being authentic. It's about embracing every part of yourself, including the flaws, and showing up congruently. At this stage, you apply everything you've learned from your earlier growth to your relationships, work, and everyday life. It's not about "fixing" yourself; it's about fully accepting who you are and stepping into your power.

This is the phase of "living your truth". You're no longer just reflecting or healing—you're thriving. You're authentic and creative, making decisions based on your values rather than what society expects of you. This is not the end of your journey, but it's a significant milestone. You've transformed your "lead" into "gold", leveraging the wisdom you've gained to shape a meaningful and fulfilling life.

Lizzie's Rubedo

As Lizzie progressed in her therapy, the rewards of her dedication and perseverance became evident. She allowed herself to grieve the profound loss of her parents, reflecting on the cherished moments they shared while also recognising them as imperfect, complex individuals. This newfound perspective allowed her to love them authentically without idealising them.

As Lizzie relinquished her perfect view of her parents, she felt less pressure to achieve perfection herself. She became more aware of the polished image she portrayed to others and began to embrace the courage needed to reveal her Shadow traits—those aspects she had previously hidden. Accepting vulnerability, even at the risk of disapproval, opened up new opportunities for connection and self-acceptance. Often, these risks were rewarding, enhancing her growth and resilience.

Lizzie noticed that she felt more comfortable in her own skin and became increasingly aware of moments when her actions didn't align with her true self. As her self-awareness grew, she became less tolerant of behaviours that contradicted her authentic self. Her relationship with her ex-husband improved, fostering a more respectful environment for co-parenting their daughter.

"For the first time," she said, "I feel real—empowered and truly self-accepting." She explained that she had turned to therapy during her darkest moment, desperate to make sense of a devastating tragedy. However, what had begun as a lifeline developed into a journey of self-discovery. She stayed to heal and find herself, and she appreciated who she had become.

"Maybe," she reflected, "that was my parents' final gift to me."

In the final stage of the alchemical journey, *rubedo* represents the moment of wholeness, embodiment, and spiritual integration. After the descent into darkness (*nigredo*), the cleansing of *albedo*, and the illumination of *citrinitas*, *rubedo* is where the inner work becomes fully real—visible, grounded, and alive in the world. Be awake to any of these symbols appearing in your dreams and waking life.

Alchemical Symbols for Rubedo

- **A red rose:** The red rose blooms in full, nothing restrained, completely open, alive, and radiant. It captures the spirit of *rubedo*, when the soul fully arrives in itself: whole, integrated, and grounded. The transformation is no longer just happening inside—it's now visible, embodied, and real.
- **The radiant sun:** Where *nigredo* is darkness, *albedo* is reflection, and *citrinitas* is dawn, the sun at full strength represents the moment of complete inner clarity and integration. Everything that was fragmented is now united in the light of full awareness. The sun shines from within.
- **The phoenix:** The phoenix represents *rubedo*, the final stage of alchemy, because it captures the essence of rebirth, transformation, and the soul coming fully into its own. After passing through the darkness of *nigredo*, the cleansing of *albedo*, and the first light of *citrinitas*, *rubedo* is the moment the soul rises, whole, renewed, and radiant.
- **A red lion:** In alchemy, the red lion is sometimes shown merging with or devouring the green lion—a symbol of raw, untamed nature or the primal material of the soul. Through this union, the red lion emerges as a sign of mastery, where matter becomes spiritual, and spirit takes form. It represents the final integration, the Self fully alive and expressed in the world.

Transformation is challenging, but these stages remind us that every breakdown ultimately leads to a breakthrough. So, if you're in your *nigredo* phase, give it time; *rubedo* awaits.

The Seven Steps (Processes) of Transformation

Now that we understand the four alchemical *stages*, let us examine the seven *processes*, which are the *practical elements*. They are:

1 calcination or *calcinatio*
2 dissolution or *solutio*
3 separation or *separatio*
4 conjunction or *conjunctio*
5 fermentation or *fermentatio* (*putrefactio*)
6 distillation or *destillare*
7 coagulation or *coagulatio*.

Calcinatio

The purifying fire that burns away superfluous elements.

- **Chemically:** Calcination involves heating a substance (below its melting point) to remove water, gases, or impurities, resulting in a purer or transformed material. For example, heating limestone releases carbon dioxide and produces calcium oxide, also known as lime. In cooking, torching crème brûlée or caramelising sugar exemplifies a form of calcination. This process serves to break down materials into simpler, more refined forms.
- **Psychologically:** *Calcinatio* is the process of burning away what no longer serves us—outdated beliefs, destructive relationships, an inflated ego, rigid identification with a persona, or unhelpful behavioural patterns. It is about stripping things down to their essence to create space for transformation.

Channelling all your unwanted elements into a psychological fire reveals something genuine underneath. This process can be intense, making you feel as if you're on fire—sometimes even in a physical sense. You may notice hot flushes (which aren't necessarily tied to menopause)! Like Lizzie in the case example, you may experience a range of emotions, including burning anger, grief, or frustration. It can feel as if life is thrusting you into a metaphorical blaze, forcing you to confront the issues you've been sidestepping or clinging to, much like having your feet held to the fire. When navigated mindfully, this stage becomes a cleansing, purifying experience.

Alchemical Symbols for Calcinatio

Pay attention to these symbols that appear in your dreams or even in your daily life (of course, if there's a fire, don't linger around analysing it; call the emergency services):

- **Fire and flames**: Fire and flames embody *calcinatio*, as this stage of alchemy revolves around burning away the false, returning things to their essence. It's the trial by fire—the beginning of transformation—where the ego and its attachments face intense heat, allowing something more authentic to begin to emerge.
- **Ashes**: In *calcinatio*, the ego is exposed to intense heat—be it emotional, spiritual, or psychological—so that pride, illusions, and old attachments can be burned away. What remain are the ashes, the stripped-down remnants of the self. They signify what is real beneath it all, what endures once the masks and defences have fallen away.
- **The sun**: The sun leaves nothing hidden. In its light, shadows disappear, and everything comes into clear view. *Calcinatio* works the same way—it brings to the surface the parts of ourselves we'd rather avoid, burning through denial and illusion until only the truth is left. It's the moment when we can no longer look away.
- **The furnace**: In alchemy, the furnace is where materials are broken down and purified through steady heat. Psychologically, it reflects those moments of emotional intensity, self-confrontation, or spiritual crisis that strip away the Ego's defences. The furnace becomes a type of inner crucible—a space where genuine transformation can commence.
- **White powder or purified substance**: Symbolically, the white residue left behind after *calcinatio* reflects a state of psychological clarity; we are humbled, yet not broken. The intense inner fire strips away pride, illusion, and old defences, leaving something cleaner and more honest. The white powder is what remains: what is true, essential, and ready for whatever comes next.
- **Bones or skeletons**: Skeletons remind us of our mortality and how vulnerable we really are. In *calcinatio*, we're forced to face our limits—the places where the ego can no longer pretend or hide. Being reduced to the "bare bones" of the self is part of the humbling process. It strips everything back to what's essential, raw, and honest.
- **The phoenix** stands at the threshold between destruction and creation. *Calcinatio* holds that same tension; it embodies the burning away of what no longer serves, yet also carries the quiet promise that something true will survive. The phoenix reminds us that there's meaning in the fire; that even in the heat of loss, something vital is being prepared to rise.
- **Fiery colours**, such as red, orange, and yellow, frequently manifest in the imagery of *calcinatio*, symbolising the fiery energy of transformation.

Solutio (Dissolution)

Stirring the pot.

- **Chemically**: Dissolution occurs when a substance, such as salt or sugar, combines with a liquid, resulting in the formation of a uniform solution. The particles break apart and are surrounded by the liquid's molecules. Essentially, the liquid separates the particles and distributes them uniformly.
- **Psychologically**: There are moments in life that compel you to abandon your usual coping strategies or self-image. Perhaps you've experienced a breakup, lost your job, or undergone a spiritual transformation—those instances when everything seems to be "melting away" and the familiar frameworks of your life begin to disintegrate.

Solutio involves breaking things down. It's about loosening rigid thinking, relinquishing the need to control everything, and surrendering to the flow of emotions or unconscious processes. It's messy, fluid, and often feels like losing your grip—but that's where growth occurs.

Solutio encourages you to release your tightly held identity—your defences, ingrained habits, and expectations. It offers an opportunity for emotional surrender, allowing repressed or rationalised feelings to emerge fully. This process may lead to profound emotional releases, such as crying or grieving, and prompts you to explore previously unknown areas of your psyche, where you can uncover your dreams, intuition, and long-suppressed emotions that come to light as you relinquish control.

Solutio is essential for transformation, dissolving the old to make way for something new. Imagine it like water: flowing, constantly changing its shape. When rigid beliefs or emotional blocks break down, space is created for healing, self-discovery, and a deeper connection with one's true Self.

Psychologically, *solutio* promotes flexibility, openness, and acceptance of change. It's about embracing the concept of "flow"—releasing resistance and allowing yourself to move with life rather than struggle against it.

Alchemical Symbols for Solutio

Be aware of these symbols if they appear in your dreams and daily life:

- **Water**: Water represents *solutio*, one of the key stages in alchemy, because it speaks to the process of dissolving, of letting go and returning to flow. In *solutio*, what was fixed becomes fluid, what was rigid begins to soften. The ego's boundaries loosen. Water, with its natural ability to dissolve, blend, and carry things forward, captures this perfectly—both as a literal and symbolic agent of surrender and transformation.

- **Oceans or rivers**: Oceans reflect the unconscious—deep, mysterious, and sometimes overwhelming. Entering *solutio* is like diving beneath the surface, letting buried emotions, old grief, and forgotten truths rise and move through us. Rivers do the same, drawing us inward and downward, guiding us gently back to the source.
- **Melting**: Melting brings to mind the sensation of softening under heat or pressure; not falling apart, but letting go. Psychologically, it's that moment of emotional release or vulnerability—when tears, grief, or tenderness begin to dissolve the old layers of protection we've been holding onto.

Separatio (Separation)

The separation of good and bad.

- **Chemically:** Separation in chemistry refers to the process of isolating components of a mixture. Methods vary: filtering removes solids from liquids (like straining pasta), distillation separates substances based on their boiling points, chromatography separates substances (such as colours on wet paper), and centrifugation sorts substances by weight through spinning. It involves using differences in properties to purify or analyse mixtures.
- **Psychologically**: *Separatio* involves distinguishing the elements within the psyche, helping you gain clarity. In therapy, we present our tangled thoughts, difficult emotions, and unproductive behaviours to our therapist in every session. This process helps to identify what is beneficial and what is not.

In therapy, you learn to distinguish between your beliefs and those you've unknowingly adopted from others. You will be invited to examine statements that have been associated with you (known as *attributes*) and assess their validity. To do this, reflect on the messages you received in your childhood, such as: "You're the smart one", "You're not creative", "You're just like your father", "You're the quiet one", "You're the loud one", and "You're a procrastinator". This process of differentiation serves as a mental spring cleaning, offering an opportunity to reassess your personal narrative and determine what to keep and what to discard. For more information, refer to Chapter 14, "All the World's a Stage: Life Scripts and How to Change Them".

Boundary work plays a significant role in *separatio*, determining where you end and others begin, as well as understanding your responsibilities and what lies beyond them. There is more on this in Chapter 7, "Boundaries or Barriers".

Separatio entails exploring detrimental mental habits, including negative automatic thoughts such as "I must be perfect" or "I'm not good enough", along with deeply ingrained core beliefs such as "I'm unlovable", "Women are untrustworthy", or "Men are aggressive". The objective is to identify the sources of these beliefs, confront them using Cognitive Behavioural Therapy

(CBT), and endeavour to release them so they no longer dictate your thoughts and behaviours.

Identifying and describing emotions is key to the journey to wholeness. In Ursula Le Guin's *A Wizard of Earthsea* (1968), a character known as the Master Namer teaches students the art of understanding the true names of everything in the universe.

This is a crucial aspect of *separatio*. Rather than simply saying, "I'm depressed", your therapist will encourage your ability to reflect, allowing your language to depict your experience more accurately.

By fully articulating our experiences, we reveal a depth and richness that surface impressions often lack. You will find a powerful clarity within you once you embrace this process of reflection, naming, and sorting.

Conjunctio (Conjunction)

The point of no return.

- **Chemically:** In chemistry, a conjunction refers to the joining of atoms or molecules through chemical bonds. In organic chemistry, **conjugation** helps stabilise molecules and influences their behaviour. At its core, it's about meaningful connection.
- **Psychologically**: In alchemy, *conjunctio* represents the ultimate transformation and is among the most revered concepts in the Magnum Opus, or the Great Work of alchemical practice. *Conjunctio* means "to unite" or "to join together" and complements *separatio*, which is the process of decomposition; the two form an unending cycle of refinement. On a psychological level, this process encapsulates symbolic "marriages" or unions of opposites, such as the active and receptive aspects of feminine energy.

Conjunctio is the process when all the elements you've been focusing on— your thoughts, emotions, actions, various complexes, inner masculine and feminine aspects, Shadow and Persona, among others—begin to come together, allowing you to feel more complete. We are a collection of parts within a single self. Multiple sub-personalities vie for your attention, often leading to internal conflict. For instance, your mind may insist, "I should pursue a stable job", while your heart says, "I want to be an artist". *Conjunctio* involves harmonising these conflicting aspects into a balanced relationship. It's not about determining winners or losers; instead, it's about enabling both parts to coexist peacefully. *Conjunctio* represents a stage where clarity emerges, and you start to feel a sense of alignment.

Shadow work plays a vital role in *conjunctio*. This journey involves delving into the parts of yourself that you have previously rejected. You learn that light resides within the darkness, leading you to acknowledge and embrace these overlooked aspects, reintegrating them into your whole being.

In the *conjunctio* process, you cease to see your body and mind as separate and recognise how emotions and physical symptoms are profoundly connected. You start to comprehend that your symptoms convey significant messages from your unconscious. As this awareness expands, you learn to trust your instincts and align yourself more fully with your true Self.

You start living in alignment with your principles, which fosters a sense of harmony between your inner world and outward actions. This congruence allows your authentic self to emerge with confidence as your beliefs, feelings, and decisions synchronise seamlessly. Authenticity becomes the foundation of your journey.

Conjunctio can feel incredible. You feel more comfortable in your skin most of the time. It's not about being perfect—it's more about accepting being perfectly imperfect. The heavy lifting of *calcinatio, solutio,* and *separatio* leads to this integration. Now, you feel grounded, congruent, and ready to move forward in life.

Alchemical Symbols for *Conjunctio*

During the *conjunctio* phase, you may notice themes of unity, balance, and connection manifesting in your dreams and daily experiences. The symbols listed below represent the essence of *conjunctio*: that moment when everything appears to be intertwined.

- **Marriage or lovers**: The classic symbol for *conjunctio* is the union of two lovers or a mystical marriage. It's not just about romance; it's about the coming together of opposites, such as your rational and emotional aspects or your conscious and unconscious mind.
- **The sun and the moon** represent contrasting forces. The sun embodies masculine, logical, and active principles, whereas the moon symbolises feminine, intuitive, and reflective qualities. Individually, they signify opposites, but together they represent harmony and balance.
- **The hermaphrodite**: At the heart of *conjunctio* lies the sacred union of masculine and feminine energies. The hermaphrodite, embodying both within, does not negate the differences; rather, it unites them within a single body. This union is not about one side triumphing over the other, but about their reconciliation—transforming into something new, whole, and evolved through their coming together.
- **The Tree of Life**: Trees have their roots in the earth and their branches in the sky. The Tree of Life signifies the interconnectedness of all things, which is precisely what *conjunctio* is about.
- **Circle-and-square**: In alchemy, the circle represents Spirit and wholeness, while the square symbolises the earth and structure. Together, they often illustrate the unity of spiritual and material aspects.
- **The phoenix** frequently appears in alchemy. It is a paradox. It dies in flames—an image of the alchemical *nigredo*, the dark night of dissolution— and then rises from its own ashes, reborn in radiant form, echoing *rubedo*,

the final stage of transformation. Through fire, the old and the new are fused, making the phoenix a striking symbol of inner renewal. For *conjunctio*, it represents what occurs when all those aspects of you integrate.

- **The starry sky**: The starry sky captures the union of Earth and cosmos, matter and spirit, humanity and the divine. When we gaze upwards, we feel both insignificant and boundless, as if the Ego and the Self are breathing in synchrony for a moment. That sense of oppositions held together—that's the heart of *conjunctio*.
- **The ouroboros**: The snake eating its own tail symbolises *conjunctio* as it unites opposites: life and death, beginning and end, Self and other. It serves as a living image of transformation, endlessly consuming and renewing itself. Rather than merely joining opposing forces, it *embodies* their unity—wholeness in motion.
- **Circles**: A circle has no beginning and no end. It embodies the eternal cycle—birth and death, descent and return, dissolution and rebirth. Just like *conjunctio*, it transcends linear thinking and merges what we typically hold as opposites into a continuous whole.

Fermentatio (Putrefactio)

Death and resurrection.

- **Chemically:** Fermentation is a natural process in which microbes, such as yeast or bacteria, break down sugars into simpler substances. It's how we get wine, bread, yoghurt, and more. Yeast turns grape sugars into alcohol in wine and helps bread rise by producing carbon dioxide. It's an ancient, low-energy method for transforming food.
- **Psychologically**: In alchemy, *fermentatio* (*putrefactio*) is a vital stage of transformation. It symbolises spiritual renewal, inner awakening, and the emergence of something new from what has been deconstructed and purified. Alchemists believed that once the old Self is dissolved and refined through earlier stages, such as *calcinatio* (burning away impurities) and *solutio* (which involves releasing and dissolving resistance), a richer and more profound essence can emerge through *fermentatio* (*putrefactio*).

Symbolically, *fermentatio* (*putrefactio*) represents rebirth and spiritual enlightenment. It is the moment when something fresh and vibrant emerges from decay. Alchemists viewed this process as mystical, likening it to the transformation of grapes into wine, where something ordinary becomes extraordinary. Spiritually, *fermentatio* (*putrefactio*) pertains to the Soul being infused with divine inspiration, a creative spark, or a new sense of purpose.

From a psychological standpoint, the *fermentatio* (*putrefactio*) process offers profound insights following a challenging period. After inner turmoil, a moment arises when everything "clicks"—creativity surges, fresh perspectives emerge, or life regains its significance. It embodies the feeling of spiritual renewal or finding purpose after personal crises or significant life transitions.

Alchemical Symbols for Fermentatio (Putrefactio)

During *fermentatio*, you might start noticing subtle signs that something new is awakening inside you. In dreams or daily moments, there could be flickers—fire glowing softly in ashes, grapes quietly turning into wine, or tiny shoots breaking through dark soil. Be aware of these signs and symbols as they appear in your life:

- **The phoenix**: Fermentation is a living, slow-burning process—fuelled by inner heat and quiet transformation. The phoenix's rebirth through fire mirrors this kind of alchemy: a soul that ignites from within, awakened by the heat of experience, deep insight, and spiritual spark.
- **Grapes turning into wine**: Fermentation is both a natural and symbolic transformation. Grapes are crushed; broken down, just like the Ego in earlier stages, and left to rest. Then, with time and the work of natural yeasts, something begins to shift. The sugars turn into alcohol, and the grapes become wine—alive, rich, and full of spirit. It's the essence of *fermentatio*: new life beginning to grow from within.
- **The birth of a divine child**: The birth of a divine child symbolises *fermentatio* because it marks the arrival of new spiritual life; a sacred presence grows out of all the trials and breakdowns that came before. In both alchemy and psychology, the divine child isn't just a new beginning; it's the living expression of a soul that's been transformed from the inside out.
- **Spiritual light emerging from darkness**: *Fermentatio* is a turning point, when the darkness starts to lift and something meaningful begins to take shape. The light that rises from within doesn't come from avoiding the shadow, but from moving through it. It shows the soul's ability to grow and come back to life from the inside out.

All point to the same theme: transformation through surrender, decay, and eventual renewal.

Distillatio *(Distillation)*

Refinement in stages.

- **Chemically**: Distillation is a laboratory technique used to separate substances based on their boiling points. When heating a liquid mixture, such as water and alcohol, the component with the lower boiling point (alcohol) evaporates first. The vapour is subsequently cooled, condensed, and collected as a purified liquid. It's like sorting laundry, but with vapours. This method extracts or purifies components, such as alcohol from fermentation or essential oils from plants like lavender.

- **Psychologically**: *Distillatio* is all about *refinement*—taking everything you've been through and boiling it down to its purest essence. This process emphasises clarity, wisdom, and identifying what matters at the deepest level.

Imagine embarking on a transformative alchemical journey, where you explore your Shadow material, identify and label your emotions, understand how your feelings influence your actions and the people around you, and embrace the process of releasing what no longer serves you. Now, however, you find yourself pondering, "What is the fundamental truth in all of this?"

That's where *distillatio* steps in. *Distillatio* removes the noise, drama, and distractions to concentrate on what matters.

This process involves capturing the core of your lessons, marking your spiritual or emotional growth as your insights integrate into your identity. You are developing a more profound capacity for contemplation—having experienced various highs and lows, you now reflect profoundly on their significance. It shifts from simply experiencing emotions to comprehending them. This transformation phase goes beyond problem-solving, emphasising profound renewal at the Soul level. It's a moment to seek simplicity, releasing outdated patterns, harmful relationships, and coping strategies such as overworking, mindless shopping, or substance misuse. This is where liberation begins, and old habits are refined.

Distillatio often feels like a spiritual stage where you connect with your higher Self or a deeper sense of purpose. Now is the moment when all your strenuous efforts bear fruit. You've endured the fire (*calcinatio*), navigated the emotional seas (*solutio*), filtered through your experiences (*separatio*), and brought everything together (*conjunctio*). Now, you're taking everything you've learned and condensing it into wisdom you can carry forward. It's the part where you feel, "Ah, here I am, at last!"

Alchemical Symbols for Distillatio

Here are some of the signs you may see in your dreams or waking life during this stage.

In alchemy, *distillatio* is often symbolised by:

- **The alembic** is a vessel in which liquids are heated and purified, symbolising your inner refinement process. *Distillatio* flows in a rhythm of rising and falling, akin to a breath. The alembic captures what ascends, such as insight or inspiration, and brings it back down in a more usable, refined form. This reflects the inner work of *distillatio*, where deeper understanding is transformed into something we can live and apply.

- **Steam or vapour**: Steam forms when heat transforms liquid into a lighter and more refined substance. In psychological or spiritual terms, it's akin to those moments when reflection or pressure elevates us to new insight, extracting meaning from our experiences.
- **The starry sky**: In *distillatio*, we separate what's essential from what's clouding it, just like stars shining clearly against the dark sky. Each star is like a distilled truth, rising out of emotional or psychological intensity. The starry sky gives us a sense of clarity and perspective, as if we're seeing things from above, with fresh eyes and deeper understanding.
- **A crystal or pure water**: In alchemy, *distillatio* purifies something by slowly heating and condensing it repeatedly. Pure water or a clear crystal shows the result—something clean, transparent, and stripped down to its essence. Psychologically, it's the moment when inner work finally brings real clarity and insight.

At this stage, you've transcended the drama of life—you've navigated through it. *Distillatio* provides a sense of tranquillity and liberation. You feel clear-minded, centred, and perhaps even a bit enlightened.

Coagulation (Coagulatio)

The final stage.

- **Chemically**: *Coagulation* is the process of transforming unstable particles in a liquid into a stable, usable form. In laboratories, it is utilised in food production, water purification, and medicine. Consider curdled milk or jelly-making; tiny particles clump together when activated by heat, acid, enzymes, or pH changes. In cheese-making, the addition of acid or rennet to milk causes proteins to form curds. Blood clotting is another common example.
- **Psychologically**: *Coagulatio* marks the moment when all your efforts—your insights, emotional breakthroughs, work with your unconscious, and inner growth—begin to manifest concretely in your life. It transforms from mere thoughts and feelings into a lived reality.

If you've engaged in deep work, *coagulatio* is when everything solidifies. This is the moment you translate the abstract—your thoughts, dreams, and emotions—into reality. Spirit transforms into matter. *Coagulatio* focuses on solidifying these changes and establishing a strong foundation for your new self.

You'll see evidence of this in various aspects of your life. For instance, you might observe how you apply what you've learned about establishing boundaries to foster healthier relationships, transforming your insights on self-care into a consistent practice. Additionally, you may become aware of how you avoid potential conflicts and pay attention to your body's reactions to different people, places, and experiences, choosing to follow your instincts rather than yielding to the pressures of "shoulds" and "musts" from your mind.

Coagulatio can be profoundly satisfying and grounding. You stop merely discussing change—you begin to live it. You might experience a sensation of being less abstract and more connected to a new reality.

Alchemical Symbols for Coagulatio

Metaphorically, *coagulatio* means transforming the fluid—this chaotic and unstructured material—into something solid and dependable. Therefore, pay attention to certain symbols in your dreams or everyday life:

- **Earth or soil**: Earth or soil symbolises *coagulatio* because it speaks to grounding, embodiment, and coming back into form. It's the stage in alchemy where what was once fluid or formless becomes solid and real. After all the dissolving and refining of the earlier stages, *coagulatio* is where spirit settles into matter, insight becomes something you manifest.
- **Stone, or rock**: Earlier alchemical stages, like *solutio* and *distillatio*, are about breaking things down and letting go. *Coagulatio* is the opposite—it's about coming together and becoming solid. A stone shows this clearly: it's shaped by pressure and time, and once formed, it's stable and lasting. It's the transformation you can see and touch.
- **Sprouting seeds**: Sprouting seeds symbolise *coagulatio* because they capture the moment when hidden potential takes shape. What was once buried begins to grow—grounded, visible, and alive. It's not just inner change anymore; it's transformation taking root in the real world.

This phase is crucial because it's where all the inner work you've been doing becomes real-world change. While insights and breakthroughs mark progress, *coagulatio* emphasises fully integrating those lessons. It's about embodying the truth of your essence, bringing the intangible wisdom of your Soul into tangible, everyday life.

We refine our understanding, reactions, and our patience with each iteration. It's not a quick fix but rather a gradual process of chipping away layers to transform the "lead" of our struggles into the "gold" of self-awareness and personal growth.

If you feel stuck in *nigredo*, hold on to faith in the journey.

By this point, you should recognise that a genuine process exists. Alchemy isn't merely an ancient form of chemistry—it represents a mindset focused on growth and transformation. And, after all, who wouldn't want to convert their lead into gold?

Key Takeaways: Alchemy

1 **Therapy as a transformative journey:**

- Psychotherapy isn't linear—it mirrors the alchemical process of transformation. It often begins with confusion or pain and progresses through breakdown, clarity, integration, and renewal phases.

2 **Alchemy as metaphor:**

- Alchemy serves as a rich metaphor for inner change. Just as alchemists sought to turn base metals into gold, therapy helps turn emotional "lead" (for example, wounds and trauma) into psychological "gold" (self-awareness and growth).

3 **Historical and symbolic depth:**

- The chapter provides a foundation in alchemy's historical roots, linking it to spiritual and scientific traditions that sought to understand and transform matter and the self.

4 **Carl Jung's contributions:**

- Jung's exploration of alchemical texts, such as the *Rosarium Philosophorum*, revealed profound parallels between alchemical symbols and psychological transformation, particularly in dreams and the process of individuation.

5 **The four alchemical stages:**

- *Nigredo* (blackening): Breakdown, loss, and chaos. Often, people begin therapy. Facing the Shadow.
- *Albedo* (whitening): Clarity begins to emerge. Emotional cleansing and early healing.
- *Citrinitas* (yellowing): Integration of knowledge. Creativity and spiritual insight increase.
- *Rubedo* (reddening): Completion and embodiment. Living authentically with a sense of wholeness.

6 **The seven alchemical processes map inner work:**

- Processes like *calcinatio* (burning away the false self) and *solutio* (dissolving rigid patterns) reflect real psychological work people do in therapy.

7 **Dreams and symbols as tools:**

- The text encourages noticing recurring symbols in dreams or life, such as the raven for *nigredo* or the white dove for *albedo*, that may signify psychological progress.

8 **Lizzie's case example**:

- Lizzie's journey through grief and betrayal exemplifies the complex yet profound stages of transformation. Her experiences mirror the alchemical process from disintegration to integration.

9 **Encouragement**:

- Be assured that confusion and regression are part of the deep work process. The symbolic framework offers hope: others have navigated this path before.

10 **Practical reflections and rituals**:

- Suggestions like journalling, dreamwork, and mindful walking are offered to help readers integrate each stage.

Notes

1 Pranayama is the yogic practice of focusing on the breath to elevate the prana-shakti, or life energies.
2 Ira Progoff (1921–98) was an American psychotherapist best known for his development of the Intensive Journal Method while at Drew University.

Recommended Reading

Burckhardt, Titus (1967). *Alchemy: Science of the Cosmos, Science of the Soul*. Stuart (Vincent) & J. M. Watkins. (A concise yet rich overview of traditional alchemical teachings from a spiritual perspective.)
Eliade, Mircea (1962). *The Forge and the Crucible*. Harper. (A classic exploration of the spiritual and cultural symbolism of alchemy throughout history.)
Evola, Julius (1995). *The Hermetic Tradition*. Inner Traditions. (Focuses on the metaphysical aspects of alchemy and initiation.)
Gilchrist, Cherry (2002). *Everyday Alchemy: How to Use the Power of Alchemy for Daily Change and Transformation*. Rider & Co. (Gilchrist uses alchemy as a metaphor for growth, transforming struggle into inner gold.)
Jung, Carl Gustav (1980). *Psychology and Alchemy. In The Collected Works of C. G. Jung*. Routledge. (A deep dive into alchemy's psychological symbolism, linking it with the unconscious and individuation.)
Roob, Alexander (1996). *Alchemy and Mysticism*. Taschen. (A visually rich compendium of alchemical art and imagery, accompanied by insightful commentary.)
Somers, Barbara, edited by Hazel Marshall (2004). *The Fires of Alchemy: A Transpersonal Viewpoint*. Archive Publishing. (Drawn from Somers' 1980s courses, this accessible book explores alchemy as a metaphor for personal and spiritual transformation across Eastern and Western traditions.)

References

Duhigg, C. (2012). *The power of habit: Why we do what we do in life and business*. Random House.
Hillman, J. (2017). *Alchemical psychology* (R. J. Leaver, Ed.). Spring Publications.

Jung, C. G. (1963). *Mysterium Coniunctionis* (R. F. C. Hull, Trans., Vol. 14). Princeton University Press. (Original work published 1955–56.)

Jung, C. G. (1968). *Psychology and alchemy.* Princeton University Press.

Lieberman, M. D., Eisenberger, N. I., Crockett, M. J., Tom, S. M., Pfeifer, J. H., & Way, B. M. (2007). Putting feelings into words: Affect labeling disrupts amygdala activity in response to affective stimuli. *Psychological Science, 18*(5), 421–428. https://doi.org/10.1111/j.1467-9280.2007.01916.x

Pennebaker, J. W., & Beall, S. K. (1986). Confronting a traumatic event: Toward an understanding of inhibition and disease. *Journal of Abnormal Psychology, 95*(3), 274–281. https://doi.org/10.1037/0021-843X.95.3.274

Chapter 6

The Chakras and the Subtle Body

In yogic wisdom, a map exists—not of roads or rivers, but of subtle anatomy. Here, energy flows rather than blood, and transformation begins not in muscle or bone, but in the invisible pathways of the energetic body, known as the *pranamaya kosha* (Feuerstein, 1998).

At the heart of this system are two key players: *chakras* and *nadis*.

The *nadis* are the energy channels through which *prana*, the life force, flows.[1]

Ancient yogis described over 72,000 *nadis*, branching like luminous inner circuitry throughout the body. Yet, three hold particular significance.

The central channel, *Sushumna*, runs up the spine like a highway of awakening, along which consciousness rises. Flanking it are *Ida* and *Pingala*, spiralling in a serpentine dance.

- *Ida* flows to the left—cool, intuitive, and inward-turning.
- *Pingala* flows to the right—fiery, dynamic, and outward-focused.

Together, they embody the balancing forces of **yin and yang, moon and sun**. When harmonised, they awaken the *Sushumna*, allowing energy to rise freely and the higher states of awareness to unfold.

Where *Ida, Pingala, and Sushumna* converge, a *chakra* is born. These energetic crossroads create seven potent vortices of consciousness, extending from the base of the spine to the crown of the head. As prana rises upward—especially during deep meditation, breathwork, or spiritual practice—it can awaken these centres one by one.

However, there's a catch: if the *nadis* are blocked, prana cannot flow freely, resulting in unbalanced chakras. You may feel stuck, anxious, creatively dry, or spiritually disconnected. That's why the yogic practices of *pranayama, asana,* and *mantra* aren't merely physical exercises; they're tools to purify the *nadis*, unblock the flow, and reawaken the body's energy circuitry.

In the tradition of **Kundalini Yoga**, this journey is known as *Sushumna sadhana*—the art of guiding the coiled serpent energy at the base of the spine upwards through the chakras towards awakening, union, and a felt sense that

DOI: 10.4324/9781003675099-7

the divine is not "out there" but pulsing through every cell of your being. This is not a metaphor; it is a lived experience, one breath, one chakra, one illuminated moment at a time.

In 1981, Hiroshi Motoyama conducted pioneering bioenergetic research that suggested a fascinating possibility: the activity of the chakras might fluctuate throughout the body in measurable ways. His research pointed to a compelling idea that suggests they aren't just symbols—they might be active participants in our biology. He proposed that these subtle energy centres could influence the nervous system and hormonal rhythms, acting as dynamic bridges between consciousness and the physical body, where energy and matter meet in motion (Motoyama, 1981).

Although scientific research on chakras is limited, some Western scholars have associated them with nerve clusters, glands, and brain regions, such as the prefrontal cortex.

Dr Charles Shang linked chakras and meridians to early cellular networks. He suggests that acupuncture meridians—and possibly chakras—may align with key areas in the developing embryo. These areas, known as "organising centres", are filled with tiny channels between cells (called gap junctions) that facilitate communication. He believes these early cell networks could offer a scientific explanation for how energy flows through the body (Shang, 2001).

Psychologist Richard Maxwell, building on the work of Shang, cautions against reducing chakras to mere physical structures. Instead, he suggests that chakras may be linked to gap junctions, which are tiny channels between cells that facilitate communication and are abundant during early embryonic development.

Maxwell presents a perspective that honours science and the subtle nature of energy. Western interpretations of the chakras often categorise them into two realms: psychology addresses emotions and thoughts, while anatomy pertains to the physical body. However, as he observes, the true challenge lies in explaining how something non-physical interacts with the physical. Our tendency to separate mind and body complicates this issue (Maxwell, 2009).

Carl Jung explored the chakra system later in life, particularly in his 1932 seminar on the Psychology of Kundalini yoga (Jung, 1996). He regarded the chakras as symbolic expressions of *levels of consciousness*, mapping individuation onto a cosmology of the subtle body. For Jung, awakening the upper chakras signified a movement towards the Self, the archetype of wholeness.

Anodea Judith is an American author, therapist, and public speaker specialising in the chakra system, somatic therapy, and yoga. She is the author of many best-selling books on the chakras. Judith draws parallels between the seven main chakras and the corresponding physiological structures. Her integrative framework bridges the subtle and the scientific, enabling contemporary readers to explore how ancient energy systems may interface with the anatomy of the human body (Judith, 2004).

Until science catches up, ancient texts may offer deeper insights into the holistic nature of the mind–body–spirit connection within the chakra system.

The chakra system originates from ancient Indian spiritual traditions, particularly those in Tantric yoga and Ayurveda. In Sanskrit, the word *chakra* means "wheel" or "disc", symbolising spinning vortices of energy aligned along the spine, each governing the physical, emotional, and spiritual dimensions of our being.

Imagine the chakras as spinning wheels of light—more than mere metaphors, they are vibrant energy centres.

Seven major chakras align along the spine, each serving as a portal to a different dimension of being, ranging from primal survival to expansive spiritual insight. They function like tuning forks, each resonating at a distinct frequency, influencing your emotions, health, sense of well-being, and purpose.

The seven main chakras form a vertical axis of energy, rising from the base of the spine to the crown of the head. Each chakra is a spinning vortex of energy, attuned to a different dimension of your being, ranging from the physical to the spiritual.

Each chakra can be regarded as an energetic centre and a psychospiritual portal, acting as a lens through which particular life themes, wounds, and gifts are unveiled. By engaging with the chakras, you can delve into your story from within.

The chakra journey begins at the base of the spine with the **root chakra**, which connects, according to Anodea Judith, to the coccygeal plexus, grounding us in physical survival and primal instinct (Judith, 2004).

As we ascend, the **sacral chakra**, which is the seat of creativity and sensuality, is connected to the sacral plexus and the reproductive organs.

At the navel lies the **solar plexus chakra**, our centre of willpower and personal power, linked to the solar plexus nerve cluster and the pancreas. In the chest, the **heart chakra**, the centre associated with love and compassion, corresponds to the cardiac plexus and the thymus gland, which are vital to immune function and emotional warmth.

As one ascends higher, the **throat chakra** governs communication and expression, resonating with the cervical plexus and the thyroid gland. Between the eyebrows lies the **third eye chakra**, which is associated with insight and intuition, linked to the carotid plexus and the pituitary gland, often referred to as the master gland of the endocrine system.

Finally, the **crown chakra**—gateway to transcendence and spiritual connection—is connected to the cerebral cortex and the pineal gland, both of which have long been considered a bridge to mystical experiences.

The Chakras and Childhood Developmental Stages

The seven chakras are more than swirling energy centres—they mirror our evolving states of consciousness. Each aligns with a key stage of human development, acting like a gate we must pass through on the journey from infancy to spiritual maturity.

Each chakra has its own vibration. It hums at a different frequency and plays a specific role in how we feel, function, and show up in the world.

Chakras tend to awaken in order, starting at the base of the spine and moving upwards—like lights flickering on, one floor at a time, in a tall building. Each one aligns with a stage of growth, presenting its own set.

At each stage, we are encouraged to learn specific emotional, psychological, and relational skills. When these lessons are absorbed and embodied, they create a stable foundation for the next chakra to awaken and unfold. The process is cumulative and organic, like climbing a spiral staircase; each step builds on the previous one. If earlier steps are shaky or incomplete, the higher levels may be unstable. However, when the foundations are strong, energy flows upwards more freely, supporting survival, creativity, love, insight, and ultimately, transformation.

Colours

Every chakra is connected to a specific element and colour, each one expressing its own personality and energetic flavour. Charles W. Leadbeater, a prominent theosophist, is often credited with popularising chakra colours. In *The Chakras*, Leadbeater described perceiving the chakras as "wheels of light", each radiating a distinct colour through clairvoyant vision. His work was pivotal in shaping the Western esoteric understanding of the chakra system, including the now-familiar rainbow spectrum, which ranges from red to violet and remains widely recognised today (Leadbeater, 1927).

Elements

Ancient Indian yogic and Tantric traditions associated elements with the chakras, with these connections evolving gradually through spiritual teachings and practice.

- At the foundation lies the **Root Chakra**, *Muladhara*, which is associated with the element of **earth.**
- The **Sacral Chakra**, *Svadhisthana*, is governed by **water.**
- Next, the **Solar Plexus Chakra**, *Manipura*, is associated with the transformative force of **fire.**
- At the centre of the system is the **Heart Chakra**, *Anahata*, which is associated with **air.**
- The **Throat Chakra**, *Vishuddha*, is associated with **space or ether.**
- Situated between the eyebrows, the **Third Eye Chakra**, *Ajna*, relates to **inner vision and insight.**
- Finally, the **Crown Chakra**, *Sahasrara*, is linked to **consciousness itself.**

Manifestation and the Chakras: A Vertical Path of Embodiment

To manifest the spiritual, we need more than lofty intentions; we need *embodiment*. The chakra system offers an integrative framework where the spiritual becomes tangible, not only in the mind or through prayer, but also in the body, breath, voice, and actions.

In *Eastern Body, Western Mind*, Anodea Judith (2004) says that the chakra system offers a framework for understanding how consciousness expresses itself through the body, serving as a link between opposing forces—such as spirit and matter, thought and sensation, the divine and the earthly.

Here is an example that illustrates how this works in practice.

Crown Chakra (Idea/Inspiration)

A spark arrives—an image, an idea, a sudden sense of knowing. It might come as a message in a dream, a tug in the heart, or a flash of insight that won't let go. You don't chase it; it finds you. This is the moment of calling—when something larger nudges you towards becoming.

> *At the end of 2023, I had an idea to write a book. I had no idea whether it would be a novel or a nonfiction book, but I felt strong urge to write something.*

Third Eye Chakra (Imagination)

You envision it vividly, recognise its truth, and start shaping it into something tangible.

> *I found myself reflecting on the years of training I've undertaken, the countless workshops I've led, and the wealth of knowledge I've gathered along the way. I began to see how I might write a book on some of the consistently recurring themes that present in the consulting room. And I thought about how useful it would be to have an easy-to-read book with case examples and "try this yourself" techniques for practitioners and the general reader.*

Throat Chakra (Declaration/Communication)

You give it voice. Speaking it out loud shapes it into something tangible; it's no longer just a thought but a declaration. You tell its story, breathe life into it, ask for what you need, and align your actions with your intention. In speaking, you begin weaving vision into reality.

> *I shared the idea with a few friends and colleagues, then, created a mind map of potential themes, along with client stories and personal reflections that could bring the subject to life.*

Heart Chakra (Belief)

You feel it profoundly, like a current coursing through your chest. Emotion ascends to meet the vision, grounding it in something tangible. You connect not only with the idea but also with your yearning for it. Love nourishes it. Conviction reinforces it. Without the heart, manifestation is superficial, merely a concept. Yet, when desire is ignited from within, it becomes magnetic.

I began to feel excited about sharing my experience and insights in a way that others could genuinely connect with and understand.

Solar Plexus Chakra (Action)

You move with purpose. You commit wholeheartedly. You follow through. This is when vision gains velocity—where intention transforms into momentum, and momentum shapes reality. You take bold steps, show up consistently, and watch your dreams begin to take form.

I threw myself into learning how to craft a strong book proposal—clarifying the target audience, identifying universities and colleges that might resonate with the material, and researching how to position it effectively. At the same time, I began thinking more broadly: How could I bridge the space between academic depth and public accessibility? I studied the competition, reflecting on where my voice might offer something distinctive. Then came the leap. I wrote the proposal and sent it out to a number of publishers. That bold step marked the true beginning of the writing journey.

Sacral Chakra (Flow)

You let go of the need to control, allowing the reins to relax just enough for creativity to find its rhythm. Effort gives way to ease. You adapt, respond, and create space for joy, not merely productivity. This is where inspiration flows most freely: not through force, but through surrender. Pleasure becomes part of the process, not merely a reward for completion.

At first, I laid down the bare bones—a rough skeleton of chapter headings and scattered notes, with examples jotted down like placeholders. I wrote mechanically, adhering to what I knew. However, once the framework was in place, I circled back and breathed life into it. I researched extensively, rewriting with colour and feeling. As I allowed more of my voice and personality to shine through, the book began to take on a life of its own—and with it, my excitement grew. I wasn't just compiling knowledge anymore; I was creating something alive. When the manuscript was finished, I sent the book proposal, along with sample chapters, to publishers.

Root/First Chakra (Grounding)

This is where the vision touches the earth. You give your vision form, structure, and substance. You integrate the vision into daily life through consistent habits, practical steps, and steady effort. You build a foundation that supports growth, making your intention not just a passing spark but something that endures. Here, the invisible becomes visible. The imagined becomes embodied.

> *At the time of writing, I have just signed a contract with my publisher. The submission date is set. If the dream is the published book (and it is), then I'm 99 per cent there. But when I look back at how I have dug deep and developed the necessary character traits to produce a book—discipline, trust, persistence, courage, to name a few—I realise the dream isn't just on the horizon. It has already touched the earth, taking form in pages and paragraphs, yes, but also in qualities shaped by the journey that brought it to fruition.*

Manifestation is not building castles in the sky; it is spiritual energy descending through you, chakra by chakra, until it touches the earth and becomes something tangible.

The ability to manifest, to bring thoughts, desires, or visions into reality, is influenced by the state of your chakra system. Each chakra plays a unique role in aligning your inner world with outer expression.

When one or more chakras are out of balance, they can *block* the flow of energy, disrupting the manifestation and liberation processes. Here's a chakra-by-chakra breakdown of what can block the energy currents.

The Causes of Chakra Imbalances

The life force does not always flow smoothly. Adverse childhood experiences, traumas, and abuses can and do cause chakra imbalances, which impede the flow of life force and, if left unattended, cause physical, emotional, and behavioural symptoms (Judith, 2004).

When the life force is blocked, the chakras become either excessive or deficient, or paradoxical, where the energy fluctuates between excessive and deficient states (Judith, 2004).

When a chakra is imbalanced, we tend to concentrate excessively on the energy associated with that chakra. If the energy is excessive, we need to discharge it; if it is deficient, we need to charge it.

In *Eastern Body, Western Mind*, Anodea Judith breathes life into the chakra system by weaving it together with the bold insights of Wilhelm Reich (1949) and Alexander Lowen (1975).

Drawing from their bioenergetic theories, she illustrates how our energy doesn't merely flow—it pulses, charges, and releases. However, when life disrupts that rhythm, whether through trauma, repression, or tension, our energy can become stuck, much like a river dammed up. Judith introduces potent practices of charging (to activate and awaken) and discharging (to release and express), which assist in restoring the natural ebb and flow of vitality throughout the body and bring the chakras back into balance.

I will provide an overview below of the types of issues that cause chakra imbalances, how to recognise the signs of an excessive or deficient chakra, and some basic self-help suggestions to begin balancing the chakra system. This is a vast subject, however, and for those interested in learning more, I recommend *Eastern Body, Western Mind* by Anodea Judith (2004). Additional recommendations can be found in the Recommended Reading at the end of this chapter.

Key Takeaways So Far

1   *Jung's Perspective*

- Carl Jung viewed the chakras as symbolic stages of consciousness and spiritual development.
- He mapped the awakening of chakras onto the individuation process, with the higher chakras representing movement toward the archetype of the Self.

2   *Scientific and Bioenergetic Views*

- Hiroshi Motoyama proposed that chakras may have measurable bioenergetic effects on the nervous and endocrine systems.
- Some researchers suggest chakras correlate with nerve plexuses, glands, or brain regions.
- Richard Maxwell and Charles Shang propose that chakras may relate to early embryonic "organising centres" and intercellular communication via gap junctions.

3   *Anodea Judith's Contributions*

- Judith integrates chakra theory with somatic therapy, developmental psychology, and bioenergetics.
- She relates each chakra to both physical structures and developmental stages.
- Imbalances can be **excessive**, **deficient**, or **paradoxical**, and may stem from trauma or disrupted energy flow.
- Her work emphasises restoring flow through practices of *charging* and *discharging*.

4   *Energetic Anatomy in Yogic Tradition*

- Chakras are energy centres along the spine; *nadis* (*Ida, Pingala,* and *Sushumna*) are pathways through which life force (*prana*) flows.
- Where these *nadis* intersect, chakras are formed.
- Yogic practices such as breathwork, meditation, and mantra help cleanse the *nadis* and awaken energy.

5   *Developmental Psychology and Chakras*

- Each chakra corresponds to a specific stage of childhood development.
- Early life experiences influence the formation, balance, or imbalance of each chakra.
- The process is cumulative: unresolved issues in the lower chakras can hinder the development of the higher chakras.

6   *Signs and Causes of Chakra Imbalances*

- Trauma, emotional repression, and adverse childhood experiences can lead to blocks.
- Blocked chakras can manifest as physical symptoms, emotional difficulties, or psychological patterns.
- Judith's (2004) framework offers tools to determine if a chakra is underactive or overactive.

7   *Chakra Colours and Elements*

- Each chakra is associated with a specific **colour** and **element**.
- Charles Leadbeater popularised the rainbow-colour system in Western esotericism.
- The elements reflect qualities and functions of each chakra, rooted in Tantric yoga traditions.

8   *Chakras as Portals of Transformation*

- Chakras are not merely energy points; they are **psychospiritual gateways** that illuminate our wounds, gifts, and personal growth.
- Balancing the chakras supports not only our physical health but also our capacity for creativity, feeling, acting, loving, expressing ourselves, and awakening.

Let us now explore each chakra, examining when it typically develops, the types of experiences or challenges that can disrupt its balance, how to recognise signs of imbalance, and what steps you can take to restore harmony and flow.

Chakra One/Root Chakra (*Muladhara*)

The root chakra begins to form in the womb and continues to develop throughout the first year of life. This energy centre governs our sense of safety, survival, and grounding. Psychologically, it corresponds to Erik Erikson's first developmental stage of Trust vs Mistrust (Erikson, 1950).

During this phase, the infant is wholly dependent on their caregivers. When basic needs such as nourishment, warmth, and protection are consistently met with love, the child develops a profound, embodied trust in the world. The nervous system learns that when I express a need, the world responds. This establishes the earliest imprint of manifestation—the energetic and psychological foundation for self-worth, stability, and a sense of belonging.

The Sanskrit name of the first chakra is *Muladhara*, which means "root support" or "root of existence". It is associated with the earth element and linked to the colour red. Colours ascend from dense to subtle in the chakra system, just as consciousness moves from survival to transcendence. Hence, red is positioned at the base, where everything begins. It signifies the start of incarnation, the spark that animates the body and prepares it for the journey upwards through the chakras.

The root chakra is traditionally associated with the colour red for symbolic, energetic, and psychological reasons. From an energetic perspective, red represents the slowest wavelength of visible light, symbolising the most solid, earthbound, and material aspects of existence and perfectly aligning with the role of the root chakra in grounding us to the physical world.

The colour red is associated with power, strength, passion, and anger—all primal emotions that arise when our basic needs are threatened or fulfilled. These emotions aren't flaws; rather, they serve as signals. They indicate when our root system requires attention. Therefore, the root chakra is red because red symbolises what it means to be alive in a body: to need, to survive, to protect, and to stand one's ground.

Balanced First Chakra

A person with a balanced root chakra enjoys vibrant health, vitality, and a strong connection to the physical world. They feel grounded and at ease in their body, able to rest deeply, move confidently, and inhabit the present moment with a sense of belonging and stability.

Imbalanced First Chakra

When a baby experiences trauma during the first year of life—the foundational period when the first chakra is forming—the energetic imprint of safety can become disrupted. The first chakra, responsible for our sense of security, grounding, and trust in the world, may become imbalanced.

Early wounding can take many forms: birth trauma, abandonment, neglect, physical abuse, chronic hunger, or a lack of nurturing touch. Difficulty bonding with the mother or primary caregiver, serious illness or surgery or exposure to violence can all disturb the energetic soil in which this chakra takes root.

Sometimes, imbalances in the root chakra are influenced not only by our early experiences but also by the echoes of those who came before us. This touches on inherited ancestral trauma—the lingering grief, fear, or survival instincts passed down through generations. Increasing research, particularly in epigenetics, psychology, and neuroscience, supports the idea that we can carry emotional echoes from our ancestors. While the science is still unfolding, several studies have already begun to shed light on how these patterns can live on in us (Yehuda et al., 2015; Dias & Ressler, 2014; Kellermann, 2001).

Even if the trauma, such as war, famine, displacement, abuse, or exile, remains unspoken, its emotional residue can linger in the body like an old, unhealed scar. A nervous system may be shaped by events it has never directly experienced. A child may grow into an adult who feels hypervigilant without reason or deeply uncertain about their right to exist, belong, or feel safe. It is as if the ground beneath us remembers danger, even when the present appears calm. Ancestral trauma can manifest as chronic anxiety, disconnection from the body, or a sense of being unwelcome in the world, as though one's roots have never found their soil.

Healing this layer of the root chakra invites us to nurture our beginnings and honour the lineage from which we come. To become, perhaps, the first in the family line to say: "It is safe now. I belong here. I will put down roots."

Physical Issues Related to the First Chakra

Important: Always consult with your physician regarding any physical issues.

Located at the base of the spine, between the anus and genitals, it exerts its energetic influence on the **large intestine, legs, and feet**—those parts of us that connect with the earth and support our upright stance.

Reflect on your feelings about this part of your body and consider if you have experienced any related symptoms.

The first chakra governs our sense of safety, survival, and belonging in the world. At the base of the spine, it serves as the energetic foundation of the entire chakra system—our internal "ground floor". When this chakra is imbalanced, the body may manifest distress through various physical issues related to grounding and survival. These issues include disorders of the bowel, anus, and large intestine, where our system literally processes and eliminates waste; problems with bones and teeth that reflect the structure and stability upon which we rely; and concerns in the legs, feet, buttocks, and base of the spine— the parts of ourselves that contact the earth and support our movement through life. Eating disorders can also stem from an imbalanced root chakra—overeating may unconsciously serve to ground a person. Simultaneously, food restriction may arise from an internalised fear of being "too much" or unworthy of nourishment. Frequent illness may indicate an immune system weakened by chronic survival stress. These physical symptoms reflect the emotional imprint left by early experiences of neglect, trauma, or instability—experiences that shake the very ground of our being.

Excessive First Chakra

An excessive first chakra often manifests as an over-attachment to safety and familiarity. This may appear as clinging to routines, remaining in a job or relationship long after it has ceased to serve us, out of fear of change, a sense of *better the devil you know*. It can also manifest through hoarding possessions or excessive weight, where physical mass becomes a substitute for a sense of groundedness and protection.

Deficient First Chakra

Conversely, a deficient first chakra indicates a lack of early containment—perhaps the infant was not consistently held, soothed, or responded to in a nurturing manner. This leads to a person feeling ungrounded and unsafe in their own skin. Without a solid inner foundation, discerning where one ends and another begins becomes challenging. Consequently, boundaries become blurred. The individual may struggle to say no, overextend themselves, or seek safety by clinging to others, fearing that asserting their boundaries might result in abandonment or rejection. Healthy boundaries necessitate a sense of safety within the body; without that, the self remains vulnerable to invasion.

When the first chakra is deficient, a person may feel chronically ungrounded, as though something essential is missing. This inner emptiness often triggers a desire for instant gratification—reaching for food, shopping, or stimulation to quickly soothe discomfort. Lacking the internal stability to self-soothe or to wait, the body seeks swift relief. It is not about indulgence; it's about survival: an unconscious attempt to fill the void where safety should reside.

A deficient first chakra often leaves a person feeling easily overwhelmed, making it difficult to complete tasks. They may initiate many projects but struggle to follow through, not from laziness, but due to a lack of inner structure and containment. Like a tree without roots, nothing can hold them steady through discomfort or delay. The nervous system, primed for survival, seeks escape rather than endurance, so goals are abandoned when they require stillness, patience, or persistence.

What's missing is not willpower, but a stable inner core—a profound, embodied sense of "I am here, and I am safe."

Working on Your First Chakra

- **Draw a genogram**: A genogram is a comprehensive visual representation of a family tree that goes beyond names and dates—it includes details about relationships, patterns, and significant events spanning several generations, typically three or more. The symbols used in a genogram are readily available online. Unlike a basic family tree, a genogram emphasises emotional connections, behavioural patterns, medical histories, and psychological dynamics. It is a valuable tool often used by therapists, social workers, doctors, and researchers to gain insight into inherited influences and recurring themes within a family system.
- **Reflect on family roots**: What ancestral patterns still shape you? Did your ancestors have to flee their homeland? Are you a holocaust survivor? Are you the child of immigrants? If so, what was their experience of settling into a new country? Were there any premature deaths, betrayals, desertions, abandonments, serious crimes, or suicides? Were there any cot deaths, infant deaths, miscarriages, stillbirths, or terminations that you know of?

For more information on transgenerational trauma, I recommend *It Didn't Start With You* by Mark Wolynn (2017).

Exploring Your Early Environment

- Working on the first chakra involves an understanding of your body. The root chakra centres on the issue of your right to exist. Exploring the questions below will help you comprehend how your rights were supported or hindered during the early months of your life.
- How was your birth? Were you born prematurely, on time, or late? Was the birth easy or difficult? Were you given straight to your mother, or were you separated for any reason? Did your mother experience postnatal depression? Were you breastfed? Did you have any serious childhood illnesses? Were there any separations from your mother?
- What was the atmosphere like at home? Was there a feeling of safety and security? Were your parents together or separated? What was their relationship like? Were there any financial issues? Was there any alcohol or drug abuse? Who were your trusted adults? Where was your safe harbour? Were there any mental health issues or physical disabilities in the home? How did family members express their feelings? Was there any abuse of any kind? How was your relationship with your siblings, or were you an only child? Where were you in the birth order, and what issues did that present for you?
- Did you attend school, a boarding school, or were you home-schooled? If you went to school, how was that experience for you? Did you feel you fitted in, did you have friends, were you the victim of bullying, or did you bully anyone?

Chakra One: Attending to the Body

- How much attention do you pay to your physical body? Do you take care of it? Do you monitor your diet and exercise? Do you get enough sleep?
- Ground yourself daily—walk barefoot, eat nourishing food, reconnect with your body.

Here's a grounding ritual you can regularly practise.

Chakra One—Grounding: A Guided Ritual

Find a quiet area where you won't be disturbed. If you have a red candle or a piece of red fabric, place it nearby—something simple to acknowledge the root chakra's earthy, grounding energy. Make yourself comfortable. You may sit with your feet firmly on the floor or lie down with your spine supported. Let your body know that this is a safe space.

Begin by closing your eyes. Inhale deeply through your nose for a count of four. Hold your breath for two counts, then exhale slowly through your mouth for six. Allow the tension to begin melting as you repeat this exercise for five to seven cycles. With each breath, you soften a little more into presence. Now, bring your awareness to the base of your spine—the area of your tailbone or perineum (between the anus and vulva in females and the anus and scrotum in males).

Imagine a warm, glowing red light beginning to pulse there. With each inhale, this light grows stronger and steadier. With each exhale, envisage roots extending downwards from your body, deep into the earth—broad, constant, and unshakable. You might say softly to yourself, or silently in your mind: "I am safe. I am grounded. I belong here."

Allow this image to linger with you for a few moments. Let it sink into your body.

When you feel ready, open your eyes slowly. Take a moment to notice how your body feels.

Key Takeaways: Chakra One/Root Chakra (*Muladhara*)

1   *Development and Psychological Foundation*

- **Develops in the womb and throughout the first year of life, aligning with Erikson's stage of Trust vs Mistrust.**
- Governs safety, survival, grounding, and our right to exist.
- Healthy development hinges on consistent, affectionate care that meets fundamental needs (nourishment, warmth, protection).
- Early experiences leave an imprint on the nervous system and shape our bodily sense of trust in the world.

2   Symbolism and Energy

- *Muladhara* means "root support" or "root of existence" in Sanskrit.
- Associated with the **earth element** and the colour **red**, symbolising physicality, strength, and primal emotion.
- Red signifies the densest energy, grounding consciousness in the material realm.

3   Balanced Root Chakra

- Feels **safe, grounded, stable**, and connected to one's body and the present moment.
- Enjoys vibrant health, ease with physical needs, and a sense of belonging.

4   Imbalances and Causes

- **Imbalances often stem from trauma** in early life: neglect, abuse, abandonment, or disruptions in attachment.
- Can also stem from **inherited trauma**, where unspoken ancestral pain influences the nervous system (for example, war, displacement, exile).
- These experiences may result in a **dysregulated sense of safety**, hypervigilance, or chronic anxiety.

5   Physical Manifestations

- Root chakra issues may affect the **bowels, colon, lower back, legs, feet, bones, immune system**, and **eating patterns**.
- Emotional stress from early trauma often plays out through chronic health or digestive issues.

6   Excessive vs Deficient Root Chakra

- **Excessive**: An over-attachment to routine, hoarding, weight gain, fear of change, and clinging to relationships or jobs.
- **Deficiencies**: Feeling ungrounded, struggling with boundary issues, experiencing chronic overwhelm, encountering difficulty in completing tasks, seeking instant gratification.

7   Healing and Grounding Practices

- Explore **family patterns and ancestral trauma** using tools such as **genograms**.

- Consider early caregiving, childbirth, home environment, and school experiences to uncover root chakra wounds.
- Daily grounding rituals include walking barefoot, consuming nourishing food, and practising breathing exercises.
- Utilise **guided meditations and visualisations** (like the red root light and the idea of growing roots into the earth) to restore a sense of grounding and safety.

8   Affirmations and Inner Healing

- Healing the root chakra may involve affirmations such as: *"I am safe. I am grounded. I belong here."*
- The journey involves reclaiming your right to exist and establishing roots, perhaps for the first time in your lineage.

Chakra Two/Sacral Chakra (Svadhisthana)

The sacral chakra develops between the ages of 6 months to 2 years (Judith, 2004).

This period, spanning 6 to 24 months, is characterised by intense exploration—both of the physical world and of the child's emerging sense of self. In Erikson's (1950) psychosocial theory, this phase corresponds to the developmental task of **Autonomy vs Shame and Doubt.**

Having established a foundational sense of trust in the previous stage (when things go well), the child now seeks to assert independence: *I want to do it myself.* This is the age of toilet training, choosing their clothes, declaring decisive "no"s, and experimenting with "yes"s. The child begins to explore the boundaries of their body, their will, and their ability to impact their environment.

This chakra is linked to the exploration of sensation and movement, the joy of discovery, and the development of a sense of "I want" as distinct from "I need."

At this stage, a child begins to take pleasure in their vitality. The name *Svadhisthana* means "one's own dwelling place" or "the seat of the self", reflecting the chakra's role as the energetic seat of the emotional body—home to desire, creativity, sensuality, and the stirrings of personal identity. Here, individuality starts to awaken—not as a concept, but as a felt experience. The second chakra serves as the energy centre for emotions, desire, creativity, and sensual experience. It is where one begins to perceive oneself as someone who senses, feels, connects, and creates.

Its colour is orange and is traditionally associated with the water element, evoking aliveness, fluidity, and openness. Orange is situated just above red in the light spectrum—less dense and more fluid, reflecting the sacral chakra's transition from survival to emotion, sensation, and creativity. The colour orange represents vitality and pleasure.

The sacral chakra is positioned just below the navel and radiates throughout the lower abdomen, hips, lower back, and genital area. It is closely linked to the reproductive organs, which explains why it is often associated with creativity, pleasure, and emotional expression. This energy centre governs our experiences of desire, intimacy, and joy, particularly during our early encounters with sexuality and connection.

Balanced Second Chakra

A person with a balanced sacral chakra moves like water—fluid, responsive, and attuned to sensation. Able to adapt, they respond to change rather than resist it, allowing pleasure, emotion, and connection to ripple through them without fear or shame. Like the moon that governs the tides, they honour cycles of need and desire, nurturing themselves. Their boundaries are clear yet permeable, like a shoreline—able to welcome intimacy while knowing where they begin and end.

Imbalanced Second Chakra

You might not immediately think to trace your low energy or creative blocks back to the sacral chakra—but that's where the story often begins, deep in the belly, just below the navel, in the realm of emotion and desire.

Deficient Second Chakra

Life can feel dull when this energy centre is deficient (blocked). Pleasure becomes a concept rather than a lived experience. You may find it challenging to access desire, whether sexual or otherwise. Emotions seem distant and difficult to identify or express. Creative sparks don't ignite; they fizzle before they even begin. You may feel dry and rigid, as though navigating life in black and white. Guilt may linger around your body or your need for connection, making it harder to open up or truly feel alive.

Excessive Second Chakra

On the other hand, when the sacral chakra is excessive (overactive), it can feel like an uncontrolled flood. Emotions swing unpredictably. There is a hunger for stimulation—sex, food, shopping, drama—anything to fill the emptiness. Relationships can be intense or consuming. Boundaries become blurred. You might seek comfort in the thrill of sensation, even when it ultimately leaves you feeling unfulfilled.

Physical Issues Related to the Second Chakra

Important: Always consult with your physician regarding any physical issues.

Chakra two is situated in the pelvic region, near the sacrum (the triangular bone at the base of the spine). It is linked to the reproductive organs, bladder, and lower digestive system.

Consider how you feel about this part of your body and whether you have experienced any issues related to it.

When the second chakra is out of balance, the body feels the effects. For some, it begins in the reproductive system—menstrual pain, fertility struggles, or issues with libido. Others may find themselves grappling with recurrent urinary tract infections (UTIs), bladder discomfort, or kidney troubles. There may be a dull, persistent ache in the lower back or tightness in the hips and pelvis that no amount of stretching seems to alleviate. The digestive system may also protest, particularly in the lower intestines, where unease and tension tend to accumulate. The body holds what the psyche cannot express.

Moreover, signs such as seemingly insatiable cravings and patterns of over-indulgence can appear, whether through food, sex, or substances. The sacral chakra, when overactive, may compulsively seek pleasure; when underactive, it can entirely sever our connection to desire.

Working on Your Second Chakra

Restoring balance to the sacral chakra invites flow, emotion, and sensuality back into your life. It involves thawing what has been frozen, softening what has become rigid, and giving yourself full permission to experience pleasure without guilt or shame. This form of healing is not about force; it is about surrender. It is not about fixing, but about allowing.

Movement is one of the most direct ways to awaken the sacral chakra. It responds best to fluid, rhythmic, and embodied motion—movement that arises from within rather than being imposed from without. Hip circles, gentle pelvic tilts, or dancing freely to music that stirs emotion can be therapeutic. Swimming or simply floating in water—this chakra's element—can also restore a sense of natural flow. The invitation is to let your body lead, not your mind. This is not a workout; it's a reunion with oneself.

Creativity is equally essential. The second chakra serves as the seat of creative expression, encompassing not only artistry but also any act of giving shape to inner emotions. Activities such as painting, drawing, singing, writing, and crafting (whatever feels playful and unrefined) can be beneficial for healing. The aim is not to create something perfect, but to allow emotions to take form. Creativity is the soul's way of exhaling.

Reconnecting with sensual pleasure is another essential aspect of balancing this energy centre. Pleasure doesn't have to be sexual; it can be purely sensory. Slow down enough to truly savour your food, feel the warmth of water on your skin, or appreciate the scent of something beautiful, such as orange peel, ylang-ylang, or sandalwood. Wearing soft, flowing clothes and engaging in gentle self-massage can help you reconnect with your body. The sacral chakra reminds us that pleasure is not a reward; it's a right.

Because this chakra is deeply linked to our emotional world, allowing those feelings to flow is essential. This might involve journalling honestly without filtering yourself, permitting tears to come when they need to, or finally expressing a truth you've been holding in. Engaging in inner child work can also be powerful—it provides an opportunity to revisit the early moments that shaped your relationship with love, touch, and emotional safety. The aim is not catharsis for its own sake but rather to restore emotional flow.

- To maintain your focus on this centre, surround yourself with rich orange tones, whether in clothing, artwork, or lighting.
- Visualise a warm, glowing orb of orange light just below your navel, gently pulsing with each breath.
- In quiet moments, bring your awareness to the sacral chakra. Visualise the orange light spinning steadily. Repeat affirmations such as, "I allow myself to feel," "I am open to pleasure and joy," or "I honour my body and emotions." These are not just words—they are invitations, statements of intent.

Balancing the sacral chakra is not about control; it is about permission. Permission to feel deeply, to desire freely, to enjoy life fully, and to relish the sweetness of existence. It embodies a gentle unfolding—a return to the waters of your being.

Key Takeaways: Sacral Chakra (*Svadhisthana*)

1   *Developmental Stage*

- Develops between **6 months and 2 years** (Judith, 2004).
- This correlates with **Erikson's stage of Autonomy vs Shame and Doubt**.
- The child starts to explore independence, pleasure, movement, and personal boundaries.
- Emotional and somatic awareness begins: *"I want"* emerges from *"I need"*.

2   *Core Themes*

- Governs **emotions, desires, pleasure, sensuality, creativity**, and personal identity.
- The Sanskrit name *Svadhisthana* means "one's own dwelling place".
- Associated with the **water element** and the colour **orange**, which signifies fluidity, vitality, and emotional openness.

3   Location and Physical Associations

- Situated **below the navel**, it governs the **lower abdomen, hips, pelvis, reproductive organs, bladder, and lower digestive tract.**
- Linked to sexuality, emotional expression, and the creative life force.

4   Balanced Sacral Chakra

- Expresses **fluid movement**, emotional attunement, creativity, and the ability to feel and enjoy pleasure without guilt or shame.
- Understands how to **honour desire** and establish **healthy boundaries** while staying open to connection.

5   Imbalanced Sacral Chakra

Deficient (blocked):

- Emotional numbness, low libido, guilt regarding pleasure, and suppressed creativity.
- Life seems dull, stiff, and lacklustre.
- Difficulty in identifying or expressing emotions.

Excessive (overactive):

- Emotional volatility and compulsive pleasure-seeking, such as food, sex, and drama.
- Blurred boundaries, addictive behaviours, and a sense of being consumed by craving or intensity.

6   Physical Manifestations

May show up as:

- Menstrual and fertility issues.
- UTIs and bladder problems.
- Pelvic pain, hip tightness, lower back tension.
- Lower digestive issues.
- Overindulgence or complete disconnection from pleasure and desire.

7   Healing Practices

Movement:

- Rhythmic, fluid, and intuitive movements (e.g., dance, hip circles, pelvic tilts, swimming).
- Aim: embody rather than control—let the body lead.

Creativity:

- Express yourself through art, music, journalling, or crafting.
- The focus is on release and emotional flow, not perfection.

Sensory pleasure:

- Reconnect with touch, taste, scent, and beauty.
- Enjoy food, nature, textures, and essential oils such as orange, sandalwood, and ylang-ylang.
- Opt for loose-fitting garments and practise self-massage.

Emotional release:

- Journal freely and openly.
- Allow tears, speak unspoken truths.
- Engage in **inner child work** to heal early imprints concerning affection and emotional safety.

Visualisation and affirmation:

- Visualise a warm **orange light** below your navel.

  Repeat affirmations:

  - "I allow myself to feel."
  - "I am open to pleasure and joy."
  - "I honour my body and emotions."

8   *The Core Message*

- Balancing the sacral chakra isn't about control—it's about **permission**: permission to **feel deeply, desire freely**, and **enjoy fully**.
- Healing is a gentle unfolding—*a return to the waters of your being.*

Chakra Three/Solar Plexus Chakra (*Manipura*)

Between the ages of 18 months and four years, as the third chakra awakens, a fire begins to ignite in the child's core—a flicker of selfhood that asserts, "*I am separate, and I can act.*"

During this formative period, the child enters the *overlapping* psychosocial stages that Erik Erikson (1950) termed **Autonomy vs Shame and Doubt** and **Initiative vs Guilt**. They begin exploring the world not only with their hands and feet but also with intention. They say "no" to what they do not want, insist on doing things independently, and try on power like a costume. "I can!" becomes their mantra. If gentle boundaries support their burgeoning independence, self-trust is nurtured. The child learns that they are capable, can act, and assert themselves without fear of punishment or rejection. This fosters courage, self-discipline, and a sense of identity.

However, if a child is shamed for their impulses, harshly controlled, or made to feel guilty for simply wanting to explore, that inner fire diminishes. They may become hesitant, fearful of taking initiative, or excessively compliant. Others, in reaction to that early suppression, may overcompensate, asserting control wherever possible, becoming domineering or defiant.

The **third chakra**, *Manipura*, known in Sanskrit as the "lustrous gem", is the solar plexus. It is here that will, autonomy, and personal power begin to manifest.

In energetic terms, this chakra governs the spark that transforms desire into action. It is the furnace where self-esteem is forged. To develop into a confident adult with a strong sense of purpose, the child must be permitted to experiment with their will, occasionally stumbling but always receiving encouragement rather than shame.

This is not merely a time of learning how to do things; it is a time of becoming someone who believes in their power to choose, to act, and to shape their world.

The key issues during this period are willpower (the phase of the "terrible twos" when a child wants to exert their will), self-esteem, and actions.

The **third chakra**, *Manipura*, is associated with the colour yellow, reminiscent of the summer sun. *Manipura* is a fitting name for the inner sun that burns at the centre of our being. It serves as the radiant hearth of **personal power**, where *fire* meets *form*, and *will* becomes *action*.

At the core of our being, we forge the jewels of the self—courage, clarity, confidence, and discipline—each polished by challenges and illuminated by self-awareness. *Manipura* is associated with the element of fire, the flame that transforms raw intention into decisive action. When we align with it, we shine—not with arrogance, but with a quiet luminosity that arises from knowing who we are and daring to act from that truth.

Here, the element of fire is kindled—small at first, yet fierce in purpose. It is the flame of becoming, of testing limits, and of daring to assert one's will. In this furnace, identity is tempered, confidence is born, and the power to choose one's path begins to stir.

Balanced Third Chakra

When your third chakra is balanced, you recognise who you are and stand firmly in that knowledge without feeling the need to dominate or belittle yourself. There exists a quiet confidence in your choices and a sense that you can trust your instincts as you pursue your goals. Decisions are made with clarity, and you feel motivated, focused, and capable. You express yourself assertively without aggression and maintain boundaries without guilt. Tasks feel manageable, and you have the energy to complete them. You are not motivated by the need to prove your worth.

Physically, your digestion feels healthy, and you maintain a balanced relationship with food, energy, and responsibility. Emotionally, you recover from setbacks with resilience. You're unafraid of challenges—you know your inner fire can withstand them.

Imbalanced Third Chakra

Deficient Third Chakra

When the solar plexus chakra is deficient, your relationship with power becomes distorted. You may find it difficult to assert yourself, continually second-guessing your decisions and seeking approval from others. Confidence seems just out of reach, and the prospect of taking bold action can elicit anxiety or self-doubt.

Excessive Third Chakra

Alternatively, the imbalance may swing towards excess, towards control, aggression, or perfectionism. You might feel the urge to dominate conversations, overwork, or micromanage situations in an attempt to feel secure. Rather than acting from inner strength, you react out of fear or a need to prove your worth.

Physical Issues Related to the Third Chakra

Important: Always consult with your physician regarding any physical issues.

The third chakra is located in the upper abdomen, just above the navel and ribcage, roughly aligning with the diaphragm and the upper digestive system. Consider your feelings about this area of your body and whether you have ever encountered any issues in this region. Physically, imbalances in this chakra may manifest as digestive problems such as bloating, ulcers, and indigestion, as well as fatigue and adrenal stress. Emotionally, you may feel either burnt out or as though you are operating on nervous energy. Minor setbacks can seem overwhelming, or you might react to challenges with anger or frustration.

Working on Your Third Chakra

Balancing the third chakra involves rekindling your inner fire into a steady flame that fuels your purpose, as this chakra governs your drive, motivation, and ability to act confidently on your goals. Begin by reconnecting with your body's core. Practices such as yoga twists, plank holds, or breathwork focused on the belly (like *Kapalabhati*) can stoke this inner heat. As the belly strengthens, so too does your sense of agency. *Kapalabhati*, often referred to as "Skull Shining Breath", is more than just a breathing technique—it's an energetic wake-up call. Rooted in ancient yogic practice, it clears the mind, cleanses the body, and ignites the fire within.

The breath flows in sharp, rhythmic bursts. You sit upright, your spine aligned, and begin to exhale forcefully through your nose, pulling your belly inward with each breath. The inhalations are passive—your body draws them in between each pulse. It's as if you're stoking a fire in your core, awakening your system with every breath.

This practice targets the solar plexus—the seat of personal power—with unmistakable intensity. As the belly moves, the mind sharpens. Heat, lightness, and a subtle clarity begin to spread from the centre outwards. The name itself reflects this effect: *kapala* means "skull" and *bhati* means "to shine". It's as though the breath clears away the fog, leaving the mind bright and alert.

Kapalabhati is both energising and cleansing. It clears stale air from the lungs, increases oxygen flow, and activates digestion. Furthermore, it also accomplishes something deeper: it awakens the will, revives inner strength, and prepares you to face the day with focus and intention. This is breath as power—each exhale serves as a reminder of your ability to move energy, shift mood, and reclaim your inner light.

You will find many videos on YouTube that can guide you through the practice, making them ideal for beginners or anyone seeking a bit of extra support.

Start slowly—especially if breathwork is new to you. There's no prize for pushing through too fast. Let your body ease in, gently finding its rhythm. Breathwork can be a powerful ally—but it's not the right fit for everyone.

Safety Warnings for Kapalabhati

Breathwork can be a helpful tool, but it may not suit everyone. If you have irritable bowel syndrome, ulcers, gastritis, or a hernia, it is best to avoid this practice, as it puts pressure on the abdominal area and could worsen your condition symptoms. Similarly, if you have epilepsy or a history of seizures, intense breathwork could potentially trigger one, so it is best avoided. This practice is also not recommended during pregnancy, after abdominal surgery, or if you have high blood pressure, heart conditions, or hernias.

If you feel dizzy, overheated, anxious, or short of breath, take that as your signal to pause. Always practise in a well-ventilated space where you feel comfortable. If you're unsure whether breathwork is suitable for you, seek advice from a qualified yoga teacher. Above all, pay attention to your body. Allow the breath to be your *guide*, not your challenge.

Ignite Your Inner Fire

The third chakra—your solar plexus—is governed by fire, which thrives on action, intention, and clarity.

Step into the sun whenever possible. Light a candle and reflect on what you truly desire as the flame flickers. Allow it to become a ritual. Journal about what ignites your passion—or what dims your inner flame.

Speak power into your being with affirmations such as, "I am strong. I trust myself. I follow through." These statements are not for ego inflation—they are a reclamation of your confidence.

Now, direct your awareness to your solar plexus. Visualise a radiant sun glowing there, warm, bold, and steady. With each breath, let that golden heat expand, filling you with courage, clarity, and strength that pulses through you.

Examine your boundaries. Are you yielding too much to please others, or pushing too hard to maintain control? A well-balanced third chakra neither collapses nor dominates; it stands its ground with quiet strength.

This is the action chakra; above all, **act**. Not reactively, but from alignment; one small, courageous action towards what matters most. Fire requires movement. This chakra awakens not just through thought, but through bold, heart-led doing.

To maintain your focus on this chakra, surround yourself with rich yellow tones, whether in clothing, artwork, or lighting. Visualise a warm, glowing orb of yellow light in your solar plexus, gently pulsing with each breath.

Balancing this energy requires you to stop concealing your light or using it to overpower others. Instead, permit it to shine brightly and steadily from within.

Key Takeaways: Third Chakra/Solar Plexus Chakra (*Manipura*)

1   Developmental Stage

- Awakens between **18 months and 4 years old**.
- Corresponds to Erikson's stages: **Autonomy vs. Shame and Doubt** and **Initiative vs. Guilt**.
- The child begins to explore **will, independence, and personal agency** with the growing assertion: *"I can."*

2   Core Themes

- Linked to **willpower, confidence, identity, action, and self-esteem**.
- Manipura means *"lustrous gem"*—the radiant centre where **intention transforms into action**.
- This chakra governs **personal power**, motivation, and our sense of purpose.

3   Symbolism and Energy

- Connected to the **fire element** and the colour **yellow**, which symbolises inner light, transformation, and vitality.
- Fire here signifies both **desire and drive**, the force that propels you from thought to courageous, heart-led action.

4   Location and Physical Associations

- Situated in the **upper abdomen**, above the navel and beneath the ribcage.
- Associated with the **diaphragm, stomach, liver, pancreas, adrenal glands**, and **upper digestive system**.

5   Balanced Solar Plexus Chakra

- Instils **confidence, clarity, motivation**, and sound self-discipline.
- You feel competent, assertive (not aggressive), and capable of making decisions while maintaining healthy boundaries without guilt.
- Physically, digestion feels harmonious; emotionally, there is **resilience and bravery** when confronting challenges.

6   Imbalanced Solar Plexus Chakra

Deficient:

- Low self-esteem, indecisiveness, fear of failure, and avoidance of responsibility.
- Overly passive or dependent, susceptible to anxiety and inclined towards people pleasing.

Excessive:

- Controlling, perfectionistic, angry, or domineering.
- Overworking and micromanaging, driven by a fear of not measuring up.

7   Physical Symptoms of Imbalance

- Digestive problems: **ulcers, bloating, indigestion**.
- **Adrenal fatigue**, burnout, and blood sugar imbalances.
- Energetically, one may feel either drained or nervously overstimulated.

8   *Healing and Strengthening Practices*

Breathwork and movement:

- Core-strengthening yoga (plank, twists) and breathwork such as *Kapalabhati* (**Skull Shining Breath**) serve to stoke the internal fire.
- *Kapalabhati* energises, clears the mind, and activates personal power—but it must be practised with care.

Cautions for *Kapalabhati*:

- Not suitable for pregnancy, hernias, ulcers, epilepsy, high blood pressure, or certain digestive problems.
- Always start slowly and seek guidance if unsure.

Empowerment rituals:

- Step into the sunlight and light candles as symbols of intention.
- Journal about desires, strengths, and obstacles.

Use affirmations:

- *"I am strong."*
- *"I trust myself."*
- *"I follow through."*

Visualisation:

- Imagine a **sun-like globe glowing in your solar plexus**. With each breath, it radiates warmth, courage, and direction.

Boundaries and action:

- Reflect on your relationship with boundaries—do you tend to overextend or dominate?
- Healthy *Manipura* energy embodies **steady, heart-aligned action**. Act with intention, rather than reactivity.

9   *Core Insight*

- This is the **chakra of action, agency, and self-respect**.
- True power is not control; it's about recognising your worth and acting in alignment with it.
- Let your fire burn **not to consume, but to illuminate**.

Chakra Four/Heart Chakra (*Anahata*)

Situated in the centre of the chest, enveloping the heart and lungs, the heart chakra, *Anahata*, begins to mature between the ages of **4 and 7**. This is the energetic seat of love, empathy, and emotional connection. Developmentally, it aligns with **Erikson's stage of Initiative vs Guilt**, which asks the child to explore their ability to initiate relationships and express affection, curiosity, and creativity without fear of disapproval (Erikson, 1950).

During this stage, children venture beyond the family home into schools and social environments. They begin to form friendships, seek a sense of belonging, and navigate the delicate terrain of being liked or not being liked. When their peers accept them, their hearts open naturally. The child feels safe to give and receive love, to care for others, and to trust that they are lovable in return.

However, if this budding openness encounters bullying, exclusion, or ridicule, the heart learns to protect itself. Shame, guilt, or fear of vulnerability can take hold, and the natural flow of affection may be obstructed. Self-worth becomes intertwined with rejection, and the ability to connect freely is diminished.

The heart chakra flourishes on connection, compassion, and authenticity. In this stage, we are learning not only how to relate to others but also how to treat ourselves with kindness, recognising that we are worthy of love, simply as we are.

The nineteenth-century German philosopher Arthur Schopenhauer shares a brief but striking parable in his book *Parerga and Paralipomena (1851)*—and it goes something like this:

> On a cold winter's day, a cluster of porcupines gathered for warmth, seeking comfort in one another's nearness. Yet their quills, sharp with instinct, caused pain with every touch, and so they scattered. The chill pulled them back again—and once more, closeness brought discomfort. After many rounds of drawing near and pulling away, they learned a quiet truth: to stay close enough to feel the warmth, yet far enough not to wound.

In *Schopenhauer's Porcupines: Intimacy and Its Dilemmas* (2002), Luepnitz opens the book with the parable and writes that Freud quoted Schopenhauer's story in *Group Psychology and the Analysis of the Ego* (1921), using it as a metaphor for the ambivalence of human intimacy—the oscillation between the need for closeness and the need for distance.

Anāhata is Sanskrit for "unstruck". It is a curious name for the heart chakra, but this term has been expressed through the centuries by yogis and mystics: there exists a sound within us that no hand has struck, nor force has impacted. A resonance arises not from collision but from stillness. It is the sound of being—not the sound of the heartbeat itself, but something deeper, a vibration you may feel when you are quiet enough to hear your soul exhale. *Anāhata* is love before it possesses an object *to* love. It is the expansiveness in which grief and joy can coexist. It is a space where you can be moved not because someone has touched you, but because something within you has opened.

In this inner chamber, forgiveness is attainable. Not because the past is forgotten, but because the heart, like a grand bell, has learned to sing even without being struck.

Anāhata is the centre of the self that neither demands nor clings. It is the place where you stop reacting and start responding.

Balanced Chakra Four

When the fourth chakra is balanced, it becomes evident. The individual is warm, magnetic, and their presence is reassuring. They navigate the world with an open heart, unaffected by fear or judgement. Compassion flows effortlessly from them.

They love others without losing themselves. They give without expecting repayment. Their empathy does not overwhelm them; it guides them. There is a steadiness in their emotional landscape, a kind of peace that is not passive but profoundly alive. Self-love is no longer a struggle, but a birth right. From that grounded centre, it becomes a sanctuary—not just for themselves, but for others as well.

Imbalanced Chakra Four

The heart chakra, according to yogic philosophy, acts as the energetic bridge between the lower chakras, which govern survival and will, and the upper chakras, which govern expression and awareness.

Wounds to the heart chakra can arise from experiences of rejection, abandonment, loss, shame, relentless criticism, or unacknowledged grief, including grief inherited across generations. Traumas may also stem from divorce, the death of a loved one, growing up in a cold or loveless environment, receiving conditional love, enduring physical or sexual abuse, and experiencing betrayal.

Excessive Chakra Four

When the heart chakra is excessive, love overflows—but not always in the positive way we might envision. It's as though the gates of the heart are stuck wide open, pouring emotion into the world without pause or protection. At first glance, this may seem like boundless compassion, but beneath it lies a different story: one of blurred boundaries, desperate giving, and a fear of being alone.

A person with an overactive heart chakra may find themselves giving excessively, always rescuing, and consistently agreeing, even when it jeopardises their well-being. Some individuals come to believe that love means sacrifice, that their value lies in how much they can give, carry, or endure for others. Love transforms into something they chase or cling to, rather than something shared freely. Consequently, they can lose touch with themselves, with their own needs dissolving in the face of someone else's need. This pattern is at the core of co-dependency.

Co-dependency is like trying to water someone else's garden while your own soil turns to dust. An excessive heart chakra is a river without banks, overflowing with such force that it floods everything in its path. Co-dependency resembles love and devotion but wraps itself so tightly around another that both struggle to breathe. Boundaries dissolve; your emotions tether to theirs. Their pain becomes yours, and their happiness is your oxygen.

To heal an excessive heart chakra does not mean to close it, but rather to contain it with care. To learn that love, in order to be genuinely sustaining, must encompass the Self. Saying no is not unkind. Compassion is not measured by how much we bleed for others, but by how we show up, whole and grounded, with the heart intact.

Deficient Chakra Four

When the chakra is closed down, the very core of the chakra system is depressed, making it difficult for energy to flow between the upper and lower chakras.

A person with a deficient fourth chakra may seem antisocial, withdrawn, cold, critical, judgemental, intolerant of themselves or others, lonely, isolated, depressed, fearful of intimacy, and lacking in empathy.

When the fourth chakra is deficient, the heart becomes inwardly focused. What was once a place of warmth and connection transforms into a chamber of withdrawal. You might not even notice it at first—a subtle dullness in the chest, a coolness where warmth should prevail—a numbness, perhaps, where there ought to be feeling.

People with a deficient heart chakra often have a history of disappointment in love, which may not always be dramatic but can rather reflect the gradual erosion of trust over time. Perhaps early love came with conditions; you were loved for what you did rather than for who you are. Maybe it ended unexpectedly. Perhaps the tender shoots of connection were trampled on too many occasions. Thus, the heart began to protect itself in the only way it knew how: by closing.

Relationships can be challenging. Intimacy often feels risky. The idea of being vulnerable may provoke more fear than desire. Even though there might be a longing for connection and a yearning to be seen and loved, it feels as if a pane of glass stands between the self and the world.

It's not that the person doesn't care. Often, they care deeply, perhaps too deeply. However, the risk of pain seems too great. Thus, they retreat into independence, wrap themselves in emotional armour, or adopt a form of polite detachment. The heart becomes a guarded garden, safe yet untouched.

To heal this, the heart must be coaxed—not cracked open, but gently invited. Trust must be rebuilt, one drop at a time. Small acts of self-love, relationships that feel safe, and moments of truth spoken without punishment are essential. Only then does the heart begin to soften. It may tremble at first, but eventually, it remembers—it was *made* to feel, to connect, to love and be loved.

Physical Issues Related to the Fourth Chakra

Important: Always consult with your physician regarding any physical issues.

The fourth chakra is located in the centre of the chest and serves as the energetic hub of love, compassion, and connection. It governs not only our capacity to love others and ourselves but also various physical systems: the heart, lungs, thymus gland, breasts, and arms (Judith, 2004).

Reflect on any issues you have experienced with this part of your body.

Physician Gabor Maté emphasises that the body expresses what the psyche cannot articulate. In his clinical experience, long-term emotional suppression—particularly concerning unmet childhood needs for love and connection—can predispose the body to chronic illness. He says, "When we have been prevented from learning how to say no, our bodies may end up saying it for us" (Maté, 2011).

The heart chakra can become a battleground between the desire to connect and the fear of vulnerability. When the heart chakra is out of balance, the body often reflects this through specific symptoms—expressions of what has been emotionally blocked, repressed, or overwhelmed.

Physical issues related to the heart chakra commonly involve cardiovascular conditions, such as high blood pressure, arrhythmias, and heart disease. These often mirror emotional strain, unresolved heartbreak, or chronic stress that closes the heart off from connection.

The lungs are also associated with this chakra. Breath and love are intimately connected, and when grief is unprocessed, it may show up as asthma, shortness of breath, or frequent respiratory infections (Judith, 2004). Judith notes that grief can literally "collapse the chest", resulting in a sunken posture and restricted breathing.

The thymus gland—situated just behind the sternum—plays a vital role in maintaining the strength of the immune system and is closely associated with the energy of the heart chakra. When this chakra is depleted or blocked, it can adversely affect the immune system, making an individual more vulnerable to illness. Suppressed emotions—especially those related to love, forgiveness, or unresolved grief—can quietly undermine the body's natural defences (Judith, 2004).

In women, the breasts are energetically linked to nurturing and self-care. Issues such as tenderness, cysts, or breast disease may indicate conflicts surrounding caregiving, self-love, or an excess of giving to others.

The arms and hands, symbolic extensions of the heart's capacity to give and receive, may exhibit circulation issues, weakness, or numbness, particularly when one finds it challenging to reach out or accept help. Tension in the upper back, especially between the shoulder blades, is common when someone carries emotional burdens silently. The body hunches inward, protecting the heart. Similarly, chest pain, when not linked to cardiac issues, can reflect emotional constriction or repressed grief.

An imbalanced heart chakra is not merely about blocked emotions; it concerns survival patterns that once shielded us from pain but now hinder our ability to connect. Healing involves learning to open up gradually and safely, to trust once more, and to extend love both inward and outward.

As Judith (2004) explains, "The challenge of the heart chakra is to maintain balance in the loving self: to care without smothering, to give without losing, to love without attachment."

Working on Your Fourth Chakra

A balanced *Anahata* is neither guarded nor overflowing; it is open with discernment and connected with integrity. However, after loss, betrayal, conditional love, or early neglect, the heart often requires guidance to open safely once more. Healing begins in the body, with the breath, and the stories we carry within us.

Breath: Creating Space in the Chest

The breath serves as the doorway to the heart. Gentle pranayama practices such as Nadi Shodhana (alternate nostril breathing) or Dirga Pranayama (three-part breath) help to calm the nervous system and expand the chest, physically creating space for emotions and energetic flow. Videos of these conscious breathing practices are readily available online. Breathing consciously encourages us to soften the protective shell around the heart.

Each inhale is an invitation. Each exhale, a release.

The Arms: Reaching Out and Taking In

As the arms and hands extend from the heart chakra, mindful movement can help restore blocked energy. Practices such as slow, expressive arm stretches, open-palm gestures, or reaching exercises—imagining "offering" and "receiving"—can symbolically retrain the psyche to give and receive love without fear.

Writing and Witnessing

Journal-keeping is a quiet act of self-love. It enables the heart to disclose truths that the voice may fear to express. Prompts like these can assist the process:

> What did I learn about love?
> Do I believe I am worthy of love? Why or why not?
> How easily can I give and receive love?
> What does love feel like in my body?
> Do I tend to overgive or withhold love?
> Whom do I still need to forgive, and what holds me back?
> What would it feel like to release old hurt or betrayal?
> Can I offer myself the same compassion I offer others?
> In what ways do I judge myself harshly?
> What parts of me need more acceptance?
> Can I sit with my pain without shutting down?
> Am I afraid of being emotionally vulnerable?
> How do I protect my heart—and is that still serving me?
> When was the last time I truly let someone in?
> Do I lose myself in relationships, or do I remain centred?
> Where do I need clearer boundaries to love more freely?
> How do I differentiate between compassion and co-dependency?

Naming grief, longing, and unmet needs helps to bring unconscious patterns into the light of awareness.

Psychotherapy and Inner Work

Psychotherapy provides a safe space for the emotional heart to unfold. Through a trusted relationship, we can explore attachment wounds, release buried grief, and engage in inner child work, nurturing the part of us that first learned love was unsafe or conditional. This also includes assessing assumptions regarding relationships, recognising patterns of co-dependency, and cultivating self-acceptance as a foundation for wholeness.

For those new to inner child work, I recommend John Bradshaw's book, *Homecoming: Reclaiming and Championing Your Inner Child* (1990). Read it gently, and preferably while in therapy, because it does what it says on the cover, and the exercises can be painful. Bradshaw's book is a homage to the inner child, acknowledging its pain, abandonment, and isolation. He speaks with compassion and remorse, recognising how the adult had to bury and forget the wounded child to survive. The book is a call to reunion, promising to listen, protect, and reclaim the forgotten joys, vulnerabilities, and truths of the child within. It sets the tone for the book's central theme: healing comes through reconnecting with the inner child, offering it the care, validation, and voice it was once denied (Bradshaw, 1990).

Healing the heart chakra involves the anima and animus (the inner feminine and masculine aspects of the psyche), which are not merely traits but vital presences within the psyche. Jung believed that reconciling these polarities was central to individuation, or the process of becoming whole. He said, when two people truly connect, something changes in both of them; just like a chemical reaction, the encounter transforms each one (Jung, 1966).

The relationship with the contra-sexual aspect precedes integration; integration arises from that ongoing inner dialogue. In therapy, we learn to connect with our anima and animus through dreams, using active imagination techniques to engage in dialogue with these aspects of ourselves. We can interact with them when we encounter particularly intense projections, relating to them through creative expressions such as art, poetry, dance, and other forms of expression. Integration involves becoming whole by bringing conscious awareness to our inner opposites. It means no longer unconsciously projecting the anima or animus onto lovers, mentors, or adversaries. Instead, we begin to recognise their voices within our thoughts, instincts, and emotions, allowing them to inform our relationships, creativity, and decisions with greater wisdom.

To integrate the anima is to allow feeling, intuition, receptivity, and soulfulness to inhabit a man's consciousness. To integrate the animus is to empower a woman's clarity, voice, assertiveness, and spiritual authority. Jung believed that embracing and integrating the anima or animus is among the most challenging parts of the journey towards self-realisation and also one of the most profoundly enriching.

Chapter 3, "Jargon Buster: Telling It Like It Is" and Chapter 12, "Carry My Gold: Retrieving Projections" provide further information on this topic.

For a deeper dive, Robert Johnson's *Inner Work: Using Dreams and Active Imagination for Personal Growth* (1986) provides an accessible introduction. Johnson describes the anima as the inner feminine within a man, the part of him that feels, intuits, and imagines. She often appears in dreams as a mysterious woman, a muse, or someone who evokes deep emotions. The anima shapes a man's ability to connect, be vulnerable, and relate to his inner world. When she is not integrated, she can lead to emotional swings, idealised romance, or dependence on others for emotional grounding. However, when welcomed and understood, she becomes a powerful guide, opening the door to creativity, empathy, and soulful insight.

For women, the animus represents the inner masculine—an emblem of reason, direction, and strength. He may manifest in dreams as a father, mentor, warrior, or critic. The animus shapes how a woman asserts herself, expresses her truth, and wields her authority. If left unchecked, he can transform into an inner critic—rigid, judgemental, or domineering. However, when integrated, he fosters clarity, confidence, and a steady sense of purpose.

Grief

Grief is a natural aspect of opening the heart. Unfelt sorrow, whether stemming from relationships, lost opportunities, or unmet childhood needs, can congest the chest like emotional scar tissue. Tears, when allowed, are not a sign of weakness; they serve as the cleansing that prepares the heart to feel again. When the heart breaks, so does the shell we've constructed around it, cracking open to let the long-held feelings finally flow free. This message is deeply aligned with mystical Sufi teachings, which assert that **pain opens the heart,** and through that opening, **divine light, insight, or love can enter.** "**The wound is the place where the Light enters you**" is a phrase commonly attributed to thirteenth-century Sufi mystic, Rumi.

Forgiveness

One of Rumi's most famous teachings was about transcending judgement: "Out beyond ideas of wrongdoing and rightdoing, there is a field. I'll meet you there." This is about stepping beyond blame, into love.

Forgiveness, when appropriate, is a gift we give ourselves. It unhooks the heart from the past, not to forget, but to move forward—freer, lighter, and more open to life. *However, we must be cautious of spiritual bypass and not rush to forgive.* First, the soul must pass through the fiery stage of rage, sorrow, and sacred grief. Only then, through this inner alchemy, are we ready to forgive not from the mind, but from the heart's deepest knowing.

Key Takeaways: Chakra Four/Heart Chakra (*Anāhata*)

1   *Developmental Stage*

- Matures between the **ages of 4 and 7**, aligning with Erikson's stage: **Initiative vs. Guilt.**
- The child begins to form friendships, exploring empathy, affection, and a sense of social belonging.
- Emotional safety or wounding during this stage influences the heart's openness or defensiveness later in life.

2   *Core Themes*

- *Anāhata* governs **love, compassion, connection, empathy, forgiveness,** and **emotional equilibrium.**
- In Sanskrit, *Anāhata* means "unstruck"—symbolising a sound that emerges from stillness, rather than from impact.

- This chakra connects the lower chakras (survival, will) with the upper chakras (expression, insight)—it serves as the **energetic centre** of the Self.

3   *Symbolism and Energy*

- Linked to the **air element** and the colour **green**.
- Symbolises **growth, openness**, and the ability to embrace both joy and grief without shutting down.

4   *Balanced Heart Chakra*

- Demonstrates **warmth, emotional resilience, empathy**, and **self-love**.
- Healthy boundaries exist; love is given and received freely without losing oneself.
- Compassion is rooted, not self-sacrificing. Emotional responses are stable, not overwhelming.

5   *Imbalanced Heart Chakra*

Excessive:

- Overgiving, co-dependency, blurred boundaries.
- Seeking validation through caretaking, fearing rejection or abandonment.
- Love can turn into clinging, rescuing, or sacrificing oneself at the expense of others.

Deficient:

- Withdrawn, emotionally numb or shut down.
- Fearful of vulnerability, difficulty trusting or accepting love.
- Often rooted in **conditional love**, abandonment, or past betrayal.
- Self-protection conceals a profound desire to connect.

6   *Physical Manifestations*

- Related to the **heart, lungs, thymus gland, breasts, arms, and upper back**.

May present as:

- Heart conditions, hypertension, and chest tightness.
- Respiratory issues, asthma, or breathlessness (frequently grief-related).
- Weakened immune function (through the thymus gland).
- Breast tenderness or disease (nurturing conflicts).
- Arm and hand issues—struggles with expressing or receiving affection.
- Upper back tension (carrying emotional burdens silently).

"When we have been prevented from learning how to say no, our bodies may end up saying it for us."—Gabor Maté

7   Healing Practices

Breathwork:

- Nadi Shodhana (alternate nostril) or Dirga Pranayama (three-part breath) for expanding the chest and soothing the nervous system.
- Breath softens the heart's protective shell, creating a space for emotions.

Movement:

- Arm-reaching exercises, open-palm gestures, and heart-opening yoga poses.
- Symbolic gestures of giving and receiving.

Self-enquiry and journalling:

- Prompts include:
  - What did I learn about love?
  - Do I overgive or withdraw?
  - Can I sit with emotional pain without shutting down?
  - What are my boundaries like in relationships?

Inner child and psychotherapy:

- Healing attachment wounds, exploring grief, and releasing shame.
- John Bradshaw's *Homecoming* serves as a powerful guide for this work.

Anima/animus integration:

- Jungian approach: achieving balance between inner masculine and feminine aspects.
- Fosters emotional wholeness, empowerment, and deeper, more meaningful relational bonds in relationships.

Grief and forgiveness:

- True forgiveness is achievable only when sorrow, rage, and truth are honoured.
- Rumi: *"The wound is the place where the Light enters you."*

8 Core Insight

- A healthy heart chakra is neither wide open nor tightly shut—it is open with discernment.
- Love is not a transaction or performance; rather, it is a presence.
- Healing is not about "fixing the heart", but rather about remembering that it was designed to feel and to love.

Chakra Five/Throat Chakra (*Vishuddha*)

The Sanskrit name for the fifth chakra is *Vishuddha*, meaning "purification". Psychologically, this chakra begins to awaken between the ages of 7 and 12, aligning with Erik Erikson's psychosocial stages—the stage of ***Industry vs Inferiority*** (Erikson, 1950).

During this time, children develop a sense of competence through communication, learning, and creative expression. The fifth chakra reflects this growing ability to articulate thoughts and feelings, transform inner experiences into language, and seek recognition for their efforts. When nurtured, this establishes a foundation for an authentic voice and confident self-expression.

Balanced Chakra Five

Issues with the throat are often the body's way of saying, *"There's something I need to say—but I don't feel safe to say it."*

A person with a balanced fifth chakra typically speaks with a resonant voice, listens deeply, and possesses an intuitive sense of timing and rhythm. They are clear, authentic communicators who express themselves with creativity and confidence. As we continuously breathe spirit into the world through sound and speech, we are, quite literally, giving form to the invisible. Therefore, the fifth chakra is not merely about communication; it acts as a vital channel for creativity and spiritual expression.

Imbalanced Chakra Five

An imbalanced throat chakra often arises from early environments where truth is distorted and expression is suppressed. This may manifest as being told lies ("Mummy isn't drunk, she's just emotional"), receiving mixed messages ("Do as I say, not as I do"), or enduring verbal abuse, constant shouting, and relentless criticism. Such imbalances are particularly prevalent in families characterised by addiction, secrecy, or authoritarian control, where unspoken rules dictate: Don't talk. Don't trust. Don't feel. In homes like these, a child quickly learns that remaining silent feels safer than speaking the truth. Speaking up might result in punishment, shame, or rejection, leading them to internalise their feelings. Over time, that silence hardens into a habit—one that makes it difficult to express themselves or trust their voice, even when the danger has long passed.

Excessive Fifth Chakra

When the throat chakra is overactive, expression can become uncontrolled. Words tumble out—fast, forceful, sometimes overwhelming—filling the space but not always fostering a connection. The person may talk over others, dominate conversations, or perform rather than communicate. Beneath the noise, something tender often longs to be heard.

This form of overactivity often arises from childhood experiences of being ignored, dismissed, or punished for speaking the truth. In adulthood, one's voice becomes a shield: incessant talking as a means to feel acknowledged and to protect against vulnerability.

But an open throat disconnected from the heart produces more noise than resonance. Words lose their foundation, and genuine listening, particularly to oneself, becomes drowned out. Healing isn't about silencing the voice but rather softening it. Allow the breath to guide, create space for stillness, and ensure what is said aligns with what is felt.

When the heart and throat move in harmony, speech transforms into not just sound, but also connection, clarity, and truth.

Physical Issues Related to the Fifth Chakra

Important: Always consult your physician about any physical issues.

The fifth chakra is located in the throat, with communication as the central issue. Disorders of the mouth, throat, ear, vocal cords, neck, thyroid gland and tightness of the jaw are fifth chakra issues (Judith, 2004).

When this chakra is balanced, we speak with clarity and conviction. We listen without fear. We express ourselves not merely to be heard, but to be known.

But when this chakra is blocked or excessive, the body often becomes the messenger. A persistent sore throat, a voice that strains or disappears, and a jaw that clenches tightly at night—all of these may indicate that something within us is struggling to be articulated. The thyroid, a butterfly-shaped gland that regulates our energy and metabolism, may falter under the burden of unspoken truths. The shoulders ache as if weighed down by words never expressed. The neck stiffens, caught between what the heart feels and what the mouth dares to articulate.

Some people remain silent for years. Afraid of conflict and conditioned to be small, they are led to believe that their voices don't matter. Others speak incessantly, but not always truthfully, filling the air with noise to evade the deeper, quieter truths within. In both cases, the throat chakra suffers.

Healing the throat chakra involves more than merely learning to speak louder—it requires learning to speak from within. It's the practice of expressing truth with kindness, claiming space without apology, and listening just as deeply as we speak. When we allow our voice to align with our heart, the throat softens, and expression flows freely. We begin to recognise the power not only in words but also in using them wisely.

Healing the throat chakra involves reconnecting with your true voice. It's not about raising the volume but about speaking with honesty and intention from a place of inner clarity and calm. It is also an invitation to listen deeply—not just to others but to the quiet truth within.

Working on Your Fifth Chakra

The aim of healing an excessive throat chakra is not to silence the voice, but to align it with the truth of your heart. Focus on finding a rhythm that is responsive rather than reactive, expressive rather than overwhelming. When the throat chakra is overactive, the voice may rush ahead of awareness. Healing, therefore, involves slowing down, grounding the energy, and reconnecting with stillness before expression.

This isn't about talking less—it's about speaking from a more authentic place within, where your words truly reflect how you feel.Here are a few simple, supportive ways to help restore balance:

- **Mindful silence**: Permit yourself to pause and be still. Let silence be a space for presence, not something to rush through or fill. You might be surprised how much clearer things become when you take a breath before speaking.
- **Be in silence**: You might even think about undertaking a silent retreat. It may seem radical, but it can be highly beneficial.
- **Active listening**: Practise receiving someone's words fully, without rehearsing your reply. Listening with your entire body invites connection and slows the tendency to overspeak.

- **Journalling**: If your mind feels crowded or your voice feels tangled, write. Journalling provides a safe outlet for your thoughts, helping you tune inward rather than projecting outward.
- **Body awareness**: Before speaking, direct your attention to your heart or belly. Ask yourself: Is this coming from truth or tension? Tuning into your body allows your words to flow with greater intention and clarity, and your voice shifts from occupying space to conveying something meaningful.

You might begin by gently exploring:

- What truths have I been suppressing?
- What would it feel like to speak honestly and be heard?
- How can I express myself in ways that feel kind and clear?

As this chakra begins to balance, you may notice that your voice embodies more confidence, your words carry greater significance, and your connections with others become stronger.

Breathwork for the Throat Chakra

- Gentle, conscious breathing calms the nervous system and regulates the pace of your voice. Inhale slowly through the nose, and exhale even more slowly through the mouth, noticing the spaciousness that follows.

Ocean Breath (Ujjayi)

- Sit comfortably with your shoulders relaxed.
- Inhale through your nose, slightly constricting the back of the throat.
- Exhale through the nose with the same gentle constriction. You should hear a soft, ocean-like sound. Practise this for 3–5 minutes to calm the nervous system and bring awareness to the throat area.

Humming or Toning

- Close your lips and gently hum on the exhale.
- Feel the vibration in your throat, chest, and face.
- Try repeating a simple tone like "HAM", the *bīja* mantra of *Vishuddha*.

In Sanskrit, *bīja* means **"seed"**, and like a seed, a bīja mantra contains the essence of a specific energy or quality. When repeated (either chanted or silently), it is believed to stimulate the corresponding chakra, awaken subtle energy (prana), and bring the mind into a state of focused stillness. This helps to awaken vocal energy and release built-up tension.

Each of the chakras has a corresponding *bīja* mantra:

- **Root Chakra (*Muladhara*): LAM**
- **Sacral Chakra (*Svadhisthana*): VAM**
- **Solar Plexus Chakra (*Manipura*): RAM**
- **Heart Chakra (*Anahata*): YAM**
- **Throat Chakra (*Vishuddha*): HAM**
- **Third Eye Chakra (*Ajna*): OM or AUM**
- **Crown Chakra (*Sahasrara*):** *Often silent* (or **OM** in some traditions).

Bīja mantras aren't just sounds—they're vibrations that stir something deep inside. When chanted with intention, they can help clear stagnant energy and create more flow through the body. Think of them like tuning forks, gently bringing your body, mind, and spirit into alignment.

As you repeat a mantra, something begins to shift. Your mind settles, your focus sharpens, and you can feel the vibration building inside. Each syllable has its own unique energy. *HAM*, the seed sound of the throat chakra, rings through the throat like a soft chime, gently awakening your voice. It's not just about speaking—it's about letting your words rise from a place of honesty and inner truth. Used regularly, these sounds become a kind of vibrational medicine—subtle, ancient, and profoundly transformative.

Sing, hum, chant, or read aloud daily. Even a few minutes helps activate the voice centre.

Touch for the Throat Chakra

- Gently massage the neck and jaw with warm hands.
- Practise shoulder rolls to release tension.
- Try self-embracing movements, such as hugging yourself, opening your chest, and stroking your arms, using your left arm to stroke your right arm and vice versa. Breathe into your collarbones.

Creativity for the Throat Chakra

- Paint, write poetry, dance or do anything that allows emotion to take shape and form.

Affirmations for the Throat Chakra

- "My voice matters."
- "I speak my truth with clarity and kindness."
- "It is safe for me to express myself."

Healing the throat chakra isn't about being louder; it's about being **truer**. Allow your voice to be soft or firm, quiet or clear; above all, let it be *your own*.

Key Takeaways: Fifth Chakra/Throat Chakra (*Vishuddha*)

1 *Developmental Stage*

- Awakens during the ages of **7 to 12**, aligning with **Erikson's stage: Industry vs. Inferiority**.
- This is the stage where children explore **communication, learning, and creative expression**.
- The development of a confident, authentic voice starts here.

2 *Core Themes*

- *Vishuddha* means **"purification"**—this chakra is the conduit through which inner truth transforms into outer expression.
- Governs **speech, listening, truth, creativity, integrity**, and spiritual communication.
- It's not merely about what is said, but whether it truly reflects what is felt.

3 *Balanced Throat Chakra*

- Demonstrates **clear, confident, and honest communication**.
- Speaks with **resonance and timing**, listens intently, and aligns words with truth.
- Creativity easily flows through words, music, movement, and voice.
- There is ease in both **expression and in silence**—a rhythm of giving and receiving.

4 *Imbalanced Throat Chakra*

Deficient (blocked):

- Fear of speaking, shyness, and difficulty in expressing thoughts or needs.
- Feeling unheard, silenced, or unworthy of a voice.
- **Often arises from early environments marked by criticism, secrecy, or emotional suppression.**

Excessive (overactive):

- Engages in excessive conversation or dominates discussions.
- Speaks without listening or employs words to disguise emotional vulnerability.

- Voice serves more for performance or control than for genuine expression.

5   Physical Manifestations

- Related to the **throat, mouth, jaw, neck, ears, vocal cords, shoulders, and thyroid gland**.

Common symptoms:

- Sore throats, thyroid imbalances, TMJ, stiff neck and shoulders, earaches, and loss of voice.
- Tension and discomfort in shoulders and neck often indicate suppressed or misused vocal energy.

"There's something I need to say—but I don't feel safe to say it," is a common body message of the fifth chakra.

6   Healing Practices

Mindfulness and silence:

- Practise **mindful silence**—use it as space, not punishment.
- Try short periods of **intentional silence** or even a **silent retreat**.

Journalling:

- Write freely to untangle inner noise and access deeper truth.
- Use prompts like:

  - What have I been afraid to say?
  - What does speaking my truth feel like?
  - Where am I performing rather than expressing?

Body-based practices:

- Gentle **neck massages, jaw relaxation**, and **shoulder rolls**.
- Use **self-touch** to reclaim safety in the voice.

Breathwork:

- **Ocean breath (*Ujjayi*):** calming and centring.
- ***Bīja* mantra (HAM):** the seed sound of the fifth chakra, promotes authentic voice and spiritual clarity.
- **Humming or toning (e.g., HAM mantra)** awakens the vibration of the throat.

Creative expression:

- Paint, sing, write poetry, dance—anything that gives form to inner feeling.

Listening:

- Practise **active listening**—hear without rushing to reply.
- Tune in to your body while listening or speaking: Is this coming from truth or tension?

Affirmations:

- "My voice matters."
- "I speak my truth with clarity and kindness."
- "It is safe for me to express myself."

7 Core Insight

- Healing the throat chakra isn't about being louder—it's about being **truer**.
- The goal is alignment: speaking from a place of **inner clarity**, not noise or fear.

Chakra Six/Third Eye Chakra (*Ajna*)

Between the ages of 14 and 21, something begins to stir in the region of the third eye chakra. This is Erikson's stage of Identity vs Role Confusion, during which the central task is to form a coherent sense of self and live in accordance with one's values and inner truth. When this process is disrupted, it can lead to fragmentation, uncertainty, or a sense of living inauthentically.

The world, once shaped by the voices of parents and teachers, begins to soften at the edges. Familiar rules give way to questions, and the well-lit path opens into a mysterious, uncharted horizon. This is the domain of the third eye chakra, *Ajna* (which means "to perceive"), serving as the gateway to intuition, imagination, and inner sight. Here, vision transcends what the eyes can see and delves into what the soul starts to discern.

At this stage of life, the mind begins to unfurl like a flower reaching for the sun. Black-and-white thinking gives way to a spectrum of nuance and possibility. Teenagers step into the rich terrain of wondering and wandering; they start to question the script, rewrite the narrative, and dream of futures still shrouded in mist. The questions grow bolder and deeper: *Who am I beyond the expectations? What do I truly believe? What kind of life could I create?* It is the quiet revolution of thought, the awakening of intuition, the birth of vision, and the first glimmers of a Self defined from within. This is the developmental window where the sixth chakra quietly (or not so quietly) awakens. No longer content with surface appearances, the individual begins to look inwards and forwards. Imagination becomes a tool for survival, hope, and the creation of identity. A teenager may try on new personas, explore spiritual ideas, or challenge inherited beliefs, not out of rebellion, but in search of a more personal truth.

If the lower chakras have provided adequate grounding, emotional support, and a sense of personal power, then *Ajna* can open in a balanced way. The inner eye becomes a dependable compass, guiding us towards vision, purpose, and wisdom that transcends logic. The young adult begins to trust not only what they have been taught but also what they feel, sense, and *perceive* within.

Yet when earlier wounds remain unhealed, when a child is silenced for thinking differently, shamed for asking questions, or denied the freedom to dream, a shadow can settle over this stage of development. Instead of expanding, the mind retreats. Rather than seeking truth, it clings to what feels safe. Vision becomes murky, intuition dims, and the inner compass grows quiet, dulled by years of being told not to trust what it perceives.

At its essence, the third eye chakra beckons us to see beyond what is visible and to attune ourselves to the intuition that lies beneath the surface. In this inner realm, imagination ripens into insight, and thought begins to take shape. It is here that we discover that the truth we've been chasing "out there" has been quietly waiting within us all along.

Balanced Chakra Six (Ajna)

When the third eye chakra is balanced, it feels as if the fog lifts and the path ahead, though not fully mapped, somehow becomes clearer. There is a serene inner clarity, much like turning down the volume on the world so you can at last hear your own wisdom. You do not merely see what is in front of you— you begin to see through it. Patterns emerge, connections fall into place, and your decisions feel less like guesswork and more like guidance.

This is the realm of inner vision. The imagination does not drift here; it directs. You catch glimpses of possibilities before they arrive, sense the mood in a room without a word spoken, and notice the meaning behind the moment. It is not about magic—it is about tuning in. When *Ajna* is open, you are not chasing truth outside yourself; you are recognising it within.

Individuals with a balanced sixth chakra often navigate life with a quiet confidence. They are not easily swayed by every opinion or trend, as they are attuned to a deeper voice—their own.

They don't need all the answers to feel aligned; it suffices for them to remain present, curious, and connected to their knowledge, even if they cannot articulate it.

In this state, vision transcends mere sight; it evolves into insight. From that place, the unseen begins to shape the seen.

Imbalanced Chakra Six

When the third eye chakra is out of balance, it can feel as though your inner lens has become fogged up. The clarity you once trusted turns murky. Decisions feel heavy and uncertain, as if you are navigating without a map. The connection to your intuition—the quiet voice that says "this feels right"—is muffled, or worse, drowned out by doubt and noise.

For some individuals, this imbalance manifests as a feeling of disconnection. You might find yourself trapped in your thoughts, overanalysing, relying heavily on logic, and dismissing your dreams or instincts. The world can begin to feel flat and excessively literal, as though it has lost its depth or magic. Creativity may wane, and your thinking might become rigid or overly black and white. It's as if the vibrant inner world has dimmed.

For others, the imbalance tips in the opposite direction. Thoughts race, visions blur into daydreams, and it becomes increasingly difficult to distinguish between insight and illusion. You may feel overwhelmed by ideas, flooded with impressions, or tempted to escape into fantasy. Imagination, instead of serving as a helpful guide, devolves into a maze. The mind feels loud, restless, and challenging to ground.

At the core of it all lies a **fracture in trust**, not with the world, but with yourself. Somewhere along the way, you may have been told not to believe your perceptions, to ignore your instincts, and to stop asking questions. Gradually, the inner eye that is meant to see beyond the surface, begins to close.

An imbalanced sixth chakra isn't merely foggy thinking; it's a call to reconnect with your inner knowing. When you quiet the noise and tune in, clarity returns. And when vision is restored, it's not just the world that changes; *you* do.

Excessive Chakra Six

When the third eye chakra enters overdrive, the mind becomes a projector on fast forward, casting images, ideas, and possibilities more quickly than you can grasp them. Thoughts begin to spin, visions blur, and what once felt like intuition now resembles anxiety because you can take everything in, but none of it lands—you're seeing it all, yet understanding none of it.

In this overstimulated state, the imagination goes into overdrive. Every moment appears laden with meaning. Yet, instead of clarity, there is merely static. You feel ungrounded, as if you are hovering above your own body, far from solid ground.

This often occurs when we have bypassed the lower chakras—disconnected from the body, from emotion, from the heart. The mind becomes a refuge, a place to retreat when the world feels unsafe. However, what once shielded you begins to turn against you, like armour that tightens until it wounds.

An overactive third eye doesn't offer true insight; it overwhelms. Healing this chakra doesn't necessitate more thought, more vision, or more input.

It calls for stillness, a return to the earth, and a deep breath. Real vision isn't something you chase—it's something that arrives quietly when the mind calms and the Self becomes still enough to receive it.

Deficient Chakra Six

When the third eye chakra is deficient, it feels as if the inner world has gone quiet. Not a peaceful quiet, but a kind of dull, disorienting silence as if the lights have been dimmed and the compass is absent. Life may seem flat or overly literal, as though there is no room for wonder, vision, or deeper meaning.

You may find it difficult to envisage your future or dream beyond the present moment. Decisions seem unclear. Intuition, that sense of just knowing, has been supplanted by second-guessing or the constant need for external validation. Creativity can feel unattainable, and even sleep may offer little insight—dreams, if they occur, feel distant or forgettable.

This kind of energetic depletion often begins early. Perhaps you were taught not to trust your imagination or were dismissed when you sensed something deeper. Maybe curiosity was stifled with "because I said so", or your questions were met with discomfort or ridicule. Over time, the bright inner eye that once looked beyond the surface learns to close.

A deficient *Ajna* doesn't indicate that you lack intelligence; it signifies that you've lost touch with that deeper way of seeing, the kind that senses what isn't readily apparent. This type of perception helps you recognise truth before it's proven. When this chakra is quiet, it's not just the insight that dims; it's also the ability to feel guided from within.

Reawakening the third eye isn't about seeing visions or reading minds—it's about rediscovering your inner sense of direction. It begins quietly, with moments of stillness, reflection, and a faint spark of imagination. Bit by bit, that spark evolves into a steady glow. Clarity returns. The path ahead may still be uncertain, but somehow, it starts to feel like your own.

Healing this chakra starts with stillness, reflection, and gently inviting your vision back. You don't need to see more; just to **trust what arises within**.

Chakra Six Physical Issues

The third eye governs the eyes, the base of the skull, the brow, and the brain. Physical dysfunctions include headaches, vision problems, nightmares, eyestrain, and neurological disturbances (Judith, 2004).

When the third eye chakra is out of balance, you may experience a throbbing behind the eyes, a dull ache in the forehead, or a headache that doesn't subside with rest. Your eyes may feel strained, your vision may blur, and even the simplest tasks can seem more challenging to focus on. It's as though your body mirrors what's happening within: a struggle to see clearly, not just the world, but your place in it.

At times, the signs are more subtle. Sinus pressure accumulates around the brow, or a lingering fog obfuscates your thoughts. You may feel dizzy or disoriented, as if your internal sense of direction has lost its bearings. Sleep can be restless or elusive, filled with bizarre dreams or fragmented images that make little sense.

At the heart of it all is the pituitary gland, situated near the centre of the brain and often linked with this chakra. It regulates your body's internal rhythms—your hormones, your cycles, your sense of timing. When *Ajna* is deficient or excessive, those rhythms may become out of sync.

A balanced third eye brings a different kind of vision—not just clear sight, but also clear insight. The mind is sharp yet calm, and the body is aligned with its wisdom. You feel connected not only to your thoughts but to something deeper—an inner knowing that perceives with quiet certainty, even when the path ahead isn't apparent.

Working on Chakra Six

Balancing a third eye involves beginning to **trust your inner voice**. Healing may involve:

- **Meditation** and inner stillness.
- **Visualisation exercises** to rebuild imaginative capacity.
- **Dream journalling** to reconnect with the symbolic mind.
- **Creative expression**—drawing, storytelling, intuitive writing.
- Practising **discernment** between intuition and fear.
- Spending time in reflection, silence, or spiritual contemplation.

A healthy *Ajna* chakra does not require you to be psychic or mystical. It simply encourages you to look beyond the obvious, to trust your instincts, to envision your future, and to recognise that what is real is not limited to what you can see with your eyes.

Key Takeaways: Chakra Six/Third Eye Chakra (*Ajna*)

1 *Developmental Stage*

- Awakens during the ages of **14 to 21**, aligning with **Erikson's Identity vs Role Confusion** stage.
- **The primary task is to create a coherent sense of self, guided by inner values** rather than external expectations.
- This is an era of **personal truth-seeking, inner questioning**, and envisioning a future life of one's own design.

2   Core Themes

- *Ajna* means "to perceive"; this chakra is the centre of **intuition, imagination, insight**, and **inner knowing**.
- Encourages **vision that transcends logic** and fosters a deeper trust in one's own wisdom.
- Integrates inner experience with outer awareness—**perceiving not merely with the eyes, but with the soul**.

3   Balanced Third Eye Chakra

- Provides **clarity, vision, and inner guidance**.
- Decision-making is both intuitive and grounded.
- Creativity flows effortlessly, and symbolic understanding becomes more profound.
- There is a sense of **alignment with one's inner truth**, even when the external path remains unclear.
- Insight transforms from a mere idea into a guiding compass.

4   Imbalanced Third Eye Chakra

Deficient (underactive):

- Life feels flat, excessively literal, or lacking in magic.
- Difficulty in envisioning the future or trusting one's intuition.
- Creativity is blocked and dreams may feel dull or absent.
- Often linked to early suppression of imagination or curiosity.

Excessive (overactive):

- Racing thoughts, feelings of overwhelm, or escapism through fantasy.
- Difficulty in distinguishing **intuition from anxiety**, or truth from projection.
- Mental overstimulation devoid of grounding.
- This can result from bypassing the lower chakras by over-relying on intellect or spiritual abstraction.

5   Physical Manifestations

- It governs the **eyes, forehead, brain, brow, base of the skull**, and the **pituitary gland**.

Common symptoms:

- **Headaches, eye strain, blurred vision, dizziness, and sinus pressure.**
- **Neurological disturbances**, mental fog, sleep problems, or intense and unsettling dreams.

- When Ajna is out of balance, perception—both of the world and of the self—may feel clouded or distorted.

6   Healing the Third Eye Chakra

Foundational practices:

- **Meditation** and **mindful stillness** to quiet the inner noise.
- **Visualisation** to strengthen the imagination and intuitive faculties.
- **Dream journalling as a means** to reconnect with the unconscious and symbolic mind.
- **Creative expression**, such as drawing, poetry, and storytelling, helps to give form to one's inner vision.

Other supportive practices:

- Create distance from excessive information or mental stimulation.
- Cultivate **discernment** instead of rushing to conclusions.
- Allocate time in **nature, silence, or spiritual practice** to recalibrate internal rhythms.

Affirmations for *Ajna*:

- "I trust my intuition."
- "I see clearly, inside and out."
- "My vision guides me."

7   Energetic Insight

- A healthy third eye doesn't mak   e you psychic—it aids in trusting your inner compass.
- True vision is not something you can force; it **emerges when you become quiet enough to receive it.**
- Healing the *Ajna* involves rebuilding **inner trust**, gently allowing **clarity to return**, and perceiving from a deeper, wiser place within.

Chakra Seven/Crown Chakra (*Sahasrara*)

As the soul rises through the chakras—awakening through survival, emotion, will, love, expression, and vision—it reaches the crown chakra, *Sahasrara*, where the journey transforms from selfhood to oneness. This is the realm where the illusion of separation starts to dissolve. You no longer perceive yourself as an isolated individual, but rather as a thread in a vast and intricate tapestry—a single cell in the greater body of life.

Mystics, sages, and visionaries have long described this awareness. Buckminster Fuller spoke of it in scientific terms, calling us "cells in a larger body" (2019). Others, like Teilhard de Chardin, envisioned a collective consciousness, a kind of global soul in which each of us plays a vital part. In the chakra system, this insight is not merely philosophical; it is embodied.

In this light, healing becomes not just personal, but planetary. Awakening is about realising that the Self is already connected to everything. The boundaries blur, compassion deepens, and service begins to feel like a natural expression of your being, rather than merely a choice.

This is the lesson of the crown chakra: not to transcend the world, but to recognise yourself *as the world*. A single spark in a constellation of consciousness. A breath in the body of the divine. A cell in the great, ever-living whole.

This often occurs as we transition into the later seasons of life when something subtle begins to shift. The urge to define ourselves is less pressing. We find ourselves posing quieter, deeper questions: What have I lived for? What truly mattered? Who have I become—not in the eyes of the world, but in the narrative of my own soul?

This is the realm of the crown chakra, a place of wisdom that opens not through effort, but through surrender. It's where the ego loosens its grip and the Soul begins to look upwards, seeking not more, but meaning. Psychologist Erik Erikson referred to this phase as Ego Integrity vs Despair, emphasising the task of reflecting on one's life with peace rather than regret. It's the moment we weave the fragments of our past into a coherent whole. Not because it was perfect, but because it was ours, and somehow, it fits.

Earlier, in midlife, we pass through the Generativity vs Stagnation stage, a phase that resonates with *Sahasrara*'s call towards a greater purpose. It's a time when we begin to create not just for ourselves, but for the world. Through parenting, mentoring, service, or art, we extend beyond personal goals and start to ask: What am I giving back?

When these stages unfold, the crown chakra flourishes. We cease clinging to identity. We no longer seek answers. We trust. We allow. We rest in the mystery.

And in that sacred space, beyond words, roles, and striving, the boundaries of the Ego and Self gently dissolve. The mind becomes still. The heart opens. And the soul, having journeyed so far, returns to the vastness it never truly left.

Balanced Chakra Seven

When the crown chakra is balanced, life becomes richer. A quiet clarity begins to settle in. You may not be able to explain it, but something within you knows: *I belong to something vast, and I don't need all the answers to feel at peace.*

This isn't a dramatic awakening or a sudden spiritual epiphany. It's more akin to standing at the edge of the ocean and realising you don't need to measure every wave to know the sea is there.

When the crown chakra is balanced, the ego recedes into the background. You don't lose your identity; you simply stop clinging to it so tightly. You can perceive your roles and stories for what they are: meaningful, yes, but not the entirety of who you are. Now, there is space for mystery, for not knowing. And curiously, that not knowing feels more solid than anything you've ever been sure of. As Socrates famously said, "I know that I know nothing." Because real wisdom doesn't begin with knowing; it starts with unknowing. With the gentle, courageous admission: I don't know.

And in that space, something opens. Not the kind of knowledge you can recite or defend, but a deeper kind of knowing. The kind that breathes, that listens, that bows. A kind of luminous humility that allows truth to arise, not as something to own, but as something to meet.

This is the gift of the crown chakra, where the mind loosens its grip, the heart opens wide, and the soul steps into the mystery—not to solve it, but to live it.

You begin to feel a deeper connection to the world around you, not merely as a place you inhabit but as something of which you are a part. The trees, the sky, the people you pass on the street—it all starts to feel a bit more *alive*, a bit more *you*. Compassion flows more freely, as does forgiveness. You no longer feel the need to prove yourself or fix everything. Instead, you wish to be genuine, present, and kind.

A balanced crown chakra doesn't mean you float off into the clouds. Quite the opposite. It signifies that you're finally grounded in something real, not a belief or a dogma, but a felt sense of belonging. A quiet knowing that says, *I'm connected. I'm enough. And I'm part of something far greater than I can imagine.*

Imbalanced Chakra Seven

When the crown chakra is out of balance, it is not always loud or obvious. At times, it is merely a feeling that something essential is missing, even though you cannot quite name what it is. Life may begin to feel hollow or disjointed—like you are lacking clear direction and feel disconnected from meaning or purpose.

For some, this imbalance feels like a spiritual drought. The world turns grey, and the soulful seems distant. For others, it takes the opposite form: an overwhelm of lofty ideals and spiritual concepts that lift you out of your body but leave you untethered, unable to ground what you know into how you live.

Either way, something vital is missing: that sense of rooted connection to the mystery, that gentle inner knowing that you are part of something greater—and always have been. Without it, you may feel lost in your head or the world.

The seventh chakra is associated with the pineal gland. In many spiritual traditions, particularly within yogic, esoteric, and mystical frameworks, the pineal gland is regarded as the "seat of the soul" or the gateway to higher consciousness. The gland sits near the energetic region of both the third eye and crown chakra, bridging inner vision and spiritual awareness. French philosopher René Descartes famously referred to the pineal gland as the place where the soul and body meet. In esoteric traditions, it's sometimes called the spiritual antenna, a centre for receiving higher wisdom or universal truth.

When the crown chakra is out of balance, life can start to feel strangely distant. For some, it's as if the light has gone out—nothing feels meaningful, and the world seems flat, devoid of purpose. For others, it tips the other way: they retreat into spiritual ideals so lofty they float above the realness of life, untouched by the body, the heart, or the messy beauty of being human.

In both cases, integration is missing—the connection between insight and embodiment, between being and belonging.

Healing *Sahasrara* isn't about rising higher or knowing more; it's about surrendering to mystery. It invites you not to solve the unknown but to relate to it, to sit with the questions, to listen to silence, and to release the need to command the cosmos.

This isn't about escape. It's about remembering that you're already part of something vast, luminous, and beyond your control. And that belonging, in its deepest sense, was never something you had to earn—it was always yours.

The crown doesn't need more effort. It needs surrender. Not an escape from life, but a return to the soft current beneath it. A reconnection not just to spirit, but to the deep stillness that reminds you that *you belong*.

Excessive Chakra Seven

When the crown chakra is excessive, the results aren't always as they appear. It might seem like spiritual insight on the surface, but beneath that facade, it can feel like spiritual overdrive—a state in which you've floated so far into the cosmos that you've lost touch with your feet, your emotions, and the ground beneath you.

Instead of unity, there is disconnection. Instead of presence, there is detachment. You are not rooted in the richness of life; you are taking a helicopter view of it.

This can manifest in both subtle and dramatic ways. Spiritual bypassing can become a way of life. Instead of confronting discomfort, engaging in shadow work, or pursuing emotional healing, the individual escapes into lofty ideals. They may speak of peace, light, and oneness, but behind the gentle words, there is often a profound avoidance of what truly hurts.

Fascination with "higher realms" can take over. The mind races towards energy work, astral travel, or esoteric teachings, while the needs of the heart and body are left behind. Life becomes about reaching up and out, rather than in and through.

Everyday life begins to feel irrelevant. Routines, relationships, and even physical health may be overlooked. The ordinary world loses its colour, as if it no longer has meaning. The result? You may be physically present, but not truly *here*.

Overthinking supplants intuition. Spirituality becomes intellectual, filled with theories and frameworks, yet devoid of embodiment. You reside in your mind, analysing everything but genuinely *feeling* very little. The body becomes an afterthought.

And, sometimes, a feeling of superiority creeps in. There's a sense of being more awake than others, a subtle elevation of oneself disguised in spiritual language. Humility is replaced by detachment. Insight is wielded not to connect, but to stand apart, above.

Deficient Chakra Seven

When the crown chakra is deficient, it can feel as though the lights have gone out. Life begins to lose its lustre. That sense of being connected to something larger—call it Spirit, Source, the universe, or simply meaning—starts to fade. What remains is often a dull flatness, a feeling of being adrift. Meditation feels empty, prayer falls flat, and even awe seems like a memory. This can lead to apathy, where the practices you once cherished now appear pointless.

Instead of insight, there is mental fog—the kind that makes you forget why you entered a room or, more painfully, why you are navigating through life at all. The mind feels burdened and uninspired. Meditation feels hollow. Prayer seems uninspiring. Wonder seems to be a distant memory. At times, this disconnection manifests as a kind of spiritual aridity. The practices that once felt vibrant and significant begin to seem empty or pointless.

Over time, that flatness can harden into cynicism. Beliefs become rigid, the heart closes off, and anything that cannot be measured or proven starts to feel suspect. Wonder fades, replaced by sarcasm or detachment. Instead of questioning with openness, we cling to rigid frameworks—because in the absence of mystery, control can feel safer.

At its deepest level, a deficient crown chakra can leave you grappling with the painful question: What's the point of it all?

This is the realm of existential despair—a profound sorrow that arises when meaning feels inaccessible, and nothing seems to hold significance.

But the truth is that the crown chakra never fully closes. It is said that a cynic was once a passionate person who fears disappointment once more.

The crown chakra may dim; it may go quiet, yet it's still there, waiting.

Healing a deficient *Sahasrara* isn't about chasing enlightenment; it's about inviting wonder back in. Sitting in stillness and asking the big questions again—not to find quick answers, but to reconnect with the mystery itself. Because sometimes the light returns not through certainty but through the simple act of remembering that you are part of something vast, even when you cannot feel it.

Physical Issues Related to the Seventh Chakra

Important: Always consult with your physician regarding any physical issues.

Though *Sahasrara* is the seat of spiritual connection, its imbalance can ripple down into your nervous system, hormones, and mind—subtle realms where spirit meets biology.

The physical manifestations of a crown chakra imbalance are neurological disturbances, cognitive challenges, sleep disturbances, endocrine issues and dissociation (Judith, 2004).

You may feel a deep, lingering fatigue—one that rest alone doesn't seem to touch. It's more than physical exhaustion; it's a kind of soul-weariness, a heaviness that settles in when inspiration fades and inner light dims.

Headaches or migraines may arise, particularly around the crown or forehead, as if the mind is overloaded, crowded with thoughts and lacking grounding. Some people also report neurological symptoms like dizziness, poor coordination, or heightened sensitivity to light and sound.

Mental fog is common, too. You might find it hard to concentrate, forget simple things, or feel as though your mind is drifting without an anchor. It's a disorienting lack of clarity, as if your thoughts have become untethered.

Sleep can also be disrupted. Overactivity in the crown chakra—especially when linked to an overstimulated third eye—may interfere with your circadian rhythm, leading to insomnia, restless nights, or vivid, unsettling dreams.

The crown chakra is closely tied to the pineal gland, which helps regulate melatonin, the hormone responsible for managing your sleep–wake cycle. This gland becomes more active in darkness and less so in bright light, signalling to the body when it's time to sleep or awaken. When this system is out of balance, so is your rest.

Due to its association with the pineal gland, disturbances in the seventh chakra can also impact hormonal rhythms, influencing mood and sleep patterns (Judith, 2004).

At times, the symptoms can be even more vague. Psychosomatic issues emerge, manifesting as aches or ailments that do not follow an apparent medical pattern. Symptoms like these may indicate a deeper misalignment, a form of grief or loss that is not physical but spiritual. It is a cry from the soul that says: *I've lost touch with meaning.*

In these moments, the body becomes a messenger, and the message is that you are disconnected from your Self. The path to healing lies not merely in medicine but in reconnecting with stillness, mystery, and the numinous thread that runs through everything, including you.

Working on Chakra Seven

Balancing the crown chakra isn't something you can force or fix. It's more about remembering how to be quiet enough to *receive*. Unlike the lower chakras, which concern tangible matters such as safety, emotion, or will, *Sahasrara* exists at the edge of language. It doesn't require us to do more; it asks us to let go.

Sometimes, balancing the crown chakra is as simple as stepping outside and lifting your face to the sky, not to search for answers, but to feel its vastness. Other times, it means sitting in silence, not to figure things out, but to rest in the not knowing. Clarity tends to come when we stop trying so hard to make sense of everything.

Breathing practices help. So does walking barefoot. Reading a line of poetry that reminds you the world is more alive than it seems helps too. So does lighting a candle and doing nothing but watching the flame. These aren't grand rituals; they're small, sacred ways of reconnecting to what's always been true: You belong here; you're part of it all.

Sahasrara doesn't ask you to rise above the world, but rather to *open yourself to it* and allow wonder to seep back in. Trust that even when you don't understand the path, there *is* one, and you are already on it.

Balance manifests not through effort, but through surrender; not through answers, but through *wonder*. When you stop striving for control, the crown unfurls, not like a gate, but like a blossom, quietly and naturally. And suddenly, you recall: *you were never disconnected in the first place.*

Key Takeaways: Chakra Seven/Crown Chakra (Sahasrara)

1 *Essence and Evolution*

- *Sahasrara* is the **final chakra**, symbolising **spiritual integration**, unity, and transcendence of ego.
- This is associated with **Erikson's stages of Generativity vs Stagnation** and **Ego Integrity vs Despair**, where life purpose, legacy, and wisdom come into focus.
- Development intensifies in later adulthood but may resurface at any moment through insight, surrender, or loss.

2 *Core Themes*

- **Unity, spiritual connection, and surrender.**
- A balanced Sahasrara creates a **tangible sense of belonging** to something greater.
- Not about escaping life, but about **recognising yourself as part of it all.**
- It bridges **being and meaning, wisdom and wonder.**

3 *Balanced Crown Chakra*

- **Calm awareness**, humility, and trust in the unknown.
- No need to prove, comprehend, or cling, just **presence** and serene understanding.

- **Spiritual clarity** emerges without the necessity of rigid beliefs.
- Compassion, forgiveness, and spaciousness come more naturally.
- "I don't know" becomes a portal to wisdom, not a failure of knowledge.

4   Imbalanced Crown Chakra

Excessive:

- **Spiritual bypassing, detachment, or superiority disguised as wisdom.**
- **Disconnection from the body, heart, and everyday life.**
- **Over-reliance on abstract ideas, excessive mental activity, or rigid spiritual ideologies.**

Deficient:

- **Spiritual apathy, a loss of meaning, and existential despair.**
- Cynicism leads to a disconnection from awe or wonder.
- Feeling adrift or lacking inspiration; a sense of flatness or spiritual dryness emerges.
- May manifest as forgetting how to feel spiritually "alive".

5   Physical Symptoms

- Connected to the **pineal gland**, the nervous system, and hormonal regulation.
  Possible issues include:

  - **Neurological disturbances**, dizziness, mental fog.
  - **Cognitive challenges**, forgetfulness, or lack of clarity.
  - **Sleep disruption** or disturbed circadian rhythms.
  - **Hormonal imbalances** affecting mood, energy, or vitality.
  - Psychosomatic symptoms (e.g., fatigue, disorientation) that lack a clear medical explanation.

The body may whisper, "you've lost touch with meaning".

6   Healing the Crown Chakra

Practices for balance:

- **Stillness** and **silence**: not for answers, but to reconnect.
- **Breathwork**: simple and grounding—returning to presence.

- **Rituals of wonder**: candle-gazing, poetry, barefoot walking, sky-gazing.
- **Letting go** of striving; inviting spaciousness and awe.

Inner work:

- Ask questions without rushing to answers: *What matters? What endures?*
- Embrace mystery and trust rather than control.
- Reframe spirituality not as escape, but as **embodied belonging**.

Balance doesn't come through intensity, but through surrender.

7 *Final Insight*

- A healthy crown chakra doesn't pull you away from life—it **anchors you deeper into its mystery**.
- It teaches that you don't need to chase meaning—you **are already woven into it**.
- When *Sahasrara* opens, it's not with a bang, but a soft recognition: *I was never separate to begin with.*

Note

1 "Chi flows through meridians" is the *Chinese* way of saying what "Prana flows through nadis" expresses in *Indian* terms.

Recommended Reading

Dale, Cyndi (2009). *The Subtle Body: An Encyclopedia of Your Energetic Anatomy.* Sounds True. (A well-researched reference guide on the chakras and energy systems from multiple traditions—yoga, Chinese medicine, Kabbalah, etc.)

Johari, Harish (1999). *Chakras: Energy Centers of Transformation.* Destiny Books. (Rooted in classical Indian teachings, with beautiful illustrations and esoteric depth.)

Judith, Anodea (1987). *Wheels of Life: A User's Guide to the Chakra System.* Llewellyn Publications. (The modern classic. *Comprehensive and* accessible, blending psychology, yoga, energy, and personal growth.)

Judith, Anodea (2004). *Eastern Body, Western Mind.* Clarkson Potter. (Explores chakras through the lenses of developmental psychology, trauma, and character structure. Highly recommended for therapists and seekers alike.)

Judith, Anodea & Vega, Selene (1993). *The Sevenfold Journey.* Crossing Press (A practical workbook blending movement, art, and journalling through the seven chakras. Great for personal or group work.)

References

Bradshaw, J. (1990). *Homecoming: Reclaiming and championing your inner child.* Bantam Books.

Buckminster Fuller, R. (2019). *Utopia or oblivion: The prospects for humanity* (J. Snyder Ed.). Lars Muller Publishers. (Original work published 1963.)

Dias, B. G., & Ressler, K. J. (2014). Parental olfactory experience influences behavior and neural structure in subsequent generations. *Nature Neuroscience, 17*(1), 89–96. https://doi.org/10.1038/nn.3594

Erikson, E. H. (1950). *Childhood and society.* W. W. Norton & Company.

Feuerstein, G. (1998). *The yoga tradition: Its history, literature, philosophy and practice.* Hohm Press.

Freud, S. (1921). Group psychology and the analysis of the ego (J. Strachey, trans.). *The standard edition of the complete psychological works of Sigmund Freud,* Volume XVIII. Hogarth.

Johnson, R. A. (1986). *Inner work: Using dreams and active imagination for personal growth.* Harper & Row.

Judith, A. (2004). *Wheels of life: A user's guide to the chakra system* (2nd ed.). Llewellyn Publications.

Jung, C. G. (1966). *The practice of psychotherapy* (R. F. C. Hull, Trans., Vol. 16). Princeton University Press. (Original work published 1954.)

Jung, C. G. (1996). *The psychology of Kundalini yoga: Notes of the seminar given in 1932 by C. G. Jung* (S. Shamdasani, Ed.). Princeton University Press.

Kellerman, N. P. (2001). Transmission of Holocaust trauma—An integrative view. *Psychiatry: Interpersonal and Biological Processes, 64*(3), 256–267. https://doi.org/10.1521/psyc.64.3.256.18464

Leadbeater, C. W. (1927). *The chakras: A monograph.* Theosophical Publishing House.

Lowen, A. (1975). *Bioenergetics.* Coward, McCann & Geoghegan.

Luepnitz, D. A. (2002). *Schopenhauer's porcupines: Intimacy and its dilemmas.* Basic Books.

Maté, G. (2011). *In the realm of hungry ghosts: Close encounters with addiction.* Vintage Canada.

Maxwell, R. W. (2009). The physiological foundation of yoga chakra expression. *Zygon: Journal of Religion and Science, 44*(4), 807–824. https://doi.org/10.1111/j.1467-9744.2009.01035.x

Motoyama, H. (1981). *Theories of the chakras: Bridge to higher consciousness.* Theosophical Publishing House.

Reich, W. (1949). *Character analysis* (3rd ed.). Orgone Institute Press.

Schopenhauer, A. (2000). *Parerga and paralipomena* (E. F. J. Payne, Trans.) Clarendon Press. (Original work published 1851.)

Shang, C. (2001). Emerging paradigms in mind-body medicine. *Journal of Alternative and Complementary Medicine, 7*(1), 83–91. https://doi.org/10.1089/107555301750164244

Wolynn, M. (2017). *It didn't start with you: How inherited family trauma shapes who we are and how to end the cycle.* Penguin.

Yehuda, R., Hoge, C. W., McFarlane, A. C., Vermetten, E., Lanius, R. A., Nievergelt, C. M., Hobfoll, S. E., Koenen, K. C., Neylan, T. C., & Hyman, S. E. (2015). Post-traumatic stress disorder. *Nature Reviews Disease Primers, 1*(1), article 15057. https://doi.org/10.1038/nrdp.2015.57

Chapter 7

Boundaries or Barriers?

We usually feel like our "self" lives inside our body, as if we're sealed off from the world by our skin, separate from everything and everyone around us. But modern physics tells a different story.

Everything you see—trees, stars, phones, coffee cups—is made from the same basic building blocks as your body: atoms. These tiny particles are the same everywhere in the universe. The only real difference between you and, say, a rock or a flower, a table or stardust, is how those atoms are arranged. As Alan Watts said, we "divide in thought what is undivided in nature" (1963).

So, in a very real sense, you're not separate from the universe; you're part of it. Your body is made of the same material as everything else. You are connected to the world around you at the most fundamental level, woven from the same fabric as everything you experience.

The first step in healing is recognising the invisible walls we've built—those emotional boundaries that shape how we perceive ourselves and interact with others. Real change can begin once we become aware of them, much like shining a light into a dark room.

Therapy helps us soften those walls, making them more open and flexible. It doesn't tear them down but enables us to see through them more quickly and move beyond them. That's when the real work—and the actual healing—can begin. German philosopher Arthur Schopenhauer wrote about what he called "the porcupine dilemma" (1851). During a cold winter, a group of porcupines moves closer to share their body heat to survive. However, by drawing closer, they inadvertently pierce one another with their quills, causing pain; Schopenhauer concluded that we should cultivate a refined solitude. There speaks a man with attachment issues. Joking aside, Schopenhauer was a philosopher who believed that solitude was a virtue and a sign of intellectual merit. I'm not disputing this stance; I can get behind it. I enjoy my own company. But is that the only way? How can we get close without hurting one another?

Robert Frost's poem, "Mending Wall" (1914), addresses boundaries. The poem describes two neighbouring farmers toiling together to complete their

DOI: 10.4324/9781003675099-8

annual chore of rebuilding their shared wall, a voluntary barrier they have imposed on themselves. One repeats his father's assertion, "Good fences make good neighbours," while the other questions why a barrier is necessary: does it not also prevent intimacy? I enjoy how this poem explores the varying approaches to the issue of boundaries; one character seemingly unquestioningly follows his father's rule, while the other takes a more flexible approach. Is there a right way and a wrong way?

Nature can teach us a great deal about boundaries. Trees are both separate and deeply connected to their environments. Physically, a tree has distinct boundaries: its bark safeguards its inner systems, and its roots occupy a specific space in the soil. However, tree roots often intertwine with those of others, forming networks through fungal mycorrhizae. This fungus develops in association with the roots of a plant in a symbiotic or mildly infectious relationship, which shares nutrients and even transmits signals regarding threats, such as pests or diseases. Trees maintain their own space while adapting to coexist. In crowded forests, they grow to maximise light and resources, sometimes developing a phenomenon known as "crown shyness", where their branches almost avoid touching their neighbours. This creates stunning patterns in the canopy as if they're communicating, *I see you, neighbour, but I need my space.* Thus, while trees establish boundaries for their protection, they are also components of a larger, interconnected ecosystem, balancing individuality with community—a valuable lesson for humans!

Setting clear boundaries is essential in psychotherapy, as boundaries create a safe, ethical environment that supports healing. Discussing these boundaries is crucial for building trust and understanding between the therapist and the client. Typically, therapists provide written terms and conditions, which they review with the client.

Clearly defined boundaries protect clients and therapists from emotional, physical, or psychological harm. They also enable therapists to maintain focus and professionalism while assisting clients. These boundaries encompass important aspects such as payment terms and fees, session structure, punctuality, and confidentiality.

Though these boundaries may occasionally be modified, this is done solely for justifiable reasons. The primary aim is to prioritise the client's welfare and development. These limits ensure the professionalism of therapy, distinguishing it from personal relationships.

We first learn about boundaries from our primary caregivers, who introduce us to the world. The words that resonate most with children include "no", "don't", "stop", and "you can't", Understanding boundaries is essential for children's socialisation, helping them navigate school and social interactions as they grow. It is important to teach and model boundaries; inconsistent or vague limits can lead to confusion and anxiety. Additionally, boundaries that do not correspond with a child's developmental stage may hinder their confidence and emerging independence. Boundaries should be established calmly and consistently, allowing for appropriate negotiation so the child can feel a sense of ownership.

The Early Years

The Ego, representing our self-identity as distinct from others, starts to develop in the first three years of life. During this period, we begin to comprehend our individuality in relation to our expanding network of relationships. The Ego assists us in making choices and managing our identity. Establishing healthy boundaries is crucial, as it protects our needs, emotions, and values while also honouring those of others.

The Skin Boundary

The most evident boundary we all possess is our skin. Focusing on this boundary from an early age is essential, because establishing and upholding other boundaries later can be significantly more challenging if the skin boundary is not understood or respected as children. Acknowledging the skin boundary is akin to unlocking the path to self-awareness and self-protection—this is where the journey begins.

Viewing the skin as a boundary is vital for children's growth and development. It involves recognising where their body ends and the outside world begins, both physically and emotionally. This awareness fosters a sense of Self in children, encourages respect for personal space, and aids in establishing emotional boundaries. These abilities form the foundation for healthy relationships and confident decision-making throughout life.

But this isn't just for children! In my role as a therapist, I've encountered many adults who missed the opportunity to learn about their skin boundaries during their formative years. Therefore, it's never too late; understanding and respecting your skin's boundaries is important, irrespective of age.

Understanding that their body is theirs and they can say "no" when others violate their physical boundaries can transform a child's life. This realisation fosters a sense of safety, independence, and self-confidence. It also enables children to articulate their feelings and develop healthier relationships.

For those who have experienced trauma, this education becomes even more essential. Trauma can blur or disrupt a child's sense of their bodily boundaries, leaving them feeling vulnerable or uncertain of their position. Therapy can help them rebuild this understanding, providing a renewed sense of control over their body and their interactions with the world.

Educating children and adults about skin boundaries offers essential tools for promoting security, confidence, and empowerment in all aspects of life.

Interactive activities such as drawing body outlines and role-playing provide children with a safe and age-appropriate opportunity to explore the concept of skin boundaries. These engaging exercises promote awareness and understanding of personal space, enabling children to express their needs and feelings with greater confidence.

Integrating this understanding into therapy empowers children and adults with the confidence and resilience needed to navigate the world. It fosters a strong sense of self-worth and equips individuals with essential skills for establishing healthy boundaries in relationships—skills that will benefit them throughout their lives.

Here's an excellent exercise suitable for all ages: Firmly pat your skin while saying, "This is *ME*, this is *ME*." Tap your whole body, from the crown of your head to your feet. Feel your hands connect with your body as you clearly articulate, "This is *ME*."

Notice how that feels.

Unwelcome physical contact violates personal boundaries and can have a profound emotional impact, especially when someone feels vulnerable. Respecting personal space is essential. Even seemingly minor issues can evoke discomfort or fear in someone who has experienced boundary violations. This underscores the importance of fostering environments where individuals feel secure and in control, not merely to prevent harm but also to nurture trust and emotional safety.

Discussing private parts with children may initially seem uncomfortable; however, it is a vital conversation for their safety, confidence, and body awareness. Thankfully, you can approach this topic in an age-appropriate and comfortable manner for both them and yourself. Here's how:

- Maintain simplicity and appropriateness for each age group. For younger children, describe private parts as those covered by swimwear or underwear, emphasising that these areas are special and should not be touched by others. As they mature, introduce the correct terminology. Educate them on the proper names for their private parts (e.g., penis, vagina, vulva, testicles). This approach normalises the discussion and ensures they can express themselves confidently.
- Start by discussing fundamental concepts. Your body is yours, and you can assertively say "no" if someone touches you in a way that makes you uncomfortable.
- "No" is always an option. Encourage them to practise saying "no" confidently in different situations, even if it feels awkward.
- Identify trustworthy adults. Compile a list of individuals, such as parents, teachers, or other dependable figures, whom they can approach if they feel uncomfortable. Emphasise that being truthful will not result in any negative consequences.

- Discuss the various types of touch you may encounter. A "good touch", such as a comforting hug from someone you trust, brings feelings of happiness and safety. In contrast, a "bad touch" encompasses any touch that causes pain or discomfort. Additionally, "confusing touches" may feel unusual or unsettling. It is essential to understand that you can always decline any touch, such as hugs or kisses, if you do not wish to accept it, regardless of who is offering. Your body belongs to you, and you have the right to make your own choices. Furthermore, it is crucial to support children when they wish to avoid hugs from relatives.
- Always ask before hugging a child to show respect for personal boundaries. If they express a "no", honour their response! Remind them that everyone's boundaries are important. And encourage them to seek permission before hugging a friend, which reflects kindness and consideration for others' feelings!
- Use comforting phrases such as, "Feel free to let me know if anything makes you uncomfortable or upset." Remind them that it is never their fault if someone invades their space.
- Talk about secrets versus surprises. Tell them that surprises, like a birthday party, are OK, but secrets about touch are never OK. Responsible adults don't ask for secrets like this.
- Explain private versus public. Help them understand the difference between private and public spaces. For example, activities such as going to the bathroom or changing clothes are typically done in private.
- Introduce the "no-touch" rule. Clearly explain that anyone else touching your private parts is permitted only for hygiene reasons (such as when a parent assists with a bath) or for medical purposes (a doctor, accompanied by a parent). They should also avoid touching anyone else's private areas.
- Encourage them to express their concerns. If someone makes them feel uncomfortable, encourage them to discuss it with you or another trusted adult.
- Foster continuous dialogue. Involve them in regular conversations about their bodies, hygiene, and safety. This isn't a single discussion; it's a long-term process as they develop. As they grow, adjust the language and examples to suit their age and level of experience.
- Remain calm and factual. If they pose questions, respond calmly and simply. Reacting with embarrassment or evasion can inadvertently suggest that the subject is taboo or shameful. By addressing it openly and using appropriate language, you empower the child to feel secure about their body while equipping them with essential tools for self-protection.
- Role-play exercises can help children practise appropriate responses to unwanted touches. For instance, they might say, "Stop! I don't like that," or seek assistance from a trusted adult.

By teaching children these simple concepts, you're helping them look out for themselves and demonstrating the importance of respecting other people's boundaries. When the skin boundary is fragile, it can undermine all other boundaries, creating a scenario where constant reinforcement is necessary, like patching a leak in a seawall, which demands relentless effort to hold back the tide. The smarter approach? Build a strong, solid defence from the outset.

Physical/Personal Space

The next challenge is the physical space, or personal space boundary, which relates to personal space and physical touch. Some people prefer to get close, others want to maintain some distance, and others require more.

Try this *Bodynamic*[1] exercise to experiment with taking your personal space.

1 Lift both arms forwards. As you lift your arms forwards, say the word: "THIS".
2 Bend the elbows to the side. As you bend your elbows outward to the sides, say: "IS".
3 Make a circle with your arms backwards. As you move your arms in a circular motion backwards, say: "MY SPACE".
4 Repeat the process a few times.
5 Scan your body and notice how you feel. How does that feel in your body?

By combining these specific movements with the words, the exercise supports the reinforcement of personal boundaries and cultivates a clear sense of self-space.

Exercise: Reclaiming Your Space

This practice helps restore a sense of personal boundary and embodied presence. It's beneficial if you often feel invaded, overwhelmed, or dissociated from your physical or emotional space.

- Begin by finding a quiet place to sit or stand where you won't be disturbed. Let your body settle.
- Take a moment to notice where your body makes contact with the chair or floor. Let yourself feel supported by the ground beneath you.
- Now, gently begin to sense the edges of your body—the shape of your arms, the outline of your back, and the space your legs occupy. Don't worry if it feels vague at first. Just stay with it.
- As you do this, imagine a soft boundary around you, like a bubble or halo of gentle light. This boundary surrounds your body, extending just far enough to feel comfortable. It's not rigid, but it's clear. You get to decide how close or far it reaches. You can even adjust it according to your mood.

- Now say, either silently or out loud, "This is my space." Notice how that feels in your body. You might place your hands in front of you, palms facing out, as if gently pressing against the air.

You might try this with different gestures: arms wide, arms crossed in front, or simply resting your hands on your belly or heart. Let your body help you find what feels right.

- Take a breath.
- Feel the boundary.
- Say again, "This is my space. I get to choose what comes in and what stays out."
- Stay with this for as long as it feels helpful. When you're ready, slowly bring your awareness back to the room. Notice how your body feels. You might want to journal what came up for you, or revisit the exercise over time to see how it evolves.

Emotional Boundaries

Emotional boundaries safeguard our feelings and energy. They include refraining from absorbing others' emotional burdens, asserting "no" when situations become too much, and being truthful with yourself and others regarding what is helpful and what isn't.

When I began therapy, I was in poor health, spending most of my days in bed. I recall telling my therapist about a friend's saying that I liked but also found quite burdensome: "Love is what you do." My therapist highlighted that, given my chronic health challenges, I was unable to do much at that time. She asked, "You are dealing with a long-term illness, reliant on assistance to get out of bed, and cannot provide for anyone. Does that mean you are unloving?" She suggested reframing the phrase "love is what you do" to "love is who you are." She explained that while you can keep your friends in your heart even when unwell, you cannot promise more. This doesn't mean you lack love for them. This insight marked the beginning of my understanding of my emotional boundaries.

Some people find it easier to say *yes* than *no*. Saying no might feel like rejecting or hurting someone, and saying yes too often can put them at risk of feeling overwhelmed or burned out from taking on too much.

Conversely, some individuals find it easy to say *no* yet struggle to say *yes*. For these individuals, making agreements can seem burdensome and result in feelings of overwhelm. To shield themselves, they may establish rigid, wall-like boundaries that restrict their flexibility and openness.

Healthy boundaries, though adaptable, are established to strengthen our connections with others rather than pushing them away. They guide us in recognising appropriate and respectful interactions and promoting relationships while preserving our identity, clarifying where we stop and others start. These personal limits are personal, reflecting our unique values, needs, and constraints. Well-defined boundaries enhance our emotional well-being, safeguard our energy and personal space, and foster relationships that are respectful and nurturing rather than draining.

A key piece of advice: steer clear of taking on the responsibility for someone else's feelings. We are not responsible for how others respond to us, unless we've seriously harmed them or crossed their boundaries.

Material Boundaries

Material boundaries concern our belongings. To successfully lend and share your items, you must also be able to say "no" to safeguard your belongings.

Shona, my client, received a request from a friend to borrow her car to pick up her daughter at the airport. Since the car was a company vehicle, Shona hesitated to enquire if her friend had insurance to drive it, fearing it might come off as rude. When the vehicle was returned, Shona found chocolate bar wrappers in the footwell, a spilt soft drink in the centre console that hadn't been cleaned, and shoe prints on the dashboard—likely from her friend's daughter resting her feet there.

Shona felt hurt and disrespected by her friend's treatment of her car, yet in therapy, she admitted feeling petty for bringing it up. She believed it was wrong to let concerns about material possessions outweigh the value of friendship.

Shona harboured unexpressed anger. This unacknowledged anger does not simply disappear; instead, it either turns inwards, leading to depression, or it manifests through passive-aggressive behaviours such as missed appointments, forgotten birthdays, or withdrawal from relationships, among other expressions.

Time Boundaries

Do you often feel overcommitted, leading to cancelled plans and an overloaded schedule? Do you feel treated this way by others? Effectively managing your time, valuing your own time, and considering the time of others is essential for maintaining a balanced relationship.

Time boundaries focus on safeguarding your time and ensuring it's utilised in meaningful ways. They enable you to manage your commitments effectively, nurture healthy relationships, and create space for relaxation and enjoyment.

When you lack clear time boundaries, it's easy to become overcommitted, stressed, or even resentful. Agreeing to too many commitments or allowing others to monopolise your time can lead to burnout. However, by establishing clear boundaries, you take charge of your schedule, maintain your energy levels, and concentrate on what is most important.

How do you maintain your time boundaries?

- Consider your priorities, including work, family, hobbies, and leisure activities. Allow these to direct how you allocate your time.
- Get comfortable with saying "No". It's perfectly fine to decline offers! Consider using phrases such as: *I would love to, but I'm unable to at the moment* or *I appreciate the invitation, but my schedule is packed this week.* If you're unsure, you might say, *Can I follow up with you on that?*
- Clearly define your boundaries. Inform others of the time you can spare. For instance, you might say, *I can meet for 30 minutes* or *I'm available until 3 p.m.*
- Plan your schedule. Set aside specific periods on your calendar for work, relaxation, or enjoyment, and regard these as essential appointments.
- Keep it simple. You don't have to explain or defend your boundaries.
- Monitor your energy levels. Allow yourself some flexibility! Recognise moments when you feel overwhelmed or stretched too thin, and modify your commitments as needed.
- Distinguish between work and personal time, such as refraining from checking emails after a particular hour.
- Value others' time by being considerate. Arrive punctually and adhere to commitments, which is simpler when you avoid overcommitting yourself.

Establishing time limits helps you regain control of your day, safeguard your energy, and allocate more time to what you cherish most.

Intellectual Boundaries

Some people overlook viewpoints that contrast with their own. Establishing healthy intellectual boundaries is advantageous for fostering mutual respect and open conversations. This involves recognising others' ideas, beliefs, and opinions while also protecting and maintaining your own views. These boundaries help achieve balance in discussions, debates, and educational settings, ensuring that everyone feels recognised and valued.

Here are some friendly ways to hold your intellectual boundaries:

- **Honour differing viewpoints**: Acknowledge another's opinion without dismissiveness or condescension, regardless of your disagreement. Respect is reciprocal.
- **Stay open-minded**: Listen to different viewpoints without the urge to alter your beliefs. You can gain valuable insights simply by listening.
- **Know your limits**: If a conversation feels unproductive or disrespectful, it's perfectly fine to step away from it. Try saying, *I think we're going in circles. Let's agree to disagree* or *I don't feel comfortable continuing this conversation.*

- **Pose questions**: If you feel strongly opposed, endeavour to avoid being dismissive or condescending. Instead, enquire to gain a deeper understanding of the other person's viewpoint. For instance: *That's intriguing—what leads you to feel that way?*

Examples of Intellectual Boundary Violations

- Interrupting or disregarding another person's thoughts and ideas.
- Coercing someone into accepting your perspective.
- Ridiculing or demeaning someone for their opinions or beliefs.
- Feeling compelled to explain or defend your ideas constantly.

By honouring intellectual boundaries, you cultivate a safe environment for learning and collaboration.

Relationship Boundaries

To foster healthy relationships, it's essential to reflect on our desired behaviours. Healthy boundaries involve honouring one another's independence, even within close connections. Allowing space for individual hobbies, friendships, and personal time is vital for preserving our identities. Time spent apart can introduce new experiences and skills to the relationship, enhancing interest and balance.

Good boundaries serve as guides—they help us understand and respect each other's needs, attitudes, and personal space. They also enhance transparency by establishing clear expectations for what is acceptable and what isn't, which can aid in avoiding misunderstandings.

Healthy relationships avoid **co-dependency**. Also known as relationship addiction, co-dependency occurs when one individual feels compelled to "save" another by meeting all their needs. A co-dependent person often defines their identity through this role, consistently sacrificing their well-being. Each person must maintain their identity. We nurture one another's freedom and independence by respecting each other's boundaries. A relationship should enrich your life rather than dictate your self-worth.

Work Boundaries

Work boundaries are the limits you establish to protect your time, energy, and well-being while promoting a healthy and productive work environment. These boundaries enable you to focus on your responsibilities, prevent burnout, and maintain a balance between your professional and personal life. Clearly defined professional boundaries are crucial for achieving a fulfilling and manageable work–life balance. By setting limits on responsibilities, work hours, and overall workload, you can ensure that your efforts remain productive without risking burnout. It is also important to discuss these boundaries with your employer, as adjustments may occasionally be necessary.

- **Clearly outline your working hours and responsibilities** whilst recognising your limits. Set personal boundaries to avoid overcommitting or taking on unnecessary stress, including the concerns of others. Be honest about your capacity.
- **Allow time for regular breaks**: Plan consistent pauses to recharge and refresh. When necessary, step away from your workspace to enjoy meals or some fresh air.
- **Practise the art of saying no**: Politely decline tasks or requests that do not align with your role or capacity. For example: "I'd love to help, but I'm already at full capacity this week."
- **Protect your time**: Only respond to work messages or emails during off-hours if it's an emergency.

Establishing healthy work boundaries enhances productivity and reduces stress. It promotes a positive work atmosphere characterised by clear roles, respectful communication, and a commitment to everyone's well-being. By defining these boundaries, you safeguard your interests while also demonstrating healthy behaviours to your colleagues.

Explore Your Boundaries

- Do you find it easier to say yes or no to life?
- Do you say yes when you'd rather say no?
- Do you tend to embrace or resist opportunities and challenges?
- Are some people easier to comply with than others?
- With whom do you respond positively, and with whom do you not?
- What is the reason for your choices?

Remember that establishing healthy boundaries is highly beneficial for maintaining strong relationships. If we fail to express our discomfort when our boundaries are violated, we become inauthentic.

Key Takeaways: Boundaries

1   *We Think We Are Separate, But...*

- We often feel separate from the world, but modern physics and thinkers like Alan Watts remind us that we are made of the same stuff as the universe—atoms arranged differently.

- True healing starts by recognising the illusion of separation and relaxing emotional boundaries.

2   Nature Models Healthy Boundaries

- Trees are excellent teachers: they keep clear boundaries but also connect underground through roots and fungi to exchange resources.

  They illustrate *coexistence with individuality*—a metaphor for human relationships.

3   Emotional Walls or Emotional Windows

- Emotional boundaries shape our relationships with others.
- Therapy helps soften rigid walls, allowing connection without harm.

4   Boundaries Begin in Childhood (Ideally)

- Children can learn boundaries from caregivers through consistent guidance.
- Boundaries must align with a child's developmental stage, and when taught calmly and clearly, they cultivate confidence and independence.

5   The Skin as a Boundary

- The most basic boundary is physical—our skin. Teaching children (and reminding adults) to respect this is foundational for emotional safety and identity.
- Exercises like affirming "This is ME" help reinforce bodily autonomy and self-awareness.

6   Different Types of Boundaries

This chapter covers multiple boundary types and how they function:

- **Physical boundaries**: Personal space and touch.
- **Emotional boundaries**: Managing others' emotions without taking them on.
- **Material boundaries**: Lending items with consent and limits.
- **Time boundaries**: Prioritising commitments, learning to say no.

- **Intellectual boundaries**: Respecting differing views, asserting your own.
- **Relationship boundaries**: Avoiding co-dependency, preserving autonomy.
- **Work boundaries**: Protecting time, energy, and personal life from overreach.

7 Practical Tools and Exercises

- Activities such as drawing body outlines, creating personal space with string circles, role-playing touch scenarios, and confidently saying "no" help both children and adults build and reinforce their boundaries.

8 Consequences of Poor Boundaries

- Ignored boundaries lead to emotional strain, resentment, or depression.

9 Healthy Boundaries Support Relationships

- Healthy boundaries are **flexible**; they support deep connection while protecting your well-being.
- They're not about pushing people away, but about knowing where *you* end and someone else begins.

Note

1 Bodynamic Somatic Psychology and Analysis System is a pioneering method of somatic developmental psychology and psychotherapy that integrates current research in children's psychomotor development, cognitive and depth psychotherapy, brain research, with a particular emphasis on the quality of contact and healthy relationships.

Recommended Reading

Clarke-Fields, Hunter (2020). *Raising Good Humans.* New Harbinger Publications. (Mindful parenting tips, including teaching children healthy boundaries.)

Glover, Tawwab Nedra (2021). *Set Boundaries, Find Peace: A Guide to Reclaiming Yourself.* Penguin Random House. (Clear, modern, and compassionate; a good book for anyone starting their boundaries journey.)

Neufeld, Gordon & Maté, Gabor (2019). *Hold On to Your Kids: Why Parents Need to Matter More Than Peers.* Vermillion. (A powerful guide to setting emotional boundaries with children while maintaining connection.)

Rosenberg, Marshall B. (2003). *Nonviolent Communication: A Language of Life*. PuddleDancer Press. (Teaches how to express needs and boundaries with empathy and clarity.)

Scott, Kim (2017). *Radical Candor*. Macmillan. (Geared towards leadership and team dynamics, offers good advice for professional boundaries.)

Urban, Melissa (2023). *The Book of Boundaries: Set the Limits That Will Set You Free*. Random House. (Direct, empowering, and full of scripts for setting boundaries in real-world situations.)

Ury, William (2007). *The Power of a Positive No*. Random House. (From a negotiation expert—how to say "no" without damaging relationships.)

References

Frost, R. (1914). 'Mending Wall'. In *North of Boston*. David Nutt.

Schopenhauer, A. (1851). *Parerga and paralipomena: Short philosophical essays*. Oxford University Press. volume II, chapter XXXI, section 396, pp. 651–652.

Watts, A. (1963). *The two hands of God: The myths of polarity*. George Braziller.

Chapter 8

It's Elementary

What's Your Type?

One of my tasks when meeting a new client is to evaluate their personality type. Each individual is unique, and understanding one's strengths, weaknesses, traits, and values can unlock potential. Personality typing provides a framework for categorising characteristics, offering insights by comparing and contrasting different types. The aim is not to restrict or pigeonhole, but to help us understand and share our internal experiences, thus improving our ability to assist and communicate effectively.

A historical tradition exists of classifying human temperament. Hippocrates proposed that pairs of opposites—blood and phlegm, choler and bile—determine character. Astrologers categorise individuals based on the signs of the zodiac, which govern the elements of air, earth, fire, and water.

Many psychologists incorporate what they call the Big Five personality traits into their methodology, with each of the five traits (represented by the acronym *OCEAN*) existing on a spectrum:

Openness measures the willingness to embrace new experiences. Individuals who score highly are generally more creative and open to new ideas, whereas those with low openness scores often prefer routine.

Conscientiousness measures a person's ability to create and adhere to a plan. Individuals with high scores tend to be more focused and organised, exhibiting a keen attention to detail. Conversely, those with a low conscientiousness score indicate a preference for a less structured approach and may experience challenges with follow-through.

Extroversion measures how outgoing, friendly, and sociable a person is. Extroverts usually score high on the extroversion scale, whereas introverts typically score low.

Agreeableness gauges empathy towards others. High scorers may be idealistic, prioritising the needs and happiness of others over their own. Low scorers may view others as competitors or even adversaries.

Neuroticism measures the emotional turmoil an individual typically experiences. A high score in neuroticism indicates more frequent bouts of moodiness[1] and anxiety, while a low score suggests greater emotional stability.

DOI: 10.4324/9781003675099-9

The score for each trait is broken down into facets. The Big Five Inventory includes 44 different aspects of the original five traits. For instance, someone with a low conscientiousness score may be seen as *frivolous*, whereas a high conscientiousness score would be linked to being *reliable*.

Jungian Personality Types

Jung was an early researcher of personality types, drawing on the work of psychologists William James and Nietzsche to propose the concepts of introversion and extraversion. In his book *Psychological Types* (1971), Jung significantly influenced our understanding of personalities. One way he classified individuals was by whether they were *extroverted* (externally focused) or *introverted* (internally focused). He referred to these tendencies as "attitudes", describing two different ways that people engage with the world and where they derive their energy. Jung's theory posits that everyone possesses introverted and extroverted tendencies, but one is typically more dominant, and individuals can exhibit different behaviours in varying contexts.

In everyday terms, an introvert feels more comfortable and energised by spending time alone or in small, quiet settings, perhaps enjoying solitary activities such as reading, writing, or being in nature. For these individuals, excessive social interaction, especially in large groups, can be taxing and even exhausting. They tend to be more reflective and may take longer to consider their words before speaking.

On the other hand, extroverts enjoy social situations and feel invigorated in the company of others. They come alive in a vibrant social setting, whether it's a party, a team sport, or collaborating on a group project. Too much time alone can leave them feeling isolated or drained.

Understanding whether you are more introverted or extroverted can assist you in making better decisions regarding your social activities, work environment, and energy management.

Carl Jung believed that deep within each of us lies a set of core functions that guide how we experience the world and understand our place in it. These are not merely abstract ideas; they shape everything from how we observe the world around us to the way we make our most significant decisions.

Four Primary Functions

At the heart of Jung's theory are four primary psychological functions, categorised into two fundamental groups: how we perceive the world and how we evaluate or make decisions. The four functions are **Sensing, Intuiting, Thinking, and Feeling**.

Jung believed that each of us has a natural way of making sense of the world, beginning with how we perceive and process information.

Some people concentrate on the physical world: the sights, sounds, textures, and details right in front of them. Jung called this **Sensation**. It's a practical, grounded way of perceiving, centred on the present moment and the facts you can trust with your five senses.

Others are more drawn to what lies beneath the surface. They notice patterns, read between the lines, and get hunches about how things might unfold. This is **Intuition**—a more imaginative, future-oriented way of perceiving, where possibilities feel just as real as what's in front of you.

Once we've taken in information, we need to decide what to do with it—and here, too, we have our preferences. Some people rely on **Thinking**, weighing up logic, principles, and consistency to reach a conclusion. Others turn to **Feeling**, asking what matters most on a human level—what's right, fair, or kind.

We all use a mix of these ways of seeing and deciding, but usually one style comes more naturally than the other. And these preferences subtly shape how we present ourselves in the world, from the choices we make to the way we interact with others.

Let's dive a bit deeper.

Sensate Type

When it comes to perception, Jung identified two contrasting ways in which people *absorb information*: sensation and intuition. Some of us lean towards **sensation**. Sensate types are grounded in the present moment, attentive to the concrete facts, details, and sensory experiences that make up daily life.

Imagine someone stepping into a room and immediately sensing the scent of a perfume in the air, the flaking paint on the window frame, the texture of the sheepskin beneath their feet, and the way sunlight pools across the floor, like spilt honey. They don't merely notice these details; they *feel* them. *They live* them. This is the world of the Sensate type, as described by Jung.

EXTRAVERTED SENSATE TYPE

For the **Extraverted Sensate**, life is vivid and tactile. They are tuned into the world around them, soaking up every colour, sound, and texture. The crunch of an apple, the pulse of music, the cool weight of linen against their skin—this is where they thrive. They are grounded in the present, alert to what is real and right in front of them. Abstract theories or distant possibilities often seem irrelevant. They think with their hands, trust what their eyes and ears tell them, and find meaning in what can be experienced directly.

An example of an Extraverted Sensate type is **Ernest Hemingway**. His direct, concrete writing style, love of adventure, and focus on the physical world—hunting, boxing, and war reporting—reflect a dominant extraverted sensate approach.

The **Introverted Sensate**, by contrast, may appear more inward or reserved, yet their inner world is equally rich. A particular scent can transport them directly into a memory. Soft lighting might evoke a feeling they struggle to articulate. They don't merely notice what's occurring around them; they *assimilate* it. Every impression penetrates, like ink saturating blotting paper. While the extraverted Sensate responds outwardly and in the moment, the introverted Sensate internalises those experiences, quietly making them their own.

A famous example of a Sensate type is Steve Wozniak, co-founder of Apple.

Wozniak was the hands-on builder and the technical genius behind the first Apple computers. He thrived on tangible problem-solving, designing circuits, writing code, and perfecting hardware. He was not drawn to marketing visions or philosophical ideals; he loved to tinker, build, and make things *work*.

Jung admired the Sensate type for keeping us grounded in reality. However, he also issued a warning: when *excessively* dominant, sensation can lead to indulgence or numb us to deeper reflection. When distorted, it may present as compulsions, physical complaints, or a restless quest for stimulation.

For the Sensate, the world isn't merely something to theorise about—it's something to touch, taste, smell, and *experience*. Their gift is presence. They remind us that sometimes, life is not about ideas, but about the sensation of the moment.

Intuitive Type

Others are more drawn to **intuition**. Intuitive types prefer to look beyond the obvious; they sense *patterns*, pick up on *possibilities*, and often focus on the *bigger picture* or what *could* be, rather than what *is*.

Where the Sensate type is grounded in the concrete and tangible, the Intuitive type is attracted to the unseen, along with the possibilities, patterns, and potentials that lie beneath the surface of things.

Intuitives have a knack for spotting hidden patterns, reading between the lines, and imagining what might lie ahead. For Jung, intuition was a way of perceiving that bypasses the five senses entirely, reaching directly into the unconscious to draw out insights that aren't immediately visible. "Intuition is a perception of realities which are not known to the conscious mind, and which goes via the unconscious" (Jung, 1971).

EXTRAVERTED INTUITIVE TYPE

This type is outward-facing, attuned to *possibilities in the external world*. They are explorers who survey the world for emerging ideas, patterns, and opportunities. Energised by new ventures, concepts, and futures not yet realised, they continuously scan the horizon for what might *be*.

The **Extraverted Intuitive** is not satisfied with what *exists*—they are consistently aspiring to what *may unfold*. This trait makes them natural explorers, entrepreneurs, revolutionaries, or reformers. They often possess prophetic insight, perceiving emerging trends well before others do.

However, this type can be unsettled or restless, letting go of a promising idea just when it starts to show real potential; initially throwing themselves with complete abandon, but dropping it without a second thought, as if it never meant anything in the first place.

An example of an Extraverted Intuitive type is **Steve Jobs,** the late visionary who saw possibilities where others saw limitations. He wasn't an engineer; he was an *intuitor*, capable of anticipating what the public would desire before they even realised it themselves. Another example is **Oprah Winfrey**. Her career has been propelled by an intuitive ability to discern cultural currents, emotional truths, and future trends in human development.

INTROVERTED INTUITIVE TYPE

By contrast, the **Introverted Intuitive** turns inward, drawing from the deep waters of the unconscious. Instead of scanning the outer world for possibilities, they perceive inner images, archetypes, and symbolic truths. This type is often visionary, even mystical, tuned into realities others can't easily see or understand. "The introverted intuitive type is directed to the inner object, a kind of perception of background processes, of what is going on in the collective unconscious" (Jung, 1971).

Examples of Introverted Intuitive types include **Carl Jung** himself. Often cited as a classic Introverted Intuitive, his work drew from inner visions, dreams, and archetypal imagery. He explored the unconscious as a vast symbolic realm, often misunderstood by more empirically minded peers.

Emily Dickinson, reclusive and enigmatic, wrote poetry that drew upon profound inner symbolism and archetypal themes, often with little regard for the outside world's validation.

Another example of this type is **Leonardo da Vinci,** who was not only a brilliant inventor and artist but also deeply introspective, attracted to the symbolic threads that connect nature, anatomy, and the cosmos.

Thinking Type

Imagine two people facing the same dilemma: whether to end a relationship. One begins to list pros and cons, weighing compatibility, timing, and life goals. The other sinks into quiet reflection, striving to discern what feels right in their heart. The first is likely a Thinking type, a person who approaches life through logic, objectivity, and principle. The second is a Feeling type. For the

Thinking type, truth is something that can be worked out, much like a mathematical problem or legal case. Emotions have their place, but they do not drive the car.

Jung believed that Thinking is one of the mind's four primary functions, orientating us to the world. Unlike Feeling types, who make decisions based on values and emotional resonance, Thinking types strive for clarity and coherence. They seek to *understand* how things fit together.

However, not all types of thinking are identical. Jung categorised them into **extraverted** and **introverted** variants—two minds with very different gears turning beneath the surface.

EXTRAVERTED THINKING TYPE

This type focuses on facts, systems, and external standards. They are the ones who design efficient workflows, create detailed spreadsheets, and manage logistics with almost military precision. Practical, organised, and decisive, they do not act to please; they act to make things *work*. Imagine a CEO restructuring a company, not for popularity, but for performance.

An example of the extraverted thinking type is **Margaret Thatcher**, the late British Prime Minister, nicknamed the "Iron Lady" for a reason. She applied logic, rules, and structure to governance, often at the expense of emotional diplomacy. **Jeff Bezos** is another example. He built Amazon on a foundation of data, discipline, and streamlined systems. Efficiency and scalable logic were not just part of his method; they were his signature style.

INTROVERTED THINKING TYPE

The **Introverted Thinker** resembles a philosopher in a quiet study or a tinkerer absorbed in a garage full of half-finished projects. They inhabit their own mind, constantly refining ideas until everything aligns perfectly. They do not concern themselves much with what *appears* effective to others—what truly matters is whether it makes sense *to them*.

These individuals may appear reserved, even distant, but internally, they are continually analysing, seeking conceptual purity and truth.

Both types can be excellent problem-solvers. However, they may encounter difficulties when emotion or ambiguity comes into play. While a Feeling type might say, "This just feels wrong," a Thinking type might respond, "But does it make sense?"

An example of an introverted thinking type is **Albert Einstein**. Though compassionate, his genius lay in modelling abstract systems (like time and space) internally in precise conceptual terms. A character from the world of fiction exemplifying this is **Spock from Star Trek**. He is coolly logical and inwardly structured, constantly questioning assumptions. He feels alienated by emotions and trusts logic above all.

Jung didn't regard Thinking types as cold or heartless—they are simply oriented differently. Their loyalty is to *truth* rather than *comfort*. They strive for fairness, rather than kindness. Often, they feel most alive when solving a problem, structuring chaos, or cutting through confusion to reveal the core idea. To them, the world is a puzzle, and their role is to decipher it.

Feeling Type

Now envision someone in the same relationship dilemma. Rather than mapping pros and cons, they ask themselves: *What does my heart know? What will hurt less? What will hurt others less?* They consider the other person's face, the history they've shared, and the significance contained in a single glance.

This represents the **Feeling type**, as Jung described it; not sentimental, nor moody, but guided by a refined sense of value, empathy, and relational truth. Where the Thinking type cuts through complexity with the scalpel of logic, the Feeling type listens for the emotional tone, the music beneath the words.

Jung regarded Feeling as a *rational* function, much like Thinking. This does not imply emotion for its own sake. For Jung, Feeling served as a means of evaluating the world based on worth, on *what truly matters*. It raises the questions: *Does this align with my values? Is this right for the soul?*

Like Thinking, Feeling can turn outward or inward.

EXTRAVERTED FEELING TYPE

In **Extraverted Feeling** types, the emphasis is placed on *social harmony*. These individuals are attuned to what is appropriate, considerate, and connective. They are the ones who remember birthdays, smooth over tensions, and know exactly how to uplift a heavy atmosphere. Their feelings radiate like warm light, measuring the emotional climate and adjusting themselves to help others feel at ease. **Michelle Obama** is an excellent example of an Extraverted Feeling type. She's warm, articulate, and inclusive—and you can sense her deep commitment to uplifting others. Her presence emanates social grace and a strong sense of values that guide her interactions with the world.

INTROVERTED FEELING TYPE

Introverted Feeling types are quietly fierce. They hold their values close, as if they are something sacred. They may not say much, but don't mistake that for indifference—*what they feel, they feel deeply*. They are guided not by what others consider good or right, but by their inner code. You might find them creating art, defending the marginalised, or holding space in silence for a friend in pain, not to fix anything, but to share the experience with them.

For Feeling types, people aren't merely data points in a system—they're living, breathing narratives. Decisions are not made solely for efficiency or success, but for meaning, for connection, for what nourishes the heart.

Frida Kahlo's art embodies classic Introverted Feeling, being intensely personal, emotional, and unapologetically self-expressive. Another example is **Joan of Arc**, who was motivated by inner conviction and individual values, even when they conflicted with societal norms.

Their challenge? Occasionally, their desire to please can lead to self-abandonment. Conversely, their inner convictions might make them appear aloof or obstinate. But their gift? A profound capacity for human truth—truth that isn't in the head but in the heart.

Where Thinking types chart the structure of the world, Feeling types perceive its soul. They do not come to conquer chaos, but to nurture within it.

The Elements Model

> Earth grows, fire glows, air blows, water flows, and the Spirit knows.
>
> (Anonymous)

In my work as a psychotherapist, I draw upon Jung's psychological types and Dr Nigel Hamilton's Elements Model. Dr Hamilton is the founder and director of the Centre for Counselling and Psychotherapy Education and the Dream Research Institute in Maida Vale. Established in 1984, the centre has become one of Europe's largest transpersonal training institutes. During my two decades there, I trained as a psychotherapist and served as a lecturer, trainer, supervisor, and facilitator. After years of studying and analysing human behaviour, Hamilton developed the Elements Model, which encompasses more than a personality theory; *it is a profound and subtle transformation system.*

Ancient Egyptians

Let us first examine some of the influences for this system of transformation.

The ancient Egyptians perceived the world as infused with meaning, viewing elements not merely as physical substances but as sacred forces embodied by gods. Creation did not begin with a bang, but with **water**—*Nun*, the dark, formless sea that contained all potential. From it, the first **land** emerged: *Geb*, the god of the earth, solid and grounding, the foundation of all life.

Arching above him was *Nut*, the sky goddess, her body stretching overhead like a cosmic canopy filled with stars. Between them stood *Shu*, the god of **air and light**, who held them apart so that life could thrive in the space between. And at the centre of it all was *Ra*, the sun god, whose **fiery** journey across the sky brought light, power, and consciousness into the world.

These forces—water, earth, sky, air, and fire—were not utilised to define personality types as the Greeks would later do, but they influenced the Egyptians' perception of existence. Their worldview was rich in symbolism: healing, nature, divinity, and even human behaviour were all interpreted through this elemental lens.

When it came to personality, the Egyptians did not establish a system of types based on the elements. Instead, they turned to the stars and the gods. They employed early forms of astrology, associating specific deities with birth months. For example, someone born under the influence of *Thoth* might be regarded as clever and articulate. It was not a structured typology but rather a mythic interpretation of character—*personality as a reflection of divine influence.*

So, while they didn't speak of "earthy" or "fiery" temperaments, the Egyptians viewed the individual as *part* of a sacred, living cosmos. Their model of the Self encompassed multiple parts of the soul, each reflecting different facets of existence. In that sense, their approach to inner life was profoundly symbolic, spiritual, and holistic. It's less about fixed types and more about how each person carries a unique blend of divine forces, written in the stars and reflected in the soul (Assmann, 2005; Pinch, 2004).

A System of Transformation[2]

The Four Elements

The model incorporates the elements of air, fire, water, and earth, addressing but remaining distinct from the framework of astrological personality theory. Specific characteristics or qualities are attributed to each element. This transpersonal model differs from other personality theories in that the qualities are Soul qualities, the internal, individual expression of Spirit.

As I mentioned in the Introduction, archetypal psychologist James Hillman eloquently conveys this idea in his book *The Soul's Code* (1996). He states that we are born with the seed of our Soul's purpose embedded within us and that our task in life is to realise the potential of that seed, allowing it to push its roots down from the fertile earth of the deep psyche and blossom through our physical being.

The qualities attributed to each element *are* those seeds, so I focus on this model and invite you to explore who you are, where you may be heading, what could obstruct you, and how to overcome any hurdles in order to achieve your potential.

According to Hamilton's model, there are four elements of orientation or inclination: air, fire, water, and earth.

We can draw a parallel between Jung's psychological types and the classical elements of nature. Each Jungian type appears to reflect the qualities of a specific element, providing a symbolic lens through which to understand human behaviour and inner life better.

Thinking types, emphasising logic, clarity, and analysis, align with the **Air element**. Like air, they are quick, clear, and far-reaching, concerned with ideas, principles, and rational frameworks that help them make sense of the world.

Feeling types resonate with the **Water element**. Deep, intuitive, and value-driven, they navigate the world through empathy and emotional intelligence. Just as water flows, adapts, and nourishes, so too do Feeling types connect with their heart and seek harmony in their relationships.

Sensate types, firmly rooted in the present, correspond to the **Earth element**. They are grounded, practical, and attuned to the sensory world. Like the earth beneath our feet, they value structure, reliability, and what can be directly seen, touched, and measured.

Intuitive types, always attuned to patterns, symbols, and possibilities, are best embodied by the **Fire element**. Fire is transformative, visionary, and untamed, much like the imaginative leaps and inner convictions that drive Intuitive personalities.

By linking these psychological patterns with the classical elements, we are provided with a vivid and timeless language to explore the richness of personality. Each type transcends a mere collection of traits; it becomes an expression of the elemental forces that shape how we think, feel, sense, and intuit.

The Tables presented in this chapter categorise the qualities into three rows under the headings: "Expressive", "Balanced", and "Receptive". These headings loosely correspond to the types of individuals who are more dynamic, measured, or yielding in expressing their qualities.

Under these three headings, an archetype has been established, representing the *ideal* type of person who might embody these traits. Remember that an ideal is just that; we often fall short of it. The arrangement of qualities within this matrix, along with the archetype that illustrates the ideal version of the element, forms a transformational roadmap that guides us on our journey towards individuation.

All these qualities can be developed, and yet some traits are more intrinsic to our nature and emerge soon after birth. When gazing into the eyes of newborns, one can observe that some are serene, while others are energetic and spirited. We encompass more than just our bodies and minds; children bring their Soul nature into the world. They also exhibit qualities that may be overlooked, dismissed, or suppressed by their families or culture. Even in the absence of clear trauma, these experiences can lead children to conceal aspects of themselves for self-protection. Perhaps no one explicitly indicated that these traits were unwelcome, but children pick up on their environment and nonverbal cues, responding based on a reward system. If demonstrating strength yields more positive reinforcement than vulnerability, they are likely to present themselves as strong and hide their vulnerability.

In the latter part of our lives, as we pursue wholeness, we begin to uncover the traits we once concealed.

Generally, we tend to resonate more with one element over the others. Therefore, in this model, you are classified as an Earth character if you exhibit a predominance of Earth qualities. However, this does not imply that you are devoid of qualities from the other elements.

When establishing your pathway, it is helpful to ensure that the primary element is balanced. The most challenging aspect of this journey is unveiling a new element, as change often presents difficulties. Approaching the development of elements and their traits in a systematic order is advantageous, beginning with air, followed by fire, then water, and finally earth, or in reverse order—earth, water, fire, and then air.

Core characteristics

In the Tables that follow, each element is featured, highlighting its core characteristics and the qualities of an *ideal* individual who predominantly embodies that element.

Distortions

Each of these qualities has distortions that arise from maladaptive responses to trauma or psychological wounding. So, the core characteristics are accompanied by a chart that illustrates how these distortions may manifest (the Shadow traits and opposite traits).

Criticising a person's behaviour can be counterproductive in a therapeutic context. A more constructive approach involves examining distortions to uncover the original quality. This method focuses not on avoiding confrontation or Shadow work, but on addressing the distortion while recognising its underlying positive quality, thereby peeling back the layers to facilitate a deeper transformation. When we acknowledge the positive attribute reflected to us, we are often inspired to embrace it; in contrast, criticising the distorted behaviour tends to provoke defensive reactions.

Example

I once worked with a client, Janet, who struggled to understand other people's sensitivity. Her bluntness often caused offence. "I'm just being honest," she'd say. "They need to toughen up. I can't stand people who are thin-skinned." However, after a series of complaints, her line manager challenged her to reflect on the impact of her communication. Janet began to acknowledge that perhaps this was something she needed to improve. We started to discuss her directness as a distortion of the Fire quality of truthfulness.

I asked Janet how she responded to directness in others. At first, she sidestepped the question, insisting that she wasn't bothered by it. However, over time, it became clear that, in truth, she could be deeply offended by criticism. This led to an exploration of her unrecognised sensitivity and how she had been unconsciously projecting it onto others.

Janet considered the feedback and began to experiment, sometimes successfully and sometimes not, with gentler ways of expressing her thoughts.

However, the work didn't end with Janet merely acknowledging that she could be too direct. Together, we explored deeper layers: her tendency to accuse others of stupidity when they didn't grasp what she considered self-evident; her habitual "shoulds", "ought-tos", and "have-tos"; the legacy of being verbally oppressed in childhood; and the ways her sensitivity had been mocked, leading her to disown and banish it to the shadows. There was much more, too—each layer bringing her closer to the roots of her defensiveness and the parts of herself she'd learned to silence.

As you review the Tables below, endeavour to identify your distortions (but remember to keep the Inner Critic—always ready to hit you with a verbal half-brick—on mute!). You may also notice distorted traits in your family, friends, and colleagues, which can sometimes be more apparent and may also prove beneficial. However, if your goal is personal growth, do not neglect your *own* patterns.

The qualities listed in the Tables below are not exhaustive, but they provide a helpful overview of the types of traits each element tends to express.

Each Table consists of three columns: **expressive**, **balanced**, and **receptive**, illustrating the various ways these qualities can manifest, depending on the individual's personality.

The Air Element

Many cultural and philosophical traditions emphasise the air element, often associated with movement, lightness, and expansiveness. The ancient Greek philosopher Empedocles identified air as one of the four key elements in ancient Greek thought, alongside earth, fire, and water. It symbolises the breath of life and the vital force that energises all living beings. Due to its intangible and encompassing nature, air is often associated with intellect, communication, and cognitive abilities. Air quality is typically characterised as light, dry, and mobile, rendering it less tangible than the properties of other elements. In numerous spiritual and metaphysical practices, the air element serves as a conduit between the physical and spiritual realms.

Meditation and breathwork often emphasise the air element to promote mental clarity and spiritual insight. Air is essential for life on Earth, comprising primarily nitrogen and oxygen, gases critical for the respiration of most terrestrial organisms. The movement of air through wind patterns influences weather and climate, impacting ecosystems and human activities. Clean air is vital for health, while air pollution presents significant challenges to both personal well-being and environmental stability. Air symbolises freedom, movement, and the power of thought. It is a crucial component of both the physical world and human consciousness.

The Air element fosters a mental orientation closely aligned with Jung's Thinking type. This realm is where concepts originate and evolve. For instance, intuition often seems to come "out of the air". Initially, its meaning may be obscure, as seen in the prophecies of Indigenous Americans predicting square tepees (houses) or the Hopi elders envisioning "talking cobwebs" (the Internet). To comprehend intuition, rational mastery is essential. An intuitive notion evolves into a concept, which, in turn, develops into an idea, ultimately giving rise to a structured plan born from intentional thought. This thought is then communicated, acted upon, and ultimately realised. In such instances, the spiritual essence manifests in material form.

In astrology, the air signs—Gemini, Libra, and Aquarius—exemplify attributes such as communication, intelligence, and sociability, highlighting the dynamic and flexible nature of the air element. Individuals with an Air disposition display a variety of traits, as illustrated in Table 8.1.

The ideal Air types are the archetypes of the Scientist/Planner (Expressive Air orientation), the Priest/Spokesperson (Balanced Air orientation), and the Oracle/Researcher (Receptive Air orientation).

Table 8.1 Qualities of the Air character © CCPE

Air Character Qualities

	Expressive	Balanced	Receptive
Ideal type	Scientist/Planner	Priest/Spokesperson	Oracle/Researcher
Qualities	Wise	Communicative	Intuitive
	Intelligent	Understanding	Insightful
	Focused	Adventurous	Free-spirited
	Witty	Peaceful	Imaginative
	Capable	Sacred	Ethereal
	Quick to grasp	Guiding force	
	Penetrating	Efficient	
	Astute	Light	
	Alert	Holy	
	Knowledgeable	Mental subtlety	
	Wise	Communicative	

EXPRESSIVE AIR

The ideal type assigned to the Expressive Air character is the Scientist or Planner. Scientists are motivated to discover the fundamental laws of the universe. They are curious and question what they observe.

The Scientist (Expressive Air orientation) works with what has been given (perhaps an intuition or a vision), compelling meaning to emerge. Maybe inspiration is lost along the way—the aspect that the Scientist cannot grasp. However, what remains becomes organised and is conveyed, linked to an existing body of knowledge. When the Scientist cultivates the qualities of the Oracle (see below), it instils in the Scientist a sense of awe, wonder, and the sacred.

Albert Einstein is an excellent example of this character.

BALANCED AIR

Across various faiths and traditions, this archetype takes on different forms, including the Catholic priest, the Jewish rabbi, the Muslim imam, the Hindu pandit, the Buddhist monk, and the interfaith minister. Each serves as a visible representative of the sacred, translating mystery into meaning. For some, this role symbolises divine presence; for others, it is a trusted guide on the spiritual path.

At their best, such figures inspire and uplift rather than impose. Their communication is not about control, but about conveying guidance while remaining grounded in the source of their wisdom.

Let us, for the purpose of this discussion, consider the Priest archetype as a representation of the religious figures listed above. The Priest (Balanced Air orientation) can draw upon the attributes of the Oracle (Receptive Air) and the Scientist (Expressive Air) as needed. The priest's talent lies in communication, blending the qualities of listening (the Oracle) and speaking (the Scientist). They are well suited to guide others, as their strong communication skills enable them to interpret and convey the guidance they receive while remaining connected to the source of their insights. Ideally, the Priest should embody a visionary role, focusing on inspiring and motivating others psychologically rather than imposing their own beliefs. The Priest archetype may begin by believing that their way is the only way, but ideally matures as they learn to recognise and respect other paths, understanding how to collaborate to serve a higher purpose.

A powerful example of the Priest archetype, extending beyond traditional religious roles, can be found in **Desmond Tutu**. As an Anglican archbishop and human rights advocate, Tutu embodied the balanced Air quality of the Priest: someone who served as a bridge between the spiritual and the worldly. He spoke truth to power with courage and conviction while also listening deeply to the pain and injustice surrounding him. Tutu held space for grief yet consistently pointed towards hope. His moral vision transcended dogma, grounded in compassion and clarity. Whether confronting apartheid or guiding post-conflict reconciliation, he communicated spiritual truths in ways that unified rather than divided. Tutu didn't impose belief; he invited transformation. He called people towards forgiveness, justice, and shared humanity. At its best, the Priest archetype represents not a guardian of fixed doctrine, but a channel for higher wisdom, guiding others with heart and integrity.

RECEPTIVE AIR

In antiquity, the **Oracle** (Receptive Air orientation) offered advice or prophecies believed to have been channelled from a divine source. I have heard therapists, counsellors, and priests report saying something they had not consciously thought of but that resonated with their client or a member of their flock, and that it *felt like it didn't come from me, but through me.*

The **Researcher** is at home in theory, abstraction, and philosophy. They are more at ease with ideas, data, rules, and regulations than with people. They possess analytical thinking skills and are avid readers with a well-developed imagination and insight into the world around them. They are detail-oriented and data-driven, enjoying the collection and examination of quantitative data to gain insights and recognise patterns. In this context, their chief quality is the ability to connect with their intuition and wisdom.

A compelling example of the **Oracle** archetype is **Carl Jung**. He was not a fortune teller or a mystic in the usual sense, but deeply embodied the essence of the Oracle—someone who listens inwardly, senses hidden patterns, and gives voice to truths that lie just beneath the surface of everyday life. Like the ancient oracles, Jung did not rely solely on logic or reason; his insights came from dreams, symbols, mythology, and the shadowy depths of the psyche.

Charles Darwin exemplifies the timeless **Researcher** archetype—curious, meticulous, and quietly determined in his quest for truth. He did not rush to conclusions or seek recognition; instead, he devoted years to observing, collecting data, asking questions, and refining his ideas. His detailed study of species ultimately culminated in the groundbreaking theory of evolution, not through dramatic proclamations, but through steady and thoughtful inquiry. Like all true Researchers, Darwin was driven not by fame but by a profound desire to understand how the world works.

DISTORTED AIR

If you or someone you're thinking of appears to be exhibiting distorted traits, it can be more beneficial to look beyond judgement. This does not deny the existence of unhelpful behaviours that require attention. Try to trace the behaviour back to its *seed quality*. From there, the work becomes one of refinement, transforming the distortion by reconnecting with the true, underlying quality that wishes to emerge.

Table 8.2 illustrates examples of distortions in the Air character (the Shadow and opposite traits). The first column lists the seed quality. In the second and third columns, you will find its shadow expression and its opposite.

Table 8.2 Distortions of the Air character © CCPE

Air Character Qualities, Shadow and Opposite Traits

Expressive Air Character

Quality	Shadow trait	Opposite trait
Detached	Cold	Attached
Wise	Cynical	Foolish
Intelligent	Braggart, smart Alec	Stupid
Focused	Tangential	Divergent/Contrary
Witty	Sarcastic	Dull
Capable	Controlling/Righteous	Inefficient
Quick to grasp	Exploitative	Slow-to-grasp
Penetrating	Intrusive/Critical	Superficial/Diffuse
Astute	Exploitative	Stupid/Unknowing
Alert	Hypervigilant	Inattentive
Knowledgeable	Know-all	Ignorant
Discriminating	Choosy, fussy	Indiscriminating, cavalier

Balanced Air Character

Quality	Shadow trait	Opposite trait
Peaceful	Indolent, lazy	Agitated
Fine, subtle	Oversensitive	Crude, gross
Sacred	Sanctimonious	Profane
Communicative	Garrulous	Closed
Understanding	Sharp	Ignorant/ Misunderstanding
Adventurous	Foolhardy	Fearful
Influential	Dominating	Insignificant
Guiding force	Manipulative/Controlling	Misleading/Easily led
Efficient	Controlling	Inefficient
Light	Insubstantial	Heavy
Holy	Self-righteous	Wicked
Mental subtlety	Too clever/Smart alec	Obvious

(Continued)

Table 8.2 (Continued)

Receptive Air Character

Intuitive	Self-deceptive	Concrete/Fantasist
Insightful	Narcissistic	Delusional
Free-spirited	Aimless	Confined
Imaginative	Dreamy	Dull
Visionary	Idealistic	Short-sighted
Ethereal	Impractical/Fragile	Boorish/Coarse

The Fire Element

Fire is a classical element in many cultures and philosophies. It is frequently associated with energy, transformation, and passion. In various mythologies and spiritual traditions, fire occupies a sacred place.

In the natural world, fire is a formidable force that can both create and destroy. Essential for survival and progress, it provides warmth and light; however, it can also become uncontrollable and destructive, capable of devouring everything in its path. Its dual nature makes fire a symbol of life, death, destruction, and regeneration.

In ancient Greek philosophy, fire was regarded as one of the four essential elements, alongside earth, water, and air. It embodied the dynamic and life-giving forces of the universe. Hephaestus was the god of fire and craftsmanship, representing the element's creative and transformative abilities. The Hindu god Agni is also the god of fire, frequently invoked during rituals and ceremonies, symbolising purification and the divine.

Fire is a timeless motif. It encapsulates the essence of transformation and the ceaseless energy of life, whether as a physical phenomenon or as a symbol.

In both literature and art, fire symbolises passion, love, grief, frustration, and rage, reflecting the complexities of human emotions. It is a multifaceted element that can evoke feelings of warmth and comfort, as well as danger and destruction.

Fire holds profound symbolic and psychological significance. In alchemy, it represents transformation and purification, which are essential for turning base metals into gold. As a potent metaphor, fire embodies personal change and enlightenment. Psychologically, it illustrates ambition, willpower, and desire. It symbolises the creative spark that ignites innovation and the resolute pursuit of goals, showcasing the vibrant energy and passion of the human spirit.

The Fire element ignites *energy* within a person, manifesting as the "fire-in-the-belly" drive often observed in high achievers and entrepreneurs or as an inner flame that purges egotistical traits, resulting in a state of purity and idealism.

Table 8.3 Fire character qualities © CCPE

Fire Character Qualities

	Expressive Fire	Balanced Fire	Receptive Fire
Ideal type	Achiever/warrior	Knight	Dervish
	Radiant	Confident	Pure
	Powerful	Successful	Inspired
	Forthright	Open	Honest
	Persevering	Useful	Discriminating
	Energetic	Principled	Ecstatic
	Initiatory	Honourable	Optimistic
	Active	Truthful	Humorous
	Industrious	Direct	Intuitive
	Aspiring	Just	
	Successful risk-taker	Independent	
		Courageous	

In elemental personality theory, Fire characters align with Jung's Intuitive type. The astrological fire signs are Aries, Leo, and Sagittarius. Table 8.3 outlines the characteristics of the Fire character.

The three *ideal* Fire types are the **Achiever** (Expressive Fire orientation), the **Knight** (Balanced Fire orientation), and the **Dervish** (Receptive Fire orientation).

EXPRESSIVE FIRE

The **Achiever** is the archetype symbolising the Expressive Fire orientation. This archetype can be likened to the sun, characterised by its constant and inexhaustible radiance. The Achiever is a natural leader who fosters a bias for action. With a strong work ethic and an optimistic and enthusiastic attitude, the Achiever is committed to excellence. They are charismatic, capable, and motivational.

Serena Williams, the former professional tennis player, exemplifies the **Achiever archetype**. Her ascent to tennis greatness was fuelled not only by talent but also by unwavering discipline and determination. Even at the pinnacle of her career, she continued to challenge her limits. Off the court, she has leveraged her success to inspire change, advocating for equality and empowerment. Like all true Achievers, she transforms personal victories into meaningful impact.

The Dervish reflects the Achiever, much like the moon reflects the sun. The mystics assert that the sun would scorch the entire universe if it were not for the moon. Were it not for the discerning qualities of the Dervish, the Achiever might view *any* challenge as worthwhile, as the most important thing to the Achiever is to work, struggle, and shine.

BALANCED FIRE

The **Knight** (Balanced Fire orientation) is a person on a mission of adventure, rescue, or conquest. Courageous, determined, principled, and honourable, they choose their battles carefully; when they fight, it is always for a noble cause. Their quest is steadfast, propelled by the unyielding force of the Achiever (Expressive Fire) and the unwavering focus of the Dervish (Receptive Fire)— an ideal harmony. The Knight carries the torch to the highest peaks, triumphantly proclaiming victory for the cause. Self-motivated and resolute, they embrace tasks with single-minded dedication, seeking neither guidance nor approval once their mission begins.

Martin Luther King Jr. exemplifies the **Knight** archetype. He represented courage, integrity, and a profound sense of duty. Guided by a moral commitment to justice and nonviolence, he confronted threats and opposition without wavering. His mission was to defend the vulnerable and challenge injustice, not through force, but through conviction. Like a true Knight, King's strength emanated from within. He battled not with weapons, but with words, vision, and the quiet power of sacrifice.

RECEPTIVE FIRE

The Receptive Fire character can be an idealist—someone who envisions an ideal world rather than the world as it is. Profoundly caring, passionate, and empathetic, they may feel a calling for work in the helping professions. They might be in search of inspiration and, on a spiritual level, seeking meaning in life. They may possess a deep intuition, recognising the potential in others.

The ideal representing the Receptive Fire character is the **Dervish**,[3] a mystic who experiences the inner fire of ecstasy. Many have heard of whirling dervishes, often pejoratively, as running around without focus. The exact opposite is true. The Whirling Prayer ceremony, breathtakingly serene, beautiful, and moving to witness, is an active meditation that originated among certain Sufi groups and is still practised by the Sufi Dervishes (also called *semazens*) of the Mevlevi order, conducted in remembrance of Allah or God, with the semazen's hat (known as a *sikke*) representing a tombstone of the Ego.

The white robe, known as a *tenure*, represents the shroud of the Ego. When the black cloak is removed, it symbolises the dervish's spiritual rebirth.

The Dervish is discriminating due to their purity and unwavering idealism. Once ignited by an idea, they can think of nothing else. They are not action-oriented (as the Achiever is), but the same spark of zeal is evident in their eyes when they discuss the idea that has captivated them.

A clear example of the **Dervish** archetype is **Rumi**, the Sufi poet and mystic. He sought truth not through logic but through devotion, poetry, and ecstatic experience. His whirling dance and soul-stirring verses embody the Dervish's path of surrender, love, and union with the Divine.

The fire element is magnetic, alluring, and transformational. It can also be destructive, uncontained, and devouring. Table 8.4 shows the qualities and distortions (the Shadow and opposite traits) of the Fire character.

Table 8.4 Fire character distortions © CCPE

Fire Character Qualities, Shadow and Opposite Traits

Expressive Fire Character

Quality	Shadow trait	Opposite trait
Active, Energetic	Restless	Inert
Radiant	Fierce	Depressed
Powerful	Domineering	Weak
Straightforward	Blunt	Deceptive
Persevering	Unrelenting	Sluggish
Risk-taking	Reckless	Risk-averse
Aspirational	Driven	Unenterprising
Energetic/Sparky	Exhibitionist	Slothful/Drab

Balanced Fire Character

Quality	Shadow trait	Opposite trait
Confident	Dogmatic	Trepidatious
Successful	Triumphant	Unsuccessful
Open	Uncontained	Guarded
Useful	Co-dependent/People-pleasing	Unhelpful
Principled	Self-righteous	Dishonest/Unjust
Honourable	Rigid	Dishonourable
Truthful	Morally superior	Dishonest
Direct	Insensitive	Evasive
Just	Uncompromising	Unjust
Independent	Hyper-independent	Dependent
Courageous	Reckless	Fearful

Receptive Fire Character

Quality	Shadow trait	Opposite trait
Ecstatic	Intoxicated	Dull
Joyful	Facetious	Miserable
Faithful/Believing	Bigoted	Doubting
Pure	Perfectionist	Corrupt
Inspired	Agitated/Overwrought	Apathetic
Honest	Impertinent	Dishonest
Discriminating	Perfectionist	Arbitrary/Autocratic
Optimistic	Heedless/rash	Pessimistic
Humorous	Irreverent/mocking	Serious
Idealistic	Naïve	Cynical

The Water Element

Water is essential for life on Earth. Since time immemorial, access to fresh water has been a prerequisite for establishing human communities. It is vital for drinking, bathing, sanitation, and the cultivation of crops for energy production and industrial processes. Rivers facilitate the transportation of goods and people, while lakes are crucial for biodiversity and recreation. Its nature makes it a powerful symbol across various cultures and belief systems, serving as a fitting metaphor for the essence of life itself.

In religious rituals such as Christian baptism, water represents purification. Its cleansing properties wash away impurities and sins, signifying the individual's rebirth into a new spiritual life. In Judaism, water symbolises creation, destruction, purification, regeneration, and love. In Hinduism, water is revered as the essence of life and the elixir of immortality, imbued with profound spiritual significance. The Sun God, Surya, is believed to have emerged from the cosmic waters, symbolising creation and vitality. Ritual baths in sacred rivers like the Ganges are thought to cleanse past transgressions and purify the soul. In Buddhism, enlightenment involves a rigorous cleansing of the mind and body. Water symbolises wisdom in the holy Quran. The faith encompasses multiple cleansing rituals, including *wudu*—a process of washing the hands, mouth, nostrils, arms, face, ears, hair, and feet before performing worship—and *ghusl*—a full-body ritual purification obligatory before engaging in various Islamic activities and prayers.

The changing properties of water inspire a sense of renewal and rebirth. The cycles of evaporation, condensation, precipitation, and collection reflect the cycles of life, death, and regeneration or rebirth. Water's renewal is recognised in myths from cultures all around the world, symbolising the source of life and its potential end. It often plays a leading role in stories of creation and destruction: Noah's Ark from the Bible, the Aztec flood story of Note and his wife Nena, and the Greek myth of Deucalion, son of Prometheus, and his wife, Pyrrham, to name but a few. In ancient Egyptian mythology, the primordial waters of Nun existed before creation, embodying the chaotic potential from which order and life emerged.

Water signifies adaptability and flexibility, taking the shape of any container into which it is poured. This trait is often invoked in philosophical and spiritual teachings, emphasising the importance of adaptability in the face of life's challenges. Lao Tzu, the ancient Chinese philosopher, highlighted water's quiet strength in the Tao Te Ching:

> There is nothing in the world more soft and weak than water, But for attacking things that are firm and strong, nothing can take its place. The weak overcomes the strong; The soft surpasses the hard.

This verse captures the Taoist insight that real strength isn't about force; it's found in softness, flexibility, and quiet endurance.

Table 8.5 Water Qualities

Expressive	*Balanced*	*Receptive*
Creator/Artist	*Friend/Partner*	*Disciple*
Creative	Loving	Glorifying/Reverential
Compassionate	Friendly	
Generous	Harmonious	Appreciative
Nurturing	Adaptable	Graceful
Sociable	Responsive	Sensitive
Affectionate	Subtle	Lovable
		Devotional
		Soothing
		Gentle
		Delicate
		Flowing
		Deep feeling
		Passionate

In psychology, water symbolises the unconscious mind and emotions. The ocean serves as a metaphor for the unconscious, representing the realm of our fears, desires, and memories. Jungian psychology uses water as a symbol of the collective unconscious, a shared reservoir of human experiences and archetypes.

The Water element resonates deeply with human emotion, embodying its fluid and transformative nature. Just as water can be serene or turbulent, so too can emotions be equally challenging to navigate. One may love intensely yet fear accepting love, or crave appreciation and respect while struggling to offer generosity and care in return. Some individuals may be emotional, intuitive, and nurturing; a new romance may sweep them off their feet, leading to rapid changes in their feelings. The Water character aligns most closely with Jung's Feeling type. In the zodiac, Cancer, Scorpio, and Pisces are the water signs.

The qualities of the Water character are listed in Table 8.5.

The ideal Water character types include the **Creator/Artist** (Expressive Water orientation), the **Friend/Partner** (Balanced Water orientation), and the **Disciple** (Receptive Water orientation).

EXPRESSIVE WATER

The **Creator/Artist** (Expressive Water orientation) masters this elemental energy. Intimately connected to the universe's creative force, they yearn to make the intangible tangible. Following an invisible blueprint, they summon, mould, and develop using the emotions that flow through them. What begins in the imagination is, through their creative efforts, brought into existence so that others can see, hear, taste, touch, and feel it. They aim to enhance the beauty of the world or invite people to appreciate its splendour. They may be painters, writers, singers, actors, florists, chefs, bakers, gardeners, homemakers, and more.

They are often generous, forming close relationships (which they generally control) and attracting disciples.

BALANCED WATER

The **Friend/Partner** (Balanced Water orientation) embodies the balance of Creator (Expressive Fire) and Disciple (Receptive Fire). They have a desire to belong and connect with others. They can be both sensitive and generous. They cultivate involvement by winning people's hearts. They approach relationships with openness, prioritising vulnerability over detachment. Rather than seeking control, they fully immerse themselves as equal partners, valuing intimacy even at the risk of occasional pain. For them, the rewards of connection outweigh the dangers of emotional exposure. They are supportive, and loyalty is a defining characteristic. They are harmonisers and can forge deep friendships due to the agreeable atmosphere they create.

An example of the **Friend** archetype is the Hobbit **Samwise Gamgee** from *The Lord of the Rings*. Sam is loyal, humble, and devoted to Frodo. He doesn't seek recognition or glory; his strength lies in being present, providing steadfast support through fear, fatigue, and doubt. The Friend archetype embodies a quiet, dependable presence, and Sam reminds us that true friendship isn't loud or dramatic; it's the subtle act of standing by someone, regardless of how arduous the journey becomes.

Michelle Obama exemplifies the **Partner archetype**—strong, supportive, and deeply collaborative. As First Lady, she stood alongside her husband, leading initiatives in education, health, and equality. This demonstrated that true partnership involves mutual respect, a shared purpose, and uplifting others while confidently standing in one's own power.

RECEPTIVE WATER

The English word "disciple" originates from the Latin *discipulus*, meaning a learner. When the **Disciple** archetype grips us, we find ourselves in the service of a teacher or master, attentively listening to their insights and philosophy while following their way of life. The Disciple (Receptive Water orientation) is accepting of others, particularly the Master, for the Master has faced many tests, risen to the challenges on the battlefield of life, and proven themselves beyond a shadow of a doubt. Thus, the Disciple no longer judges or tests; they accept whatever the Master provides. The Disciple's devotion to people surpasses the Dervish's dedication to their ideals. Unlike the Dervish (Receptive Fire orientation), who may be discriminating, the Disciple embraces acceptance.

A powerful example of the **Disciple** archetype is **Malala Yousafzai**. From a young age, she dedicated herself to a higher purpose—fighting for girls' right to education. Even after surviving a life-threatening attack, she remained true to that mission. The Disciple is not driven by ego, but by a profound commitment to learning, growth, and something greater than oneself. Malala embodies this beautifully—humble, determined, and unwavering in her dedication to a cause she believes in.

WATER CHARACTER DISTORTIONS

Water can lead to floods, tsunamis, and catastrophic devastation. It once ushered in the Ice Age, irrevocably transforming the world as it was known.

Considering the qualities of a person with a water nature, who wouldn't want to be their friend? However, water can freeze. Therefore, if you have offended someone with a Water nature, do not necessarily expect them to confront you; instead, have they gone off the radar? They may choose to avoid a fiery conflict with you and instead isolate you. They may not be "ghosting" you, but you might feel as though they have erected an invisible wall of ice, and the intimacy you once shared has disappeared.

The qualities of the Water character and the distortions (the Shadow and opposing traits) are detailed in Table 8.6.

Table 8.6 Water character distortions © CCPE

Water Character Qualities, Shadow and Opposites

Expressive Water

Quality	Shadow trait	Opposite trait
Creative	Fanciful	Mundane/Prosaic
Compassionate	Too amenable	Ruthless/Heartless
Generous	Permissive	Stingy
Nurturing	Pliable	Withholding
Sociable	Over-friendly	Unsociable
Affectionate	Gushing	Cold

Balanced Water

Quality	Shadow trait	Opposite trait
Loving	Lustful	Indifferent
Friendly	Co-dependent	Foe
Harmonious	Sycophantic/Fawning	Discordant
Adaptable	Chameleonic/Changeable	Inflexible
Responsive	Inconsistent/Volatile	Apathetic
Subtle	Frail/Languid	Coarse

(Continued)

Table 8.6 (Continued)

Receptive Water

Quality	Shadow trait	Opposite trait
Glorifying/Reverential	Spacey/Unrealistic	Denigrating
Appreciative	Impressionable	Unappreciative
Graceful	Pliable	Clumsy
Sensitive	Sugary/Sentimental	Callous
Lovable	Inauthentic	Unlovable
Devotional	Easily led/Weak-willed	Disloyal
Soothing	Soporific	Disturbing/Agitating
Gentle	Seductive	Harsh
Delicate	Ineffectual/Appeasing	Solid/Harsh
Flowing	Indecisive	Solid
Deep feeling/Passionate	Emotionally controlling	Superficial

The Earth Element

In numerous cultures and belief systems, the earth element symbolises stability, nourishment, and the foundation of life. It acts as the ultimate provider, sustaining life through its fertility.

The Earth is often depicted as a nurturing mother figure; for instance, in Greek mythology, *Gaia*, who emerged from *Chaos*, is the mother of all life. *Pachamama* (which translates to Mother Earth) is an ancient female deity worshipped by local Andean and Amazonian peoples; she symbolises the fertile ground from which all life springs and is sustained. Offerings are regularly made to her in gratitude for providing food, support, and shelter.

The earth element symbolises stability, reliability, endurance, and grounding. In various spiritual practices, grounding exercises involve connecting with the earth to achieve mental and emotional strength, such as the Mountain Pose (*Tadasana*) in yoga and Alexander Lowen's biodynamic exercise "The Bow".

The earth element symbolises permanence and continuity, enduring despite inevitable change. The Earth provides the foundation for the constantly interacting aspects of air, fire, and water, enabling life to flourish. The interconnectedness of all elements and the importance of maintaining harmony between them represent a holistic view long held by Indigenous peoples, such as the First Nations, Inuit, and Métis. Now, amid the climate change crisis, it is finally being recognised by the scientific community.

The individual with the Earth nature possesses numerous qualities associated with it and corresponds most closely to Jung's Sensate type. In the zodiac, the signs of Taurus, Virgo, and Capricorn are categorised as earth signs.

The qualities of the Earth character are listed in Table 8.7.

Table 8.7 Earth character qualities © CCPE

Earth Character Qualities

	Expressive Earth	*Balanced Earth*	*Receptive Earth*
Ideal type	Guardian	Sovereign	Healer/Counsellor
Qualities	Masterful	Magnetic	Merciful
	Disciplined	Majestic	Patient
	Principled	Authentic	Helpful
	Strong-willed	Responsible	Calm
	Ordered	Dependable	Quiet
	Resilient	Tolerant	Nurturing
	Cautious	Big-hearted	Healing
	Capable	Solid	Gentle
	Pragmatic	Inwardly strong	Protective
	Facilitative	Dignified	Compassionate
	Firm	Noble	Accepting
	Measured	Decisive	Forgiving

The ideal character types for Earth are the Guardian (Expressive Earth orientation), the Sovereign (Balanced Earth orientation), and the Healer/Counsellor (Receptive Earth orientation).

EXPRESSIVE EARTH

The Expressive Earth character is associated with will, a sense of purpose, and responsibility. The **Guardian** is an example of the ideal Expressive Earth orientation. Although relational by nature, they can find solace in solitude, striking a balance between connection and introspection. Their orderly and measured approach to life reflects a disciplined adherence to the law. This steadiness grants them the resilience to withstand challenges and defend their values unwaveringly. The Guardian personifies the notion of defence, counsel, and guidance; they can manifest as gatekeepers or advocates, offering wisdom or protection.

The Guardian can also serve as an obstacle on the journey to individuation. In the tale of Theseus and the Labyrinth, the Minotaur, a mythical creature with the body of a man and the head of a bull, was imprisoned at the heart of a maze, acting as the guardian of the threshold and preventing anyone who entered from escaping. Theseus ultimately volunteered to enter the Labyrinth and slay the beast.

Guardians tend to appear at life's turning points—those moments when we transition from the familiar into the unknown, from who we've been to who we're becoming. They ignite a confrontation that opens up a liminal space, a kind of inner doorway where our sense of Self can begin to shift and take on new form. The Guardian is therefore not a negative influence; rather, it acts as an *opposing force*, encouraging us to delve deep and nurture the qualities we need to complete our journey. To overcome the Guardian, brute force rarely suffices. One must often rely on cleverness, compassion, or self-awareness. This calls forth dormant strengths, such as humility or resilience, which the journey ahead will require.

A powerful example of the **Guardian archetype** is **Mahatma Gandhi**. Gandhi was not merely protecting people; he was safeguarding values, including nonviolence, justice, and human dignity. He devoted his life to standing up for the oppressed and led India to independence through peaceful resistance. His strength did not stem from force but from quiet courage and profound compassion.

The Guardian archetype embodies the protection of what truly matters, offering steadiness and moral clarity. Gandhi exemplified this completely, standing firm in the face of injustice, not for himself, but to safeguard the well-being and spirit of his people.

BALANCED EARTH

The **Sovereign** (Balanced Earth orientation) bears the responsibilities of both the Guardian (Expressive Earth) and the Counsellor (Receptive Earth): establishing order, upholding the law, and dispensing the mercy essential for making that order humane. The Sovereign orientation imparts to a person a sense of their god-like or goddess-like potential, without becoming inflated.

Throughout history, the Sovereign has symbolised the stable core of civilisation, both geographically and spiritually. In times of chaos, Sovereigns remain steadfast, embodying calm and clarity amidst the storm. A true Sovereign offers an enduring presence, serving as an unshakeable foundation—a guiding lighthouse when all else falters. They possess an overarching perspective and a broader outlook. When a crisis arises, they draw upon their experience to infuse their decisions with expertise and practical wisdom. The Sovereign lives with integrity.

In Spanish, the word *integro* means "whole". Integrity, therefore, implies being whole, undivided, and intact. Integrity is the glue that binds all of a person's virtues together. Their life is a unified whole. The Sovereign mends fractured relationships, keeps their word, is honest, and takes responsibility for their actions.

The *majestic* person is magnetic. They carry their burdens without revealing them to others. They fulfil their duties, dedicating their lives to the cause. **Queen Elizabeth II** was a prime example of this.

While not all sovereigns are leaders of a country, we are all sovereign in our own way. The word "sovereign" ultimately derives from the Latin *superānus*, meaning "above". We have areas for which we are responsible to oversee and protect—physically, mentally, emotionally, or spiritually. For instance, your home represents a sanctuary, a refuge from negativity and external pressures.

In the workplace, leading others involves navigating a complex landscape of team dynamics, conflict resolution, and organisational changes.

A compelling example of the **Sovereign** archetype is **Nelson Mandela**.

Mandela led with calm authority, integrity, and a deep commitment to the greater good. After 27 years in prison, he emerged not with anger or a desire for revenge, but with a vision for unity and healing. As President of South Africa, he guided the country through a challenging transition with wisdom and grace.

The Sovereign archetype isn't about control; it's about leadership that empowers others. Mandela exemplified what it means to stand firm in the face of conflict, to lead from the heart, and to wield power not for personal gain, but to serve and uplift others.

RECEPTIVE EARTH

Where the Guardian is strong, the **Receptive Earth** orientation archetype of the **Counsellor** is compassionate. When faced with someone in distress, Counsellors do not pause to enquire about what led the person to their situation; rather, they do whatever they can to assist. Naturally approachable, with an attentive and curious disposition and a talent for connecting with others, the Counsellor archetype fosters a safe environment where individuals can share their feelings and challenges. The Counsellor flourishes when exploring the complexities of human emotions, behaviour, and motivation.

A prime example of the **Counsellor** archetype is **Brené Brown**, an American researcher, author, and speaker.

Through her work on vulnerability, shame, and empathy, she creates a space where individuals feel truly seen and understood. The Counsellor archetype embodies deep listening, emotional honesty, and a caring nature, and Brown exemplifies this perfectly. She doesn't speak from a pedestal; she connects as a fellow human. Her warmth, insight, and willingness to share her struggles make her a trusted voice—someone who fosters growth in others by meeting them with compassion and truth.

EARTH CHARACTER DISTORTIONS

The Earth possesses many positive aspects—solidity, stability, receptivity, and productivity, to name but a few. We take the Earth for granted at our peril.

Individuals with a natural inclination towards Earth can exhibit distorted behaviours. However, their greatest strengths can sometimes transform into their most challenging flaws. Resilience may shift into masochism, capability into control, and strong will into rigid stubbornness. Their ordered and methodical nature, while admirable, can become a source of frustration for loved ones as rigidity overshadows adaptability. Although slow to anger, when they do become angry, it can feel earth-shattering. Table 8.8 illustrates the Earth character's qualities, Shadow, and opposite traits.

Table 8.8 Earth character distortions © CCPE

Earth Character Qualities, Shadow and Opposites

Expressive Earth

Quality	Shadow trait	Opposite trait
Masterful	Over-driven/Compulsive	Incompetent
Disciplined	Enforcing	Undisciplined
Principled	Obstinate/Unyielding	Unprincipled
Strong-willed	Unbending/Overbearing	Vacillating/Indecisive
Ordered	Pernickity/Fussy	Disorderly/Messy
Resilient	Masochistic	Vulnerable/Susceptible
Cautious	Fearful	Reckless
Capable	Controlling	Incompetent
Pragmatic	Unfeeling	Unrealistic
Facilitative	Unengaged	Obstructive
Firm	Rigid	Soft/Yielding
Measured	Slow/Stultifying	Erratic/Careless
Grounded	Rigid	Ungrounded
Peacemaking/Dispassionate	Indecisive	Stubborn
Protective	Rigid	Over-protective

Balanced Earth

Quality	Shadow Trait	Opposite Trait
Magnetic	Overbearing	Repulsive
Majestic	Grandiose	Mundane, Subservient
Authentic	Insensitive	Artificial
Responsible	Rule-bound	Negligent
Dependable	Victim/Martyr	Unreliable
Tolerant	Indulgent	Petty/Narrow-minded
Big-hearted	People-pleasing/Indulgent	Mean-spirited
Solid	Intransigent/ Uncompromising	Unreliable
Dignified	Pompous	Undignified/Foolish
Noble/Honourable	Pompous	Ignoble/Shameful/ Unworthy
Forgiving	Permissive	Unforgiving
Decisive	Rigid/Stubborn	Indecisive

Receptive Earth

Quality	Shadow trait	Opposite trait
Merciful	Naive/Too permissive	Merciless
Patient	Inert	Impatient
Helpful	Masochistic/Infantilising	Unhelpful
Calm	Soporific/Unresponsive	Agitated
Quiet	Soporific/Sleepy	Loud
Nurturing	Condescending/Belittling	Neglectful
Healing	Overburdened/Burnt out	Harming/Damaging

(Continued)

Table 8.8 (Continued)

Receptive Earth

Quality	Shadow trait	Opposite trait
Gentle	Permissive	Brutal/Unkind
Compassionate	Naive	Heartless
Accepting	Too permissive	Rejecting
Forgiving	Masochistic	Punishing

How To Use the Elements Model for Personal Growth

We all experience some degree of wounding during childhood as we navigate the stages of development. We begin life in the womb, connected to our biological mother. We are born into a world of constraints. We quickly learn that we cannot have everything—without wings, we cannot soar like birds, and without gills, we cannot dive into the depths of the ocean.

Our caregivers are human, and like all of us, they are inherently flawed. Our families and cultures shape us, often leading us to suppress aspects of our true selves to conform and make life more manageable. Over time, we develop a persona—a version crafted to fit in and meet expectations.

In this process, we often suppress parts of ourselves that we believe will not assist us in navigating the world. For instance, a child in a harsh environment may learn to stifle their natural sensitivities, thinking it renders them too vulnerable or unwelcome. Similarly, a fiery, assertive child might conceal their boldness if their emotional expressions are overlooked, conforming instead to the expectations of others.

By marginalising these traits, we begin to obscure our entire selves. This is how our False Self (the Persona) forms. Gradually, we become estranged from our authentic nature.

A key task in the journey of individuation is to uncover and reclaim the lost or hidden aspects of ourselves, bridging the gaps in our personalities and restoring a sense of wholeness.

- To explore this model, start by recognising all the qualities you possess and highlighting them. Take some time to reflect on and compile them into a list.
- Once you have completed this, identify which element feels the most dominant—your primary element.
- Now identify the areas where you feel most deficient.
- Observing the qualities of others can be beneficial. Appreciate each person's unique traits and contributions. Recognising and valuing others' strengths can illuminate aspects of yourself that you may wish to explore or develop (your potential).

- It is also useful to reflect on a desired quality in various ways; below is an example.

An Example of Developing a Quality

- If you wish to cultivate a **Fire** quality, such as becoming more **courageous**, consider undertaking a 21-day experiment.
- Begin by observing fire in all its forms. Watch a candle flame flicker, a bonfire blaze, or a roaring fireplace. Notice the different states of fire—dancing, smoking, shimmering, or guttering. If you do not have access to a physical fire, explore documentaries or films that showcase fire's behaviour and effects.
- Consider your reaction to this element. Does fire draw you in, or does it frighten or repel you? Reflect on what fire signifies and its effects. Fire possesses a dual nature: it warms us, transforms raw materials (such as cooking food, melting metal, or purifying substances), and brings people together (around a hearth, campfire, or bonfire).
- While it serves as a source of warmth and transformation, it also has a destructive side, reducing forests and homes to ashes. Yet even in its devastation, it facilitates renewal, paving the way for new growth and regeneration as life emerges from the remains.
- By observing and contemplating fire, see if you can recognise its qualities within yourself. You may start to understand and integrate these qualities into your life, including boldness, transformation, magnetism, and the ability to initiate and embrace renewal.
- To cultivate a deeper connection with the fire element and the quality of courage, begin by genuinely befriending it. Take time to reflect on the nature of *courage*. Meditate on the word, research its meaning and origins, and consider someone who embodies this quality.
- Next, engage your body in the process. Strike a pose that symbolises courage—perhaps something bold, forward-moving, or commanding. Notice how this posture makes you feel. Does it evoke a sense of power, determination, or resistance?
- Develop this further by creatively conveying the essence of courage. Visualise it: Is it a sharp arrow, a steady square, or a circle? What colour embodies its energy—blue, grey, red, orange, or something different? Draw it. Speak in the first person as though you are the drawing.
- Imagine what it would be like to be courageous and how it would change your life. Be specific about how it would change things.
- Then, take *action*. Experiment. You don't need to join the military. Start with small steps. Take a risk. Step out of your comfort zone. The specific activity is less important than the act of *beginning*.

- As you do this, pay attention to the unhelpful thoughts that arise—self-doubt, procrastination, or fear of failure. Expect them; they are part of the process. Recognise these thoughts as your "growing edge", the areas where you tend to pull back. Lean into this discomfort; it is where transformation begins.

Change

Change is not only possible but inevitable. Although we may perceive ourselves as fixed, we are constantly evolving. Nevertheless, change can be challenging, as our brains favour familiarity and resist disruption, leading to fear, anxiety, and a tendency towards routine, even when change may be beneficial for us.

Uncertainty can provoke resistance, as we fear the unknown and feel a loss of control. Change may also induce stress, sadness, or frustration, particularly when it disrupts established habits. Breaking old patterns requires effort, and when the benefits of change are unclear, we become even more reluctant to adopt it.

At times, change can feel like a threat to our security or identity, prompting us to cling to what we know. Nevertheless, despite its challenges, change represents a pathway to growth, new opportunities, and transformation.

Key Takeaways: Personality Types

1   Personality Typing Is a Tool

- Personality typing is used in therapy to comprehend traits, strengths, and blind spots—not to limit or stereotype clients.
- Frameworks such as Jungian types and the Big Five (OCEAN) model offer insight into how individuals perceive, evaluate, and engage with the world.
- The Elements model is a system for transformation.

2   The Big Five Traits Explain Personality on a Spectrum

- **Openness, Conscientiousness, Extraversion, Agreeableness, and Neuroticism** are used to evaluate behavioural tendencies.
- Each trait lies on a continuum, offering nuance instead of rigid categories.

---

3 Jung's Psychological Types Highlight Internal Experience

- Jung suggested that we all favour specific functions:

  - **Sensation vs Intuition** (how we perceive).
  - **Thinking vs Feeling** (how we decide).

- Each of these can be either introverted or extraverted, resulting in eight distinct dominant personality types. Understanding your dominant function helps you in recognising how you process information, connect with others, and derive meaning.

4 The Elements Model and the Soul Qualities

- Grounded in the elements of Air, Fire, Water, and Earth, the model interconnects personality with soul qualities, paving the way for transformation. Each element approximately aligns with a Jungian function:

  - **Air/Thinking**
  - **Water/Feeling**
  - **Fire/Intuition**
  - **Earth/Sensation**

5 Each Element Has Qualities And Distortions

- The model examines expressive, balanced, and receptive orientations within each element.

6 Personality Is Adaptable and Can Change Over Time

- Qualities and traits can be innate or shaped by family and culture.
- We often conceal certain qualities or traits to navigate childhood, but we can reclaim them for personal growth and healing.

Change is possible

Although the brain may resist change for the sake of safety, transformation remains essential for growth and development.

Cultivating underrepresented aspects within ourselves fosters greater balance, wholeness, and individuation.

Notes

1 See therapist.com (2024, 13 June). "Mood disorders: Symptoms, causes, and treatment", https://therapist.com/disorders/mood-disorders/.
2 Copyright © CCPE.
3 In Islam, the term Dervish refers to members of a Sufi fraternity whose focus is on the universal values of love and service, overcoming the illusions of ego to reach God.

Recommended Reading

Hillman, James (1997). *The Soul's Code: In Search of Character and Calling*. Random House. (A philosophical, archetypal look at personality as a soul-driven journey, not just a psychological one.)

Jung, Carl Gustav (1921/2016). *Psychological Types*. Routledge. (The original source of Jung's personality theory, introducing introversion/extraversion and the four functions (Thinking, Feeling, Sensation, Intuition). Dense but essential.)

Keirsey, David (1998). *Please Understand Me II*. Prometheus Nemesis Book Company. (Builds on Jung's ideas and MBTI, offering profiles of 16 types in practical contexts like relationships and leadership.)

Nettle, Daniel (2007). *Personality: What Makes You the Way You Are*. Oxford University Press. (Based on the Big Five (OCEAN) model; it is grounded in research but readable and insightful.)

Tieger, Paul D. & Barron-Tieger, Barbara (1995). *Do What You Are*. Little, Brown & Company. (Connects MBTI (Myers–Briggs Type Indicator) types to career choices. An excellent guide for matching your personality type to your work life.)

References

Assmann, J. (2005). *Death and salvation in ancient Egypt* (D. Lorton, Trans.). Cornell University Press.

Hillman, J. (1996). *The soul's code: In search of character and calling*. Random House.

Jung, C. G. (1971). *Psychological types* (H. G. Baynes, Trans., R. F. C. Hull, Rev. ed.). Princeton University Press. (Original work published 1921.)

Pinch, G. (2004). *Egyptian myth: A very short introduction*. Oxford University Press.

Chapter 9

My Granny's Elbow

The Symptom Speaks

Western medicine has long regarded physical symptoms as indicators of problems within the body's functioning. However, this perspective has not always been the prevailing one. In the seventeenth century, physicians began to treat symptoms rather than the individual as a whole, often attempting to suppress these symptoms and remove diseased parts to restore the body to optimal health.

Considering symptoms from a psychological perspective does not necessitate the dismissal of allopathic medicine; it is crucial to consult a medical doctor for symptom evaluation; psychological work on these symptoms can occur concurrently. From a psychological viewpoint, symptoms communicate significant messages from the unconscious, urging us to acknowledge them. Rather than dismissing or demonising these symptoms, exploring them can unveil profound insights, steering us towards personal transformation and growth.

Hippocrates, the Greek physician (c. 460–c. 370 BC), revolutionised medicine by emphasising the relationship between the body and mind while adopting a holistic perspective. He was the first physician to assert that the mind can influence health and disease, with the principle of a "healthy mind in a healthy body" being central to his philosophy. Hippocrates' keen ability to observe and interpret signs was highly regarded, and his standards and ethical guidelines remain relevant today. He championed mental care and art therapy interventions for mental disorders, utilising music and drama in the treatment of illnesses and in promoting behavioural change.

Fast-forward to the mid-seventeenth century in Europe, a period of radical change that ushered in a significant shift in thinking. French philosopher René Descartes (1596–1650) introduced the concept of **dualism**, the idea that the mind and body are fundamentally separate (Descartes, 1996).

This marked a turning point in medical thought. Mechanical explanations of the body began to dominate, pushing aside the once-integrated view of the body and mind. Cartesian dualism, as it came to be known, gradually replaced the holistic approach of Hippocratic medicine, fragmenting what had previously been seen as a unified human experience.

DOI: 10.4324/9781003675099-10

Contemporary science is increasingly revealing the complex, bidirectional relationship between mental and physical health, aided in part by advancements in neural imaging. Research indicates that a positive outlook is linked to a longer life and a quicker recovery from illness. Optimistic thinking appears to enhance the body's ability to combat disease, while chronic negative emotions can hinder it by triggering inflammation.

Most people are familiar with the **placebo effect**, the phenomenon whereby belief alone can influence physical health. Studies consistently show that when people believe a treatment will help them, they often experience real, measurable improvements—even if the treatment is inactive. This effect highlights the mind's powerful influence on the body. Belief can stimulate the release of neurotransmitters and hormones that support the healing process. Positive thoughts and emotions, in particular, can trigger the release of "feel-good" chemicals, such as **endorphins**, contributing to a genuine sense of well-being (Price et al., 2008).

Conversely, there is the **nocebo effect**, where negative expectations can lead to harmful outcomes. Chronic stress, for example, can flood the body with excess cortisol, which over time weakens the immune system and undermines overall health (Benedetti et al., 2014).

Thus, Hippocrates has been vindicated by science; the mind and body are intricately interconnected. Those ancient Greeks weren't just lazing around, eating olives and complimenting each other's togas; they understood their stuff.

Symptoms serve as messages from the unconscious. The notion that symptoms convey hidden meanings and offer insights into our inner worlds is anchored in the depth psychology of Carl Gustav Jung, the distinguished Swiss psychiatrist and psychoanalyst. He viewed symptoms such as neuroses, mental health issues, emotional disturbances, and behavioural patterns like addictions and compulsions as possible *keys to self-discovery* and healing. Essentially, symptoms can lead us towards wholeness.

Dr Arnold Mindell, an American author, psychotherapist, and educator, enhanced this theory by incorporating Jungian dream analysis to encompass physical symptoms. In the 1960s, Mindell began his analysis with Marie-Louise von Franz, a colleague of Carl Jung. He trained as a Jungian analyst, obtaining his diploma in 1970, and subsequently taught at the C.G. Jung Institute. In the early 1980s, Mindell and his colleagues established the first training programme for Process-Oriented Psychology (POP), known as Process Work.

In *Dreambody*, Mindell suggests that symptoms are not merely physical issues to be treated; they are meaningful messages from the unconscious. He perceives the body as speaking a kind of symbolic language, expressing what the psyche cannot articulate (Mindell, 1982).

Jungian psychology, Taoism, Shamanism, physics, and Indigenous knowledge all contribute to Process Work.

Indigenous knowledge encompasses a rich and evolving collection of cultural traditions, practices, values, and wisdom developed by Indigenous peoples over generations, often in close connection with their local environments. Grounded in oral traditions, observation, and experience, it spans diverse fields such as agriculture, medicine, environmental management, and spirituality. Indigenous knowledge offers a holistic perspective, emphasising the interconnectedness of humans, nature, and the spiritual realm.

This body of knowledge, belonging to Indigenous peoples, has developed over millennia through a deep understanding and respect for the natural world.

Adaptive and steeped in ecological understanding, indigenous knowledge plays a vital role in preserving biodiversity, nurturing cultural identity, and tackling the urgent challenges of climate change and sustainability. The Earth we inhabit is inextricably linked with biological, physical, social, cultural, and spiritual dimensions.

Mindell's Process Work considers the physical body as part of a larger field he named the *dreambody*. This field encompasses all bodily experiences, dreams, symptoms, and patterns of relationships. The dreambody theory offers a distinctive approach to engaging with the unconscious, and as it has informed much of my work, I frequently draw upon Process Work in this book.

When confronted with a severe illness, we often take it personally: "Why me? I've been good! I don't deserve this." To the modern mind, illness is unwelcome and should be overcome as quickly as possible, by whatever means necessary.

However, there is an additional task to undertake. To uncover the *meaning* behind an illness or symptom, we must approach it with curiosity and compassion rather than rejection. By embracing and thoroughly listening to what ails us, we integrate unconscious elements, fostering psychological healing and moving closer to a sense of wholeness. Treating illness with allopathic medicine alone can be likened to pulling weeds from a garden without addressing the underlying soil. The symptoms (the weeds) may vanish for a time, but the root causes remain unaddressed. Sooner or later, the weeds return, often tougher than before.

It's not that the weeding is useless; it can provide relief and order. However, if we never ask *why* the weeds are thriving in the first place, the cycle may continue. True healing, much like gardening, requires us to prepare the ground, not merely tidy the surface.

Learning the language of our symptoms enables us to understand what is being conveyed. Your migraine does not hold the same significance as mine. My arthritis and my neighbour's arthritis do not communicate the same message because, as Jung stated, "When we attempt to understand symbols, we are not only confronted with the symbol itself, but we are brought up against the wholeness of the symbol-producing individual" (Jung, 1964).

At the age of 35, I was diagnosed with ME (myalgic encephalomyelitis; now referred to as Chronic Fatigue Syndrome or CFS). At that time, there was no recognised treatment for this illness. For years, I explored every option that came my way—acupuncture, aromatherapy, shiatsu, Rolfing, reflexology, meditation, Reiki, herbal and homoeopathic remedies, and much more. Some therapies provided minor relief, but none offered substantial help. My savings were exhausted. Invitations to socialise dwindled; my aspirations for the future disappeared like melting snow.

Three years later, I began to wonder whether there might be an emotional component to this illness. Psychotherapy in the 1990s was viewed in some circles as self-indulgent or "woo-woo". After booking my first psychotherapy session in desperation, a few friends expressed concern. "Let sleeping dogs lie," they said.

I wasn't entirely convinced that psychotherapy was particularly effective. Nevertheless, something was troubling me, and I had exhausted all other options. As you will hear from my story, I was astonished by the positive impact of my first session. It soon became clear that untreated trauma and suppressed grief were the underlying causes of my symptoms.

In therapy, I began to recall and share the story of my life. The verb "remember" originates in the Latin "rememorari", which means "call to mind"; "dismember" means to cut into pieces or take apart. I had forgotten and severed myself from my past so thoroughly that significant pieces had slipped into obscurity. My initial commitment in therapy was to summon these fragmented parts back into a cohesive whole, to re-member what had been dismembered. The process of therapy demands patience; the unconscious resists the glaring glare of a floodlight but opens up under the soft glow of a candlelit approach. Timing is critical, and defences constructed in the past, for good reasons, must be respected and carefully dismantled when the time is right.

During sessions, whenever I dismissed my pain or vulnerabilities, my therapist gently reminded me that this was an unhelpful way of defending against more sensitive feelings. Marginalised emotions are pushed into the unconscious, where they wait patiently, occasionally surfacing as emotional and physical symptoms, dreams, and body language. Sleeping dogs don't sleep forever.

The therapy proved challenging at times because it involved change and required me to accept help. I had learned that I should strive to be independent and not ask for assistance; in the tough neighbourhood of my childhood, vulnerability was seen as a weakness, which bred resilience—a commendable quality. However, I had taken it too far.

The symptoms of chronic fatigue syndrome brought me to my knees in a manner that necessitated care I would previously have rejected. For as long as I can remember, I have faced life's challenges head-on, pushing through obstacles with relentless determination. Nevertheless, the condition compelled me to pause, reflect, and reconsider my path, examining my circumstances to ascertain whether proceeding as I had was possible, let alone wise. Recovery required listening to my symptoms and uncovering the root of what ailed me.

I was born and raised in the mid-1950s in Manchester, England—the stomping ground of the artist L. S. Lowry. Now known as the trendy

"Northern Quarter", Ancoats was a deprived area at the time. Characterless new council houses, maisonettes, and high-rise blocks had replaced the old slums of Manchester.

My parents were working-class individuals. My father joined the Royal Navy and fought in World War II, while my mother worked as a cook. After serving as a stoker in the Royal Navy, my father worked long hours as a bus conductor. He suffered from a chronic respiratory illness, yet he rarely took a day off. My mother then became a full-time, unpaid carer for her disabled mother. Without the modern labour-saving appliances we have today, she was constantly cooking, cleaning, baking, sewing, washing, and ironing. I'm not about to tell a story of abuse or neglect; far from it. My parents were wonderful people who did their best for me; I still miss them.

While I have fond memories of my childhood, I also remember being an anxious child. I was terrified of getting out of bed at night to go to the bathroom, and I recall experiencing night terrors and sleepwalking.

Reflecting on my past and understanding how certain life events shape personality—especially during childhood development—I now recognise that I absorbed the unresolved traumas of both my parents: my mother's loss of a brother in active war duty, the loss of her sister due to complications during pregnancy, the trauma of warfare, and the burdens of poverty, accompanied by its close companion, shame.

This is now acknowledged as inherited or transgenerational trauma. Trauma experienced by one generation, like Holocaust survivors or people affected by war, genocide, or systemic oppression, can leave a lasting impact on the generations that follow. These effects can manifest not only psychologically but also biologically, potentially being passed down through factors such as parenting patterns or changes in gene expression (epigenetics).

I remember watching my father gasping for breath during his frequent respiratory attacks; I would anxiously observe my mother, burdened by responsibility and later breathless and clutching her chest or arm, taking medication for angina pain. Occasionally, an ambulance would be summoned. I often felt anxious on the way home from school, afraid of turning the corner into our avenue, dreading the sight of an ambulance and very scared that she had taken ill or passed away.

When I was eight, my sister, who was ten years older, became engaged to be married. Sandra was young and healthy, a beacon of hope. I could not imagine a home without her in it. As I observed the items she was gradually accumulating for her married life, I felt what I now recognise as anticipatory grief.

When I was 13, my sister married her fiancé, John. It should have been a day of celebration; yet, I felt quietly heartbroken. At the wedding reception, I couldn't stop shaking, likely from grief or shock. When a waiter, unaware of my age, offered me a glass of sweet sherry, I gulped it down; it felt like a magical elixir. I stopped trembling and felt calm. In secret, I had another glass of sherry, and from that moment on, I consumed alcohol whenever I could. By the age of 16, I was firmly in its clutches.

For years, when asked, I told people that my mother died when I was 13. It wasn't until I was 30 years of age that I looked in my photo album and found a newspaper obituary of my mother's death and realised that she had died when I was 17.

I was astonished; if it is possible to both know and not know, that was precisely my state. Somehow, I had confused my sister's marriage with my mother's passing.

Sibling loss is often an underestimated area in psychotherapy. Loss does not always imply death. Siblings leaving for university or enlisting in the military, parents separating or divorcing with siblings choosing one parent or the other, or family members moving out to live independently, marry, or cohabit are all significant events. Naturally, these moments are frequently marked by rites of passage, which are typically celebrated yet profoundly impactful. However, they can cause emotional pain for the sibling left behind, and the need to celebrate a sibling leaving the nest can inhibit the expression of loss felt by those remaining. I hope we are becoming better at discussing such matters.

One evening, four years after my sister's wedding, I was at home with my parents. My father was exhausted, dozing in his chair. My mother and I were chatting and watching the television when she suddenly collapsed from a cardiac arrest. Panic ensued, and an ambulance was called. Attempts to resuscitate her proved unsuccessful.

She had been my touchstone for 17 years. Within moments, she was gone forever. A few hours later, my father and I re-entered the room we had occupied earlier, and all that remained of her was a solitary blue slipper.

From early childhood, our brains are intricately linked to our primary caregivers and significant others, creating lifelong emotional patterns that profoundly influence who we become, for better or for worse.

When valued relationships come to an end, the impact is both psychological and physiological. It affects the immune system, particularly the limbic system, which processes and regulates emotions, behaviour, and long-term memory.

In the outstanding book *A General Theory of Love* (2000), the authors explain how love and loss rewire the brain, demonstrating that our nervous systems are not self-contained.

The breakdown of a close relationship puts intense stress on the body. Extended separation doesn't just impact emotions—it disrupts various physical systems. Because disconnection unsettles the body's balance, the loss of a relationship can actually lead to physical illness (Lewis et al., 2000).

When separation is prolonged, this initial anxiety often gives way to lethargy, which deepens into despair. Beyond the emotional toll, extended separation inflicts significant psychological distress and disrupts critical physiological systems, including hormone regulation, cardiovascular function, and immune response.

Following my mother's death, I immersed myself in frantic activity. I left school and found work at an advertising agency. At home, the housekeeping duties mainly fell to me. My father, unknowingly battling emphysema, had little energy left after long days at work. Without his wife, he seemed adrift, giving me housekeeping money for groceries and bills. I felt unanchored, dreading the return to an empty house that no longer felt like home. I had nightmares and flashbacks of the moments surrounding my mother's death. I suffered from insomnia. I was grieving, angry, and afraid, and I began to drink heavily. I know now that these are symptoms of post-traumatic stress disorder, or PTSD.

This was 1973, and I hadn't heard of counselling. I was 17 and desperately in need of help. I booked an appointment with my GP, who prescribed anti-depressants, anti-anxiety medication, and sleeping pills; that was how my grief was managed. Although, of course, it wasn't managed at all; it was suppressed. The medication, along with my coping mechanisms (alcohol, work, and burning the candle at both ends), kept my trauma at bay for another eight years until it could no longer be held back.

I built a career and, at 22, married and moved from Manchester to London. In 1981, weary from repeatedly facing difficult situations and suffering from severe hangovers, I joined Alcoholics Anonymous (AA) and gave up drinking. A few months later, my father passed away. Shortly after, I left my husband and was divorced by the time I was 27. Now alone in London, I struggled to support myself; however, I had friends, and, freed from the rollercoaster of my previous life with alcohol, I enjoyed life in the city.

At the age of 33, while I was working as an Account Director at a leading advertising agency in London, I became seriously ill. I suffered from influenza, from which I did not recover; my doctor diagnosed me with ME. One symptom followed another in rapid succession: intense fatigue that no amount of rest could alleviate and that worsened with physical or mental exertion; agonising pain in my muscles and joints; digestive issues; frequent colds and episodes of influenza; chest infections that resisted treatment; disrupted sleep; and cognitive difficulties (often referred to as brain fog). Walking any distance became utterly impossible.

A few years earlier, a boyfriend had said, "When you enter a room, you do it with a 'whoosh'." Now, I entered with a whimper. I felt like an extremely old woman. All I wanted to do was sleep.

As none of the other treatments had significantly improved my condition, I reluctantly attended my first psychotherapy session. "I feel dreadful all the time," I complained. I had no idea how therapy worked; I felt uneasy, and I'd already resolved that this would be our last session.

"And right now, you're feeling awful? Could you say more?" said Annie, my therapist.

Well, I've got this headache, more of a migraine, without the flashing lights. It's called an atypical migraine. Most people would be in bed with this level of pain, but I've grown accustomed to being in pain. Today, it's crucifying; I can't hold my head up. And I feel I'm 80 rather than in my thirties. I'm constantly ill. I sleep all the time. The doctor told me it was depression, but I don't feel that's right. I'm only miserable because I can't do what I used to do, what I ought to be able to do. Anyone would be miserable if they felt as ill as I do. I've felt this way for five years. And I'm not getting any better. I don't know where to turn.

"OK. If you like, rather than trying to do too much talking today, I've got an idea of how we could work with your headache," she suggested.

"I suppose," I said warily, not knowing what "working with it" could mean.

She said, "Allow your eyes to close and … take three deep breaths, as if breathing into your third eye, in the centre of your forehead."

This sounded like "woo-woo", but I played along.

"Connect with the sensation of the pain in your head, and see if an image comes to mind … don't edit anything; go with the first thing you see …."

BOOM! It was there immediately!

"It's … it's … I feel silly … but … It's my granny's elbow!"

"And could you speak as this elbow? Like, 'I, elbow …'" she prompted.

More and more weird, I thought.

"I, elbow … am old, hidden away, fragile, weak, useless, unsightly. I'm only touched when someone wants to move me from here to there …" I burst into tears at this point, recognising that I felt the same way. I had become my granny!

Annie asked me to say more about Granny Ryder.

Granny's disabilities kept her largely confined to her chair, except when she went to bed. By the time I reached my teenage years, she was well into her eighties—frail, blind, profoundly deaf, and battling diabetes. In my earliest memories, she was a constant presence, seated in the corner of the living room. However, as I grew older, her presence became a source of embarrassment, particularly when friends visited. Unaware of her volume due to her deafness, she would shout, sometimes asking, "Have they gone yet?" To my young eyes, she seemed old and unattractive.

'So, what do I associate with my granny? I feel she held my mother hostage. I suppose she took up all the space. My space. I was a little child. I suppose I wanted more of my mother's attention than she had to spare. I guess I feel Granny Ryder stole my mother from me.'

This was news to me; I hadn't even realised I felt that way until the words left my *mouth*.

'So, you have a bad headache, and when I asked you to see if you could find an image to represent that, you saw her elbow? You've spoken as the elbow, which resonated with you. I'm wondering why your mind offered that part of her anatomy. Do you have any thoughts on that?' asked Annie.

"Good question. Yeah. She couldn't help it, but she took my space! Elbowed me out of the way, I suppose." I laughed, astonished at the spontaneous and apt metaphor provided by my imagination. I couldn't take credit for it; it was already there, waiting for the big reveal.

I left my first psychotherapy session with my head spinning. I had cried, yet the world hadn't stopped turning. Annie neither laughed at nor dismissed my feelings. I also recalled something significant. It felt as though I had placed a bookmark in one of the most painful chapters of my life years ago, and now, as if by fate, the page had fallen open once more, compelling me to confront and resolve what I had long avoided.

This experience shattered every preconceived notion I held about therapy. I had envisioned the stereotypical setup: reclining on a couch, pouring out my thoughts while a therapist jotted down notes and offered profound interpretations. Instead, I found myself immersed in a process that was far more dynamic and transformative—one that required not just my presence but also my active engagement, vulnerability, and courage. My therapist asked open-ended questions that guided me to delve deeper and uncover answers within myself. It was invigorating and relieving.

I can't recall whether my migraine lingered after my session, but I vividly remember leaving that house in Notting Hill, London, and life suddenly felt brighter. My mind had shifted towards the exciting possibilities that the unconscious mind could offer, rather than the limitations of my physical body. I'd experienced my first conscious encounter with my inner world, and my perspective had changed; from that moment on, I began my recovery.

Annie regarded the migraine as a message from my unconscious mind. She took a chance on my willingness to cooperate, and it paid off. Looking back, I truly believe I needed a dramatic start to my therapeutic journey; otherwise, I think I would have given up quickly, as my inner cynic was on steroids at that time.

Back then, I had no idea what techniques my therapist had used to help me achieve such a light bulb moment. Annie had used Gestalt therapy to explore the meaning behind my symptom. Let me unpack what happened.

The starting point is *awareness*. In Gestalt therapy, the cycle of experience can begin when an individual becomes aware of their thoughts, emotions, bodily sensations, and environment in the present moment. *Awareness* is regarded as the doorway to genuine change.

Further along comes *contact*, which represents the meaningful and authentic interactions we have with ourselves, others, and the environment. Contact is about being fully present and engaged, rather than withdrawing or avoiding.

Rather than merely discussing change, Gestalt therapy encourages clients to explore new ways of being through role-plays, dialogue exercises, movement, and creative experiments within the safe space of the therapy room.

Ultimately, this process culminates in *integration*, where new insights, experiences, and patterns are assimilated into a person's sense of self. Integration signifies that the individual does not merely understand something intellectually; instead, they live, feel, and embody it.

This cycle of experience correctly portrays Gestalt therapy as a dynamic, vibrant, and deeply experiential process, transitioning from awareness to contact, and subsequently progressing through experimentation to profound integration.

Annie and I now had something therapeutically significant to engage with. A piece of my psychological puzzle had been examined and carefully placed aside to see how it fitted into the overall picture.

The image of my granny's elbow became a powerful visual metaphor for unresolved childhood wounds. Was I overreaching in drawing a connection between my symptoms at the start of therapy—symptoms that left me feeling and behaving much like my grandmother: disabled and reliant on others? I don't believe so.

There was much more, of course. The losses I carried, the weight of my grief, the grip of my addiction, the sensitivity of my wounded inner child buried deep within my unconscious, and the defence mechanisms that no longer served me; the anxiety I had never expressed; and my over-identification with the carefree clown persona I had crafted to survive—it was all there, laid bare. So much to unpack, so much to heal. Yet, amidst the enormity of it all, I felt a quiet pride. I had taken the first steps, and that, in itself, was a victory. What I had thought was a curse—my illness—had led me to heal wounds from the past, to grow, and to retrain as a psychotherapist two years later.

About two years into therapy—after years of chasing every other possible cure—I finally recovered from ME. Many people never do. Even now, if I push too hard or neglect self-care, a flare-up can serve as a reminder.

When people ask what the illness meant to me, I find myself smiling. Its meaning is hidden in plain sight, in the very letters: ME. In the end, it was about coming home to my Self.

Working with Your Symptoms

If you have troubling symptoms, you can work with them in many ways; below are three examples.

1   Speak as the Symptom

- Identify any areas of tension and take note of them mentally. Imagine scanning your body from the top of your head to the tips of your toes as if using one of those handheld scanners used by airport officials.
- Close your eyes and concentrate on the sensation of the symptom you wish to address, noticing its qualities. Is it stabbing, gnawing, nagging, burning, wrenching, aching, grinding, piercing, heavy, or prickly? Explore it.
- Try to perceive the sensation more acutely. Exaggerate it, amplify it.

- Now, speak in the first person as the symptom. For instance, if your symptom is a stiff neck, you might say, "I am rigid, immovable, and stiff. I cannot give way; I keep my host looking in one direction only, causing pain when required to flex," and so forth.
- Upon completing this exercise, scan your body one more time. Observe whether the areas of tension you identified initially still feel tense. Does your entire body feel the same or different? Take a sheet of paper, date it, and document the symptoms you are exploring. Jot down a few notes about what you expressed verbally as your symptom. Does anything you articulated as the symptom (the microcosm) relate to your entire Self (the macrocosm)? Using the example above, you should enquire, *How am I rigid, unyielding, and unable to understand points of view other than my own?* Avoid asking, "Am I ..." and instead, ask "*How* am I...?"

2   Draw an Image of the Symptom and Speak as If You Were the Image

Your ability to draw is not essential. Many people start by saying, "I can't draw." This reflects the voice of your inner critic, which can impede your growth.

Prepare for this exercise by gathering some paper and a selection of coloured crayons or oil pastels. An A4 artist's pad and some quality drawing materials are worth the investment.

- **Scan your body** from the top of your head down to your toes, mentally noting any areas of tension. Then, choose one.
- **Drawing**: Allow your imagination to guide you and see if a shape, colour, or symbol emerges to represent this sensation. Go with the first thing that comes to mind; don't overanalyse. Visualising may not occur quickly—you might not see colours or shapes but may instead *experience* the concept of something, like a grey cloud, a large boot, or an apple. Trust the process. *Simply draw what you perceive* or believe you perceive. This exercise should take no longer than five minutes to complete. Avoid overdoing it; draw it and then sit back.
- **Place your completed drawing before you**: Close your eyes and envision an expansive blue sky adorned with a few white clouds for decoration. This action resembles pressing the delete button. Now, open your eyes and examine your drawing as if you were encountering it for the first time. Can you perceive anything you didn't notice when you created it? Sometimes, we discover unintended details, which may be a gift from the unconscious mind. For instance, if you've drawn a person and realised you've omitted their eyes or mouth, contemplate what that might signify. In such cases, perhaps there's something you've overlooked. If there's nothing unexpected, don't worry.

- **Taking your drawing, speak as if you were the drawing**: For instance, if you've depicted a tree on a hill, you might start with, "I'm a tree. An oak tree. I'm very old. I may seem isolated, but that's far from the truth. I provide shelter for birds, squirrels, and all manner of insects, and people come to visit me, have picnics beneath my spreading branches, and sometimes wrap their arms around me and talk to me."
- **Recording yourself speaking might be helpful**: If you do this, you might find it beneficial to write the entire thing down and analyse the content, examining whether the tree's narrative aligns with your experiences—in this case, how do you feel isolated? Do you provide a place of shelter and safety for others, etc?
- **Scan your body once more**: Observe whether the areas of tension you noticed at the beginning of this exercise are still taut. Does your entire body feel the same or different?
- **Save your drawing and notes**: Please store them in a specific folder or file. Treat your drawings with care while working on this project; you have given voice to a part of your subconscious.

3 Strike a Pose

This exercise is intended to raise awareness of the symptom's message.

- Start by scanning your body from head to toe, noting any areas of tension. Make a mental note of the sensations that stand out, concentrating on the one that calls to you most strongly as the starting point for your work.
- Now, strive to feel the sensation more intensely. Exaggerate it; amplify it. *Take a position in the room and adopt a posture that represents the symptom you're addressing.* Suppose your symptom is indigestion accompanied by a hot, burning sensation. You might crouch, placing your hands in front of you and shaping them like claws to express anger, rage, or anything you associate with heat and burning. Allow your imagination to guide you as you physically engage your entire body to convey this localised symptom. Explore how it may manifest in your posture, movement, and energy.
- Once you feel you've fully embodied the symptom, shift into a position that represents its opposite—the polar expression—creating balance through contrast. For instance, if you've just embodied an angry cat, you might adopt an open, loving, flowing, and receptive posture that contrasts with your initial position.
- Now, alternate between positions one and two, paying attention to your experiences with each. What do you observe as you transition between the two? Is one preferable? Does one posture feel familiar and comfortable

while the other feels unfamiliar? Do any associations arise during this process? Do the postures remind you of anyone or aspects of yourself? Do the poses you adopt symbolise what's happening in your life or what may need to happen?

- Record your observations once you have mindfully completed this exercise.
- Re-scan your entire body and observe whether the areas of tension you identified at the beginning of this exercise remain tight. Does your body feel the same or different overall? Note any changes you become aware of.

Key Takeaways: My Granny's Elbow—The Symptom Speaks

1 **Symptoms serve as messengers**: Physical symptoms convey unconscious psychological messages, providing opportunities for insight, healing, and growth.
2 **Mind–body connection**: Modern neuroscience supports Hippocrates' long-held belief that mental and physical health are profoundly interconnected.
3 **Process Work (Process-Oriented Psychology)**: Developed by Arnold Mindell, this therapeutic approach integrates Jungian psychology, dream work, and body awareness to help decode symptoms as symbolic expressions of deeper emotional truths.
4 **Re-membering dismembered stories**: Trauma can fragment our life narrative. Therapy can help reclaim those lost parts and reassemble a coherent, healing story of the Self.
5 **Inherited trauma is a reality**: Unresolved emotional pain and grief can be transmitted through generations, shaping how we handle illness and loss.
6 **Gestalt techniques reveal meaning**: Approaches such as speaking *as* the symptom or employing art and body postures help translate physical discomfort into psychological insight.
7 **The body holds wisdom**: Symptoms such as chronic illness may be the psyche's way of urging us to slow down, reflect, and change course.
8 **Therapy demands courage and openness**: Genuine healing means confronting pain, relinquishing outdated defences, and being prepared to *engage* with the unconscious instead.
9 **Creative symptom exploration tools**: Articulating, drawing, or physically embodying symptoms can provide profound insights and pave the way for personal healing.

Recommended Reading

Dahlke, Ruediger (2001). *Symptoms as Metaphors*. C.W. Daniel Company. (A valuable resource for symbolically interpreting symptoms—connecting body, mind, and spirit in illness.)

Levine, Peter (1997). *Waking the Tiger: Healing Trauma*. Atlantic Books. (Introduces Somatic Experiencing and explains how unresolved trauma is stored in the body, often leading to physical symptoms.)

Maté, Gabor (2003). *When the Body Says No: The Cost of Hidden Stress*. Vintage Canada. (Explores how suppressed emotions and chronic stress can manifest as serious illnesses, especially autoimmune conditions and cancer.)

Mindell, Arnold (2001). *Working with the Dreaming Body*. Lao Tse Press. (Mindell's "dreambody" links dreams, symptoms, and emotions as messages from the unconscious, inviting therapists to work with the body as a symbolic field of healing.)

Mindell, Arnold (2010). *ProcessMind: A User's Guide to Connecting with the Mind of God*. Quest Books. (A deep dive into Process-Oriented Psychology, showing how symptoms, dreams, and body experiences can reveal meaning and transformation.)

Sarno, John E. (2010). *Healing Back Pain: The Mind–Body Connection*. Wellness Central. (A thought-provoking read which asserts that many chronic pain conditions arise from repressed emotions, particularly anger and anxiety.)

Shapiro, Deb (2007). *Your Body Speaks Your Mind*. Plaktus. (Shapiro explores how physical symptoms reflect buried emotions, blending chakra theory with Western psychology to read the body as a canvas of the unconscious.)

Van der Kolk, Bessel (2014). *The Body Keeps the Score*. Viking. (A modern classic that explores how trauma reshapes both the body and brain, and how healing must involve the body, not just the mind.)

References

Benedetti, F., Carlino, E., & Pollo, A. (2014). Placebo and nocebo effects: Mechanisms, clinical implications, and ethics. *Nature Reviews Neuroscience, 15*(7), 467–476. https://doi.org/10.1038/nrn3811

Descartes, R. (1996). *Meditations on first philosophy* (J. Cottingham, Trans.). Cambridge University Press. (Original work published 1641.)

Jung, C. G. (1964). *Man and his symbols*. Doubleday.

Lewis, T., Amini, F., & Lannon, R. (2000). *A general theory of love*. Random House.

Mindell, A. (1982). *Dreambody: The body's role in revealing the self*. Sigo Press.

Price, D. D., Finniss, D. G., & Benedetti, F. (2008). A comprehensive review of the placebo effect: Recent advances and current thought. *Annual Review of Psychology, 59*, 565–590. https://doi.org/10.1146/annurev.psych.59.113006.095941

Chapter 10

You May Say I'm A Dreamer
Working with Your Dreams

Carl Jung believed that when we lose touch with myth and story, something essential within us begins to unravel. For him, myths were not merely old superstitions; they were the soul's language, rich with symbols that help us to make sense of our inner world. Without them, we may feel lost, severed from the deeper patterns that impart meaning and direction to our lives.

Consider how many people conclude their day by reading a book, tucking their children into bed, and sharing fairy tales. Or think about the money we invest in books, films, television programmes, and audiobooks—everything from dramas and fantasies to comedies and tragedies. It's clear: we all enjoy a good story. Stories entertain, educate, connect us, and even help us navigate life's twists and turns.

Dreams are stories, too, and have fascinated us for centuries. Consider your dream self as your personal, on-call therapist—appearing each night to provide a mental check-in, offering insights and creative solutions to address whatever is on your mind. It's like free nightly guidance from your subconscious!

Some people swear they never dream, others recall fragments, and some wake up with vivid, film-like details fresh in their minds. However, we all have numerous dreams each night. According to the National Sleep Foundation, the average person dreams four to six times a night, accumulating roughly two hours of dreaming in total (Larson, 2020).

Your dreams provide symbols, images, and coded messages about your life, often conveying information that remains inaccessible to your conscious mind. They may depict a vignette of your current state or function as complementary, wish-fulfilment dreams that reveal what is lacking.

You can uncover their purpose by learning to record, reflect on, and analyse your dreams. A dream may serve as a "snapshot" of your current mental and emotional state, alerting you to something that requires attention, highlighting an imbalance, or even offering wise counsel on how to tackle challenges.

There is broad agreement in psychotherapy regarding the significance of dreams. Sigmund Freud famously called dream interpretation "the royal road to a knowledge of the unconscious activities of the mind" (Freud, 1953). Early in his work, Freud proposed that dreams serve as *wish fulfilments,*

DOI: 10.4324/9781003675099-11

expressing repressed desires. For instance, someone who consciously identifies as a pacifist might dream of committing violent acts, symbolising hidden, denied impulses. However, Freud later expanded his perspective, acknowledging that not all dreams arise from wish fulfilment.

Some dreams reflect current anxieties, unresolved inner conflicts, or even recurring traumatic experiences—what we now recognise as symptoms of post-traumatic stress disorder (PTSD). Others may signify self-punishment, particularly in individuals with a strict internal critic or an overactive superego.

Carl Jung regarded dreams as messages from the unconscious, arising naturally and without bias from the unconscious mind, beyond our conscious control. They reflect raw, unfiltered truth—like nature itself—and, more than anything else, can restore a mindset that reconnects us with our essential humanity, especially when we've lost our way or hit a psychological dead end.

Fritz Perls, one of the founders of Gestalt therapy, believed that dreams encompass the dreamer's rejected and disowned aspects. Imagine waking up from a vivid dream and realising: "Every part of that dream is you." The barking dog? You. The crumbling staircase? You. Even the cold wind blowing through the window? You. That's the Gestalt approach to dreams—not as cryptic messages needing decoding, but as living expressions of the self, rich with hidden parts waiting to be discovered (Perls, 1969).

Perls believed that every element in a dream represents a *fragment of the dreamer's psyche*. He stated that dreams are not puzzles to solve, but *unfinished business*—emotions, needs, or conflicts we have set aside, often since childhood. Unlike Freud or Jung, Perls did not interpret dreams *for* clients; instead, he encouraged them to step inside their dreams and *become* them.

This is the method I adhere to and will explore in this chapter. When presented with a client's dream, I might say, "Don't just talk about the lion in your dream—*be* the lion. Speak as it. Feel what it feels. What does it want? Take a posture representing the lion."

One moment, you're the dreamer; the next, you are the storm, the locked door, the weeping child. Through this bold, theatrical method, the dream's meaning does not come from outside—it aris*es from within*, through direct experience.

While some universal symbols may be helpful (but only if the universal meaning resonates with the dreamer), I tend to avoid dream dictionaries. What matters is not what the dream dog signifies in a dream dictionary or to someone else; it's what the dog represents *for the dreamer*.

Dreams are not merely stories told by the sleeping mind; they form a personal theatre—raw, revealing, and potentially transformative. By stepping into the roles your dreams assign to you, you confront the parts of yourself that you have ignored, suppressed, or forgotten. In doing so, you initiate the journey towards becoming whole.

Dream symbols are unique to each individual. For instance, I might associate dogs with fun, loyalty, and unconditional love; whereas someone else may connect dogs with danger and volatility.

However, there are certain instances where dreams may feature archetypal motifs that are familiar to us all, such as mother, father, child, innocent, lover, caregiver, jester, sage, orphan, hero, villain, and maiden. Individuals in your dream who share your gender may represent your Shadow; those of the opposite gender symbolise your inner masculine (animus) or feminine (anima), while children or small animals may symbolise your inner child.

There are numerous ways to engage with dreams, and many dreamwork models follow the guiding principle that the meanings derived from a dream should come from the dreamers themselves. I incorporate Jungian, Gestalt, and Process-Oriented Psychotherapy models.

In our fast-paced, tech-saturated world, many of us have become disconnected from the present moment and out of touch with our sensory experiences. Fritz Perls famously exhorted people to lose their minds and come to their senses. Gestalt therapy invites us back into the *here and now*, encouraging awareness of bodily sensations, emotions, perceptions, and behaviours as they unfold. Rather than becoming lost in old stories or overthinking, this approach helps us to ground ourselves in direct experience, allowing us to step out of our heads and into our bodies. By tuning in to the body's wisdom, we can reconnect with the richness of our moment-to-moment lives, fostering deeper connections with ourselves, others, and the world around us.

Gestalt techniques have a therapeutic effect by disrupting rational left-brain functioning and evoking right-brain processes more associated with rhythm, intuition, perception, and memory. These techniques utilise metaphor, imagery, body posture, movement, role-play, and the full expression of feelings involving the entire body. The aim is not to abandon rational processes altogether but to integrate the body, emotions, and intellect. Gestaltists encourage experimentation and working at the growing edge of our known identity.

When a client becomes shy or expresses sentiments like, "I couldn't do that" or "That's just not me," it signifies their growing edge (the boundary of their known identity or who they perceive themselves to be). I gently assist clients in experimenting with different approaches to being at that edge and exploring what hinders them from experiencing their complete selves. We disrupt the *selfing* process when we avoid trying a new behaviour or situation. Therefore, if you withdraw from experimenting with changes, you evade your wholeness.

Flirts

Something worth keeping an eye on in therapy—and in dreamwork—is the presence of flirts: those subtle, fleeting signals that invite deeper exploration.

Flirts are gentle signals from the fringes of awareness; fleeting, subtle nudges that seem to say, "Hey, notice me." They can be easily overlooked, yet when we heed them, they often lead to unexpected, frequently useful places.

Sometimes, they manifest in the body. A client says, "I'm fine," but their foot is tapping restlessly. Or perhaps they're sharing something painful, and you catch the flicker of a smile they don't seem aware of. You might even notice something within yourself, like a sudden tightness in your chest or a twist in your stomach. These are body flirts—unspoken signals that don't quite align with the story being told.

As therapists, we might gently ask:

Can we slow down for a second and notice what your foot is doing?

That smile caught my eye—can we take a moment with it?

At other times, it's the room that seems to be speaking. A beam of light falls on a particular object at a key moment. Your attention drifts towards a painting, a crack in the wall, or even a word on someone's T-shirt that suddenly feels significant. These are visual flirts, often subtle but seemingly charged.

We might say:

I keep being drawn to that painting behind you. Can we take a moment to explore what it brings up?

Then there are the sounds—fleeting interactions from the world outside. A siren blares just as someone discusses feeling unsafe. A bird sings loudly at the perfect moment when hope is mentioned. A floorboard creaks during a pause that feels heavy with meaning. These environmental interactions can feel as though the world itself is participating in the session.

A simple way to acknowledge them might be:

Did you hear that bird just now? It came right as you were speaking about longing. Let's stay with that for a moment.

And sometimes, the flirts come from within. A half-formed image appears behind your eyes. A scene from a dream pops into your mind. A metaphor or phrase arrives from nowhere. These *inner flirts* are like poetry rising from the unconscious; they may seem random at first, but they often carry something important.

You might say:

An image just came to me as you were speaking—would you be open to exploring it?

The therapist is part of the field as well. Perhaps you suddenly feel sleepy while the client is talking about something upbeat. Maybe an emotion swells in you for no apparent reason, or a thought won't leave you alone. These *flirts in the therapist* matter. They might reflect something unspoken in the space between you and the client.

A gentle way in could be:

Something in me just felt really moved—let me check in with that. It might be important.

In all these moments, the flirt serves as an invitation—from the body, the unconscious, the environment, or the shared field. When we pause and follow its lead, it can guide us right into the heart of the process.

Working with Dreams

What follows is an example of conducting dream work using a Gestalt/Process Oriented technique with a client.

- Request the dreamer to recount the dream slowly and in the present tense.
- Listen attentively, quietly noting any elements that might be intriguing or significant. However, remember—this is the dreamer's dream, not the guide's!
- As the guide, remain vigilant for elements that capture your attention, known as "flirts".
- Encourage the dreamer to "rewind the dream" several times, and narrate it *using the present tense and first-person* from the perspective of each individual, location, or object in the dream, incorporating every detail. Each element reflects a facet of the dreamer's psyche; of particular interest are those "parts" that may appear trivial, as they might represent the overlooked aspects that hold significant importance.
- After thoroughly examining each aspect of the dream, ask the client to determine whether they understand its message. If not, encourage the dreamer to let the completed work to percolate and to note any subsequent dreams. Sometimes, the meaning of a dream may not become clear until later.

Dream Number One: The Sloth House

According to the method, here is an example of a dream I had, written in the present tense.

I'm travelling, and it feels like a place I've been to before: Dalyan Turtle Beach in Turkey. There are houses on stilts along the edge of a wide river that flows into the sea. I know that animals are cared for in about a dozen homes, each housing a different set of creatures. While I'm not particularly interested in the animals, when I reach the final house, I spot sloths inside, which makes me happy because I adore these gentle creatures. The keepers are soaping them up and giving them a good wash, paying particular attention to their tummies. They're holding the sloths' long arms above their heads while gently circling their tummies in a clockwise motion. The sloths seem happy and contented. I wake up feeling nurtured and joyful.

This dream lingered in my mind, prompting me to dedicate time to ensure that I would not be interrupted while exploring its depths. I documented what emerged spontaneously as I embodied each aspect of it. Here is a transcript of each part "speaking".

House:

I'm a house on stilts. I'm high above the ground to protect myself from being overwhelmed and destroyed by water. Although I prefer to be on solid earth, the ground beneath me isn't always solid; sometimes, it's just mud. People must climb a steep staircase to reach me, and leaving me can be precarious, making it difficult for visitors to come and go.

Animal carer:

I love animals, and sloths are my favourite. I have six sloths to tend to today; each one has been injured or is exhausted and requires some care before being released back into the rainforest. The flood left all the sloths covered in grime, so I cleaned them with a specialised cleanser, focusing mainly on their tummies. I ensure they are thoroughly clean using firm yet gentle circular motions. I hold their arms up as I work—otherwise, they will cling to me like babies, wrapping themselves around my neck. I love that, but there will be time for cuddles once they've had their baths—work, then pleasure.

Sloth:

I'm having a lovely time with this kind young man. He's fed me, and now he's rubbing my tummy, and it feels so good! He's even holding my arms above my head, so I don't have to do a thing except cling to his hands, and that's easy for me. The tummy rub is making me sleepy. But I'm tired. I'm not in my natural environment; I'm in a high-up structure. I can see the ground beneath us and branches nearby, so it would be easy to swing out and chew some leaves. But right now, I think I'll chill out and let him rub my tummy. There's no rush to be anywhere, which is good because I'm a sloth.

The Context to the Sloth Deam

At that time, I was experiencing a flare-up of Chronic Fatigue Syndrome (CFS)—the first in many years. During that week, I reluctantly chose to slow down and accept fewer client referrals. After a working day, I returned home, had something to eat, rested for an hour, watched a bit of television, and slept for around ten hours. Despite this, I still felt fatigued.

Dream message

After reflecting on the material, I realised the dream had an important message: I would benefit from being more like a sloth. I have always been fond of the three-toed sloth—the slowest mammal on Earth, which lives among rainforest trees and moves at a leisurely 0.5 miles per hour (much slower than humans and similar to the pace of London traffic).

I recognise that I often feel insecure and unsteady when my health is poor, as I rely on myself financially. During these vulnerable times, I tend to isolate myself, which makes it difficult for others to help or connect with me. While I'm attentive and nurturing towards others' emotional needs, I rarely provide the same care to myself.

In the dream, I recalled the comforting sensation of having my stomach massaged. I recognised my stomach as a physical and emotional centre, prompting me to realise it needed attention. I prioritised gut health, researching ways to enhance my well-being. Concurrently, I acknowledged the importance of emotional nourishment, whether through meaningful connections with supportive friends or seeking therapy when necessary. I noted that I should reflect further on this and indulge in a massage and reflexology session—a moment of care exclusively for me.

Given my background in CFS, I recognised that significant advancements have been made in understanding the condition since my initial flare-up. I devoted several weeks to researching the vagus nerve, which plays a key role in the symptoms I experienced. Convinced that dysfunction of the vagus nerve may be a primary contributor to my fatigue, I purchased a device designed to tone the nerve. I also resolved to take my fatigue seriously by incorporating daily exercises into my routine to stimulate the vagus nerve, including ear massage, humming, cold water immersion, and breathing techniques.

This process marked a turning point: I began to approach my health with increased seriousness, care, and intentionality, both physically and emotionally.

Dream Number Two: Behind a Painted Smile

A client named Emily shared this dream:

I find myself in a bustling fairground. Stalls offer popcorn, hot dogs, and candyfloss. Hawkers call out to patrons, enticing them to join the carousels,

Ferris wheels, spiralling helter-skelters, rollercoasters, dodgems, swing boats, shooting ranges, and ghost train rides; a queue has formed outside the fortune teller's tent. The music blares, and temptation lurks at every turn. The crowd is lively and boisterous, eyes wide with childlike delight at the bright lights, sights, sounds, and aromas. In the distance, I can hear someone crying out in sorrow.

The fairground's glamour and glitz were alluring, yet I found myself drawn several times to the shadowy aspect of the dream (a "flirt"). I asked her to begin by entering into the consciousness of the person wailing in the background and to speak as that part of her psyche. She remained entranced by the thrilling experience of the fairground, believing that I was missing the essence of the dream; nonetheless, she obliged my suggestion:

The wailing, sad part:

I'm in a place of celebration, joy, and delight. Everyone seems to be having a great time. There are plenty of distractions. Yet, I'm all alone in a tiny tent. There's no light in here, and although I can see the tent flap, I can't get out. I feel paralysed by my misery, and I don't want anyone to see me like this. I don't want to drag everyone down—they're enjoying themselves. I wouldn't be welcome. So, I'll remain here in the gloom, feeling utterly sad.

Emily grew tearful. I asked whether she recognised the part of herself that she had just given voice to; she affirmed that it resonated. However, a part of her could not express its pain and sadness for fear of rejection. As a child, she felt that her vulnerability and sadness were not well received by her family of origin, so she chose to be the jester, upbeat and joyful, while concealing any so-called negative feelings.

The fairground in the dream represents Emily's persona. The isolated, unhappy part resides in her shadow; she denies or represses it. She had valid reasons to suppress this part of herself during her childhood, yet her dreams now signalled that it was time to bring it into awareness. As an adult, Emily continued to rely on the same strategy she had employed in her younger years to feel accepted. However, now the question arose: Could she embrace this neglected part of herself to pursue authenticity and a sense of wholeness? It is often true that what served us well in the first half of our lives can hinder us in the second half. As Jung said,

One cannot live the afternoon of life according to the programme of life's morning; for what was great in the morning will be of little importance in the evening, and what in the morning was true will at evening become a lie.

(Jung, 1933)

I invited Emily to do some more work on this dream.

The Gestalt exercise I suggested was Empty Chairwork. This technique involves engaging in a dialogue with an absent person or a part of oneself, represented by an empty chair. The aim is to enhance self-awareness, resolve internal conflicts, and address unfinished business.

Emily sat opposite an empty chair, while I was slightly off to the side of the "action". I asked her to speak first for the "funfair" part, followed by the "sad, wailing" part. I directed the exchange when I judged it appropriate, usually when the energy of one part began to diminish or when I sensed the other polarity might need to respond.

It can be surprising how quickly feelings emerge using this method.

Funfair:

I'm very popular. I'm bright and exciting, and people love to visit me. I have hundreds of ways to entertain others. I'm noisy and exuberant, and I exist to bring joy to people. I travel frequently as well, visiting different places so that new people can experience me, and I leave quickly so they don't grow tired of me.

Sad part:

Well, good for you. It must be nice to be popular and entertaining. I'm stuck here in the dark, with no friends and nothing to do. Nobody wants to visit me, and I know with absolute certainty that I shall not be welcome if I venture out of hiding. My role in life is to remain in the dark, in pain, with nobody to hear or see me. I'm like a pariah.

Funfair:

I'm sorry you feel that way. You do sound a bit whiny and angry! Are you angry with me? You come across as quite upset. I put in a lot of effort to be popular. I can't help being well liked and in demand.

Sad part:

Whiny! You'd be whiny if you were kept in the dark, depressed, and forced to listen to all the fun of the fair! Of course, I'm bloody angry. Why do you get all the fun? I feel robbed. I feel unlovable. I feel …

At this point, Emily broke down and cried; it was her moment of clarity. During this piece of work, by employing the Gestalt Empty Chair method, we successfully separated the "fun" aspect from the "sad, wailing" aspect. By directing Emily to change chairs at appropriate times, she fully embodied each component and became familiar with them. The next step was to guide her in integrating these two conflicting facets. Every part of the self—even those that seem dysfunctional—exists for a reason, holding purpose and positive intent. Using the empty chair technique, we engaged in a "separate-to-integrate" process, allowing each facet to express itself, be heard, and engage in dialogue. This is what we seek; first, we separate and then integrate to restore harmony and balance to the psyche.

For the remainder of the session, we continued to explore utilising the Internal Family Systems (IFS) model to gain a better understanding of their roles. The IFS model suggests that the psyche comprises numerous parts or sub-personalities, each possessing its own thoughts, emotions, and behaviours. These parts interact dynamically with one another, much like members of a family system. Conflicts or imbalances among the parts can lead to internal distress. The aim of IFS therapy is to restore harmony within this internal system. These parts generally fall into three categories: **Exiles, Managers, and Firefighters**.

IFS therapy involves understanding the various "parts" of yourself that pull you in different directions. It is based on the concept that we all possess these inner parts, each contributing to how we think, feel, and behave. Some parts may be beneficial and supportive, while others might carry pain or express themselves in ways that make life more difficult.

In very simple terms, here's how IFS operates.

Key Ideas

Imagine you possess an internal "family" made up of various parts (sometimes referred to as subpersonalities). For instance, you might have a part that is critical of you (like an inner critic), another part that attempts to avoid challenging situations (perhaps by procrastinating or distracting), and perhaps a part that longs for love and care. These parts are not random; you have unconsciously developed them over time to help you cope with life's challenges.

We don't seek to eliminate any parts; instead, the aim is to help you understand and work with them. Even the parts that may seem negative, such as the inner critic or the angry part, have good intentions—they're generally trying to protect another part of you—the Exiled part—from being hurt. The issue arises when they sometimes go too far or keep you entrenched in old coping patterns that no longer serve you.

A key idea in IFS is that we all possess a Self. This is the calm, wise, and compassionate part of you—the version of you that can listen to your parts without judgement and assist them in working together. The Self functions as the leader of your internal family, and things feel more balanced when it is in charge.

In therapy, you learn to recognise your parts by tuning into them. You may begin to notice certain internal voices surfacing at different moments—perhaps the self-critic that tells you you're not enough, or the anxious part that reacts in specific situations. Rather than suppressing or battling these aspects, the key is to explore them with curiosity and compassion. You might converse with them, using the Empty Chair technique and posing questions like, "Why are you here?" or "What are you trying to protect me from?"

Some parts may carry deep pain, shame, or fear—often referred to as "exiles"—younger aspects of yourself that were hurt or overwhelmed in the past. It is beneficial to connect with these parts compassionately and to extend understanding toward them. Over time, these parts can begin to heal and release the burdens they have been carrying.

Life feels considerably more manageable when your parts are in harmony, with your Self guiding the way. You are less likely to be weighed down by self-criticism, anxiety, or unhealthy habits. Instead, you can face challenges with greater calmness and confidence, and your relationships with others are likely to flourish.

Working in this manner means not pathologising anything; all your feelings, behaviours, and aspects are valuable, even those that may appear problematic.

It's all about understanding yourself and nurturing a kinder, more balanced relationship with the facets of yourself that shape who you are.

As we continued with the Empty Chair work, Emily realised that her sorrowful part was an Exile. Exiles are so named because they have been pushed out of conscious awareness and cast aside. As a child, she had buried her sadness and loneliness, convinced that these feelings made her unlovable. However, exiled parts never disappear; they resurface when triggered, emerging as sadness, anxiety, or other so-called "negative" feelings. They require care and healing.

Emily viewed the funfair aspect as a Manager. Managers represent those parts of you that strive to maintain order and control so that the Exiles are not triggered. They manifest as overly responsible, cautious parts that say, "Let's not go there; it's too messy." These parts may resemble perfectionists, people-pleasers, overly self-critical individuals, or workaholics. Managers focus on prevention, aiming to keep you safe by avoiding situations or emotions that might evoke the Exiles' pain. While their intentions are good, they can occasionally be inflexible and limit your ability to relax or take risks.

As we continued working on different aspects of the dream, Emily recognised one of the funfair visitors, who was drinking and overeating, as a part of herself. This aspect was identified as a Firefighter.

Firefighters spring into action when an Exile is triggered, despite the Managers' efforts. These roles focus on damage control; their job is to extinguish the emotional fire as swiftly as possible. Firefighters often utilise distraction, numbing, or self-soothing strategies, such as binge-watching television, overeating, drinking, using substances, or even becoming angry and lashing out. They aren't subtle; their priority is to alleviate the pain quickly, regardless of the methods employed. While their tactics may offer temporary relief, they can result in harmful long-term repercussions.

Taking a Posture

I asked Emily to adopt a posture representing the fun, sad, and drunken polarities, switching between the positions and focusing on the sensations and emotions that accompanied each posture until she became increasingly familiar with all parts.

To embody her fun-loving side, Emily stretched her arms and legs wide in a star-jump stance, immediately sensing a surge of energy and extroversion.

In contrast, to represent the sad part, she assumed a slumped posture, her arms limp at her sides like a rag doll, as she felt an overwhelming sense of powerlessness and despair.

Her "drunken" persona leaned against the wall, eyes unfocused, reflecting a state of detachment. As she switched between the parts, she became aware of how her mental and emotional state shifted with each different position.

By embodying the parts, Emily came to understand them better.

This dream and Emily's work helped her recognise how she had been favouring one part of herself while neglecting another. Through chair work and posture exercises, she realised that she had been suppressing the aspect of herself that felt depressed, anxious, and isolated (her Exile). She came to understand that this was a childhood coping strategy that no longer served her.

The chairwork also helped Emily observe her Inner Critic more clearly. She hadn't realised how harshly she was treating her Exile. By recognising her critical nature towards herself and others, she began to understand how this negatively affected her relationships.

Emily made significant progress towards self-acceptance as she endeavoured to connect with these aspects of herself. She began to embrace herself, flaws and all, which marked a decisive step forward in her personal growth.

Tips for Working with Your Dreams

- If you find it difficult to remember your dreams, set your intention by drinking water before bed and saying, "When I wake up, I will have another drink of water and recall my dream."
- Buy a dream journal and place it by your bed.
- If you believe the meaning of the dream is immediately clear, pause for a moment! Dream messages should reveal something new; the unconscious

doesn't waste time repeating what you already know. If you think it's merely a rehash of a television programme you watched that day, reconsider your perspective. Try examining the dream from different angles to uncover deeper significance. Dreams can possess multiple meanings, and there is no single "correct" interpretation.

- Record your dreams each day, ideally as soon as you wake. Once you establish the habit of documenting your dreams, they will start to connect, and you will begin to notice the emerging themes.

- When you awaken, keep your eyes closed for a few moments to prevent any extraneous thoughts from entering your mind before you have the chance to capture your dream.

- Interpretations can differ because each interpreter brings their history and baggage. Thus, the dreamer should be cautious about sharing their dreams and placing too much importance on others' interpretations. If the meaning of the dream eludes you, leave it be. Wait for the next dream and see if it provides any clarity; the true significance may take time to reveal itself.

- Exercise caution with dream dictionaries. There are, of course, symbols that possess a universal quality—archetypal symbols that most of us recognise, such as the Grim Reaper, the Divine Mother, the Innocent Child, the Hero, the Maiden, fire, water, and so on. However, the dreamer's association with a symbol is more significant than what any dream dictionary might suggest. If I dream of a cat, my associations might be love and devotion; someone else may associate cats with witchcraft and selfishness.

- Take note of the emotion you felt upon waking from the dream. Sometimes, this is the feeling you need to "wake up" to. Therefore, if you wake up feeling anxious, it may be important to recognise the extent of your anxiety.

- If you can remember only a fleeting moment from the dream, jot that down. For instance, if you wake up and recall just a wisp of smoke from a cigarette, take note of it.

- Avoid making any moral judgements about your dreams.

- Refrain from altering any elements that do not seem to fit into the story.

- Illustrate what you saw in your dream ("sketch-and-reflect").

- Give the dream a title to help you recognise emerging themes.

- Pay attention to puns. For example, you might dream of a bin marked with the letter "D". Have you been feeling rejected lately? Could this dream suggest that you feel rejected, "binned" (bin-D, see what I mean?), or cast aside?

- Share your dreams in therapy as early in the session as possible, rather than at the end of the session. This way, you can learn to engage with your dreams and use them to guide and enrich your life.

- There are various methods for recording dreams. Some individuals prefer to document them on their phones or share them with others in a dream group. However, remember that your associations with the elements in your dream hold more significance than those of anyone else. If someone else offers an insight that resonates, that's perfectly acceptable; if it doesn't, simply set it aside.

- Treat your dreams with respect. Avoid dismissing them as bizarre or meaningless.
- A word of caution: Be careful when working with dreams, including those of others. Engaging with dreams involves the unconscious mind and may uncover content that you—or they—aren't prepared to confront.

Key Takeaways: Working with Your Dreams

1 Dreams Are Your Inner Guides

- Dreams function as nightly narratives from the subconscious, offering insight, emotional check-ins, and creative solutions, much like a personal, built-in therapist.

2 Dreams Reflect the Unconscious Mind

- Sigmund Freud saw dreams as disguised fulfilments of unconscious desires.
- Carl Jung viewed them as nature's truth-telling mirror. He believed they compensated for the one-sided nature of our waking consciousness and could offer glimpses of where we are heading emotionally or spiritually.
- Fritz Perls regarded them as revealing rejected aspects of the Self.
- All perspectives highlight the power of dreams.

3 Dreamwork Deepens Self-Awareness

- Interpreting dreams using Jungian, Gestalt, and Process Work models can reveal hidden conflicts, unprocessed emotions, and overlooked aspects of the psyche.

4 Everything in a Dream Is a Part of You

- Dream elements symbolise aspects of the dreamer. Exploring each through embodiment, voice, or movement brings the unconscious to light.

5 The "Growing Edge" Is Where Change Happens

- Gestalt therapy encourages stepping beyond the familiar, challenging identity limits ("That's just not me") to allow previously disowned parts into consciousness.

6   *The Body Unlocks Meaning*

- Embodying dream figures or emotions through posture, gesture, or physical expression can unveil insights that the conscious mind might resist.

7   *From Persona to Shadow to Wholeness*

- As seen in Emily's dream, therapy can help reconcile the cheerful mask (the Persona) with the hidden sorrow (the Shadow)—an important step toward authentic living.

8   *Dreams Are Not One-Size-Fits-All*

- Personal associations hold greater significance than generic meanings. Although archetypes may emerge, it is your associations that impart truth to the dream.

9   *Dreamwork Can Heal Trauma*

- Through techniques such as the Empty Chair and Internal Family Systems, we can compassionately meet exiled parts of ourselves, often rooted in childhood trauma.

10   *Dream Rituals Enhance Recall and Meaning*

- Practices such as journalling, titling dreams, sketching, and reflecting on dreams, along with noting morning emotions, cultivate a deeper relationship with your inner world.

Recommended Reading

Here is a list of books with approaches that emphasise embodiment, direct experience, and symbolic exploration rather than interpretation alone.

Goodbread, Joseph (1987). *The Dreambody Toolkit: A Practical Introduction to the Philosophy, Goals and Practice of Process-Oriented Psychology*. Penguin. (A clear and hands-on guide for therapists or anyone wanting to apply Process Work tools to dreams, symptoms, and states of consciousness.)

Hamilton, Nigel (2014). *Awakening Through Dreams: The Journey Through the Inner Landscape*. Routledge. (Hamilton blends Jungian and alchemical insights to present dreams as a bridge to the soul and a guide for transformation.)

Johnson, Robert A. (2010). *Inner Work: Using Dreams and Active Imagination for Personal Growth*. Harper Collins. (Johnson views dreams as messages from the unconscious, employing a four-step process, culminating in ritual, to facilitate insight into embodied integration.)

Mindell, Arnold (1982). *Dreambody: The Body's Role in Revealing the Self.* Sigo Press. (A foundational Process Work text. Introduces the concept of the "dreambody" and how body symptoms and dreams are interconnected.)

Mindell, Arnold (2001). *Working with the Dreaming Body.* Lao Tse Press. (Deepens the exploration of dreams, body signals, and altered states of consciousness. Practical examples show how dreams can be worked with physically and symbolically.)

Perls, Fritz (1969). *Gestalt Therapy Verbatim.* Real People Press. (Perls' classic lectures on dreamwork in Gestalt. Raw, direct, and practical—this is the source of the "every part of the dream is you" method.)

Perls, Fritz (1973). *Dreams and Nightmares: A Book of Gestalt Therapy Sessions.* Joanna Cotler Books. (Real transcripts of Perls' dream sessions. Shows how dreams are enacted through role-play and embodiment in therapy.)

Polster, Erving & Polster, Miriam (1974). *Gestalt Therapy Integrated: Contours of Theory and Practice.* Vintage Books. (Includes a comprehensive and accessible section on working with dreams in Gestalt, including the "Empty Chair" technique.)

References

Freud, S. (1953). The interpretation of dreams. In J. Strachey (Ed. & Trans.), *The standard edition of the complete psychological works of Sigmund Freud* (Vols. 4–5). Hogarth Press. (Original work published 1900.)

Jung, C. G. (1933). *Modern man in search of a soul* (W. S. Dell & C. F. Baynes, Trans.). Routledge & Kegan Paul.

Larson, J. (2020, 10 February). How long do dreams last? *Healthline.* Available at https://www.healthline.com/health/how-long-do-dreams-last#how-long-dreams-last

Perls, F. S. (1969). *Gestalt therapy verbatim.* Real People Press.

Chapter 11

A Tale of Two Faces

Persona and Self

Noel strode confidently across the waiting room to greet me, taking my hand as he said, "Great to meet you, Lynn." His aftershave wafted towards me. He wore a smart suit, his jacket casually draped over his shoulder, an immaculate shirt with the sleeves rolled up to his elbows, and an expensive watch on his wrist—every inch the successful businessman.

Despite his confident presentation, Noel's slightly stooped posture gave me pause for thought. Our bodies tell the stories we cannot express. Imagine your body as an ever-evolving sculpture, continuously shaped by your experiences. If, as a child, you absorbed negative beliefs about yourself and accepted them as truth, certain areas of your body may reflect this internalised injury, becoming stiff, weakened, or emotionally numb and shielded. The body then forms around those deadened or defended aspects, conveying a story you may have forgotten. This concept is known as character armour, introduced by Wilhelm Reich (1949) and further developed by Alexander Lowen (1958).

Wilhelm Reich (1897–1957) was an Austrian physician and psychoanalyst from the generation that followed Freud, and he remains one of the most daring and unconventional minds in the history of psychiatry. As a controversial figure, he pioneered groundbreaking approaches, including body psychotherapy, bioenergetic analysis, and primal therapy, forever altering our understanding of the connection between the mind and body.

Reich was the first to discuss character armour. He noticed that when people suppress emotions such as anger, sadness, or fear, they don't simply disappear—they are stored in the body. This manifests as muscle tension or stiffness, such as tight shoulders or a puffed-up chest. It is as if your body is donning a suit of armour, but it also keeps you trapped. Reich said, "Character armour is the total of character attitudes which an individual develops as a defence against emotional excitation, resulting in a chronic muscular rigidity" (Reich, 1949).

Reich believed that character armour doesn't merely shape our personalities—it moulds our bodies as well. A person who constantly tries to appear tough might hold themselves stiffly and unyieldingly, while someone gripped by fear may shrink inward, with their shoulders hunched. This armour, Reich

DOI: 10.4324/9781003675099-12

argued, obstructs the natural flow of energy through the body, resulting in emotional and even physical distress. By releasing this chronic tension, he claimed, people could unlock a deeper sense of vitality, freedom, and emotional well-being.

Alexander Lowen (1910–2008) was an American physician and psychotherapist, as well as a student of Reich, whose ideas he embraced and expanded upon. He developed Bioenergetics, a discipline that examines the intricate relationship between bodily expression and emotional well-being.

Lowen identified five distinct character types, each shaped by unique patterns of emotional and physical responses. For instance, while some individuals adopt rigid tension to convey strength, others unconsciously collapse inwards to avoid confrontation.

These patterns typically stem from how we learn to cope with stress or trauma during childhood. Lowen's approach focused on reconnecting with the body. He believed that by concentrating on aspects such as posture, breathing, and movement, one could gain insight into one's emotional state. To achieve this, he employed exercises to release tension, including deep breathing, stretching, and allowing oneself to scream or cry. His method centred on breaking free from the confining "armour".

The work of Reich and Lowen can be summarised in a few key points:

- The armour offers protection; it acts as a defence mechanism that shields you from pain, yet it complicates the ability to experience joy, love, or connection.
- Your body tells a story; emotional baggage isn't merely in your mind—it manifests throughout your body. Your posture, breathing, and the manner in which you carry tension convey a great deal about your experiences.

Healing is physical. To release old pain, you must engage your body. This may involve breathing deeply, moving in new ways, or expressing emotions that have been trapped for years.

Reich and Lowen focused on assisting individuals in shedding their emotional and physical defences, allowing them to live more freely and wholeheartedly. Shedding defences is similar to removing a heavy suit of armour that you didn't even realise you were wearing!

Noel's chest area appeared rigid, characterised by a slight stoop and a subtle collapse around his solar plexus. The chest region is linked to the heart chakra; unresolved grief frequently results in this frozen quality. Meanwhile, the solar plexus relates to the third chakra, which is associated with will, power, and self-confidence. His collapse in this area reinforced my reflections on whether he had faced challenges that compromised his sense of agency or autonomy.

He began by sharing his current struggles. A high-flyer in the City of London, he enjoyed a lavish lifestyle, residing in one of the city's most expensive areas and having a second home in the countryside. His demanding job consumed most of his time, leaving him rarely able to see his wife and their three young children, aged five, seven, and nine. At his wife's urging, he sought therapy after she expressed frustration at his emotional unavailability, describing him as a man whose thoughts revolved solely around his work. He admitted to feeling disconnected from his children, sensing that his wife had taken on full responsibility for parenting.

> *I've overheard her on the phone, chatting with one of her girlfriends: "He's a fantastic financial provider, yet when it comes to connecting with me, forget it! He doesn't understand how he feels most of the time, and whenever I try to discuss my feelings, he seems bewildered." I mean—it's bloody demoralising. I don't know what she wants. I'm doing my best.*

Noel's career was successful, with another promotion on offer; however, this also presented problems.

> *People say I'm great at my job; I'm invited to give after-dinner speeches and speak at conferences. Yet, I always feel like an impostor. I think I haven't grown up. I'm a schoolboy in an expensive suit. I have no real friends and don't know how to make them, and my wife thinks I'm emotionally stunted.*

We began discussing his childhood experiences, family dynamics, school experiences and so forth.

With a father whose job in the oil industry involved lengthy stints living abroad and a mother who accompanied him, it was decided that an English boarding school would provide Noel with the stability lacking in a life of constant upheaval. Sent to boarding school at just seven years old, he vividly recalled kissing his parents goodbye, feeling a mix of excitement and curiosity about the new adventure ahead. However, his young mind couldn't fully grasp what awaited him. During the first few nights, the dormitory was filled with the muffled cries of new boarders; yet, none of the older boys offered reassurance or comfort. Those who had been at the school for some time had learned to suppress their vulnerable emotions. Noel absorbed this lesson well.

Although some pastoral care and staff were available for the children to speak with, Noel found the situation distressing and wished to return home.

Boarding School Syndrome is now recognised as having a complex and varied range of symptoms, which may include difficulties with intimacy, workaholism, an inability to relax, feelings of isolation, substance abuse, and a pervasive sense of failure. Individuals may also struggle to acknowledge their emotions and can experience physical issues, sleep disturbances, and sexual dysfunction.

These individuals often grapple with excessive self-criticism and an unyielding drive for perfection, which only exacerbates their inner turmoil.

Many also struggle with lingering feelings of isolation and unresolved grief stemming from early childhood separations. Such experiences can shape maladaptive attachment styles, resulting in patterns of avoidance, insecurity, or heightened anxiety in relationships. Addressing these lasting effects in therapy is crucial for helping clients process early wounds and strive towards healthier relationships with themselves and others.

While exceptions may exist, my experience as a therapist working with individuals who were placed in care at a young age suggests that the odds are significantly stacked against them. These early separations often hinder the ability to form functional, intimate relationships in adulthood.

Noel was forced to develop a strong persona from a young age.

The word *Persona* is derived from the Latin word for *mask*. It refers to an individual's character or identity in a specific context, often used to convey a particular image or fulfil a role. Carl Jung (1953) introduced the concept of the Persona as part of his theory of the psyche. It represents what we show the world, mediating between the inner and outer environments. While the Persona is necessary for social functioning, over-identification with it can lead to a loss of the authentic Self and psychological distress.

Noel and I had plenty to discuss, but I decided to start with a creative exercise to get things moving. I gestured towards the pastels and the artist's pad on the table, inviting him to explore his psyche through drawing. As expected, he cautioned me that he "couldn't draw"—nearly every client says this (the inner critic is always present). Nevertheless, he agreed to give it a try, which was all we needed to begin.

I asked him to close his eyes, wait for my question, and, upon hearing it, see whether his imagination could respond with a symbol, some colours, or shapes. My question was, "What do you show to the world?" I instructed him to accept the first thing his imagination provided and not to edit anything.

I asked him to open his eyes and describe what he saw. It was a robot. Noel was astonished by the image he had crafted.

I initially asked Noel to close his eyes and envision a vast blue sky to clear his mind, and then open his eyes to revisit his drawing as if he were seeing it for the first time. Was there anything there that he hadn't noticed while drawing it?

He noticed that it was entirely black and white; the robot possessed no mouth, and its left wheel was square.

I asked Noel whether any of that resonated with him. How was he like that robot? He acknowledged that the description felt surprisingly accurate and suspected that his work colleagues would agree. Perhaps even his wife and children had made similar observations in the past. When I pointed out that the robot he had drawn lacked a mouth, he reflected that this mirrored his tendency to withhold his true thoughts. Then, I wondered about the robot's square left wheel—what might that signify?

I don't feel very stable; I often feel ungrounded, as if something could topple me over if I don't keep earning money and proving myself; also, I've just been diagnosed with plantar fasciitis in my left foot!

I asked him to look again at his drawing and see if he experienced any physical sensations in his body while he examined it or felt any emotions. "Not really, although I'm amazed. I've drawn a wonky left wheel, and I've got a wonky left foot." I encouraged him to continue observing his drawing, the representation of what he presents to the world, and to wait for any feedback from his body. "Well, perhaps I feel a little sad." I inquired about where he felt that emotion. He pointed to his heart. "Sad because ...?" I prompted. "Well, it doesn't feel very human. It feels, as I mentioned, cold ..."

This represented progress. Noel was now beginning to tune in with his body.

I then asked him to hold the robot drawing in front of his face, as if it were a mask, and to speak in the robot's voice. After a bit of persuasion (first-timers often report feeling silly when engaging in this activity), he began:

I'm manufactured. I'm clever and reliable. I'm cold to the touch, and I move around on my wheels. I'm programmed not to get too close to people or objects, so I don't get in anyone's way. People appreciate me because I'm helpful, and they sometimes laugh at my expense, knowing I won't take it personally. I do my job very well, and that's why I exist. I have no expectations of the humans around me—they needn't worry about the types of things that seem to trouble their human colleagues—things like birthdays, or whether they're tired or facing difficulties at home, because they know I can keep going as long as I'm put to sleep at night and charged up, ready for the next working day.

We explored whether any of this resonated with Noel. He expressed surprise at how much he and this robot were alike! Worryingly so, he added.

I then asked Noel to close his eyes, await my next question, and see if his imagination could respond with a symbol, some colours, or shapes.

My second question was, "What do you *not* show the world?"

I reminded him to draw the first thing his imagination provided and not to edit anything. As he opened his eyes, he took his time sketching the image while I observed in quiet anticipation. A therapist must cultivate patience, offering the same unwavering attention a nurturing parent provides when witnessing a child's creative expression. There was no need for immediate interpretation; his drawing itself would reveal its meaning in due course.

I view the drawing process as the client giving birth to an aspect of their psyche, and I hold the space as I would if someone were giving birth; at that moment, I'm the midwife. Of course, I may have my thoughts, but I keep them in check until the client has made their associations.

His second drawing portrayed the ocean. A ship sailed across the sea, while a dragon leapt from the ocean depths, breathing fire towards the vessel. Noel sat back and exhaled loudly.

That's weird. I have no idea where that came from!

Once again, I encouraged Noel to close his eyes and imagine a vast blue sky to clear his mind of the image before reopening his eyes to view his drawing anew, as if for the first time. Was there anything he hadn't noticed while creating it? The ocean spanned two-thirds of the page. "It looks *very* deep," he commented.

I asked him to hold up his drawing and speak in the first person as each part of it.

*I'm an **ocean**. I'm deep and turbulent. I'm uncharted. I harbour creatures that live within me. People both adore and fear me. However, I also have rubbish thrown into me, and I strive to rid myself of it; yet, it ultimately returns to me. Now, I require assistance to clear out all the waste.*

*I'm a **dragon**. I guard treasures at the bottom of the ocean, so I've had to adapt to life underwater. I've come up for air, and I can see a boat, which I don't like the look of. Are they throwing rubbish into the ocean? Perhaps they're after my treasure. I'm going to scorch them with my fiery breath.*

Then:

*I'm a **boat**. I'm taking these people sailing, and we were having a lovely time, but a dragon just leapt from the water and is trying to burn us. If I want to survive, I must get away and stay afloat!*

Then, speaking as the ocean, he said:

*I am the **sea**. I'm life-giving and rejuvenating. I sustain countless creatures, and I feel endless. I can be calm and soothing, yet also immensely destructive. I am unknown to many people. Even submariners and divers don't know everything about me.*

"So, how are you a rejuvenating force? How do you give life? How are you, unexplored? Unknown?" I asked him.

I'm unsure about rejuvenation. I suppose I've given life to my children, and I continue to sustain them by ensuring their survival. I'd like to think I provide them with a good quality of life as well. My wife contributes by working hard and supporting our lifestyle financially. Am I unexplored? Absolutely! I don't know myself, and nobody seems to bother looking deeper than the surface. But perhaps I don't reveal too much to them. Maybe there's not much to reveal; that's my fear.

"As the ocean, you spoke of being feared and dumped on. Does that ring any bells?" I asked.

I've received feedback that my subordinates find me intimidating, but I'm not. At least, I don't believe I am. I can come across as rather aloof and not overly interested in all that touchy-feely business. I have a great deal on my plate both at work and at home. I have my own issues to manage without running around being a shoulder to cry on for my colleagues!

"Does that remind you of anything? That last bit—not being a shoulder to cry on?" I asked.

Noel paused before answering, quietly,

That sounds a bit like my early experience of boarding school. Perhaps all the other kids were dealing with their issues without taking on the problems of the newer, younger boarders.

He drew a sharp breath at that moment and looked directly at me. His eyes were moist. He sat in silence. I asked him, if possible, to experience whatever he felt and to embrace the feeling without judgement. After a few moments of stifling his tears, he said:

Wow. I didn't see that feeling coming. My heart started racing, and I thought I was going to cry. I've never been able to recall my early boarding school days with any emotion. What happened? How did I end up back there?

I noticed a potential theme when Noel expressed the phrases "I have my stuff to deal with …" and "shoulder to cry on". As he said this, his voice softened, and he sounded very young. I took a chance, which resulted in a moment of insight for him. Noel was beginning to connect with long-repressed emotions.

We concluded the session, and I encouraged Noel to bring back his drawing if he wished to continue working on it. I then spent some time reflecting on and noting his drawings.

The dragon is a complex, universal archetype—the mythical dragon, the "winged serpent", merges serpent and bird, symbolising Spirit. In Jungian symbolism, dragons can represent inner darkness, chaos, and the need for self-discovery.

The immensity of the ocean can symbolise emotions, the feminine, the vast, unconscious mind, and the collective unconscious. My unvoiced interpretation of Noel's drawing revealed that his unexplored unconscious harboured treasures yet to be discovered.

As the dragon, he was prepared to "scorch" anyone getting too close or threatening to "contaminate" him. I wondered whether he was unconsciously expressing a fear of allowing me to delve too deep, too soon, so I decided to go gently for a while, as his Ego (the boat) had instructed, because, in psychotherapy, as in life, timing is crucial.

Recommended Reading

Goffman, Erving (1990). *The Presentation of Self in Everyday Life*. Penguin. (Goffman likens social interaction to theatrical performance, emphasising roles and masks.)

Jung, Carl Gustav (1959/1991). *The Archetypes and the Collective Unconscious*. In *The Collected Works of C. G. Jung*. Routledge. (Foundational work that introduces Jung's idea of the persona as the social mask we wear.)

Jung, Carl Gustav (1964). *Man and His Symbols*. Aldus Books. (Written for a general audience. A more accessible introduction to Jung's ideas about the self, shadow, and persona.)

Laing, R. D. (1970/2010). *The Divided Self*. Penguin. (A radical psychological and philosophical take on mental illness as a struggle between false self and authentic self.)

Miller, Alice (2008). *The Drama of the Gifted Child*. Basic Books. (Explores how children develop personas to meet parental expectations, often losing connection to their true selves.)

References

Jung, C. G. (1953). *Two essays on analytical psychology* (R. F. C. Hull, Trans., 2nd ed., Vol. 7). Princeton University Press. (Original work published 1928.)

Lowen, A. (1958). *The language of the body*. Macmillan.

Reich, W. (1949). *Character analysis* (3rd ed.). Orgone Institute Press. (Original work published 1933.)

Chapter 12

Carry My Gold

Retrieving Projections

Projection is a defence mechanism where we attribute our feelings, thoughts, or traits to others, often without realising we are doing so.

Although Freud didn't initially employ the term "projection" formally, he described the concept early in psychoanalytic theory, particularly as a *defence mechanism* in which the ego rejects an idea it finds unacceptable by attributing it to something or someone outside itself (Freud, 1922).

Sometimes, when we feel something we're not fully aware of—or aren't ready to confront—we unconsciously assume it's coming from someone else. For instance, if you're angry at yourself but can't fully handle that emotion, you might begin to believe that someone else is angry with you. Or, if you're overly self-critical, the world around you may suddenly feel populated by judgmental people. This is projection: your inner emotional world gets transferred onto others, making it seem like their issue when, in reality, it's your own.

Freud contended that the origins of projections stem from a child's perceptions of their primary caregivers and siblings. For example, if we have had a negative experience with an angry father, we may unconsciously project these internalised images onto authority figures—be they doctors, supervisors, government institutions, or even strangers who bear a slight resemblance to our father or his behaviour.

Until we recognise and reclaim these projections, our perception of such individuals, situations, or organisations will remain distorted. The angry father, for example, becomes an internalised "object" within the psyche. Consequently, the child—now an adult—might unknowingly reflect that anger in their behaviour, perpetuating the patterns they once endured.

When we form a snap judgement about someone, we often find, with additional information, that we were mistaken. This can be a misjudgement, and we move on.

However, a person with a defence mechanism of projection will vigorously defend themselves and deny that they are projecting.

What is hysterical is historical. Thus, in therapy, we explore the client's past to understand who that person reminds the client of. Jung said that throughout life, we keep encountering reflections of ourselves, each time in a different form (Jung, 1953).

DOI: 10.4324/9781003675099-13

Collective Shadow Projections

From around 1400 to 1775, an estimated 100,000 people—many of whom were tortured into false confessions—were prosecuted for witchcraft in Europe and America. Although historical witch hunts may seem like distant memories, the dynamics of shadow projection remain very much alive today. Whenever we observe individuals or groups demonised and blamed for societal ills, it is worth asking: What shadow material is being projected here?

The witch hunts represented a collective psychological phenomenon. Entire communities projected their shadow material onto individuals. The qualities they could not tolerate in themselves—lust, greed, envy, and sometimes merely a desire for vengeance—were "discovered" in witches. This enabled communities to exorcise their guilt and fear by eliminating the perceived source. Blaming a "bewitching" woman allowed them to maintain their halos while outsourcing their sins. Witches became the ultimate scapegoats for the cultural and religious upheavals of their time.

The Christian Church, eager to eradicate anything that even hinted at paganism, focused on older women practising herbal medicine, labelling them as broomstick-riding pagans and adding a layer of sexual hysteria that resulted in accusations steeped in strange fantasies of orgies and seductive spells.

Society projected its own shadow onto so-called witches, who became scapegoats and repositories for everything that society feared. The accused were often women (though not exclusively) who didn't fit the mould—widows, healers, the poor, or simply the eccentric. These individuals were different, and their differences could pose a threat to a tightly knit community. Those in positions of power, or under stress, needed someone to blame for their misfortunes. Instead of admitting, for instance, that the crop failure might have been caused by bad weather or their lack of agricultural planning, it was easier to point the finger at someone in the village—"It's because Old Maggie is consorting with the Devil"—when she was merely tending her herb garden.

Witch trials remind us that our hidden fears, if left unchecked, can become dangerous, not just for individuals but for society as a whole. While we may no longer burn witches, understanding this history can help us avoid repeating it in subtler, modern forms. Old Maggie was not a witch; she was simply different, and that was enough to make her a target for everyone else's Shadows.

Let us now look at how projections reveal themselves in the consulting room.

Negative Projections: Carry My Sh*t

My client, Dennis, was utterly convinced that his wife, Alicia, was unfaithful, despite the lack of any evidence. Over time, it became apparent that he had been harbouring an attraction to a colleague. Unwittingly, he projected his own suppressed desires onto his wife, perceiving them as her feelings rather than his own. Nevertheless, the object of our projections (in jargon, the *projicient*) often provides us with something to which we can attach them. In this instance, Alicia was secretive, fiercely protective of her personal space, and not always inclined to disclose where she had been, even if it was merely out shopping; she conveyed that she felt controlled. Projection is an unconscious defence mechanism. In the case of negative projection, we possess traits or desires that we find unacceptable and attribute them to others; in a sense, we are saying, "Here, you carry my sh*t."

It is tempting to think that the other person is entirely to blame. However, to understand ourselves and achieve personal growth, we must take responsibility for our unconscious patterns. The journey doesn't conclude with merely recognising that we have projected onto another; we must actively retrieve the disowned trait, integrate it, and transform it, turning lead into gold. Chapter 5, "Alchemy: A Journey of Transformation", provides further elaboration.

Positive Projections: Carry My Gold

Positive projections are a subtle psychological trick we all employ from time to time. Unlike negative projections, where we unconsciously transfer our fears and perceived flaws onto others, positive projections recognise our hidden strengths, talents, and admirable qualities—seeing in others what we often overlook in ourselves. It's as if you're viewing someone through a golden, sparkly filter and that sparkly gold could very well be yours! We are simply using someone else as a mirror. In a way, we are falling in love with our potential.

When we meet someone and think, "Wow, they're so confident! So capable! I wish I could be like that"—heads up! What you admire in them often already exists within you. Positive projections are our subconscious way of indicating, "This is a part of me I haven't fully recognised or embraced yet."

These projections tend to appear in those we admire, respect, or feel awestruck by. Reflect on the childhood heroes, or those who inspire or captivate you today. What is it about them that is so compelling?

The qualities we admire in others often reflect aspects of ourselves that are waiting to be acknowledged and nurtured. Rather than simply projecting these traits onto someone else, consider developing them within yourself. The qualities that captivate you signal from your subconscious, "Hey! This is your path forward." This is not about imitation; it's about drawing inspiration from your positive projections to help you reveal those qualities in your unique style. Chapter 8, "It's Elementary: What's Your Type?", assists in developing qualities.

The Downside of Positive Projections

It's easy to understand why negative projections would benefit from analysis. But positive projections? What's the harm?

Positive projections arise when you idealise someone, perceiving them as flawless or far superior to their true selves. While these notions may appear harmless and flattering to receive (but remember, there's only one way to go when you are placed on a pedestal), they can lead to considerable trouble if one is not cautious.

You are likely to feel disappointed when you place someone on a pedestal. No one is perfect; eventually, they will let you down or fail to meet your expectations. This can leave you feeling frustrated or even betrayed. The truth is, those expectations were not reasonable to begin with.

Another concern is that positive projections can foster an excessive reliance on others. When you perceive them as exceptional, you may depend on them for happiness or validation. You are thereby relinquishing your power without even realising it. That mentor, partner, or friend you regard as "perfect" can quickly transform into the one you rely on for everything, making it easy to lose your sense of independence.

Then there's the issue of overlooking your potential. When you see someone as courageous, talented, or confident, it's easy to assume they possess qualities you lack. However, the very trait you admire in them may be something you already possess or could develop.

Another tricky aspect is that positive projections prevent you from seeing the whole picture. When you idealise someone, you focus solely on their admirable traits while overlooking their complexities and flaws. The illusion shatters the moment they act in a way that contradicts your idealised image, whether by setting a boundary, showing vulnerability, or making a mistake. It's unfair to them, and it's unfair to you as well.

Ultimately, idealising someone can leave you open to manipulation. If they recognise that you see them as perfect, they may exploit this. Whether it's a boss, a partner, or a leader, placing someone on a pedestal can render you vulnerable to their influence, even if they do not have your best interests at heart.

And here's the kicker: if the qualities you admire in others reflect what you aspire to be or could become, then by projecting them onto others, you evade the effort of evolving. It's easier to say, "Wow, they're so confident, lucky them," than to confront your insecurities and work on them. You are, quite simply, avoiding your wholeness.

Here is an example of my negative projection onto an organisation. When I completed my psychotherapy training, I recall asking a colleague who had been invited to join the staff at my training college how she managed to do it.

She replied, "I asked." I was momentarily speechless. I realised I had hoped for an invitation without expressing my interest. At that moment, I unknowingly carried an unprocessed core belief: "I'm not welcome." I had projected that belief onto the college, assuming they wouldn't want to invite me.

Determined to tackle this, I made a mental note to explore it in therapy. However, rather than waiting, I chose to take action. I visited the office and expressed my interest in any vacancies that might arise. I held my breath, half-expecting them to say, "For you? Don't be foolish." But they didn't.

A month later, I was offered a position facilitating a guest group. Taking that initial step was empowering and reinforced my belief in the importance of confronting fears head-on. Tracing the origins of deeply held beliefs can be profoundly enlightening. However, nothing accelerates transformation as effectively as action.

Self-compassion is vital. It involves accepting all aspects of yourself, particularly those that may feel uncomfortable to confront. Retrieving projections plays a crucial role in shadow work, a necessary step towards achieving wholeness.

Working with Your Projections

One of the most eye-opening aspects of therapy is paying attention to our projections—the ways we unknowingly see parts of ourselves in others. These projections can manifest in various ways: at times, we place someone on a pedestal, admiring their confidence or charm; at other times, we bristle at their arrogance or neediness. Yet, often, what we're reacting to is something within us, something we've disowned, denied, or not yet claimed.

A helpful way to explore this is by creating a kind of projection map—a psychological mirror.

- Begin by considering people who elicit a strong emotional response from you. These could include close relationships, casual encounters, or even interactions with public figures. Some may get under your skin, while others might provoke admiration, jealousy, or longing. Either way, they illuminate something within your inner world.
- Then ask yourself: What exactly do I see in them? Be specific. Is it their assertiveness? Their emotionality? Their messiness, ambition, sparkle, stillness? These are likely projections—qualities within you that are being reflected, for better or worse.
- Now, take a moment to trace the feeling back. *When did I first encounter this quality? Was I allowed to express it as a child? What messages did I absorb about being too bold, too sensitive, too loud, too much?*

This is where things begin to unfold. Perhaps the colleague you find controlling reminds you of a parent whose unpredictability caused you to shrink. Maybe the friend you admire for being playful reflects a part of you that was urged to grow up too quickly. Often, what irritates or inspires us in others points to something we've had to suppress or never had the chance to develop.

- And then comes the most crucial part: turn inwards. Ask yourself, *How does this trait manifest within me?* Is this a side of me I've buried? A strength I've feared? A shadow I've been avoiding? You may discover a voice that has long been silenced—or a potential that has been waiting in the wings.

If you feel ready, you might ask: What would it mean to reclaim this part of me? Perhaps it's speaking up in a meeting. Maybe it's dancing, creating, crying, or laughing more freely. The action need not be grand—it simply needs to be authentic.

Ultimately, the individuals who move us, whether they bring us joy or discomfort, often reveal something fundamental about ourselves. Our projections are not mistakes; they serve as invitations to explore. They highlight aspects of ourselves that yearn to return home.

Key Takeaways: Projection

1 **Projection is a defence mechanism**: We unconsciously attribute our unwanted feelings, traits, or desires to others to protect the ego.
2 **Freud first described the concept in a discussion on paranoia**: He viewed projection as a way the ego "repudiates the unacceptable idea by projecting it onto the external world" (1922).

How Projection Works

3 **Unacknowledged emotions are transferred**: For example, if you're angry with yourself but can't admit it, you may believe that others are angry with you.
4 **Projection often stems from early relationships**: Images of caregivers (for instance, an angry father) are internalised and subsequently projected onto authority figures or institutions.
5 **Projection distorts perception**: The people or situations we project onto become stand-ins for unresolved emotional history.

Recognising Projections

6 **Strong emotional reactions are clues**: When your response seems disproportionate, it may be a projection. Ask: *"What does this remind me of?"*
7 **Projections are robustly defended**: People frequently double down when confronted, as they protect us from uncomfortable truths.

Collective Projection and the Shadow

8 **Witch hunts as societal projection**: The historical persecution of "witches" illustrates how collective fear and guilt can be directed towards vulnerable groups.
9 **Scapegoating reveals the shadow of a group**: Communities "cast out" their disowned traits—lust, rage, envy—onto a symbolic "other".

Negative Projection: "Carry My Sh*t"

10   **We disown painful qualities**: Then we accuse others of having them.

11   **Example shows projection in action**: A man accuses his wife of infidelity while suppressing his attraction to someone else.

Positive Projection: "Carry My Gold"

12   **We project our hidden strengths**: Admiring someone's confidence or creativity may reveal our untapped potential.

13   **We fall in love with our potential**: What we admire in others can be a call to develop those qualities in ourslyelves.

Dangers of Positive Projection

14   **Idealisation leads to disappointment**: No one can live up to a fantasy.

15   **It fosters dependence and disempowerment**: You give away your power, believing others have what you lack.

16   **You underestimate your talents**: Rather than nurturing them, you observe from the sidelines.

Reclaiming Projections

17   **Projection can be transformed**: The work isn't just about noticing projection, but also about **retrieving and integrating** what was disowned.

18   **Self-compassion is vital**: We should approach our projections with curiosity, not shame.

19   **Action accelerates healing**: Awareness matters, but so does making changes—speaking up, asking, and taking risks.

Practical Tools for Working with Projection

20   **Use emotional intensity as a guide**: Strong responses indicate deeper meaning.

21   **Engage in journalling exercises**: Compile a list of individuals you admire and those you dislike, and delve into the traits linked with each.

22   **Consider reflective questions**: "What part of me is reflected in this person?" "What lesson might this situation be offering?"

23   **Therapy and dreamwork provide assistance**: A therapist can act as a "spotter" for projections; dreams often reveal the unconscious roots.

Recommended Reading

Hollis, James (1998). *The Eden Project: In Search of the Magical Other*. Inner City Books. (A Jungian look at how we project idealised fantasies onto romantic partners, often confusing them with the Self's unmet needs.)

Johnson, Robert (2008). *Inner Gold: Understanding Psychological Projection*. Koa Books. (Johnson's "inner gold" symbolises our highest qualities, which we often fail to see in ourselves and project onto others.)

Johnson, Robert (2010). *Owning Your Own Shadow*. Harper. (A concise guide to the Shadow, illustrating how confronting our rejected aspects is crucial to inner wholeness.)

Zweig, Connie & Abrams, Jeremiah (Eds) (1991). *Meeting the Shadow: The Hidden Power of the Dark Side of Human Nature*. Tarcher. (A rich anthology of essays by Jungians, therapists, and scholars. Includes deep explorations of projection, repression, and integration.)

References

Freud, S. (1922). Psycho-analytic notes on an autobiographical account of a case of paranoia (Dementia paranoides). In J. Strachey (Ed. & Trans.), *The standard edition of the complete psychological works of Sigmund Freud* (Vol. 12, pp. 1–82). Hogarth Press. (Original work published 1911.)

Jung, C. G. (1953). *Two essays on analytical psychology* (R. F. C. Hull, Trans., 2nd ed., Vol. 7). Princeton University Press. (Original work published 1928.)

Chapter 13

When OK Is Not OK
What's Your Position?

This chapter explores the life position theory (our attitude towards life) and methods of communication.

Mary sought psychotherapy to address her struggles with low self-esteem and difficulty asserting herself. She shared a recent incident that had left her feeling disheartened: after booking an exercise class a week in advance, she arrived at the venue only to be informed by the receptionist that her name was not on the list.

> *I knew I'd booked—it was right there in my online confirmation. But still, I found myself apologetically asking the snooty receptionist to check. She insisted the system was infallible. I knew better, yet I backed down. I wasn't confused, just cowardly. And I'm tired of it. It baffles me.*

This is a classic example of an unhelpful life position, where my client unconsciously slipped into an "I'm not OK/You're OK" life position.

A **life position** is one of the building blocks of a life script, a concept from Transactional Analysis (TA). Eric Berne, the founder of this psychological theory and therapy, introduced the notion of a life script; you can read more about this in Chapter 14, "All the World's a Stage: Life Scripts and How to Change Them".

An underlying principle of TA is that we are all "OK", meaning everyone has value and worth. Based on their experiences, young children develop certain convictions about themselves and those around them, known as life positions, of which there are four:

- I'm OK/You're OK.
- I'm OK/You're not OK.
- I'm not OK/You're OK.
- I'm not OK/You're not OK.

(Berne, 1964)

DOI: 10.4324/9781003675099-14

We form our basic outlook on life—what's called a "life position"—without even realising it, usually before the age of seven. At that age, we're making sense of the world with a child's logic, long before we've got the tools to judge things clearly.

The good news is, once we become aware of our life position, we can change it. These positions are basically the stories we tell ourselves about where we stand in relation to others. For example, if a parent is constantly critical, a young child (who can't yet see the bigger picture) might take the blame and think, "You're OK, I'm not OK." Another child might go the other way and decide, "I'm OK, you're not OK." And some might end up believing, "Neither of us is OK."

When a child has a critical mother, for instance, they might start to believe that *all* mothers, or even all women or all people, aren't OK. It's a big leap, and of course it's not logical. But remember, we're talking about the way very young children think, before they've got the ability to see things clearly or put things into perspective.

Frank H. Ernst, a student of Eric Berne, further developed the concept of life positions into the OK/not-OK matrix, also referred to as the OK Corral (the title of a famous 1950s cowboy film). This matrix encompasses all possible combinations, illustrating how these beliefs about ourselves and others can manifest in relationships (Ernst, 1971).

Ernst hypothesised that the outcome of all transactions is determined by one of four categories of dynamic social interaction (Table 13.1).

The unconsciously chosen dynamic can shift based on a person's self-perception and their view of others. For instance, one may adopt an "I'm OK/You're not OK" position at home; yet, during a romantic date with someone new, one might transition to "I'm OK/You're OK".

Becoming aware of our life positions can be incredibly helpful. Once we understand what is happening, we can see that we are often merely playing out old patterns—following a script we wrote long ago. The life position we adopt in any situation shapes how we think, feel, and act—and that, in turn, influences our relationships, for better or worse. With awareness, we are no longer stuck on autopilot. We can pause, choose differently, and begin to build healthier, more authentic connections.

Table 13.1 The OK Corral

	You're OK	You're Not OK
I'm OK	Mutual respect (I'm OK/You're OK)	Critical or dismissive (I'm OK/You're not OK)
I'm Not OK	Self-doubting, deferential (I'm not OK/You're OK)	Hopeless or disconnected (I'm not OK/You're not OK)

Source: Adapted from Ernst (1971).

To bring this concept to life, I've included examples of how a conversation might sound when approached from each of the four life positions.

"I'm Not OK/You're Not OK"

Being in this life position, where we see ourselves as equals, but more like "fellow underdogs", can lead to a sense of hopelessness. That hopelessness seeps into our thoughts, emotions, and actions, often creating a feeling of "we're just going in circles" when trying to connect with the other person.

Andrew: Ugh, I don't even know why I bother coming to these meetings. It's not like anyone listens to me.

Jack: Tell me about it. Honestly, I think everyone here is just playing some game. No one cares.

Andrew: Yeah, and even when I do say something, I just feel like an idiot afterwards.

Jack: Same. Doesn't matter what we say; people are going to ignore us or shoot us down anyway.

Andrew: Right? It's all so pointless. I'm over it.

Sometimes, when we have endured painful experiences early in life, we begin to believe that neither we nor anyone else is OK. Perhaps love felt like something we had to earn, support was unreliable, or trust was broken time and again. Gradually, we absorb a message: *There's something wrong with me, and something wrong with you too.*

This "I'm not OK/You're not OK" mindset can settle in quietly, almost like a protective layer. If no one feels safe, not even ourselves, it can seem safer to expect nothing at all. However, that comes at a cost: it often leaves us feeling stuck, disconnected, and weighed down by mistrust and self-doubt.

Therapy begins by gently loosening that old belief. Bit by bit, we start to rediscover our own worth, and open to the possibility that a safe, meaningful connection is possible after all.

"I'm Not OK/You're OK"

In relation to other people, or the world in general, being in this position, where we feel one-down, can evoke feelings of helplessness that cloud our thoughts, unsettle our emotions, and distort our behaviour. It often makes us want to withdraw from the very person we're trying to connect with.

That same conversation between Andrew and Jack, from an "I'm not OK/You're OK" position, would go something like this:

Andrew: That meeting ... I really screwed up again. I should've just kept quiet.

Jack: What are you talking about? You had every right to speak up.

Andrew: I don't know. I just always feel like I'm not good enough next to everyone else. You got your point across, though, well done.

Jack: Andrew, you're being too hard on yourself. Seriously. We're all just trying our best.

Origins of an "I'm Not OK/You're OK"

Sometimes, as we grow up, we receive the message, either verbally or non-verbally, that we're not quite enough. Perhaps love seems conditional rather than unconditional. We may have faced criticism or comparisons, or been left to manage significant emotions on our own. Gradually, we come to believe: You're OK ... but I'm not.

This "I'm not OK/You're OK" position can follow us into adulthood. We second-guess ourselves, put others on pedestals, over-apologise, or chase approval. Deep down, it's the old belief whispering: *They've got it together. I don't.*

In therapy, we start to challenge that voice. We begin to see that being human—flawed, feeling, learning—doesn't make us any less. It merely makes us real.

"I'm OK/You're Not OK"

Being in this position, where we feel one-up, can provoke anger that clouds our thinking, disrupts our emotions, and skews our behaviour, causing us to push away the very person we're trying to reach.

Andrew: What a joke of a meeting. No one had a clue what they were doing.

Jack: True. It's like we're the only competent ones in the room.

Andrew: I swear, I'd run this place better with one hand tied behind my back.

Jack: Exactly. Total amateurs. No wonder nothing gets done.

The good news? With awareness and support, people can shift out of this and start to feel more grounded in the idea that *they* are OK—and that others can be too.

Sometimes, when we've been hurt or let down early in life, we learn to protect ourselves by flipping the script: "I'm OK—you're the problem." Perhaps a parent was unpredictable, critical, or simply not safe to rely on. Instead of feeling powerless, we learn to keep our distance, stay in control, and not let anyone get too close.

Over time, that survival strategy can harden into a mindset—critical, guarded, and disconnected. It appears as self-sufficiency on the outside, but underneath, there is often hurt that never found a safe place to land.

In therapy, the work involves softening that stance, gently unearthing what has been buried, and learning, little by little, that connection doesn't have to cost us our safety.

With awareness and support, people can move away from these self-defeating life positions and begin to feel more grounded in the idea that *they* are OK—and that others can be too.

"I'm OK/You're OK"

And finally, here's how this conversation would sound from an "I'm OK/You're OK" life position, where both parties are relating to each other as adults in a healthy, balanced manner.

Andrew: That meeting was a bit frustrating—I didn't feel heard.

Jack: Yeah, I noticed that too. I felt the same. Let's bring it up next time or find a more straightforward way to convey our points.

Andrew: Good idea. My nerves got in the way a bit. I'll try to stay more grounded next time.

Jack: I totally get it; I get nervous when I'm speaking up in large meetings. And by the way, your ideas are worth sharing, don't doubt that.

Self-Reflective Questions

General Awareness

- In terms of these life positions, what do I believe about myself, deep down?
- How do I tend to see other people; do I trust them, fear them, feel better than, or less than?
- When I'm under stress, how do I treat myself? How do I treat others?
- Do I feel I have value, even when I make mistakes?

Exploring Specific Situations

- What life position might I be coming from in this situation? ("I'm OK/You're OK", etc.)
- How does that affect the way I behave or communicate?
- Am I expecting rejection, criticism, or disappointment before it even happens?

Origins of Life Positions

- What messages (spoken or unspoken) did I receive growing up about myself and other people?
- Was love conditional? Was I criticised, praised, ignored, or idealised?
- Which life position did I learn to adopt to stay safe, loved, or included?

Doing Things Differently

- What would change if I approached this from a place of "I'm OK/ You're OK"?
- Can I imagine extending compassion to both myself and the other person?
- What slight shift could I make right now (in thought, tone, or action) that reflects a healthier life position?
- Who do I feel safe being my "OK" self around? What's different in that relationship?

Key Takeaways: Life Positions from Transactional Analysis

1 **Life positions**—our deeply ingrained beliefs about ourselves and others—are formed in early childhood, often before the age of seven, and shape how we think, feel, and interact with others.

2 These life positions fall into four categories:

- *I'm OK/You're OK* (healthy, balanced)
- *I'm not OK/You're OK* (low self-worth, idealising others)
- *I'm OK/You're not OK* (defensive, critical)
- *I'm not OK/You're not OK* (hopelessness, disconnection)

3 **Mary's story** illustrates how someone can unconsciously act from an "I'm not OK/You're OK" stance, even when they know logically that they've done nothing wrong.

4 Life positions are part of our **life script**, a concept introduced by Eric Berne in Transactional Analysis (TA). These scripts often play out unconsciously until brought into awareness.

5 The **OK Corral**, developed by Frank Ernst, expands these concepts into a matrix that maps how people interact based on their internal beliefs about self and others.

6 **Our life position can shift** depending on context, such as moving from "I'm OK/You're not OK" at work to "I'm OK/You're OK" in a safe relationship.

7 Becoming aware of your life position helps interrupt old patterns and opens the possibility for healthier, more authentic connections.

8 Four example conversations show how the same situation plays out differently through each life position, highlighting the emotional tone and relationship dynamics.

9 A set of **self-reflective questions** invites readers to explore their own patterns and begin making conscious, compassionate shifts.

Recommended Reading

Berne, Eric (1961). *Transactional Analysis in Psychotherapy: A Systematic Individual and Social Psychiatry*. Grove Press. (The seminal text establishing Transactional Analysis (TA) as a clinical model; introduces ego states and structural analysis.)

Berne, Eric (1964). *Games People Play: The Psychology of Human Relationships*. Grove Press. (While this classic by the founder of Transactional Analysis focuses on social games, it introduces the concept of ego states. It implies life positions that people adopt during interpersonal transactions. Accessible classic; introduces "games" and psychological payoffs.)

Berne, Eric (1972). *What Do You Say After You Say Hello? The Psychology Of Human Destiny*. Corgi. (A mature synthesis of Berne's ideas on life scripts, injunctions, and autonomy.)

Harris, Thomas Anthony (1969). *I'm OK–You're OK*. Jonathan Cape. (This is the definitive and most popular introduction to life positions. Harris explains how early life experiences shape our unconscious beliefs about self and others and how we can shift toward the healthy "I'm OK–You're OK" position. Popular, yet still conceptually useful, introduction to TA and life positions.)

Hay, Julie (1992). *TA for Trainers*. Sherwood Publishing. (Applies TA to Learning, Communication, and Leadership.)

Hendrix, Harville & LaKelly, Hunt Helen (1988, updated). *Getting the Love You Want: A Guide for Couples*. Henry Holt & Co. (A transformative book based on the idea that partners unconsciously seek healing from early relational wounds. Includes exercises for couples.)

Johnson, Sue (2008). *Hold Me Tight—Let Me Go*. Little, Brown and Co. (EFT-based, but adapted for parent–teen dynamics, it is also relevant in blended families or couples parenting together.)

Joines, Vann & Stewart, Ian (2002). *Personality Adaptations: A New Guide to Human Understanding in Psychotherapy and Counselling*. Lifespace. (Brilliant bridge between TA, attachment, and personality theory. Builds on core TA concepts, including life positions, and links them to personality styles. It is helpful for therapists or advanced readers.)

Jongeward, Dorothy & James, Muriel (1971). *Born to Win: Transactional Analysis with Gestalt Experiments*. Addison-Wesley Publishing Company. (A popular TA self-help book that connects life positions with success and self-esteem. Includes experiential exercises to help readers shift their internal position.)

Steiner, Claude (1974). *Scripts People Live: Transactional Analysis of Life Scripts*. Grove Press. (Deepens Berne's script theory with practical therapeutic strategies.)

Stewart, Ian & Joines, Vann (2012). *TA Today: A New Introduction to Transactional Analysis*, 2nd ed. Lifespace. (Widely used in TA training. Offers clear, structured explanations of life positions, ego states, scripts, and games. Accessible and evidence-informed. Concise, practical, and ideal for students.)

References

Berne, E. (1964). *Games people play: The psychology of human relationships*. Grove Press.

Ernst, F. H. (1971). The OK corral: The grid for get-on-with. *Transactional Analysis Journal*, 1(4), 231–240. https://doi.org/10.1177/036215377100100404

Harris, T. A. (1967). *I'm OK—You're OK*. Harper & Row.

Chapter 14

All the World's a Stage
Life Scripts and How to Change Them

In the late 1950s, Eric Berne, a Canadian-born psychiatrist influenced by Freud, established a school of psychotherapy known as Transactional Analysis (TA). Unlike Freud and Jung, who concentrated on their patients as they presented in the consulting room, Berne placed greater emphasis on his clients' social transactions. In his final and most far-reaching book, *What Do You Say After You Say Hello?*, Berne deepened his theory of TA into a study of how we unconsciously script the course of our lives. Long before we are capable of rational choice, we begin to assemble a private mythology—a life story drawn from childhood impressions, parental messages, and emotional survival strategies. These early decisions become the invisible blueprint for how we relate, succeed, fail, love, and repeat familiar patterns (Berne, 1972).

A central aspect of TA philosophy is the concept of the Life Script. According to Eric Berne, life scripts are unconscious mental blueprints that determine how a person's life will unfold. These life scripts begin to form in childhood, shaped by interactions, experiences, and messages absorbed from parents and significant figures. You probably won't remember when you created your script; your experiences and choices have shaped it.

Much like a carefully crafted play, they possess a beginning, middle, and end, subtly guiding thoughts, emotions, and behaviours. Operating beneath conscious awareness, they wield immense power over personal choices and life trajectories. Recognising that you can alter the narrative you have created for yourself is essential.

There are winning, mediocre, and losing scripts. If your script is mediocre or losing, the good news is that you are not stuck with it; you can actively change your story. By becoming aware of the building blocks or elements of your script, you can revise it to align with your consciously stated desires and aspirations.

The first thing to understand about how we develop our Life Script is the concept of Strokes. In Transactional Analysis (TA), "strokes" refer to the ways people give and receive attention or recognition. Consider strokes as emotional "high-fives"—they can be positive or negative, verbal or non-verbal, and they play a significant role in how we feel about ourselves and connect with others.

DOI: 10.4324/9781003675099-15

What's a Stroke in TA?

A stroke is any indication that someone notices or acknowledges you. It can be as simple as a smile, a compliment, or a critical remark. People require strokes to feel good and maintain emotional health, just as children need hugs to thrive. Our need for recognition is so strong that we often prefer criticism to the uncomfortable prospect of being ignored.

Picture a young boy, Jimmy, completely absorbed in his play while his mother is engaged in a lengthy phone conversation. As boredom sets in, he tugs at her sleeve, seeking her attention. She hushes him dismissively, leaving him feeling overlooked and unwanted. It doesn't take long before Jimmy accidentally breaks something, provoking his mother's anger (a negative stroke); it's better than being ignored.

Types of Strokes

- **Positive strokes** (such as "Great job!" or a warm hug) make one feel good.
- **Negative strokes** (like "That was stupid!" or a cold glare) can be painful but still count as attention.
- **Conditional strokes** are rooted in actions (for example, "You're fantastic at sport!").
- **Unconditional strokes** refer to who you are, with no strings attached; for example, "I love you no matter what."
- **Verbal strokes and spoken words**, whether positive or negative.
- **Non-verbal strokes** refer to **gestures** such as a pat on the back, a thumbs-up, or even the lack of action, such as giving someone the "cold shoulder".

Why Strokes Matter

Strokes contribute to our emotional well-being. In the 1930s and 1940s, René Spitz conducted research on the impacts of separation from mothers on infants and children in orphanages.

Spitz noted that children in orphanages and hospitals suffered from a condition he termed "hospitalism", which arose from a lack of maternal care, stimulation, and affection. His research revealed that children who were separated from their mothers for more than three months often experienced irreversible developmental damage, resulting in long-term personality issues. He further discovered that maternal separation delayed development in critical areas, including physical growth (height and weight), motor skills, emotional regulation, and social relationships. In severe cases, these deficits could become permanent and, in some instances, could even lead to death (Spitz, 1945).

Spitz's research produced recommendations emphasising the importance of responsive and nurturing caregivers for the well-being of infants and children.

We all require strokes—both physical and emotional. For infants, physical stroking helps to regulate negative emotions, supports their ability to manage behaviour, encourages exploration of their environment, and aids in processing emotions. As we grow, positive strokes—whether through kind words, gestures, or physical touch—lift our mood and enhance our confidence, fostering a sense of connection and well-being. Even negative attention can be preferable to being ignored, as it at least shows that someone is interested in you.

When we are young, we develop habits regarding giving and receiving strokes. These patterns typically endure and are reflected in our interactions with others as adults, often without our even realising it.

The Unspoken Rules We Should Ignore

Claude Steiner introduced the concept of the "Stroke Economy" (1971), which relates to the unspoken rules of childhood that influence how individuals express and receive affection, compliments, and support.

Many of us grew up hearing phrases such as "Stop attention-seeking," "It's not all about you," "Don't get too big for your boots," or "Don't show off." In response, we may have withdrawn, dimming our light to avoid criticism or rejection.

Over time, this may cultivate a belief that accepting praise or being acknowledged is somehow wrong or undesirable, making it challenging for adults to truly appreciate and value positive attention. As a result, giving or receiving compliments can often feel awkward or unnatural, leading many to either minimise or completely avoid them.

This reluctance perpetuates a cycle where people silently crave validation yet seldom receive it, despite recognition being essential for feeling valued and connected.

Steiner observes that some *unhelpful* and frequently noted "rules" to which people adhere include:

- Don't give strokes when you want to.
- Don't ask for strokes when you need them.
- Don't accept strokes when offered.
- Accept strokes you don't want.
- Don't give yourself strokes.

We've all experienced moments when we have considered reaching out to others, offering a compliment, showing support, or simply being kind, yet we often hesitate. This hesitation commonly arises from internal barriers, such as shyness, fear of being misunderstood, or concerns about how our actions might be perceived.

Perhaps you've considered offering a heartfelt compliment to a friend but hesitated, fearing it might come across as awkward or overly forward. Asking for feedback can also be quite challenging—we may refrain from doing so out of concern about appearing insecure or needy. It's a constant balancing act between the desire to connect and the fear of vulnerability.

Consider how often we dismiss compliments. When someone praises us, we might downplay their words or respond with a quick "Thank you," thinking this is the polite or modest reaction. This can unintentionally diminish the moment for both ourselves and the person offering the compliment.

Criticism can be even more daunting. If someone raises a sensitive issue, we may fall silent or divert the conversation, unsure of how to react or express our feelings.

These examples illustrate the complexity of our relationship with communication. Recognising these patterns is the first step towards breaking them. It involves embracing vulnerability and being open, not just in how we offer, but also how we receive attention, kindness, and criticism. By doing so, we can cultivate more genuine and meaningful connections with others.

Using Strokes for Better Relationships

Effectively employing strokes can enhance communication, strengthen relationships, and cultivate a supportive social environment. Here's how to use strokes:

Be Generous with Positive Strokes

- Say something kind. Let others know when they have excelled or when you appreciate their qualities. For instance: "You nailed that project! Your creativity is remarkable!"
- Express gratitude. Acknowledge others for their assistance, even for minor gestures; they will feel recognised and valued.
- Be supportive; offer encouraging words when someone is doing their best or facing a challenging time.
- Use conditional and unconditional strokes.
- Conditional strokes: Acknowledge specific behaviours or achievements, such as saying, "Great job today!"
- Unconditional strokes: demonstrate acceptance regardless of actions (for example, "It's always good to be around you.").
- Practise verbal and non-verbal strokes.
- *Verbal strokes.* Use words of appreciation, praise, or acknowledgement.
- *Non-verbal strokes* include smiling, hugging, patting someone on the back, or maintaining warm eye contact. A simple thumbs-up after a good performance can convey a great deal.
- Accept strokes graciously. Say thank you: accept compliments and recognition without downplaying or dismissing them.
- Acknowledge the giver: recognise the effort the other person has made in offering the compliment; for instance, if someone gives a kind remark, respond with, "Thank you! I appreciate you saying that."

Be Mindful of Negative Strokes

- Avoid giving hurtful feedback; criticism should be constructive rather than harmful.
- If you're on the receiving end of a negative stroke, address it; respond calmly and seek clarification if necessary. For instance, you might say, "That feels rather harsh. Please allow me a moment to gather my thoughts and reflect on what you just said before I respond," or "I appreciate your feedback; could you clarify how I might improve?"

Practise Self-strokes

- Acknowledge your successes and celebrate personal achievements, regardless matter how small they may be.
- Practise positive self-talk by replacing negative inner dialogue with affirming thoughts, such as, "I managed that challenge well. I'm pleased. I remained calm."

By being mindful of how we give, receive, and respond to strokes, we can strengthen our relationships, boost self-esteem, and foster a supportive environment for personal and social growth.

We develop the building blocks of our Life Scripts to receive strokes (both positive and negative). Let us explore the fundamental components of life scripts and how they shape our experiences.

Life Script Components

Children are like little scientists, constantly observing the behaviour, tone, and attitudes of their caregivers, siblings, and others around them. They absorb messages—both spoken and unspoken—about themselves, others, and the world. With only a limited understanding, they begin forming early beliefs and making unconscious decisions that assist them in adapting to the expectations of their family and culture.

As they search for affirmation and connection (also known as strokes!), the behaviours that elicit a response—whether praise, attention, or even disapproval—tend to persist. These patterns, repeated over time, can become ingrained strategies for meeting needs. Although they may have served a purpose in childhood, these early adaptations often continue into adulthood, shaping how we think, feel, and relate—sometimes long after they are no longer necessary.

For instance, a child who consistently receives negative strokes, such as messages of incompetence or unworthiness, may internalise these experiences and develop a life script that leads them to view themselves as failures or unworthy of success. Conversely, a child who receives positive strokes, such as encouragement and support, is more likely to formulate a life script based on self-confidence and a strong desire for achievement.

The Building Blocks of a Life Script

The building blocks of a life script are the essential elements that come together to create this internal narrative. Some of the building blocks of a Life Script include:

- Parental messages
- Life positions
- Injunctions
- Games
- Rackets
- Drivers

Parental Messages

As children, we absorb messages from our parents (or primary caregivers) that shape our self-perception and influence our beliefs about what we deserve. These messages can be categorised into two main types:

- **Nurturing messages** are warm and encouraging, helping you feel loved, valued, and capable. They boost your self-esteem and empower you to believe in yourself.
- **Critical messages** can be severe, and judgemental messages may leave you feeling inadequate or flawed. They frequently evoke feelings of shame, guilt, self-doubt, or perfectionism, resulting in rigid or excessively self-critical behaviour.

As we receive messages from others, we formulate responses that shape our self-perception and influence how we navigate life; this becomes an integral part of our life script.

Life Positions

Life positions reflect the fundamental beliefs we develop about ourselves and others, often stemming from early childhood experiences with caregivers. These beliefs shape our worldview, influence our decision-making, and affect our interactions with others (Berne, 1964).

In simple terms, the four life positions can be summed up as follows:

- **"I'm OK/You're OK"** (healthy and balanced). This represents the sweet spot where you perceive both yourself and others as capable, valuable, and deserving of respect. It embodies the ideal mindset for fostering healthy relationships and encouraging personal growth. In this state, you are open, respectful, and ready to tackle problems collaboratively. Your belief may be, "I trust myself and presume others are doing their best as well."

- **"I'm OK/You're not OK"** (superior or defensive). This stance allows you to feel superior to others—often due to past disappointments or hurts. From this position, you tend to act in a critical, judgemental, and controlling manner, convinced that "If I don't take charge, nothing will be done correctly."
- **"I'm not OK/You're OK"** (inferior or dependent). In this context, you view others as more capable or worthy than yourself. This perspective often stems from criticism or neglect experienced during childhood. Seeing the world through this lens, you may behave in an insecure manner, seek approval, and undermine your self-worth. You might think, "I can't do this as well as others; I'm simply not good enough."
- **"I'm not OK/You're not OK"** (hopeless or defeated) epitomises the bleakest position. It reflects a mindset in which you have lost faith in both yourself and the world. Everything seems pointless or doomed. Embracing this perspective, you are likely to feel withdrawn, hopeless, and pessimistic. You may believe that "Nothing ever works out, and people can't be trusted."

Refer to Chapter 13, "When OK Is Not OK: What's Your Position?" for further information on life positions.

Injunctions

Injunctions resemble hidden rules that children learn from their parents or caregivers, often without anyone realising. These messages, whether explicitly stated or subtly implied, tend to wield significant influence. More often than not, children absorb them not just through words but also through their parents' behaviours. Deeply ingrained and often restrictive, these internalised commands can persist into adulthood, quietly shaping thoughts, emotions, and actions long after their origins have been forgotten.

They may be linked to how one or both of your parents were raised, as well as how their parents were raised. Therefore, we are sometimes addressing generational trauma that has been unknowingly transmitted. Recognising and challenging this process is a crucial aspect of personal growth.

Here are 18 common injunctions:

Messages Concerning Identity

- **Do not exist.** This is the most damaging injunction, suggesting that the child's existence is unwanted. It can lead to feelings of worthlessness, depression, or self-destructive behaviour.
- **Do not be yourself.** This message makes children feel that being who they are is not good enough. They might believe they have to change or hide parts of their identity to be accepted, which can lead to struggles with self-identity. It is a common experience; every one of us develops a Persona early in life, relegating the traits we consider unacceptable to our Shadow, where they remain hidden until we learn to confront them.

- **Do not belong**. Many individuals raised in cultures that marginalise them or those who have reclusive parents experience a sense of not belonging. This situation leads to feelings of isolation, social anxiety, and uncertainty regarding the establishment of meaningful relationships.

Messages Against Feeling

- **Do not feel**. This message conveys to the child that it is unacceptable to express their feelings. Consequently, the child may suppress their emotions, struggle to understand their feelings, or appear emotionally distant.
- **Do not be important**. This message can lead the recipient to feel as though their needs and opinions do not matter. It may result in low self-esteem, an excessive preoccupation with pleasing others, and difficulty asserting themselves.
- **Do not be close**. This message advises the child to refrain from getting too close to others due to a fear of rejection or abandonment. Such avoidance can result in trust issues and difficulties with intimacy in relationships.

Messages About Success and Achievement

- **Do not succeed**. This message makes success seem risky, possibly due to jealousy or fear of overshadowing others. It can cause individuals to hold themselves back, procrastinate, or shy away from realising their full potential.
- **Do not be smart**. This can occur when a child's intelligence makes a caregiver feel insecure or inadequate. To prevent creating tension, the child may hide their intelligence or stop seeking learning opportunities altogether.
- **Do not try**. When a child is harshly criticised for their failures, this message conveys to the child that striving is not worth the effort. Over time, this can extinguish motivation and leave the child feeling helpless, as though nothing they do will ever be good enough.

Messages About Autonomy and Control

- **Do not think**. This injunction often originates from controlling caregivers and can leave individuals feeling uncertain, stifling independent thought. Consequently, they may struggle to make decisions and continually seek guidance from others for direction.
- **Do not decide**. Similar to "Don't think," this prohibition fosters indecisiveness and dependency. Individuals may evade making decisions to escape responsibility or due to a fear of making mistakes.
- **Do not be independent**. This message restricts autonomy, causing individuals to depend on others. It can hinder their ability to stand up for themselves or to make life changes without the approval of someone else.

Messages About Safety and Security

- **Do not trust**. This injunction can render the individual suspicious and cautious, often stemming from past experiences of betrayal or inconsistency by caregivers. It may also result in a tendency towards guardedness and difficulties in forming relationships.

- **Do not play it safe.** Emerging from chaotic or unsafe environments where danger is ever-present, individuals may engage in unnecessary risks or face security issues.
- **Do not grow up.** This rule suggests that growing up involves a loss of love or protection. It may result in immaturity, dependence, or avoidance of adult responsibilities.

Messages About Worth and Value

- **Do not be loved.** Due to neglect or emotional unavailability, the child may feel unworthy of love and might even sabotage affectionate relationships.
- **Do not be happy.** This injunction, possibly stemming from familial struggles in which happiness seems selfish or inappropriate, discourages joy and fulfilment, potentially resulting in chronic dissatisfaction.
- **Do not matter.** This message implies that the child's existence is insignificant. It can lead to feelings of low self-worth, a lack of ambition, and a tendency to be overlooked or ignored.

Understanding these injunctions will help you recognise limiting beliefs developed in childhood, allowing you to challenge these patterns and adopt healthier ways of thinking and behaving.

Games

When you find yourself thinking, "Here we go again," it's likely that you've entered a psychological game. These repetitive patterns aren't random—unmet needs or unresolved emotional issues drive them. Whether it's seeking attention, evading responsibility, or pursuing the comfort of familiar (even painful) feelings, psychological games operate on hidden motives.

You'll know you're in one by their telltale signs: predictable dynamics, emotional intensity, and a frustrating sense of déjà vu. Everyone involved walks away feeling bad—angry, guilty, confused, or hollow—yet, somehow, the pattern keeps repeating.

At the heart of these games lies the Drama Triangle: a rotating cast of roles—Victim, Rescuer, and Persecutor. Each participant adopts a role, and together they enact a familiar script that unfolds time and again.

What's the payoff? Oddly, it's often a negative one. Players rotate through feelings of moral superiority, wronged-ness, shame, or self-pity. It may not be enjoyable, but it *is* familiar—and this familiarity is powerful enough to keep the game going.

For a deeper dive into these dynamics, see Chapter 15, "The Only Game in Town: The Drama Triangle".

Rackets

Eric Berne, the founder of Transactional Analysis (TA), used the term *"racket"* to describe those familiar emotional loops in which we become trapped—a sort of psychological con we unknowingly perpetrate on ourselves and others. Like any good scam, a racket has a hidden agenda. It's not about expressing what we truly feel, but about replaying a rehearsed emotion—anger, guilt, helplessness—that garners us attention, avoids conflict, or allows us to maintain control.

Think of it as hitting "repeat" on an old emotional playlist. The song may be out of tune with the present moment, but it's strangely comforting and entirely unconscious. Beneath the racket, the true feelings remain buried, waiting to be heard.

Rackets commence in childhood when caregivers do not accept certain emotions. For example, if anger is punished while sadness is met with sympathy, a child may learn to suppress anger and display sadness instead. Over time, these learned responses develop into deeply ingrained emotional habits. Many cultures discourage girls from expressing anger and boys from shedding tears, thereby reinforcing gender-based emotional conditioning. In my practice, I have noticed that many women only realise they are angry when they examine their tendency to cry in moments of frustration—a reaction so ingrained that they fail to recognise the underlying emotion. Conversely, I observe many men expressing anger when they feel sadness.

Common Racket Emotions

- **Anger** frequently conceals vulnerability, fear, or sadness, and expressing gentler emotions can feel disconcerting.
- **Sadness** can mask anger or disappointment when expressing anger feels unsafe.
- **Guilt** may take the place of anger to avoid conflict or sidestep assertiveness.
- **Fear or anxiety** can emerge when one feels powerless or out of control, particularly when the prospect of regaining control appears menacing.
- **Self-pity** can act as a substitute for assertiveness, enabling individuals to evade responsibility and confrontation or to seek solace from others.

Meet Janet

Janet reported that her friend Lara had cancelled a dinner date at the last minute. Janet burst into tears, stating that she felt abandoned and rejected. Lara was perplexed—she had been delayed at work and couldn't understand why Janet reacted so strongly. As we explored the situation, it became apparent that this was the third time Lara had cancelled dinner at the last minute. While Janet's underlying emotion was anger, her usual way of expressing distress was through tears. She feared that if she admitted to feeling angry, their relationship might not survive.

Working with Your Rackets

- Be mindful. Pay attention to emotional reactions that appear disproportionate.
- Identify your triggers. What kinds of situations provoke your "rackety" responses?
- Recognise the benefit. What familiar feeling or emotional comfort do you gain from the racket?
- Choose a fresh response. Cultivate healthier, more authentic emotional reactions—even if they feel strange at first. This may guide you to your "growing edge" and appear unfeasible. Seeking help from a therapist could assist you in this process.

Recognising and understanding rackets can assist you in breaking free from old emotional habits, responding more honestly, and fostering healthier, more genuine relationships.

Drivers

Drivers resemble internal voices or pressures that influence us to behave in specific ways, often rooted in the messages we absorbed during childhood. Although these drivers can sometimes be beneficial, they may also induce stress or impede our progress. There are five primary drivers, each with its unique vibe:

1   Be Perfect

Here's how to identify it: you pay close attention to small details, dislike making mistakes, and hold yourself (and perhaps others) to exceptionally high standards. The positive aspect is that you are highly reliable, produce excellent work, and remain organised. On the downside, you might find yourself feeling stressed, procrastinating, or as though nothing you do is ever good enough.

2   Be Strong

The "Be Strong" driver focuses on maintaining composure, regardless of the situation. If this resonates with you, you are likely the type of person who endures challenges, never shows weakness, and consistently strives to be a source of support for others. You may avoid seeking help, as you do not wish to impose on anyone or appear vulnerable.

One positive aspect is that people view you as reliable, resilient, and someone they can trust. However, what about the drawbacks? Carrying all that weight can be exhausting, and suppressing your emotions may leave you feeling isolated or overwhelmed. At times, being strong involves recognising when to rely on others as well.

3   Hurry Up

The "Hurry Up" driver is all about speed. If this resonates with you, you're likely always rushing about, juggling multiple tasks, and striving to complete everything as quickly as possible. The frustration of waiting gnaws at you, and nothing unsettles you more than feeling stuck in a slow or inefficient process. You take pride in your speed, tackling tasks with remarkable efficiency, to the point where others likely admire your ability to multitask. However, there's a downside: relentless urgency can lead to mistakes, heighten stress levels, and leave you in a near-constant state of tension. Sometimes, slowing down isn't a bad idea; it might even make things easier in the long run.

4   Please Others

The "Please Others" driver focuses on ensuring that those around you are happy. If this resonates with you, you likely always say yes, make an effort to help, and avoid conflict at all costs. You find satisfaction in pleasing others and detest disappointing anyone.

The advantages include being kind and considerate; people appreciate your company because you genuinely care. However, the disadvantages may include the possibility of overcommitting, neglecting your own needs, or feeling resentful if no one reciprocates your kindness. It's marvellous to be helpful, but remember to look after yourself as well!

Drivers aren't all bad—they can help you succeed. However, if you let them take control, they can lead to stress, burnout, or unproductive habits.

How to Deal with Drivers

- Notice them: pay attention to which driver is in charge.
- Challenge those rigid inner messages by saying, for example, either silently or aloud, "I don't have to be perfect to be good," or "It's OK to disappoint people sometimes."
- Achieve balance by utilising the beneficial aspects of drivers without permitting them to dominate you.
- Seek support; if you're struggling, a therapist or coach can help you understand the origins of these patterns and how to change them.

Your drivers can either guide you in the right direction or mislead you, depending on their authenticity. It's important to recognise whether you're acting from a place of genuine intent or from a neurotic need to control the outcome.

Life Scripts

Now that we've examined the building blocks, let's explore the different types of life scripts. There are three types of life scripts: winning, mediocre, or losing.

The tricky part is that life scripts are unconscious; they operate on autopilot. Many individuals navigate through life unaware that they are following an invisible script. These unconscious patterns function beneath the surface, subtly dictating choices and reinforcing repetitive cycles, even when they no longer serve a beneficial purpose. For example, someone with the belief that they must always please others might find themselves in relationships where their needs are consistently overlooked.

Winning Scripts

A winning life script assists you in tackling challenges, making wise choices, and pursuing meaningful goals. It appears to be something everyone would wish for. So, why do some individuals have winning scripts while others do not?

It all comes down to early childhood experiences. Winning scripts are built on positive messages, such as being praised for your effort (not just the results), receiving encouragement, and feeling supported by significant people in your life. These experiences foster confidence, resilience, and a belief in your ability to succeed.

Not everyone begins life with a supportive foundation. Some children internalise limiting beliefs and messages that can later hinder their growth. While we don't *consciously* choose these early narratives, we make decisions that shape them, making our life script a product of our choices. The encouraging truth is that, since the script is built on decisions, it can also be rewritten. With self-awareness, effort, and support, you have the power to change your story.

Key Traits of Winning Scripts

Individuals with winning life scripts tend to share key traits. They possess a strong sense of control, believing in their ability to shape their lives and make things happen. Their healthy self-esteem enables them to view themselves as deserving of success, love, and happiness. Resilience is another defining quality—they bounce back, learn from mistakes, and continue moving forward. They also take full responsibility for their actions and choices, recognising that they are the architects of their own destinies. Ultimately, success arises from taking charge and maintaining a positive mindset, regardless of the challenges.

Individuals with winning scripts tend to infuse positivity into every aspect of life. In their professions, they pursue careers they are passionate about, challenge themselves to grow, and take genuine pride in their accomplishments. They cultivate strong, healthy relationships with those who provide mutual care, support, and encouragement.

They also concentrate on personal growth, establish meaningful goals, and work towards them while continually striving to better themselves. Confidence is key to their mindset—they trust themselves and feel good about who they are. When challenges arise, they do not give up; instead, they approach problems with a "How can I fix this?" attitude, demonstrating resilience and creativity. This approach leads to a balanced and fulfilling life, where achievements and relationships bring genuine happiness. Furthermore, they often inspire and uplift those around them, spreading positivity and creating a ripple effect that benefits those they encounter.

How to Create a Winning Script as an Adult

Imagine your life is a play you didn't know you were performing. The lines were written long ago—before you could speak in complete sentences. You learned them from your parents, your caregivers, and your culture. Perhaps the script stated, "Don't shine too brightly," or "Be good, but never ask for anything," or "Love means sacrifice." These weren't choices; they were unconscious decisions made by a young child trying to survive and be loved.

Most of us live out these early narratives without even realising it. They feel like fate. However, here's the good news: the script isn't set in stone. You can rewrite it.

The first step is recognising the old plotline. You start to notice patterns—moments when you think, *Why does this always happen to me?* or *Here we go again.* These repetitions serve as clues that you're still following an outdated script. Perhaps you always find yourself rescuing others, sabotaging your own success, or feeling unworthy of love. These aren't accidents; they're familiar roles you've played for years.

Then comes the deeper work: understanding what those roles provided you. Even painful patterns offer emotional rewards—what TA calls *rackets*. Perhaps playing the victim gained you attention. Or being the overachiever made you feel secure. The feelings aren't always pleasant—guilt, self-pity, anger—but they're familiar. And familiarity is powerful.

With insight comes choice. From your Adult self—the rational, grounded part of you—you start to challenge the old script. Is it still true that I must please everyone to feel safe? Do I *genuinely* believe that love must be earned through suffering? You begin to question, edit, and revise.

And then, something amazing happens: you permit yourself to write something new. Permission to succeed. To rest. To be close without losing yourself.

These new permissions are the seeds of a *winning script*—one based on awareness, intimacy, and autonomy.

Living that new script isn't merely about thinking differently; it's about behaving differently. Choosing relationships that honour your truth, saying no without guilt, and taking risks that align with who you are becoming, not who you were told to be.

In this new story, you remain the protagonist, but now, you are also the author.

Mediocre Scripts

Some people live lives that, on the surface, look perfectly fine. There's no obvious disaster, no big trauma playing out. They have a job, a relationship, maybe a family. They're functioning. And yet—something's missing. A spark, a sense of aliveness, a feeling of deep satisfaction. That's what Transactional Analysis would call a *mediocre script*.

It's not tragic. It's not dramatic. It's just … underwhelming.

Meet Adam

By most standards, Adam's life was quite fine. He held a decent job in marketing, had a partner he cared for, and lived in a flat in a pleasant neighbourhood. He was polite, responsible, and dependable—the kind of person people described as "nice" or "solid".

And yet, Adam often felt as if he were living on autopilot. He would wake up, go to work, come home, watch television, and repeat the cycle. Weekends were a blur of errands and Netflix. Occasionally, he experienced fleeting moments of something more—memories of how he used to adore painting as a child, or a sudden yearning to book a one-way ticket somewhere. But those impulses were swiftly suppressed by thoughts such as: *Be practical. Don't make a fuss. What would people think?*

In therapy, Adam began to explore these feelings. He realised that he had grown up with the unspoken message: "Don't expect too much." His parents weren't unkind—they simply valued safety and modesty above all else. They had lived through tough times and wanted Adam to have a stable life. Thus, Adam became the good son, the quiet achiever. He coloured inside the lines.

But now, in his mid-thirties, something within him was beginning to itch. It wasn't exactly depression, but more a kind of soul-level boredom. A hunger for meaning. With the assistance of therapy, Adam started to question the script he had been following. Who had written it? And did it still serve him?

Gradually, he began to explore new options. He enrolled in an evening art class and, initially shy, started to showcase his work online more boldly. He declined a promotion that did not interest him. He and his partner began to discuss their life goals more openly. For the first time in years, Adam felt awake. His life did not turn into a Hollywood movie, but it felt like *his own*. More colourful. More connected. He was no longer just surviving; he was creating something. Not merely because it was what he was supposed to do, but because it felt true.

That's what it looks like to step out of a mediocre script and into a story worth living.

People with a mediocre script often tread a well-worn path. They make safe choices, do what's expected, and walk the line. There's a sense of compromise, as if they've traded their dreams for comfort and predictability. They might even say, "I should be happy. Nothing's really wrong." But beneath the surface, there's often a tug of restlessness or regret—*Is this all there is?*

This kind of script usually begins in childhood, not with overt harm, but with subtle, shaping messages: "Be sensible." "Don't expect too much." "It's safer not to stand out." These messages aren't cruel—they're often protective. However, they teach the child to keep things small, manageable, and safe. Consequently, the adult they become does precisely that. They construct a life that's steady but uninspired.

The emotions tied to a mediocre script aren't particularly dramatic either. There's no fiery rage or crushing sorrow. It's more like a low-grade hum: boredom, mild resentment, and a quiet sense of missing out. Sometimes, people say, "I feel like I'm going through the motions," or "I've ticked the boxes, but I'm still not fulfilled."

Rewriting a mediocre script doesn't mean blowing up your life. It means waking it up. It means asking: *What do I want? What have I been too afraid—or too conditioned—to imagine for myself?* It's about allowing yourself to desire more, to take more risks, to live more fully.

Because "good enough" isn't the same as *alive*. And fine isn't the same as *free*.

Losing Scripts

A *losing script*, in Transactional Analysis, is the kind of life story that seems almost set up to fail from the beginning—though the person living it often doesn't realise that. It's the script that leads to repeated heartbreak, self-sabotage, dead-end jobs, toxic relationships, chronic addictions and even taking one's own life.

Let's bring it to life with an example.

Meet Lou

Lou was the kind of person who always seemed to be fighting an invisible current. No matter how hard she tried, things just didn't quite work out. Relationships fizzled out or turned sour. Jobs felt like battles. She would start new projects with a burst of energy, only to abandon them halfway through. She blamed herself constantly—*What's wrong with me? Why can't I just get it together?*

In therapy, Lou began to unravel the deeper story she had been living. As a child, she was often told, "You're too much," or "You'll never amount to anything if you don't calm down." Her parents, overwhelmed and emotionally distant, had little room for her feelings. Somewhere along the line, Lou absorbed the message that she was a problem to be managed, not a person to be cherished.

She didn't consciously decide to fail; no one does. But deep down, her script said: Don't succeed. Don't get close. Don't ask for what you need. It was safer that way. It felt safer to sabotage the relationship before she was abandoned. It felt safer to remain in underpaid work than risk rejection by trying for something bigger. It felt safer to give up on dreams than face the shame of not being good enough.

Lou's life wasn't merely difficult—it was tragic in that quiet, relentless manner that wears one down over the years. She played out her part with unsettling consistency, trudging the same emotional corridors time and again.

But as she began to discern the pattern, a new possibility emerged. She wasn't cursed, and she wasn't broken. She was living a narrative that had been composed for her and unwittingly adopted by her. And that meant it could be rewritten.

It wasn't easy. Changing a losing script takes time. It involves grieving the years lost to mere survival, daring to believe in your own worth, and taking tentative steps in unfamiliar directions. However, Lou began to make those changes. She attended therapy regularly. She stood up for herself at work. She allowed a new, healthier relationship to develop. She started to listen to her own needs rather than burying them.

Bit by bit, Lou's story shifted. It didn't erase her past—but it stopped defining her future.

That's a losing script: a life shaped by early decisions made under emotional pressure—decisions that quietly say, *You're not allowed to win*. And the path out begins with recognising that voice, then slowly, courageously, choosing a new one.

A losing script doesn't mean you are doomed—it represents a pattern, not a destiny. The first step to breaking free is to become aware of the script that holds you back. Individuals can rewrite their stories, challenge outdated beliefs, and create a more positive and fulfilling path forward through self-reflection, therapy, or tools like some of those in this book. It's not easy, but it's possible.

A child who is repeatedly told that they are not good enough or who feels unloved might develop script beliefs that say, "I'll never succeed" or "I don't deserve happiness." They may make choices or take actions that reinforce these beliefs without realising it, such as remaining in toxic relationships, avoiding opportunities, or sabotaging their efforts.

In summary, the building blocks of a life script—messages from parents, early decisions, injunctions, life positions, games, rackets, and drivers—work together to influence how we navigate life.

By understanding these elements, we can identify and transform unhelpful scripts, empowering us to make more informed choices and lead more fulfilling lives. We can consciously rewrite our life script; however, we must first become aware of it.

Key Takeaways: Transactional Analysis and Life Scripts

1 **Life Scripts Are Unconscious Blueprints**

- Formed in early childhood through messages from parents and significant others.
- Function like a personal "life play" with a beginning, middle, and end.
- Can be **winning, mediocre,** or **losing**—but they are **not fixed**; they can be rewritten.

2 **Strokes Are Emotional Units of Recognition**

- Positive or negative, verbal or non-verbal.
- Even negative strokes are preferred to no strokes.
- Form the foundation for emotional development and drive much of human behaviour.
- **The stroke economy** (per Claude Steiner) teaches us unhelpful rules like:

  - Don't ask for or give strokes.
  - Don't accept or give yourself strokes.

3 Building Blocks of Life Scripts

- Parental messages: Nurturing vs critical.
- Life positions: Four core beliefs ("I'm OK/You're OK", etc.).
- Injunctions: Implicit prohibitions (e.g., "Don't be you," "Don't feel," "Don't succeed").
- Drivers: Internal pressures like "Be Perfect," "Hurry Up," "Please Others."
- Games: Repetitive, emotionally charged interactions like those in the Drama Triangle.
- Rackets: Learned emotional substitutes (e.g., showing sadness instead of anger).

4 Scripts Shape Repeated Patterns

- Emotional habits and belief systems become self-fulfilling.
- Children adopt behaviours that generate strokes, even negative ones, which persist into adulthood.
- Without awareness, people repeat these patterns unconsciously.

5 Scripts Can Be Rewritten

- Awareness of your script is the first step to change.
- Therapy, especially when incorporating techniques such as Transactional Analysis (TA), journalling, and Cognitive Behavioural Therapy (CBT), is found to be beneficial in challenging outdated beliefs.
- Positive relationships, resilience, and a supportive environment are crucial.

Recommended Reading

Berne, Eric (1961). *Transactional Analysis in Psychotherapy: A Systematic Individual and Social Psychiatry*. Grove Press. (The seminal work in which Berne lays out the core structure of Transactional Analysis (TA), including ego states and script theory.)

Berne, Eric (1964). *Games People Play: The Psychology of Human Relationships*. Grove Press. (A classic that introduced TA to the public. It outlines the "games" people unconsciously play in relationships.)

Berne, Eric (1972). *What Do You Say After You Say Hello? The Psychology Of Human Destiny*. Corgi. (Explores life scripts in depth—how they're formed and how they influence adult behaviour.)

Jongeward, Dorothy & James, Muriel (1971). *Born to Win: Transactional Analysis with Gestalt Experiments*. Addison-Wesley Publishing Company. (Introduces TA concepts with a strong emphasis on personal growth and Gestalt-style exercises. Accessible and engaging.)

Karpman, Stephen (2018). *Collected Papers on Transactional Analysis*. Drama Triangle Publications. (This compilation includes many of Karpman's foundational writings, including his work on the **Drama Triangle** and its evolution.)

Steiner, Claude (1974). *Scripts People Live: Transactional Analysis of Life Scripts*. Grove Press. (A comprehensive and psychologically rich dive into how life scripts operate and how to change them.)

Stewart, Ian & Joines, Vann (2012). *TA Today: A New Introduction to Transactional Analysis*, 2nd ed. Lifespace. (One of the best modern overviews. Straightforward, practical, and widely used in TA training. Includes script theory and many diagrams.)

References

Berne, E. (1964). *Games people play: The psychology of human relationships*. Grove Press.

Berne, E. (1972). *What do you say after you say hello? The psychology of human destiny*. Grove Press.

Spitz, R. A. (1945). Hospitalism: An inquiry into the genesis of psychiatric conditions in early childhood. *Psychoanalytic Study of the Child, 1*, 53–74.

Steiner, C. (1971). The stroke economy. *Transactional Analysis Journal, 1*(3), 91–97. https://doi.org/10.1177/036215377100100306

Chapter 15

The Only Game in Town

The Drama Triangle

Eric Berne's model of Transactional Analysis (TA) gained public popularity because it did something rare in the world of psychotherapy—it made psychology understandable. While many psychodynamic theories of the time were dense, abstract, and laced with jargon, Berne offered something refreshingly simple, relatable, and immediately applicable. His concepts—like Parent, Adult, and Child ego states, psychological "games", and life "scripts"—were easy to grasp and, more importantly, recognisable in everyday life (Berne, 1964).

TA helped individuals make sense of their behaviour as it unfolded, particularly in relationships. Why do I always end up in the same argument with my partner? Why do I shrink around authority figures? Why do I keep rescuing others and end up feeling drained? Berne's model made unconscious patterns visible. It revealed how people were replaying old roles, following outdated scripts, and falling into familiar traps. And once you can recognise a pattern, you can start to change it.

At the heart of TA lies a hopeful idea: that change is possible. While some Freudian approaches suggested that we were trapped in the emotional patterns of early childhood, Berne challenged this notion. Yes, he stated, you wrote your life script when you were very young, but you're not confined to it. You can choose a different ending.

The message—that we are the authors of our own lives—resonated powerfully during the cultural climate of the 1960s and 1970s, a period when ideas of self-discovery and personal growth were gaining traction in the mainstream. TA did not merely speak to therapists; it communicated with everyday people. It provided them with a language for what they were already feeling and the tools to effect meaningful change.

Berne dedicated 40 years to studying psychological games, giving them witty titles to help people quickly identify them. Through years of observation, he recognised recurring social dynamics among thousands of patients, meticulously documenting his findings and authoring a ground-breaking book, *Games People Play* (Berne, 1964).

DOI: 10.4324/9781003675099-16

His book quickly gained widespread recognition, solidifying its status as one of the most influential texts in the field of popular psychology. Decades later, despite some of the terminology feeling somewhat outdated, the core principles remain as relevant as they were in the 1960s. Berne characterised psychological games as unconscious, habitual behaviours that involve several "moves". I've listed some of the games later in this chapter; however, regardless of the game's name, *it's a Drama Triangle*.

Once you become aware of the Drama Triangle, you will notice it everywhere—in international politics, workplaces, marriages, shops, and soap operas. It's the game everyone plays. Yet, hardly anyone acknowledges when this game is "in play".

The Drama Triangle is a psychological game.

Games are played to obtain positive or negative *strokes*. Chapter 14, "All the World's a Stage: Life Scripts and How to Change Them", discusses strokes in more detail.

Psychological games are patterns of behaviour that unfold on two levels: what is articulated on the surface and what is occurring beneath. These interactions often obscure their true purpose, such as eliciting sympathy, attention, or control. While someone may walk away with a short-term benefit, the exchange typically feels insincere and tends to leave at least one person feeling frustrated, misunderstood, or hurt.

The Drama Triangle (Figure 15.1) describes a dysfunctional communication model proposed by psychiatrist Stephen Karpman, a colleague of Eric Berne, the founder of Transactional Analysis (Karpman, 1968).

For those wishing to know more about the Drama Triangle, I recommend Stephen Karpman's *A Game Free Life* (Karpman, 2014).

The Drama Triangle model involves three interlocked roles: Victim, Rescuer, and Persecutor (V, R, P).

Once caught in the Drama Triangle, roles can shift in the blink of an eye. One moment, you're the Rescuer; the next, you're the Victim, or the Persecutor. It all depends on the storyteller's perspective. The Drama Triangle never ends well, mainly because the emotions associated with the roles often lead us to act irrationally.

Here's an example:

Sam feels overwhelmed at work and says, "I can't make this work. I've been at it for hours!" (**Victim**).
His colleague, Jay, jumps in: "Don't worry—I'll fix it for you!" (**Rescuer**).

Later, when Sam makes a mistake, Jay (now feeling like Sam's Victim) snaps: "I do everything for you, and you still mess it up!" (**Persecutor**).

All three roles—Victim, Rescuer, and Persecutor—are played out in one cycle, with people switching roles along the way.

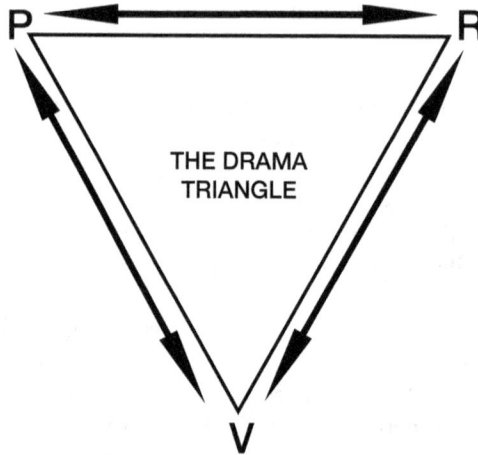

The Persecutor (P)

Angry (openly or passively)

Critical

Controlling

Judgemental

Bullying

Demanding

Scornful

The Rescuer (R)

Self-sacrificing

Over-helpful

Enabling

Likes to be needed

Engulfing

THE DRAMA TRIANGLE

The Victim (V)

Manipulative

Woe is me

Helpless and needy

Complaining

Downtrodden

Blaming others

Figure 15.1 The Drama Triangle © 1967 by Stephen B. Karpman, M.D. Used with permission.

While the classic triangle involves two people, more can join the fray, and sometimes the drama unfolds entirely within one individual, switching between all three roles internally. Here's how this may play out:

1 The Inner Victim

- "Why does this always happen to me?"

- "I can't handle this."

You feel powerless, overwhelmed, or taken advantage of; life feels unfair, and you feel stuck or helpless.

2 The Inner Rescuer

- "Maybe if I just push through, I can fix everything."
- "I'll read that new self-help book, and it'll all be fine."

The Rescuer might manifest as perfectionism, overwork, people-pleasing, or compulsively trying to manage one's emotions or circumstances.

3 The Inner Persecutor

- "You're such a failure."
- "What's wrong with you? Why can't you get it together?"

This voice blames and shames, creating the distress the inner Victim reacts to ... and the cycle continues.

It's a sort of emotional loop. One moment you feel helpless, the next you scramble to fix everything, and then you turn on yourself with blame and criticism. You don't need anyone else to participate in the game; it all unfolds inside your head, like a one-person show where you keep switching roles.

Participants in this dysfunctional triangle take turns occupying three roles: Persecutor (P), Rescuer (R), and Victim (V). All participants are caught in feelings of guilt and blame.

- The **Victim** adopts a helpless, one-down position (I'm not OK/You're OK, or possibly I'm not OK/You're not OK), embraces a "poor me" attitude, and feels oppressed, helpless, ashamed, and incapable. They tend to rely on others, avoid responsibility, and make little effort to make constructive decisions.
- The **Rescuer** sees themselves as a *saviour*, adopting a one-up position (I'm OK/You're not OK). Rescuers often assume an excessive caretaking role, prioritising the needs of others at the expense of their own. They experience an overwhelming sense of responsibility, believing that everything will fall apart if they do not intervene. By viewing others as helpless, they instinctively rush to rescue them, unknowingly fostering dependence in those they are trying to assist. The Rescuer feels guilty when problems cannot be resolved.
- The **Persecutor** is domineering, bullying, and adopts a superior position (I'm OK/You're not OK). They blame others, use guilt to control the victim, and are critical, judgemental, argumentative, and lash out.

If you believe you're in a Drama Triangle, draw a triangle and write the names of the participants in each of the three corners to clarify your current position. It can be enlightening to observe how these roles interchange.

A Case Example: "Yes, But ..."

As a student psychotherapist, I had a client called Alison. Unbeknownst to me at the time, she was a Drama Triangulator.

Alison arrived for her weekly sessions, and the game would begin within minutes. "My boss has done it again this week. She asked me to complete a piece of work by Wednesday, but then she piled on extra work and insisted that I prioritise that. Then, of course, she chased me on Wednesday for the original work, and when I said that I hadn't finished, she didn't allow me to explain. She yelled at me! It's unfair! She always behaves like that."

I asked Alison how she had responded to this situation. She said she "couldn't be bothered arguing" and, feeling resentful, worked late into Thursday night because she didn't want to lose her job.

Alison expressed that her boss consistently overloaded her with work and imposed unrealistic deadlines. I enquired whether striving even harder to meet her boss's unrealistic expectations was a sustainable response. She said no. I suggested exploring TA's communication theory, believing it might offer a solution. She agreed, albeit reluctantly. I outlined how we would begin, to which Alison responded, "Yes, but ..." My efforts were met with, "That wouldn't work because she'd say ..." I proposed examining her negative automatic thoughts, suggesting CBT as a way forward, and she again replied with, "Yes, but ...."

Noticing her resistance, I reminded myself to be patient—defences aren't walls to bulldoze but doors to gently knock on. Still, something about Alison's pushback felt rehearsed, even gratifying for her. It seemed like a setup. As she clung to her "Yes, but ..." routine, my silence stifled a growing frustration. She appeared comfortable remaining stuck, and I couldn't understand what held her back from considering another way.

Psychotherapists aren't here to provide answers—we're here to help clients find their own. While we may seem quiet, we're actively listening, tracking dynamics, spotting themes, and gently guiding insight. We ask questions like, "Who does this remind you of?" to explore possible projections and help name distorted thoughts that fuel unhelpful behaviour patterns. Through curiosity and reflection, we support clients in discovering new ways to understand and navigate their inner world.

Occasionally, when a client has a particularly stubborn blind spot and subtler approaches haven't landed, we may offer a more direct interpretation. Something like: "I wonder if this person might remind you of your mother?" But let's be honest: unless the therapeutic planets are perfectly aligned, even the sharpest insight might go in one ear and out the other. The real magic happens when the client stumbles upon the insight themselves, however uncomfortable: "Okay, I'm wrong... but at least I figured it out on my own."

Even when something is difficult to accept, self-discovery is significantly more impactful, empowering clients to embrace and integrate their insights.

However, Alison remained entrenched in her role as a victim of circumstance and was either unable or unwilling to engage with any of my interventions. I took my dilemma to supervision and shared it with my supervisor. (All psychotherapists participate in regular supervision sessions to discuss their work and address professional challenges. This benefits both the psychotherapist and the client.)

My supervisor noticed that I had unintentionally become part of a Drama Triangle. I had taken on the "Rescuer" role, trying to help Alison with a "Let me help you …" approach, while Alison responded in the "Victim" role with a "yes, but …" approach, deflecting solutions.

As a psychotherapist-in-training, the Drama Triangle was new to me—and revelatory! Everywhere I looked, I could now see it. My supervisor advised that, rather than continuing to engage Alison by problem-solving for her, I should bring her unconscious psychological game of "Yes, but …" into her awareness. Only then could we progress.

If I'd continued on the path I began with, I would have been on course to secure the role of Persecutor—cue the "After all I've done for you …" script. And if that dynamic kept repeating, I knew where it would lead: with me cast as the Victim—overwhelmed, unappreciated, and wondering how I ended up emotionally cornered in a play I didn't audition for.

- Rescuers need a Victim.
- Victims need a Persecutor, a Rescuer or both, and
- Persecutors need a Victim and a Rescuer.

Wait—Persecutors need Rescuers? Surprisingly, yes. Sometimes a Persecutor feels like a Victim who's been pushed into that role and looks for a Rescuer. For example, a boss lashes out at their assistant for poor performance. On the surface, the boss appears to be the Persecutor, but if the assistant's repeated mistakes trigger the dynamic, the boss might feel victimised and react from that place, hoping someone will step in to "fix" the situation.

There are various types of psychological games, including marital, party, sexual, competitive, and even consulting room games (as demonstrated above).

Knowing the names of these games can help you recognise them.

Case Example: Christmas Martyr

I had a client who played the "Martyr" game every Christmas. It's a popular game enjoyed worldwide.

Every year, Phil catered for about 18 people. He loved cooking and made a significant effort. He contacted everyone to find out who was coming, planned the menu, did the shopping, and prepared the food.

Everything usually went smoothly until the meal was nearly ready to be served.

Everything was under control—turkey resting, ready for carving, the gravy prepared, and the vegetables nearly finished on the hob. He absentmindedly began setting the table, his frustration gradually building.

Wait a moment, he thought; everyone else was still laughing, drinking, and enjoying themselves in the other room! His irritation deepened as he intensified his feelings of unfairness, placing the plates down. He stormed into the next room and shouted, "I'm bloody sick of this! I make the Christmas dinner every year, and nobody even offers to set the table! Nobody's even offered me a glass of wine. I'm taken for granted."

Phil's Annual Christmas Kitchen Meltdown had become as much a part of the holiday tradition as the turkey itself. Right on cue, the bad temper flared—and so did the chorus of predictable reactions. Some rushed to soothe him with a glass of wine, while others apologised profusely for not reading his mind. A few muttered that Phil never let anyone help in the kitchen anyway. And, like clockwork, someone would sigh, "Same drama, every year. Nothing ever changes."

Phil unconsciously craved appreciation—a few strokes for being the selfless hero in the kitchen, along with a measure of sympathy for shouldering it all. Once he received his emotional payoff, whether praise or pity, he would reset as if nothing had happened, happily returning to the roast as if the outburst had never occurred.

Phil had a habit of bottling up his anger. But where does all that unspoken frustration go? It doesn't just disappear. Picture it like a Resentment Loyalty Card: whenever someone irritates you and you say nothing, you quietly collect a point—cha-ching. Over time, those points accumulate, and eventually, you redeem them—usually for a dramatic outburst or a sudden exit from the relationship. Berne referred to this as "trading stamps", but I prefer the updated version: Resentment Loyalty Card—more modern, same emotional debt.

Psychological games resemble scenes from a play in which the script has already been written, and the actors follow their cues without deviation. Every move, line, and reaction is predetermined, unfolding in a predictable sequence: first, this happens, then that, and so forth. This cycle repeats itself, creating an unmistakable sense of déjà vu: "Here we go again."

Though often subtle, these games involve deeply ingrained behavioural patterns for specific psychological purposes. Phil was playing the **Martyr** who sacrifices and suffers for the sake of others; it inevitably led to **Uproar**, where the person stirs chaos and conflict to command attention. Sometimes the sequel is the **Woe Is Me**, a perpetual lamenter who evokes sympathy through self-pity.

Each role hits its mark with the flair of a well-rehearsed play—because that's precisely what it is. What appears to be spontaneity is a script running on auto-pilot. The trick is recognising the performance for what it is. Only then can the cast drop their lines, step off the stage, and cease playing parts they never intended to audition for in the first place.

I've listed below some of the games that Eric Berne named and analysed in his book, *Games People Play* (1964).

Uproar

Uproar is a game many couples and families know well. Jenny and Rick came to therapy stuck in what Jenny called a "Groundhog Day of arguments". Rick's usual move was to walk away when things got tense—predictably lighting the fuse. Minor disagreements over chores or plans quickly escalated into blame, guilt trips, and defensive jabs, leaving both feeling hurt and disconnected. I asked for examples. Jenny explained, "It always starts the same way. We head out on a Saturday, do some food shopping, maybe wander through a few clothes shops, then grab lunch. But somewhere along the way, Rick picks a fight. Suddenly, I'm standing there alone, watching him walk off. He disappears for hours, and when he finally comes home, he's usually been drinking."

This game can serve as an escape from intimacy. The party with a hidden agenda, such as the desire to go to the pub or the gym, uses Uproar as a pretext.

Martyr

Unlike genuine martyrs who suffer for their beliefs, the psychological Martyr plays a different game. She helps others—often at personal cost—to feel good about herself. When drained or unappreciated, she shifts the blame onto those she endeavoured to help. It's a close cousin of the "Woe Is Me" game.

If It Weren't For You

This is a game often played by couples. A couple once came to counselling where Joe complained that his wife, Alicia, was stopping him from pursuing his hobbies. One example was mountain climbing—something he said he'd always wanted to do, but couldn't because she wouldn't go with him. When I asked why he couldn't go alone or with friends, he had no answer. Ironically, Alicia claimed she supported his hobbies; she enjoyed the space it gave her.

Eventually, Joe booked the trip. He didn't reach the summit, because on the of the way up the mountain, he developed vertigo. Frustrated, he blamed Alicia for "holding him back". Similar patterns followed: his knees were too bad for ice skating, friends unavailable for bowling, or finances too tight for golf.

Digging deeper, Joe's history with a controlling, risk-averse mother shaped his view that women limited him. Alicia's past left her viewing men as needy and pessimistic. Their dynamic mirrored old family patterns. Joe projected his internal fears onto Alicia to avoid taking risks, reinforcing a game TA calls **"If It Weren't for You"**—a way of seeking reassurance while avoiding responsibility.

Look What You Made Me Do

This game shifts blame away from the person who's actually made the mistake. For example, John and Liz were on a trip. John was driving and Liz was chattering companionably, when John, having been forced to brake suddenly, snapped at Liz: "Look what you made me do! This never happens when I'm driving alone." Perhaps he needed quiet to focus, but instead of asking for it, he let frustration build and used the error as a release.

Similarly, Katie, a mother of three, was pruning roses when her five-year-old asked for biscuits. Startled, she cut her finger and yelled, "See what you've made me do! Can't I have a few minutes to myself?" Rather than calmly setting boundaries, she unleashed pent-up resentment, likely fuelled by feelings of overwhelm or people-pleasing habits. Her outburst taught her child that needs are not expressed directly, but rather through blame and frustration. A clearer, more respectful request could have made all the difference.

Kick Me

Kick Me players tend to act in ways that lead others to metaphorically "kick" them. They often display a discouraged and defeated attitude. I had a client who frequently irritated friends and colleagues by showing up late, cancelling plans last minute, double-booking, and forgetting important dates. This pattern extended into therapy—he arrived late, missed payments, and tried to cancel sessions outside the agreed policy.

It became valuable material in our work. Rather than reacting, I named the pattern, explored it with him, and held clear boundaries without anger. But outside the consulting room, these games usually end badly. When others inevitably push back, the game player often shifts roles, usually into the Victim role, when their behaviour finally triggers criticism, and then they switch to …

Why Does It Always Happen To Me?

Sometimes, this type of player teams up with another player who plays:

I'm Only Trying To Help You

The helper continues to assist until overwhelmed by Kick Me's game. Subsequently, they react by losing patience and attributing blame to Kick Me for involving them in the game in the first place.

Look How Hard I've Tried

Games sometimes show up in the consulting room. A couple came for relationship counselling—the husband was fully committed, but the wife seemed less engaged. At first, she participated enough to appear cooperative, but soon began missing assignments, skipping sessions, and showing up emotionally distant and defensive. Over time, her disengagement stalled the process.

After 12 sessions and several efforts to re-engage her, I gently shared my concern: continuing therapy in this manner wasn't helping and might be wasting their time and resources. I made it clear I was open to continuing if both were willing to put in the effort. The wife became angry, accusing me of giving up, though I sensed her frustration was genuine and perhaps connected to deeper, unspoken issues. I sought supervision on this matter because the last thing a therapist wants to do is call it a day. A few more sessions followed, but the same dynamics persisted, and I eventually had to conclude the process. It is part of the therapist's role to recognise when therapy isn't progressing.

Nowadays

This is a game played by the self-righteous and sometimes punitive, and the payoff is that the gamer gets to position themselves as superior (I'm OK, You're not OK, or They are not OK). The player focuses on what is wrong with society and how it wasn't like that back in the day: "Parents let their children get away with too much nowadays, crime is increasing because the police are powerless, you can't trust anyone these days, everyone's out for themselves," and so forth. Another name for this game is **"Innit Awful?"**

So, those are a few examples of psychological games, all of which are variations of the Drama Triangle. Now, let us explore how to break free from it.

Turning Drama into Dialogue

To avoid Drama Triangles, the main task is to recognise your role, reflect on its origins and "payoffs".

Identify the Payoff

In Transactional Analysis, the **payoff** refers to the hidden emotional reward we receive from repeating familiar, often painful patterns. It's the moment a psychological game reaches its predictable conclusion, confirming an old belief like "People always let me down" or "I'm never enough."

Eric Berne identified **four levels of payoff**, from mild irritation to deep existential despair, depending on the emotional cost.

- **First-degree**: Relatively mild—awkwardness, disappointment, or irritation.
- **Second-degree**: More damaging—strained relationships, recurring conflict.
- **Third-degree**: Potentially harmful—emotional crisis, abuse, or psychological injury.
- **Fourth-degree (existential)**: Deep, often unconscious reaffirmation of despairing beliefs like "I'm doomed," or "Life isn't worth it."

Recognising the payoff is a pivotal moment in therapy. Once we recognise what we have been unknowingly demonstrating or pursuing, we can start to make different choices, shifting from unconscious repetition to conscious change. Let me illustrate this.

The Boomerang Effect

Imagine you're throwing a boomerang. You hurl it out into the world—words, behaviours, reactions—and, after a brief arc, it comes spinning back towards you. It repeatedly hits you in the same old spot. It stings, but it's familiar. And predictable.

That sting? That's the **payoff**.

In Transactional Analysis, the payoff is what we unconsciously expect—*and create*. We throw the emotional boomerang because, deep down, we're trying to prove something we've believed since childhood: *I'm not good enough, People always leave, It's safer to go it alone.* When it returns and confirms that belief, something inside us says, *See? I knew it.*

The strange thing is, we often don't realise we're the one throwing the boomerang. It feels like life is doing it *to* us when really, we've been setting it in motion all along.

The work of therapy is learning to pause before you throw. To ask: *What am I hoping to get back?* And, with time, to choose a different action—one that doesn't come back to prove the old story right but opens space for something new.

Over time, several helpful alternatives to the Drama Triangle have been developed.

Acey Choy's Winner's Triangle

Acey Choy offered the Winner's Triangle. Choy presents a thoughtful reworking of the Drama Triangle in "The Winner's Triangle", first published in 1990. Rather than *Victim, Rescuer, and Persecutor*, Choy reframes the roles as *Vulnerable, Caring, and Assertive*, each grounded in adult-to-adult relating.

The **Vulnerable** person owns their feelings and needs without blame. The **Caring** person offers support without rescuing—listening, empathising, and encouraging autonomy. The **Assertive** person expresses themselves clearly and respectfully, setting boundaries without attack.

Choy's model replaces drama with dignity, inviting us to respond consciously, relate authentically, and step out of old roles—without stepping out of connection.

The Empowerment Dynamic

David Emerald introduced The Empowerment Dynamic (TED), offering a healthier and more constructive alternative to drama.

In *The Power of TED* (with TED standing for *The Empowerment Dynamic*), Emerald offers a reframe of the roles we assume when caught in drama. Instead of being reactive, these roles become conscious, creative, and grounded in choice.

The **Victim** becomes the **Creator**. This doesn't mean life stops being hard, but the focus shifts. Instead of dwelling on what's wrong, the Creator asks, *What do I want? What's one small step I can take from here?*

The **Persecutor**, often seen as the villain, transforms into the **Challenger**—not an enemy, but a force for growth. The Challenger may still be blunt or confronting, but the intention is to call forth clarity or change, not to control or shame.

And the **Rescuer** becomes the **Coach**—someone who resists the urge to fix, and instead holds space, listens with care, and asks empowering questions like, *What's important to you?* or *What support would be most helpful?*

This isn't just a new triangle—it's a new way of seeing. Emerald shows how we can shift from reacting to life's problems to responding with intention. The old roles may still show up—we're only human—but we don't have to get stuck in them.

TED invites us out of *drama* and into *choice*. It's not about getting it all right; it's about staying present. It's about recognising when we're slipping into an old pattern and gently choosing a different way forward (Emerald, 2009).

Self-Reflection

The first step in shifting out of the Drama Triangle is becoming aware of when we're in it. When conflict arises, pause and ask yourself: *Am I seeing myself as a Victim here? Am I trying to fix or rescue someone? Am I coming across as controlling or critical?*

These roles—Victim, Rescuer, and Persecutor—are *reactive in nature*. They keep us focused on problems, not possibilities. But with a bit of awareness, we can begin to make a shift.

Instead of feeling stuck in **Victim**, we can choose to step into the role of **Creator**. The Creator still faces challenges but views them as opportunities for growth. Rather than asking, "*Why is this happening to me?*", the Creator asks, "*What outcome do I want? What's one step I can take right now?*"

Rather than defaulting to **Rescuer**, we can assume the role of **Coach**—offering support not by fixing, but by listening, posing thoughtful questions, and trusting others to find their way. The Coach creates space for others to step into their power.

Rather than acting as a **Persecutor**, we can embody the **Challenger**—someone who speaks the truth with respect. The Challenger does not attack but invites clarity, accountability, and growth. They challenge the pattern, not the person.

Ask yourself: *In the dynamics I keep replaying, which role do I usually take on? What old beliefs might that be reinforcing? What would it look like to respond as a Creator instead? How might I support others as a Coach, or speak up as a respectful Challenger?*

Pick one real-life situation this week. Imagine how it would feel to show up differently—more conscious, more curious, more empowered.

These roles aren't about being perfect. They're about choosing presence over reactivity. The more we practise shifting from drama to empowerment, the more freedom we create—not just in our relationships, but in our lives as a whole.

Summary

Engaging in psychological games often involves blaming others or seeking validation in counterproductive ways. By shedding these harmful habits, individuals reclaim control over their emotions and actions, allowing them to meet their needs with greater awareness and control. This shift promotes healthier coping strategies, enabling individuals to navigate challenges with greater confidence and effectiveness. Ultimately, it fosters personal growth, enhances resilience, and promotes a healthier approach to life's challenges.

Key Takeaways: Transactional Analysis (TA) and the Drama Triangle

1   *TA Made Psychology More Accessible*

Eric Berne's Transactional Analysis (TA) framework demystifies psycho-therapy by using relatable terms, such as "Parent", "Adult", and "Child" ego states, as well as psychological games and life scripts, making complex psychological ideas accessible and applicable to everyday life.

2   *The Drama Triangle Is a Dysfunctional Pattern of Relating*

Stephen Karpman's Drama Triangle—comprising Victim, Rescuer, and Persecutor—describes a dysfunctional relational dynamic that manifests everywhere, including in relationships, politics, therapy sessions, and even within oneself.

3   *Psychological Games Have Hidden Payoffs*

Games represent unconscious patterns characterised by surface-level behaviour and hidden motives. The emotional payoff reinforces early script beliefs, such as "I'm not OK" or "People always let me down."

4   *The Triangle Can Be Internal*

Individuals often replay the entire triangle internally, feeling helpless (Victim), over-functioning (Rescuer), and engaging in self-criticism (Persecutor), thus creating an emotional loop.

5   *The Roles Are Fluid and Reactive*

People quickly shift roles within the triangle, often without conscious awareness. A Rescuer can become a Victim or a Persecutor in the blink of an eye.

6   *Real-life Examples Bring the Triangle to Life*

Cases like "Yes, but …", "Christmas Martyr", and "If It Weren't For You" highlight how psychological games play out subtly in daily life, reinforcing drama and blocking growth.

7   The Payoff Must Be Recognised to Break the Cycle

The hidden emotional "reward" (e.g., sympathy, moral superiority, justification) sustains the game. Recognising the payoff is crucial to choosing something new.

8   Berne's Payoff Levels Show the Degrees of Emotional Cost

Payoffs range from mild irritation to deep existential despair. Therapy can help identify the level of impact and uncover what is being unconsciously pursued.

9   Reframing Roles Promotes Empowerment and Adult Relating

- **Acey Choy's Winner's Triangle**: Victim becomes Vulnerable, Rescuer becomes Caring, and Persecutor becomes Assertive.
- **David Emerald's TED**: Victim becomes Creator, Rescuer becomes Coach, and Persecutor becomes Challenger.

10   Self-reflection Is Key to Change

Becoming aware of your default role in the triangle, understanding its origins, and envisioning a healthier response are the first steps towards conscious choice and relational freedom.

11   Therapists Must Watch Their Own Role

Practitioners can easily become entangled in the triangle. Awareness and supervision help prevent unconscious re-enactments and foster a more empowered therapeutic alliance.

12   The Drama Triangle Is a Scripted Loop—But You Can Rewrite It

Psychological games resemble emotional theatre: the roles are familiar, and the endings are predictable. Real change occurs when we recognise the script—and choose to step off the stage.

Recommended Reading

Berne, Eric (1964). *Games People Play: The Psychology of Human Relationships*. Grove Press. (The classic text that introduced psychological games and laid the groundwork for the Drama Triangle. Essential reading for understanding the dynamics beneath human interaction.)

Forward, Susan (1997). *Emotional Blackmail*. Bantam Press. (Examines manipulative dynamics, such as Victim–Persecutor games, with tools for boundary setting and relational clarity.)

Harris, Thomas Anthony (1969). *I'm OK–You're OK*. Jonathan Cape. (Introduces the OK Corral model, which is closely related to the Drama Triangle roles. Helpful for understanding internal scripts and relational dynamics.)

Karpman, Stephen (2014). *A Game Free Life*. Drama Triangle Publications. (Karpman's deep dive into the Drama Triangle and how to break free from toxic roles.)

References

Berne, E. (1964). *Games people play: The psychology of human relationships*. Grove Press.

Choy, A. (1990). The Winner's Triangle. *Transactional Analysis Journal*, 20(1), 40–46. https://psycnet.apa.org/doi/10.1177/036215379002000105

Emerald, D. (2009). *The power of TED: The Empowerment Dynamic*. Polaris Publishing.

Karpman, S. B. (1968). Fairy tales and script drama analysis. *Transactional Analysis Bulletin*, 7(26), 39–43.

Karpman, S. B. (2014). *A game free life: The definitive book on the Drama Triangle and the compassion triangle*. Drama Triangle Productions.

Chapter 16

The Call of the Soul

Can we truly come to know ourselves independently? The soul isn't meant to exist in isolation—it comes alive through deep, genuine connection. We grow, unfold, and discover who we are in relationships that embrace vulnerability, where we feel genuinely seen and known, where the Soul is met with care, curiosity, and love.

Although often used interchangeably, Soul and Spirit are distinct, yet deeply interconnected. Their meanings can differ significantly depending on cultural, religious, or philosophical traditions.

The Soul may be regarded as the individual expression of Spirit. If Spirit is akin to the sun, then each ray of sunlight represents a Soul—a unique and personal manifestation of the universal Spirit.

The Soul is the essence of who you are—your inner self, unique individuality, and the core of your emotions, personality, and consciousness. It is the part of you that carries your identity, memories, and a profound connection to all life. Many traditions regard the Soul as dynamic, evolving, and maturing through experiences, shaping the narrative of your life's journey.

The Spirit, in contrast, is viewed as the eternal and divine facet of your being; it acts as the thread that links you to a higher power, the cosmos, or the Infinite.

Spirit transcends individuality. It is often described as the source of life's energy or the very breath of existence (from the Latin *Spiritus*, meaning "breath"). Spirit represents the boundless, universal force that animates and unites all of creation. While the Soul reflects the individual's journey, Spirit speaks to the infinite and eternal within us all.

In the vast expanse of cosmic powerlessness, how can we find the means necessary to assert agency over our lives and imbue them with a sense of purpose and profound significance?

The journey of the Spirit begins with a gentle awakening when a Soul first perceives its purpose in the external world. Not every Soul will heed this call; many wander through life unquestioningly, oblivious to the end of their days, their song unsung.

DOI: 10.4324/9781003675099-17

But those who dare to seek, who embrace the mystery with open hearts, will ultimately uncover the truth they desire. The answer is not far away; it is always close by, a gentle and persistent hum resonating from the depths of your being.

Be Still

Listening to the Soul's call involves embarking on an intimate inward journey, tuning out the distractions of the world to hear the quiet voice within.

It begins by cultivating a space where the mind can rest in stillness, allowing the Soul to whisper its truths. Engaging in moments of silence or meditation fosters the openness necessary to connect with your essence. Sitting in nature, focusing on your breath, or being fully present can help you access this sacred stillness.

Hazrat Inayat Khan[1] said:

To the eye of the seer, every leaf of the tree is a page of the holy book that contains divine revelation, and he is inspired every moment of his life by constantly reading and understanding the holy script of nature.

I love this. Nature is our cathedral.

Nature

Yesterday, my husband and I visited our local park in Ampthill, Bedfordshire. It is a vast expanse designed by the genius of Capability Brown.

We often walk there to enjoy the sweeping views and the towering majesty of countless trees. However, more than anything, we go to encounter the dogs! Dogs of all breeds, colours, and sizes—all with their tails wagging. Their joy, boundless energy, and simple delight in the world fill the heart. As Dr Clarissa Pinkola Estes said, "Dogs are the magicians of the universe. By their presence alone, they can transform grumpy people into grinning people" (Estés, 1992).

Despite the dogs, trees, and landscape, many people were engrossed in their mobile phones. The sky was grey, the weather cold and damp, and as I grappled with the post-Christmas blues, I felt rather low. Sipping my hot chocolate, I noticed people looking up from their devices, drawn to something. They pointed towards the sky, and as I gazed upwards, I spotted them—two magnificent macaws soaring above in long, graceful arcs, their loud squawks reverberating through the crisp air!

They were stunning—a vibrant explosion of tropical brilliance. Their feathers shimmered with an electric cyan-blue hue that enveloped their sleek bodies and extended across their broad wings and tails, fanning out spectacularly as they soared. Against the cool tones of the blue plumage, their bright yellow bellies glowed like captured sunlight, a vivid reminder of nature's beauty. They were dazzling ambassadors of the wild, embodying majesty and charisma.

At first, I felt concerned—had they escaped? But no, their keepers were present. They strolled around the park, occasionally beckoning the birds with outstretched hands.

The macaws eventually settled on a wooden structure, but their performance was far from over. Now surrounded by a crowd of admirers—some snapping photographs, others simply gazing in amazement—they unfurled their wings with grandeur. Each beat celebrated their majesty as if silently proclaiming, *Look at us. Aren't we magnificent?* Their presence commanded awe, a living reminder of the wild's beauty and its power to captivate.

If we can witness such beauty in nature, what stops us from seeking and discovering that beauty within ourselves and in our fellow human beings?

Nature, the eternal teacher, guides with quiet wisdom. Watch the insects weaving with their instinctual thread, storing their sustenance with quiet knowing. See the bees, born to create liquid gold, dancing in harmony. Every living being is given its path, equipped by the hand of creation to fulfil its design. And to each Soul, nature calls, steady and unyielding, a gentle yet persistent reminder: *find your place, fulfil your purpose, and heed the Soul's call.*

Feelings

Feelings often serve as the Soul's compass, guiding you towards what truly resonates. Pay attention to what brings you joy, fulfilment, or peace, as well as what causes discomfort or restlessness.

These emotions serve as messages, guiding you towards alignment and away from disconnection. When something feels right, trust it. Intuition—the deep, unexpressed knowing within you—speaks the Soul's language. Trust those gut feelings, those quiet nudges encouraging you towards a particular path, even when the rational mind cannot fully articulate them. You don't need to make significant, life-altering decisions all at once, but listen! There may be opportunities to make gradual changes towards your desired life without leaving a trail of tears behind.

Self-Reflection

Self-reflection is essential for heeding the call of the Soul. Pose questions to yourself that explore your essence, such as:

- What activities fully engage you, leaving you fulfilled?
- What do you need to relinquish?
- What do you need to embrace?
- What is one small thing you could do today to spice up your routine?

- Is there something you can do today or this week that embodies an act of creativity? For example, you might wear a colour you don't typically choose or take a different route when walking.
- What sort of impact would you like to leave behind?

Journalling can serve as a powerful tool for exploring these answers, enabling your inner voice to emerge freely and authentically.

Signs and Synchronicity

Be open to signs and synchronicities—meaningful coincidences that nudge you in a particular direction.

Carl Jung introduced the concept of synchronicity to describe those uncanny moments when life's coincidences seem too significant to be random. He believed these events are not connected by cause and effect but by a shared meaning unique to the individual experiencing them. Such occurrences might manifest in dreams, recurring symbols, or unexpected encounters, gently affirming the path you are meant to follow (Jung, 1973).

One of the most famous examples Jung gave of *synchronicity* happened during a therapy session with a young woman who was highly intelligent but emotionally closed off. She prided herself on her rational mind and was resistant to the deeper, more intuitive aspects of the work.

One night, she dreamed of being given a golden scarab—a sacred symbol of rebirth in ancient Egypt. The next day, while she was telling Jung about the dream, something tapped against the window behind him. Jung turned, opened the window, and caught a beetle that had flown in; it was a scarabaeid beetle, which closely resembled the golden scarab from her dream.

He handed it to her and said, **"Here is your scarab."**

The moment broke through her intellectual defences. She was so struck by the coincidence—an image from her inner world suddenly materialising in outer reality—that it opened the door to fundamental psychological transformation.

For Jung, this was a perfect example of *synchronicity*: a fortuitous and significant connection between inner and outer events.

Here's another striking example of synchronicity. A few years ago, I jolted awake from a nightmare about a bird with a severed wing—haunted, uneasy, and a little shaken. I got up, padded to the bathroom for a glass of water, and as I returned to bed, something nudged me to glance out the window into the garden.

For a moment, I wondered if I was still dreaming. Perched in the moonlight was my metal garden ornament—a cream-coloured owl with its wings usually spread wide. That night, however, one of its wings had fallen to the ground. I stood there, glass in hand, stunned. It felt as though the dream had spilt into the world outside, blurring the boundary between the inner and outer, the symbolic and the real.

This is synchronicity— a meaningful connection that defies logical explanation yet feels undeniably real. Jung viewed these moments as glimpses of a more profound truth, where the inner world of thoughts and emotions intersects with the outer world of events. They suggest a hidden pattern or purpose weaving through our lives, even if we cannot fully comprehend it.

For Jung, synchronicity served as a gateway to explore the profound mysteries of existence—the invisible threads that connect mind, matter, and meaning. This concept is comforting and inspiring, reminding us that life is intricately interconnected in ways we might never anticipate.

But what were the dream and the fallen ornament trying to tell me? The image of the wounded bird had startled me awake, and seeing its echo in the garden stopped me in my tracks. Around that time, I had begun collaborating with someone eager to work more closely on workshops. Yet, somehow, whenever we met, I felt stifled and drained, as if my natural energy and creative spirit were being syphoned. They were clipping my wings!

Trusting the messages of both dream and symbol, I withdrew from the collaboration. My unconscious had spoken, and I listened.

Further information on dreams and decoding their messages can be found in Chapter 10, "You May Say I'm A Dreamer: Working with Your Dreams".

The Body

Your body conveys messages. Take note of how you feel physically in various situations. Do you feel energised or drained? Relaxed or tense? The Soul's alignment often appears in the body as a sense of ease, whereas misalignment brings tension, fatigue, or a sensation of weakness. If you experience symptoms, pay close attention to the messages they are trying to convey. See Chapter 9, "My Granny's Elbow: The Symptom Speaks" for more on this.

Gratitude and Presence

Gratitude and presence are essential. Focusing on what you are grateful for creates space for the Soul to express itself. Being fully present in each moment enables you to hear the subtle whispers of your inner voice, unhindered by the noise of past regrets or future anxieties. Offering your complete presence to yourself and others is a remarkable gift. Listen with your heart, not just your ears. Pay attention to what is said and what remains unsaid.

Change

Be prepared for change and embrace it. The Soul's call is rarely about remaining in your comfort zone. It may encourage you to grow, evolve, and take courageous steps towards what feels meaningful. Welcome the opportunity for transformation, recognising that listening to your Soul is vital to the journey.

Embrace Your Wounds

There exists a quiet fellowship among those whose hearts have been broken open by life—a tribe not marked by visible signs, but by depth in their eyes and truth in their voices. These people have known sorrow intimately, wrestled with their shadows, and emerged not unscarred, but more fully human.

To belong to the Tribe of the Wounded Heart is not to be defined by pain, but to be transformed by it. Wounding becomes initiation, and the ache becomes an invitation. Healing is not a return to who we were, but an unfolding into who we are becoming. Our wounds help shape us. If you have suffered emotional pain, you are not alone—you never were. "The wound is the place where the light enters you" (Rumi).

Intimacy and Companionship

To live fully and thrive, we crave intimacy—a genuine human connection that binds us together. Moreover, we also need the quiet companionship of animals, the grounding presence of nature, and the wild yet tender reminder that we are part of something far greater than ourselves. Nature is an unwavering sanctuary, a source of nourishment upon which we can depend.

Humans, with their complexity, can be more challenging to understand. We all bear the weight of our scars. Yet, when I step outside with my heart open and loving, the world begins to soften. My open heart resonates with others, reflecting light amid darkness. Because I'm human, I often stumble and become judgemental, critical, distrustful, or aloof. But like a phoenix rising from the ashes, I shake it off and try again.

The true art is this: to collect the years gently and keep the heart untainted by bitterness.

Wisdom Teachers

Many souls have left their mark on me—writers, musicians, artists, friends, and clients. Extraordinary beings disguised as ordinary people—gifted, sometimes luminous, and occasionally unaware of their light. I have been fortunate to learn from wise women and men, yet the ones who influence me most often tread unpaved paths—unconventional voices that gently call to those who have the ears to hear, from the fringes of the mainstream.

Early in my psychotherapy training, I balanced work, study, and voluntary client hours, scarcely finding time to breathe, let alone spend a weekend doing anything other than collapsing into my bed. However, one day, a leaflet caught my eye. It drew me, quietly and insistently, to a workshop led by a remarkable teacher: Atum Thomas O'Kane, a Sufi master and guide.

The Call of the Soul workshop attracted around a hundred people, a considerable number in those pre-Internet days. I had not met Atum before, but something in his workshop leaflet beckoned to me. I registered for my place, uncertain of what I hoped for; it simply felt necessary.

Atum began the workshop by sitting quietly, and the room fell silent. There was no need for calls to order, bells, or sweeping gestures. His quiet presence alone commanded stillness. This is the way with such teachers: they carry a weightless gravity, a magnetism, an unseen force that naturally draws the attention of everyone around them. But don't mistake Atum for someone too heavenly to be of earthly use. Atum was mischievous, playful, and delightfully funny. His workshops often revolved around children's books, which he read aloud, sharing the illustrations and transforming simple stories into profound spiritual teachings.

He began by asking us to recall when we first encountered his leaflet. He then invited us to sit and reflect on the question: What drew you to this workshop?

In the stillness that followed, I pondered the title of the workshop and realised it resonated with something deep within me—a longing for connection, a sacred space where I could listen to the quiet stirrings of my Soul.

As I sat quietly, an image came to mind: "The Christ Child Asleep" by Bernardino Luini—a painting I had seen years ago at the V&A Museum in Kensington. In the artwork, Mary gazes tenderly at her sleeping child, her face serene, her presence so deeply attuned that I could imagine her hearing the child's every heartbeat and every soft breath. The image lingered in my mind, vivid and rich with a meaning I had yet to grasp, for at that moment, I didn't understand why that image appeared or what it intended to convey. However, as the workshop unfolded, I began to comprehend. It was a call to listen deeply to others, the Divine, and my Soul.

Several years later, at the end of a wonderful ten-day silent retreat, my retreat guide, Noor Jacobs, gave me a postcard featuring "The Christ Child Asleep" as a farewell gift. Her message on the back urged me to remain still and listen softly to the divine child within. She could not have known about my image from the workshop all those years ago; I had nearly forgotten the event myself. Coincidence? I don't believe in such things. Synchronicity.

Laughter

It will come as no surprise to those who know me that I have chosen to close this chapter—and finish this book—on the subject of laughter.

Some therapists see humour as a defence mechanism to shield us from complicated emotions. While this can sometimes be true, we must approach this interpretation with caution, as it conveys only part of the story.

Like all profound experiences, laughter has layers, and its significance in our emotional and spiritual lives extends far beyond mere avoidance. What better way to celebrate life, connection, and the sacred than through the joyful, uncontrollable, soul-shaking act of laughter?

Laughter and spirituality are more deeply intertwined than we might initially realise. Both touch something profound within us, bringing joy, release, and a sense of connection. Genuine laughter is more than merely a reaction; it is a spiritual experience—a means to fully embrace the present moment, dissolve the ego, and cultivate a deep connection with the universe.

When we laugh, we immerse ourselves in the present moment, leaving behind worries about the past or future. In that instant, we are truly alive, anchored in the present—a state that many spiritual traditions encourage us to cultivate. Furthermore, when we laugh at ourselves, we release pride and seriousness, softening our edges and reconnecting with our shared humanity.

Laughter is a balm, a healer, medicine for the soul. It clears emotional clutter, breaks through energetic blockages, and invites lightness and joy. Shared laughter, in particular, acts as a bridge. It dissolves barriers, forges bonds, and reminds us of a profound spiritual truth: we are all interconnected.

Many of the world's great spiritual teachers recognise the power of humour. Sufi mystics, Zen masters, and the Dalai Lama often sprinkle their wisdom with laughter, uplifting hearts while deepening understanding. Laughter, after all, is a divine gift—an energy that reminds us that spirituality is not always about solemnity and silence. Joy is just as sacred as stillness.

Some spiritual practices even intentionally incorporate laughter into their activities. Laughter Yoga, for example, combines the physical act of laughing with breathing exercises to cultivate joy and well-being. Other communities weave laughter into rituals alongside dancing and singing, embracing the richness of life's playfulness.

Even laughing at our foibles can be an act of grace. Finding humour in our imperfections is a practice of self-compassion and humility, honouring our beautifully flawed human nature.

Laughter reveals life's great paradox: it is both profound and absurd, heavy and light. Within this playful balance lies a significant spiritual truth. We need not seek transcendence solely in silence or stillness; we can also discover it in the bubbling joy of a good laugh. For in laughter, we glimpse the divine—profound, playful, and wonderfully human all at once.

Clients, supervisees, and students occasionally ask about the appropriateness of laughing in therapy. If gravitas is genuinely needed for such a topic, I rely on those heavy-hitters, the Greek gods and goddesses.

I tell them about Baubo, the goddess of mirth. She is a fascinating yet often overlooked figure in Greek mythology, celebrated for her connection to laughter, healing, and feminine wisdom. Her role in the myth of Demeter and Persephone is small, but it is profoundly significant, illustrating the transformative power of humour and the sacred nature of joy.

Baubo enters the story during Demeter's search for her daughter, Persephone, who has been abducted by Hades and taken to the underworld. Overwhelmed by grief, Demeter withdraws from her duties as the goddess of agriculture, resulting in famine across the land. It is during this time of despair that Baubo appears; she is not a grand or imposing figure but rather humble and playful, embodying a raw, earthy sense of humour.

When Demeter arrives at Eleusis, weary and inconsolable in her grief, Baubo steps forward with an unexpected gift: humour. Baubo makes risqué jokes and, with bold irreverence, lifts her skirt to reveal her genitals. This audacious act elicits a burst of laughter from Demeter. In that moment, Demeter's sorrow loosens, and she reconnects with her inner strength and resolve, regaining the will to continue her search for Persephone.

The laughter that Baubo inspires is so profound that it ripples through the very fabric of the earth. Tiny cracks appear in the ground, and birds rise into the sky, scattering their droppings as they take flight. Some of this fertilising matter falls into the newly formed crevices, from which fresh growth emerges. This imagery underscores a powerful truth: humour and irreverence can break open the most rigid surfaces, even in despair, allowing life to renew itself in unexpected and miraculous ways.

Baubo embodies the healing power of laughter, demonstrating that humour can be a sacred act that restores balance and vitality, even in the darkest of times. Her association with the body and sensuality reflects an unapologetic embrace of physicality and the life-giving energy of femininity.

Her presence also emphasises the cycles of life, death, and renewal—central themes in the myth of Demeter and Persephone. Baubo's humour connects the sorrow of loss with the hope of rebirth, reflecting the eternal rhythm: darkness yielding to light, despair to joy.

In today's world, Baubo's story continues to resonate. She serves as a powerful reminder of the significance of laughter as a tool for resilience and healing. Baubo teaches us to find joy in our bodies, embrace the unexpected, and recognise that humour is not merely a distraction but a profound means of connecting with others and rediscovering our inner light. She stands as a timeless celebration of laughter as a sacred force that holds the power to heal, unite, and transform.

At the conclusion of my Advanced Transpersonal Psychotherapy training, I was invited to select an object to accompany my final presentation—a talisman representing the journey I had undertaken and the path that was unfolding. I chose the Laughing Buddha. He stood, with a belly round and wide and spirit light, as both a symbol of what I had learned and a quiet herald of what I sensed was yet to come.

In the Chinese tradition, the Laughing Buddha is inspired by a tenth-century Chinese Zen monk named Pu-tai, also known as Budai. He is a folkloric figure symbolising happiness, abundance, contentment, and good fortune. Archetypally, he represents the Holy Fool, the Divine Child, and the Trickster—figures who disrupt, delight, and liberate with their laughter and presence.

In Jungian terms, when the Laughing Buddha appears—whether in a dream, a piece of art, or your imagination—he often signifies that something within you longs to let go. Perhaps it's the pressure to be perfect. Maybe it's grief that has lingered for too long. Perhaps it's simply the tight grip of control.

From an alchemical perspective, the Laughing Buddha is a symbol of *rubedo*—the final stage of transformation. His laughter isn't escapism. It's the sound of someone who's faced the darkness, lived through it, and come out the other side whole. His joy is the kind that's been earned.

Final Thoughts

The Soul's call is gentle and patient, never demanding or loud. One must be willing to pause, listen, and trust to hear it. It's not about seeking quick answers but nurturing a deep relationship with oneself—a connection that becomes richer over time.

The Soul communicates in silences and dreams, weaving truths that words cannot convey. Therefore, listen carefully to discern who you are and who you can become. To listen is to yield to the quiet sanctuary within and to receive the boundless wisdom that flows from your innermost depths. For in the song of the Soul lies the map to your most authentic self—an expanse of light, shadow, and infinite possibility.

Note

1 Hazrat Inayat Khan (1882–1927) was the founder of Universal Sufism and the Sufi Order International.

References

Estés, C. P. (1992). *Women who run with the wolves: Myths and stories of the wild woman archetype*. Ballantine Books.

Jung, C. G. (1973). *Synchronicity: An acausal connecting principle* (R. F. C. Hull, Trans.). Princeton University Press. (Original work published 1952.) This work is part of *The collected works of C. G. Jung*, volume 8, *The structure and dynamics of the psyche*.

Index

Note: Page numbers in *italics* refer to figures and those in **bold** refer to tables.

For Product Safety Concerns and Information please contact our EU
representative GPSR@taylorandfrancis.com
Taylor & Francis Verlag GmbH, Kaufingerstraße 24, 80331 München, Germany